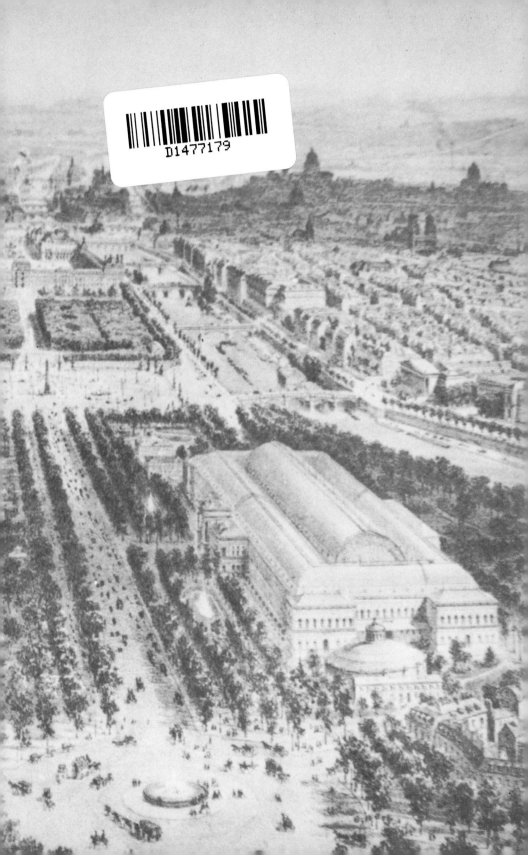

Aerial view of central Paris, taken from a tethered balloon, in the late 1850s. The line of the *grands boulevards,* marking the limits of the right bank centre, is clearly visible. [*Paris dans sa splendeur* (1861).]

STUDIES IN URBAN HISTORY I

General Editor: H. J. Dyos

Reader in Urban History at the
University of Leicester

To
Arnold Fellows

The Autumn
of Central Paris

The Defeat of Town Planning 1850-1970

Anthony Sutcliffe

Research Fellow in Modern History at the
University of Birmingham

Edward Arnold

© Anthony Sutcliffe 1970

First published 1970
by Edward Arnold (Publishers) Ltd.,
41 Maddox Street, London, W.1.

ISBN: 0 7131 5549 3

Made in Great Britain at the Pitman Press, Bath

Foreword

Sixty years ago four-fifths of Britain's population could be classified officially as urban. It might be said of this country at least that the process of urbanisation had already come to an end, since the proportion of the population living in towns and urban districts was to remain more or less constant down to the present time. It appears to us now, looking back, as something of a paradox that the study of the urban past, though never totally neglected in this country, should have been held in abeyance for so long after that phase of urbanisation had closed. And if we widen the horizon to include, not merely growing numbers, but changing attitudes, movements, structures, images, the fact of the matter seems to be that an urban culture has arisen without an historical tradition that might explain it. Yet it was Britain which led the world, however unconsciously or even prodigally it may seem to have done so in human terms, in establishing a type of urban culture in the nineteenth century which has been transplanted or transformed over a much wider field in the twentieth. How surprising it therefore seems that it is only within the last generation, perhaps within little more than a decade, that urban history as such should have come to be recognised in this country as a proper and distinctive field of study and research.

So recent are these developments that their very limits and the techniques for discovering what they were about are still in a state of flux. So multifarious are the possibilities now opening up that most of the practitioners at work in this field are not yet rid of their initial sense of confusion. Nothing could, in fact, be less surprising. What they see before them is a field in which they must pay attention, not only to particular towns in all their peculiar detail—to urban societies fixed more or less in time and space—but a field in which they are being called upon to investigate historical processes and trends that completely transcend the life-cycle and range of experience of any single community when viewed in isolation. The global demographic sweep of urbanisation is already overturning our notions of what cities are or might soon come to be. Sociological concepts of urbanism are forcing us to look deeper for the generic differences between urban and agrarian life that common experience has led us so often to take for granted. The political realities of facing urban problems that have fewer national characteristics than fundamental human ones are suggesting inter-cultural comparisons of a type which historians grounded in empirical traditions have generally viewed with alarm. The interconnections between the growth of cities and the rise of indust-rialised societies have thrown into the study of their economic relations searching questions about the extent to which urbanisation itself may be regarded as an initiator or a product of economic growth or decline.

The town, which was to historians for so long the unconsidered container of industry and trade and the anonymous masses, is therefore now assuming a new importance in its own right. Historians are addressing it *directly*, partly to understand urban changes better for their own sake but chiefly in order to relate them more coherently to economic, political, and cultural developments on an altogether wider plane. Purely 'biographical' studies of individual towns which leave no lasting impression when set in a void offer a basis for making their differences indelible when studied comparatively; investigations of urban life in microscopic detail are being matched by far-reaching research into the fundamental social processes leading towards the urbanisation of the whole world. Historians are on common ground here with other disciplines, for towns have always embodied their own history with peculiar tenacity, and this is now causing scholars across a wide front to look at the urban past with growing curiosity. Among them are geographers, economists, sociologists, demographers, archaeologists, civic designers—each of them having distinctive ap-proaches and techniques, all of them sharing the problem of inter-disciplinary communication. The present mood of urban history is therefore experimental and exploratory. The field is wide open and world-wide, as much concerned with concrete detail where it matters as with imaginative hypotheses wherever they lead, as readily approached by the geographer as by the sociologist or the historian. *Studies in Urban History* is a series designed in this mood. The volumes will have a standard format but in all other respects remain completely unstereotyped so as to give free rein to the most promising ideas, from whatever quarter or however remote their reference to time or place.

The forerunner of these volumes was what now appears to have been a seminal conference, held in 1966 by the Urban History Group operating in this country, in an attempt to promote the exchange of ideas between scholars occupied with problems of urban analysis within different disciplines which nevertheless touch each other at various points. From it came the volume I edited in 1968 under the title *The Study of Urban History*, which might be said, as one reviewer remarked, to have 'put British urban history on the map'. That book was an unconscious anticipation of the series about to be published. In writing a Foreword to it, Asa Briggs looked forward to the time 'when the field will have been cultivated still more and when the fascinating projects described in these pages have reached completion.' It is too soon to report so much. But it is fitting that the series should open with a study by one of the original group that came together in 1966 and who now takes up one of the challenges thrown out in the paper contributed at that time by François Bédarida on the growth of urban history in France. 'Historians', he wrote, 'should be trying to respond to as many of the questions thrown up by sociologists, demographers, geographers, town planners as they can. As brilliantly expressed by Lucien Febvre, "the present offers us a lot of questions to be put to our beloved documents."'

That the first volume presented here by Anthony Sutcliffe should concern itself with a contemporary problem in its historical context— the problem of the changing functions of the city centre—is a fitting start in another sense. The largest single stimulus to our present concern about the urban past comes from our growing awareness of the problems of the urban present. It is a commonplace already that the city is now history's looking-glass and that what it reflects are the conflicts of class and race and ideology that are the products in our time of historical processes that go far beyond it. Many of the most urgent problems facing advanced, if not backward, societies are or appear to be urban ones. And the problems that *seem* easy to separate by a purely academic division of labour in studying generations now gone remain tangled in our own hands today. One of the convictions underlying this series is that our understanding of the complexities of urban change in the past can be advanced only by the kind of conscious co-operation between scholars from a wide range of disciplines of the kind that are proving necessary to the ordering of our own social space today. The main challenge of urban history is not only one of exploration but of communication between disciplines that are not so much disparate as disconnected. For this reason every volume in the series will be selected with the object not only of filling some important gap in our knowledge but of demonstrating particular techniques of research or approach. But let it be understood quite clearly that urban history cannot be regarded, even in embryo, as a single coherent discipline. It is a field of study in which all cognate disciplines can engage in their own ways, and it is to be hoped that as wide a range of them as possible will find expression in this series.

The author of this first volume is an historian who has used his eyes and found a problem that transfixes the past and the present. How is it that any of the half-dozen editions of John Murray's *Handbook for Visitors to Paris* that were published in the 1870s should still be so useful a hundred years later whereas the comparable volumes for London should be so frustrating? How have the commercial and administrative pressures—not to mention the bombardments—that caused the rebuilding of one left the other virtually intact? What forces have been at work, both for and against change, and how has the balance been struck? The same question faces those looking back as those looking forward. For both there is the enduring or diminishing legacy of the past, and to understand how it was, or is likely to be, used it is necessary to be explicit about values as well as about budgets and the force of outside events. This is precisely what Dr. Sutcliffe does. The career of Baron Haussmann, the great rebuilder of Paris under the Second Empire, closed exactly one hundred years ago. His ideas proved scarcely less enduring than his familiar boulevards or their less familiar economic and social ramifications. No-one has yet explained how, in such different circumstances, this was so. This book tells us, and goes on to show just how relevant is the Haussmannic tradition, not only to Parisians themselves but to everyone concerned with the conflict between generations of buildings, between preservation and modernisation, there or elsewhere. We need to know much more about the history of the urban environment if we are to understand how cities can remain alive, or we to survive them. Dr. Sutcliffe's analysis of one case of ossification is a brilliant piece of urban pathology that has meaning far beyond the right bank centre of Paris.

University of Leicester H. J. DYOS
May, 1970

Preface

This study has developed from a piece of research which I submitted in 1966 for the degree of *Docteur de l'Université de Paris*. I owe a great debt to my supervisor, Professor Louis Girard, and to Professors Louis Chevalier and Jean Bastié, all of whom gave me substantial help and encouragement. My thanks are also due to the editor of this series, Dr. H. J. Dyos, for his invaluable guidance. He, and my colleagues Irene Binns, Penelope Corfield and Roger Smith, have been able to suggest numerous improvements to my manuscript, but I alone am responsible for any errors and obscurities that remain. I am grateful to the Faculty of Arts of Birmingham University for a generous grant which enabled me to complete my research. But my greatest obligation is to Monsieur Michel Roussier, director of the administrative library at the Hôtel de Ville. Without his constant aid and support over the last seven years, this book would certainly never have been written.

None of the illustrations could have been included without the selfless cooperation of a number of friends and colleagues. Russell and Helen Walden spent several days photographing streets and buildings on my behalf. Toshio Horii prepared a series of excellent reproductions of older photographs and engravings. And Mr. R. Swift and his staff in the photographic section of the Geography Department at Birmingham University always maintained their high standards of craftsmanship despite the heavy loads of reproductive and development work that I placed on them.

I am most grateful to Mademoiselle Geneviève Gille for permission to quote from her unpublished Sorbonne dissertation, 'Recherches sur l'histoire des emprunts de la Ville de Paris, 1814–1875'. I wish to thank Monsieur Roussier and the director of the *Archives de la Seine* for permission to quote and reproduce items from their collections.

Preface

The *Préfecture de Paris* has kindly allowed the reproduction or use of a number of copyright maps and plans and the City Librarian of Birmingham has authorised the publication of a photograph from the Benjamin Stone Collection in the Birmingham Reference Library. Monsieur Michel Fleury, secretary of the *Commission du Vieux Paris*, was good enough to allow me access to the minutes of that body for the years in which they remain unpublished. Finally, I wish to express my thanks to Mr. T. Garfield and Mr. D. Orme of the Department of Geography, Leicester University, who have devoted hundreds of hours to drawing the maps and diagrams.

University of Birmingham

January, 1970

Contents

Abbreviations

Ann. Stat.	Annuaire statistique de la Ville de Paris
A.S.	Archives de la Seine
A.P.	Arrêté préfectoral
B.A.	Bibliothèque administrative
B.M.	British Museum
Bulletin	Bulletin de la Société des Amis des Monuments parisiens
B.M.O.	Bulletin municipal officiel
C.M.	Conseil municipal
C.V.P.	Commission du Vieux Paris
H.B.M.	Habitations à bon marché
H.L.M.	Habitations à loyer modéré
I.N.S.E.E.	Institut national de la statistique et des études économiques
P.A.D.O.G.	Plan d'aménagement et d'organisation générale
R.A.A.	Recueil des actes administratifs du Préfet de la Seine
Z.A.D.	Zone d'aménagement différé
Z.U.P.	Zone à urbaniser en priorité

Note : Abbreviated titles have been given to works appearing more than once in a given chapter.

Plates

xiii

Figures

FIG. 1. *Arrondissements and wards of Paris.*

KEY TO WARDS (QUARTIERS)

1 SAINT GERMAIN L'AUXERROIS
3 PALAIS ROYAL
4 PLACE VENDOME
5 GAILLON
6 VIVIENNE
8 BONNE NOUVELLE
9 ARTS ET METIERS
10 ENFANTS ROUGES
12 SAINTE AVOYE
13 SAINT MERRI
14 SAINT GERVAIS
21 MONNAIE
24 SAINT GERMAIN DES PRES
35 FAUBOURG MONTMARTRE
36 ROCHECHOUART
38 PORTE SAINT DENIS

KEY TO BOUNDARIES

--- Ward (Quartier)
— Arrondissement

Miles

Kilometres

I

Introduction

This study sets out to answer the following question: why has the fabric of the historic centre of Paris remained almost unchanged since the middle of the nineteenth century, while the centres of most other big cities have been almost completely rebuilt? The visitor to London needs a guidebook to direct him to those corners of the City that can be described, without stretching the imagination too far, as Dickensian. But in central Paris most streets could still serve as a setting for a story by Balzac or Victor Hugo, and Maupassant would certainly be able to find his way unerringly there. The French would have us believe that the charm of central Paris reflects their aesthetic genius. But does it? And what squalor and unhappiness lie behind those picturesque façades? Is the survival of old Paris a triumph for enlightened conservation, or a defeat for material progress?

I DELIMITATION OF THE STUDY

The central area chosen as the zone of inquiry is composed of the *arrondissements* I–IV. It is usually referred to as the *centre rive droite*, and we shall henceforth call it the 'right bank centre'. Its area of 558·97 hectares (5½ square kilometres)—one-twentieth of the city area—is greater than that of the City of London. But, like the City, it was completely surrounded by fortifications, although they were maintained much longer than those of London, until the late seventeenth century. A smaller area on the left bank was also defended, but it contained none of the key organs of medieval and Renaissance Paris except the university. It has always been inferior in population, wealth, business, and administrative and political importance to the right bank centre. Furthermore, the post-1860 administrative boundaries do not coincide on the left bank with the old fortified area, and it has been excluded from this study.

Although it would be fascinating to trace the history of the right bank centre from its origins in Roman times until the present day, the scope of this volume is restricted to the period since the middle of the nineteenth century. The 1850s mark the beginning of the history of the centre of modern Paris because the first serious attempt was made then to modernise the old fortified area in order to adapt it to the needs of a city swollen by immigration and industrial growth. Moreover, certain important statistical series begin in these years. And the administrative boundaries were completely reformed in 1860, since when there have been no changes.

The basic framework of this survey is an examination of the forces working for and against change in the city centre. Among the factors leading to change have been municipal improvement and town planning policies; spontaneous building; redevelopment or conversion for residence, commerce or industry; the provision of new or improved transport systems and other amenities bringing or attracting people to live, shop or work in the centre; wars and civil unrest which damage the urban fabric, and the normal decay of that fabric leading to its disappearance or replacement. And among those factors working against change in the fabric are static or declining population, industry or commerce, bad transport, stagnant amenities, building to last, and conscious preservation. A glance at central London suggests that factors of change have had the upper hand; in Paris the opposite is apparently true. But what causes of inertia have predominated in Paris, and why? And were any factors of change operative in the past, but are no longer?

2 THE RIGHT BANK CENTRE IN THE MORPHOLOGICAL AND ADMINISTRATIVE CONTEXT OF PARIS

(a) *Morphology of the right bank centre*

The first part of Paris to be inhabited was the island of the Cité[1], which was occupied and fortified by the Parisii tribe from the third century B.C. During the campaign against Julius Caesar the inhabitants burned and left the settlement in 52 B.C., and although they were able to return soon after, it was occupied by the Romans in

---

[1] All place-names referring to central Paris may be traced on the folding street plan provided at the end of the book.

2

the following year. The Romans reconstructed it, but owing to shortage of space they soon began to lay out a new town on the left bank. Gradually, the Cité became an administrative and religious centre as well as a fortress. But after about A.D. 250 a series of Germanic invasions resulted in the destruction of parts of the unprotected town on the left bank. The Cité had to be refortified, and again became the main area of settlement. When the town began to expand again under the Merovingians and Carolingians, the right bank was increasingly favoured. The area to the north of the Cité had been marshy and prone to flooding in Roman times, but by now it was being drained and most of it was becoming suitable for the construction of houses. A hard beach opposite the eastern end of the Cité (*la grève*) began to be used for unloading and repairing boats, and merchants and ship-masters set up house nearby. From the eleventh century a market was established there, and a wall was constructed to defend the area. In about 1137 Louis VI transferred this market to a site just to the north-west of the Châtelet, which guarded the northern end of the bridge linking the Cité to the right bank. Northwards from the Châtelet ran two parallel streets, the Rue Saint-Martin and the Rue Saint-Denis. The first of these was part of the main road to Flanders, but it had become inadequate, and the Rue Saint-Denis grew up a short distance from it. Both streets were built on a ridge of land running across the more marshy fields of the right bank, and because of the growing importance of trading contacts with the industries and fairs of the north, ribbon development took place along them. It was to protect this growing urban area on the right bank that Philip Augustus built a new wall in about 1200. He also built a similar wall a few years later on the left bank, where residential development was the result of a proliferation of religious houses rather than of commercial expansion. The two walls enclosed an area of 253 hectares. At the point where the right bank wall met the Seine in the west, the Louvre was built to perform the same function as a defence against upstream attackers as the Tower of London.

Despite royal attempts to prevent the spread of settlement outside the walls, the right bank area continued to grow, and by 1370 it was necessary for Charles V to order the construction of a new wall, which increased the fortified area to 439 hectares. This provided the oppor-tunity to build an eastern fortress, the Bastille, to counter-balance the Louvre in the west. The new wall followed the line of the present *grands boulevards* in the east and north, and the Rue d'Aboukir and the Rue de Valois in the west, where it terminated at an enlarged Louvre. No extension or alteration was made to the wall of Philip Augustus on the left bank. The new fortifications took in the north-ward ribbon development along the Rue Saint-Denis and the Rue Saint-Martin, and, in the east, the expanding aristocratic district of the Marais, in which Charles V built the Hôtel Saint-Paul and other royal residences, This area had remained ill-drained longer than other parts of the right bank, and offered wide spaces for the construction of the houses and gardens of the royal family and the nobility. So by the fourteenth century the town was expanding more rapidly towards the east than the west ⟨*see* plate 2⟩. The direction was later modified by a growing royal preference for the west of the city. François Ier had the Louvre rebuilt as a palace from the 1540s, and in 1554 Catherine de Medici began to build a residence, the Tuileries, to the west of the Louvre, outside the fortifications. The Marais fell completely out of favour after Henri II was killed in a jousting accident there in 1559, and further extensions to the Louvre were undertaken by Louis XIII. Although many of the aristocracy continued to reside in the Marais, others built their mansions in the unoccupied fields to the north of the Louvre. Because part of the royal palace and many of the houses of the nobility were outside Charles V's fortifications, these had to be extended to the west in the sixteenth and early seventeenth cen-turies, along the line of what are now the western *grands boulevards*. However, under Louis XVI the power of the French monarchy and nation grew so great that the capital was in little danger of attack, and in about 1670 Louis XVI ordered the demolition of its fortifications. The wall of Philip Augustus, on the left bank, soon disappeared or was embodied in domestic buildings, but the wall of Charles V and its westward extension were pulled down and transformed into a wide promenade. The expansion of the city beyond the old fortifications, which the monarchy had previously tried to discourage, was now accelerated. It is, however, the area within Louis XIV's *grands boule-vards* that will be the primary concern of this study.

The appearance of the right bank centre was largely the result of its long period of fortification. It was densely built in comparison to the unfortified suburbs, although many gardens remained, and those belonging to mansions and religious houses were particularly extensive. It contained the main organs of civic, religious and business life, and of national administration, none of which could have been sited outside the walls before 1670, and which subsequently remained on their traditional sites. The street pattern of the area was essentially an irregular grid of streets running parallel or vertical to the Seine. The two principal elements of the grid were a north-south axis, formed by the parallel Rue Saint-Martin and Rue Saint-Denis, and a more tortuous east-west route running from the Louvre to the Bastille. Owing to the occupation by the royal family of the Louvre, the extreme west of the right bank centre was its most aristocratic district, but those parts of the west nearer the Rue Saint-Denis were made extremely commercial by the presence of the markets. The east retained the Hôtel de Ville, near the Place de Grève, and a numerous, though declining, noble population. But as the nobles left, industry and a poorer population took their place, and by the eighteenth century the east of the right bank centre provided a home for many of the city's workshops and artisanal activities. But most of it remained less densely constructed than the commercial areas of the west ⟨*see* plate 3⟩.

Throughout the right bank centre the great majority of streets were extremely narrow, and even principal routes like the Rue Saint-Denis and the Rue Saint-Honoré were not more than ten metres wide. The area's buildings were of a variety of types. In the medieval core in the Cité, around the Châtelet and the Halles, and on either side of the Rues Saint-Denis and Saint-Martin, some of the narrowest streets in the city were lined by the almost unbroken façades of its tallest houses. The great mansions that had once existed here had long since been pulled down and their sites and gardens had been divided into smaller plots. The houses which now crowded onto them could be as many as five or six storeys tall—and hardly any were lower than three storeys. Many were built on long, narrow sites, and had originally had gardens, but by the late eighteenth century most of these had been built on. Few people's dwellings opened directly onto the street, and most were approached by narrow passageways running deep into the interior of each block.

Outside this central core the right bank centre had much more open space, although this feature was more pronounced in the east than in the west, which had become the city's main area of population and business growth by the eighteenth century. Many mansions still remained, especially in the east where some had been split up into apartments or converted for use by commerce or industry. Other houses were often quite small, with two or three storeys, and the areas on the outskirts of the right bank centre looked like the small French provincial town of today.

5

(b) Administration

Even before the Revolution the local government of Paris had been distinguished from that of other towns by the extent of the control exercised by the monarchy. Subsequent régimes, whether republican, imperial or royal, sought to maintain authority over the city because the great political influence of Paris would have been strengthened by an independent municipality. Although the capital was allowed a municipal council in some form after 1789, close central control was restored from 1794. In 1800 the Prefect of the Seine *département*, which had been created to include Paris and a small area round it in 1790, was granted administrative authority over the city. Public order was placed under the control of a new official, the Prefect of Police. Both Prefects were appointed by the Government, and they shared the functions which would normally have been exercised by the mayor. They also shared the authority which in all other *départements* belonged to the departmental Prefect alone. The municipal council was allowed to decide certain questions within a very limited range, but otherwise could make only recommendations to the Prefects. Its ultimate sanction was the refusal to vote taxation, but this right was rarely, if ever, exercised because it would have brought the administration of Paris to a halt.

These arrangements were several times modified after 1790, but it is relevant here to describe only the local government situation as it developed from 1848. After the revolution of that year the Prefecture of the Seine was abolished and Paris was again granted its own mayor— a privilege which it had not enjoyed since 1789-94. But in fact, little was altered, for the mayor was appointed by the Government, and his powers were similar to those formerly enjoyed by the Prefect of the Seine. And in July 1848 the Prefecture of the Seine was re-established. Civic autonomy was now even more limited than before, for the municipal council had been dissolved in February, and although the Provisional Government passed a law in July 1848 which provided for the election of all local councils by universal suffrage, it did not apply to Paris. Instead, a nominated commission was set up to discuss the affairs of both the city and the *département* of the Seine. In 1849 two separate commissions were established, one for the city and one for the Seine, with the thirty-six members of the Paris commission also belonging to that of the *département*. But although the Government promised to re-establish an elective régime, it did not do so. So Louis-Napoleon found himself already invested with sufficient control over Paris when he took personal power in 1851, and he made few modifications to the administrative machinery established by the Second Republic. The municipal council remained a nominated body, even after provincial municipal councils were made elective in 1855.

After the fall of the Second Empire the republican Government maintained its administrative control over Paris, but allowed the election of the City Council by universal male suffrage. This had never been attempted before in Paris, for electors of previous councils had been subject to a property qualification. At first it was thought that the Council would be revolutionary and socialist in character, but in the 1871 elections the supporters of the ideals of the Commune were overborne by the many who had been frightened by its excesses. Not until the elections of 1874 was a republican-socialist majority returned, and even then its actions did not bear out the worst fears of the conservatives. To some extent it would be true to say that it had no choice but to behave itself because the range of matters over which it had powers of decision was still very limited. But its sense of responsibility was also the result of an objective appraisal of the city's problems. Disputes with the Prefect of the Seine were frequent, but they rarely obstructed the efficient working of the administration. In any case, very few of the socialist councillors were working men, and many councillors of all parties used the Council merely as a springboard into national politics. Even when the nationalist landslide of 1900 expelled many radicals and socialists from the Council, others, and an even greater number of moderates and conservatives, survived by incorporating the word 'nationalist' in their party affiliations. And they quietly dropped it a few years later when it was no longer a *sine qua non* of electoral support. In fact, at a municipal level the councillor's loyalty was reserved far more for his ward than for his political party or group.

In 1860 the enlarged city was divided into twenty *arrondissements*, each of four wards. From 1870 each of these wards returned one councillor. Members of the Council had to make sure, above all else, that their own electorates were satisfied with their performance. Low taxation, of course, was a demand common to all wards, but most of the citizens' other requirements were strictly local, especially in the days before the *Métro* encouraged people to travel about the city. The Parisian was concerned that his own area should possess wide streets, healthy houses, schools, baths and other amenities, and flourishing commerce and industry. The danger that councillors' interests would become so narrow that they would ignore the perhaps greater needs of areas other than their own was recognised very early on, and they were forbidden to form factions within the Council to promote the demands of certain groups of wards. But such arrangements were nevertheless made unofficially, and the whole Council fell naturally into two opposing groups—east versus west. The rich wards of the centre and the west usually returned moderate or conservative councillors, while the working-class wards of the north, east and south tended to elect radicals and socialists. Any direct confrontation could usually be won by the east, whose representatives were in a majority. But within and around this conflict another battle went on, between the centre and the outskirts. Here the odds were more even, for the pre-1860 city area was now composed of eleven *arrondissements* and so had forty-four councillors, while the annexed districts were represented by thirty-six. Most of the outer areas were poor and industrial, and on the whole the central *arrondissements* had more commerce and prosperous residents, with the exception of the XIe. The question was, should more money be spent on the centre, which needed rapid communications and healthy buildings in order to serve as the centre of business, services and amenities for the whole city and even the whole of France, and which, in its older parts, contained some of the worst slums in Paris? Or should it be spent on improving residential conditions in the outer ring of *arrondissments*, which predominated increasingly in terms of population and industry, yet were under-equipped and underplanned in comparison with the centre?

After 1914 this struggle began to die down as less and less money became available for spending anywhere in the city. But the existing system of representation was clearly anomalous, because the eleven central *arrondissements*, and especially those four in the right bank centre, were smaller than the others, and their population was declining. So in 1935 the wards and *arrondissements* were abandoned as electoral units, and were replaced by much larger districts which returned several councillors. The arrangements were further modified in 1945, when a system of proportional representation was introduced. These reforms eradicated most of what was left of the old spirit of local loyalty.

Although Paris is not strictly a municipality, in that it has no elected mayor, and its council has more limited powers than those of other communes, it has its own administration, separate from that of the

Seine *département*. To avoid unnecessary confusion, it will be referred to throughout as the City of Paris. City Council committees have been given English names when their functions are similar to their English equivalents. However, there is a fundamental difference between them and English local government committees in that they do not enjoy delegated powers over the administration, for the City Council has no executive powers to delegate. Their responsibility is to submit reports to the Council on matters of policy passed to them for study. Such reports are presented to the Council by the *rapporteur*, who is to all intents and purposes the chairman of the committee. And he will usually be referred to as such in this study. There may be a risk that Paris will begin to sound like Manchester or Birmingham if English terminology is used, but it would be too fastidious to use the French terms throughout. In fact, every attempt has been made to find English equivalents for all technical terms, for the great similarities between cities and their problems throughout Europe should not be obscured by linguistic pedantry.

2

The Grand Design

In terms of achievement, the history of Paris as a modern world city clearly begins with Napoleon III and Haussmann. But the seeds of the improvement policies which burgeoned then were planted long before, in the reign of Louis XVI. In the field of urban planning, as in so many others, the last decades of the eighteenth century were a turning point, from which the shape of things to come could already be vaguely discerned.

Until the late eighteenth century the major responsibility for the improvement of Paris was taken by the members of the Capetian dynasty that had made the city its capital. But their schemes, and those of individual citizens who tried to emulate them, were piecemeal, and the desire to embellish had usually prevailed over the necessity for practical improvements. But gradually the need was felt for an overall plan to coordinate public works. A royal edict of 1783 establishing minimum widths and heights for new streets and buildings was an important first step. In future, all new development would conform to these simple standards, thus preventing excessive congestion in the streets and the undesirable crowding together of tall buildings. But the city already contained about half a million people, most of them in conditions that did not conform to the edict. In whatever form the outskirts were subsequently developed, there would remain a central core where conditions could only deteriorate with time, as structural obsolescence was accelerated by the growing preference of the rich for the new suburbs, leaving the old city only to the very poor. And it is with the city centre that we are concerned here.

Although succeeding kings had usually sited their embellishment schemes in newly developing areas of the city, they had powers to deal, if they so wished, with the centre. The streets of Paris were classified as part of the royal highway network, so that the Crown had powers to fix the widths of existing thoroughfares as well as new ones. But before anything could be done there had to be an accurate map of the city, and although many plans had appeared over the years, none had the great exactitude that was essential to any overall recasting of street widths. In April 1783 Louis XVI gave official blessing to the work of Paul Verniquet, an architect who was already preparing a plan of Paris on his own initiative, and provided him with a team of assistants.[1] At about the same time he also set up a study committee to consider plans and projects of utility, salubrity and embellishment, and an architectural office.[2] The royal architect, the Comte de Wailly, prepared a new plan of 'embellishments', which appeared in 1787.[3] This scheme included a number of wide avenues on the left bank, and a new street running from east to west across the right bank centre from the Rue Saint-Antoine to the Louvre.

Although the Revolution destroyed the royal authority which would have put De Wailly's plan into effect, it allowed more people to take a positive interest in the city's problems. And the transfer of royal prerogatives almost intact to the republican administrative machine meant that the power to carry out urban improvements was scarcely impaired.[4] In fact, the opportunity to carry out public works became even greater than before the Revolution, as a result of the nationalisation of Church property. Many religious foundations had retained large closes or gardens even in the centre of the city, which were now sold to developers as building sites. But first of all they had to be split up into building blocks by new streets, and the need to plan these streets emphasised the urgency of deciding on an overall highway scheme. So in 1793 the Convention set up a body, which became known as the Commission of Artists, to continue the work of the royal study committee.

Within a few years the Commission, which was composed of architects and administrators, produced the city's first overall street scheme[5] ⟨*see* plate 7⟩. Most of the streets planned were intended to

---

[1] *Atlas des anciens plans de Paris* (1880), p. 27.

[2] Pierre Lavedan, *Histoire de Paris* (1960), p. 69.

[3] See Noël Boutet de Monvel, 'Plans de Paris, 1734–1966', *L'architecture d'aujourd'hui*, no. 138, June–July 1968.

[4] See Alfred des Cilleuls, *Origines et développement du régime des travaux publics en France* (1895), p. 296.

[5] For a reconstruction of the *Plan des artistes*, see Commission d'extension de Paris, *Considérations techniques préliminaires* (1913), plate 5.

divide up the 'national properties', some of which were in the right bank centre. But a number were clearly intended to remedy traffic congestion, in that they did not cross nationalised lands. The most important scheme in this category was for a wide thoroughfare running from the Place de la Concorde to the Bastille on a route similar to that of the east-west street planned by De Wailly. The Commission also planned several smaller new streets in the vicinity of the Halles, and the widening of the southern part of the Rue Saint-Denis between the Halles and the Seine. Three new streets were planned in the Cité, and there was to be a new artery linking it to the Marais via two bridges and the Île Saint-Louis.

The Commission retained the principle that an official width should be fixed for every street. It suggested that there should be five width categories, according to the amount of traffic using the street.[6] From the late 1790s the Government, which had inherited the royal control over the streets of Paris, began to fix improvement lines in all the narrower streets. This process was almost complete by about 1810. The owners of properties which infringed the improvement line were required, after demolition, to cede to the public highway that part of the site which lay in front of the line. Unless demolition was forced on the owner by a compulsory purchase order, he would receive compensation only for the value of the land ceded. To encourage speedy demolition, all structural repairs were forbidden on buildings infringing improvement lines. It was hoped that the application of these regulations would bring about the widening of every street at low cost within a few decades. But within a few years the widths fixed were recognised in many cases to be inadequate, and they were increased in the 1820s and 1830s, when improvement lines were also established for many streets which had been ignored under the Consulate and Empire. And there were occasional later modifications, so that the whole process of fixing and modifying optimum street widths was continuous throughout the first half of the nineteenth century.

The determination of Napoleon Bonaparte to continue the royal tradition of benefaction towards Paris resulted in the execution of a number of projects included in the Artists' Plan. The most important for the right bank centre was the construction of the western section of the big east-west artery, from the Tuileries to the Louvre, which the Emperor named Rue de Rivoli after one of his victories. He also emoved the noxious slaughterhouses from the city centre near the

[6] *Considérations techniques*, p. 21.

Halles, and established them in modern premises outside the city.[7] The cemeteries, too, were decentralised for health reasons. But these measures only scratched the surface of the city's problems, as population, congestion and disease continued to increase.

Although the Restoration set up a monarchy which could not rival in magnificence the one that the Revolution had overthrown, the Bourbons were eager to take up the traditional royal task of embellishing Paris. But they could no longer ignore the needs of the mass of the population, especially now that Saint-Simon and others were urging a more enlightened improvement policy. In 1817 the Prefect of the Seine, Comte Gilbert de Chabrol, drew up a new scheme of 'embellishments' which the Government accepted. One of Chabrol's biggest concerns was to provide better communications throughout the city. At the time, over 17,000 vehicles were circulating in Paris.[8] This was quite enough to bring about serious congestion, especially as many streets were not wide enough for two vehicles to pass each other. But resources were so limited that it could only be hoped that the application of improvement lines would slowly produce an adequate street system. Meanwhile, work proceeded steadily on the construction of embankments (*quais*) along the whole length of the Seine within the city, a process which was almost complete by mid-century.[9]

More urgency was shown under the July Monarchy. The great cholera epidemic of 1832[10] frightened the middle classes, and although some of the momentum towards public health improvements was lost when cholera did not return in the following few years, a number of important schemes were carried through. The enthusiasm of a new Prefect of the Seine, the Comte de Rambuteau, who was appointed in 1833, obtained the cooperation of the City Council. The construction of sewers, which had been slowing down after the opening of 18,000 metres of them between 1808 and 1831, was accelerated after the cholera epidemic.[11] A system was planned by the canal and sewer engineer, Charles Henri Emmery, to link the old sewers with those whose construction was now envisaged. By the mid-1830s over 8,000 metres of new sewers were being built every year, and in 1837 Emmery's system was two-thirds complete. Construction proceeded steadily

---

[7] See Richard Boxall Grantham, 'Description of the abattoirs of Paris', *Proceedings of the Institution of Civil Engineers*, vol. VIII, 1849, pp. 66–81; Félix Pigeory, *Les monuments de Paris au dix-neuvième siècle* (1849), pp. 547–8.

[8] A. J. Meindre, *Histoire de Paris et de son influence en Europe* (1854–5), vol. V, p. 333.

[9] Pigeory, *Monuments de Paris*, pp. 600–14.

[10] See Louis Chevalier (ed.), *Le choléra: la première épidémie du XIXe siècle* (1958).

[11] Pigeory, *Monuments de Paris*, pp. 554–8.

throughout the next decade, financed by annual allocations out of revenue. Regular progress was also made in the improvement and extension of the water distribution system.[12] Much of the money spent on improvements on the surface was devoted to buildings, such as the Hôtel de Ville and the Palais de Justice,[13] but more resources were devoted to street improvements than before 1830. In that year the Government immediately voted 1,400,000 francs (£56,000) for monuments and public works in Paris to employ the working classes during the economic crisis.[14] In the right bank centre work started in 1833 on the Rue du Pont-Louis-Philippe, the link between the Marais and the two islands of the Seine which had been included in the Artists' Plan. In the Cité itself three more projects planned by the Artists were carried out. The Rue d'Arcole and the Rue Constantine were built, and the Rue de la Cité was widened. But the most ambitious of the Artists' projects to be executed was the Rue de Rambuteau, which ran for nearly a thousand yards eastwards from the Halles into the Marais. Powers were obtained to build this street in 1838, and demolitions took place between 1839 and 1845. Great resources could be devoted to the Rue de Rambuteau because there was more than one good reason for building it. It improved traffic flow between the Halles and the Marais, which was already beginning to suffer from its poor communications with the west of the city, and shortened the journey to the Temple retail market in what is now the IIIe *arrondissement*. The demolition of over seventy houses in a depressed area and the creation of a corridor along which air and light could penetrate was expected to bring about an improvement in the health of the district. And, not least, it split in two a centre of political unrest which had frequently been the scene of riot and revolt.[15]

The significance of Rambuteau's work lies in his willingness to tackle improvement schemes in the very centre of the city, instead of following the traditional line of least resistance by siting his public works projects on the outskirts where land values were low and leaving the centre to rot. But he was not able to determine his priorities until the conclusion of a lengthy controversy over the future of the city centre which revolved round plans for the Halles. And before moving on to the Second Empire we must examine this debate, for its outcome

[12] Pigeory, pp. 558–9.
[13] Charles Merruau, *Souvenirs de l'Hôtel de Ville, 1848–1852* (1875), p. 339.
[14] Meindre, *Histoire de Paris*, vol. V, p. 307.
[15] Charles Rouget, 'Rue Rambuteau', p. 396, in [Louis Lurine, ed.], *Les rues de Paris* (1844), vol. I, pp. 383–96.

established the main terms of reference within which Haussmann had to work.

The Halles of Paris, which grouped all wholesale marketing functions except wine, and served as a retail market for the population of the immediate area, had remained on the same site since the middle ages. Their steady growth, in an area several hundred yards north-west of the Châtelet, had been largely responsible for the rapid expansion of the urban area west of the Rue Saint-Denis, and the relative decline of commerce in the Marais to the east and on the left bank of the Seine. As the population of Paris increased, the Halles expanded, but growth became increasingly difficult as the surrounding areas became more and more crowded with buildings. And while congestion grew in the market buildings, the narrow streets of the district became blocked by market traffic, so that the distribution of food to retail outlets in the peripheral areas became increasingly difficult. The construction of the first railways in the late 1830s accentuated the problem by creating the likelihood of increased population and the possibility of transporting foodstuffs to Paris in greater quantities by train. The City Council postponed all decisions affecting the area until it knew what the future of the Halles would be,[16] and a lengthy debate was carried on over the issue. Eventually the Government, worried that inadequate distribution of provisions might lead to unrest, took a hand. In 1841 the Secretary of State for the Department of Commerce, Cunin-Gridaine, told the Chamber that the provisioning of Paris was a matter affecting public order, and could no longer be left to chance. The Government would have to take responsibility for it.[17] So, in July 1842, Rambuteau set up an administrative commission to study means of improving the Halles so that they could once again meet the needs of the population.[18] At the first session of the commission, which was composed of officials and councillors, Rambuteau declared himself to be in favour of the extension of the Halles on their existing site.[19] Such a solution would avoid disturbing the deep-rooted interests of the market traders, who were a power to be reckoned with in the municipality. Moreover, distribution from a central point was clearly the ideal as long as it could be carried out efficiently. But

---

[16] In 1838, for instance, the Council put off any decision on the improvement lines for twenty streets in the area (Pigeory, *Monuments de Paris*, p. 535).
[17] Alfred des Cilleuls, *Histoire de l'administration parisienne au XIXe siècle* (1900), vol. II, p. 73.
[18] Commission des Halles, *Documents* (B.A.2122), nos. 3, 4.
[19] Commission des Halles, *Documents*, no. 1, p. 6.

such a solution would make it necessary to carry out extensive street improvements in the immediate area of the Halles and along all the main radial routes. Rambuteau was prepared to face up to this fact, and could point to the work that was already proceeding on the Rue de Rambuteau as proof of the feasibility of such improvements. Moreover, he was already committed to some extent by the decision to build the Rue de Rambuteau, whose main *raison d'être* would be removed if the Halles were decentralised.[20] He also knew that without the Halles there would be little chance of getting the City Council to agree to street improvements in the centre, which would be unfortunate in view of the contribution they made to public health.

Rambuteau's opinion was supported by the majority of the members of the commission. Daniel, the inspector-general of public weights and of municipal market taxation, had previously argued in an influential report that although the Halles in their existing form had driven better-off residents out of the district, owing to the presence of certain unpleasant activities and individuals, they would be much less repulsive if regularised and enlarged. And they would contribute even more to the commercial prosperity of the area. Daniel insisted that a central site was the most convenient possible for the delivery of provisions from the countryside.[21] So the commission drew up an extension project for the Halles, which it finally approved in 1843.[22]

Throughout these discussions a strong dissentient view was expressed by Councillor Lanquetin, a highly respected wine merchant.[23] He wanted the City to look beyond the immediate problem of the Halles, and to consider it as one of the overall urban problems facing Paris. Pointing to the increase in population which would almost certainly result from the construction of railways, he called for a statement of planned street improvements throughout the city. Moreover, he urged the City to consider what would be the role of the centre in an enlarged Paris. He claimed that the movement of the business district towards the north-west[24] resulted not only from the attraction of the Bourse and other financial establishments there, but from the 'intolerable and dangerous' congestion of the narrow streets of the old centre. As a result, the east of the city and the left bank were in decline.

---

[20] But for the view that strategic considerations alone justified the Rue de Rambuteau, see Charles Rouget, 'Rue Rambuteau', p. 396.
[21] Commission des Halles, *Documents*, no. 3, pp. 3-4.
[22] Pigeory, *Monuments de Paris*, p. 535.
[23] See Commission des Halles, *Documents*, no. 4.
[24] See below, pp. 151 ff.

2

Lanquetin argued that the prime necessity was to establish better communications between the new centre of activities and these declining areas, and the growing peripheral districts. But this would be impossible so long as the barrier of the Halles and the congestion they engendered remained in the centre, no matter what street improvements were carried out. On the other hand, if the Halles were moved to the suburbs and the tolls on the Seine bridges were abolished, only a few new streets and widenings would be necessary.

Although the removal of the Halles would have disturbed a powerful body of vested interests, it was not totally out of the question. The decentralisation of the abattoirs, which had been closely connected with the Halles, had been a great success, and in 1808 wholesale trading in wine had been transferred to a new market (Halle aux vins) on the left bank of the Seine in what is now the Ve *arrondisssement*. The establishment of railways seemed to offer the compensation of improved access from the provinces if the Halles were moved to the outskirts, especially as the Government did not want the lines to penetrate into the very centre of Paris because of the traffic congestion they would cause.[25] Lanquetin, however, was defeated in the administrative commission, which voted 'almost unanimously' for the enlargement scheme.[26] When, in 1844, Rambuteau laid the project before the City Council, Lanquetin was elected to the committee studying his memorandum, and he again put the case for a new site. He suggested that the Halles should be moved to the left bank, just south of the Île Saint-Louis, near the wine market. Although he found much more support here than in the administrative commission, and nearly obtained a majority, the committee eventually voted in favour of extension on the existing site in February 1845. Rambuteau then instructed his architect, Victor Baltard, to work on the details of the project with the Council committee.[27] Although no irrevocable steps were taken, there was now little chance that the decision would be reversed, and the reconstruction of the Halles on their existing site was finally decreed by an ordinance of 18 January 1847.

Rambuteau could now finalise his plans for street improvements in the centre. Lanquetin had suggested the widening of the Rue Saint-Denis south of the Halles, as proposed by the Artists, and the extension of the Rue Montmartre to the Châtelet in order to link it directly with

[25] Vivien, 'Etudes administratives: II, La Préfecture de police', p. 453, *Revue des Deux Mondes*, 1842, vol. IV, pp. 430–56; René Clozier, *La Gare du Nord* (1940), p. 26.
[26] Commission des Halles, *Documents*, no. 7.
[27] Pigeory, *Monuments de Paris*, p. 536.

the new centre of activities. On the left bank, existing streets should be widened, or a new thoroughfare built, to prolong the north-south axis of the Rue Saint-Denis. Finally, Lanquetin recommended that the monumental route from the Louvre to the Bastille should be built at some stage, although for the moment it was too much for the City's slender resources.[28] There was nothing novel in these suggestions, for they were the obvious steps to take. Improvement lines had already been fixed in 1837 along the whole length of the Rue Saint-Denis to provide an eventual width of thirteen metres. An optimum width of ten metres had been fixed for the Rue Montmartre in 1799, but this was clearly insufficient and in 1845 it was increased to fifteen metres. At the same time, powers were taken to widen the whole of the southern section of the street from the Halles to the Rue d'Aboukir. Preparations were also made to widen the Rue de la Harpe, which extended the line of the Rue Saint-Denis on the left bank. As for the east-west route, the Rue de Rivoli extension, it remained, as Lanquetin put it, 'in everybody's mind',[29] but it was generally agreed that important Government participation was essential to its execution. The effect of building it, combined with the other improvements, would be to create two main traffic routes, running from north to south and from east to west, and crossing each other at right-angles near the Châtelet.

In 1848 Rambuteau was removed from the Prefecture by the over-throw of Louis-Philippe and the establishment of the Second Republic. The Provisional Government had immediately to face the problem of high unemployment in Paris, which had helped bring about the revolution, but which now had to be reduced to avoid the risk of further violence. Although the National Workshops were expected to constitute the principal source of employment, the Government looked to street improvements to provide further jobs. And the gradual recognition of the failure of the National Workshops increased the urgency of beginning a public works programme in Paris.

Although the City was now re-established in name as an independent municipality, it was more closely under Government control than during the July Monarchy. Even the new mayor was appointed by the Government.[30] So it seemed for a time that the City could now be made the direct instrument of Government policy. In May 1848

[28] Commission des Halles, *Documents*, no. 4, pp. 49–51.
[29] Commission des Halles, *Documents*, no. 4, p. 48.
[30] (after Maurice Félix), *Le régime administratif et financier de la Ville de Paris* (1957), vol. I, pp. 107–8.

powers were obtained to extend the Rue de Rivoli, but lack of resources prevented a start being made until the June uprisings forced the City to drop its plans.[31] In July the authority of the Prefect of the Seine was again extended over Paris, and two men passed quickly through the post until Berger was appointed in December 1848. During 1849 the first signs of a rift appeared between the Government and the City. The nominated City Council[32] proved to be as devoted to the cause of economy as its predecessor, and Berger used it as an excuse for his own lack of enterprise.[33] Yet a quick start on a public works programme appeared to the Government to be an urgent necessity. A new epidemic of cholera, although not so lethal as in 1832, emphasised the need for quick action to improve public health. And a series of disorders, centred on the Arts-et-Métiers district in the present IIIe *arrondissement*, shook the Government's confidence in its ability to keep order in the narrow streets of central Paris. It was, however, an inopportune time to float loans and begin ambitious schemes. The Council agreed to a plan to isolate the Hôtel de Ville by acquiring a block of houses behind it, and Berger planned a large barracks on the site.[34] But, above all, the Government wanted the City's cooperation in its plans to complete the north side of the Louvre and extend the Rue de Rivoli along its length. The City Council, on the other hand, was interested in the scheme only if the Rue de Rivoli were to be extended right across the city centre, whereas the Government was prepared to subsidise it only as far as the eastern extremity of the Louvre.[35] The Council finally agreed that work should begin on this first section of the street, with a generous Government subsidy, after an assurance that its further extension was not ruled out. But an additional complication had been introduced by the construction of the Gare de Lyon to the south-east of the centre. Work had been proceeding since before 1848 on streets linking it to the fringes of the centre, and the City Council could not agree on the line that the Rue de Rivoli extension should take in the east to meet these new thoroughfares.[36]

From 1850 the President, Louis-Napoleon, who since his election in 1848 had taken a personal interest in the future of Paris, began to put increasing pressure on Berger to undertake more extensive public works. Louis-Napoleon had prepared a sketch plan of the streets he

[31] Merruau, *Souvenirs*, p. 75.
[32] It was officially termed 'commission municipale' until 1855, but was still frequently referred to as the 'conseil municipal'.
[33] Merruau, *Souvenirs*, p. 165.   [34] Merruau, pp. 158, 162.
[35] Merruau, pp. 148, 151.   [36] Merruau, p. 165.

wanted to see built in the city. Some of them, like the Rue de Rivoli, were established projects, but others were innovations. The revived interest in public health after 1848 led to the establishment of a number of new administrative bodies, and to the passing of legislation providing for the inspection and improvement of unhealthy dwellings in 1850. The Paris Unhealthy Dwellings Commission, in its first annual report, made a strong plea for public works, without which any general improvement in living conditions would be impossible.[37] Among the schemes which the President put forward to the City Council were the Halles rebuilding and the Rue de Rivoli, and these were eventually the first to be tackled. However, for the time being Berger continued to prevaricate by claiming that the City's finances would not stand the strain.

Before taking any final decisions the City Council again discussed the problem of the Halles. Although various possibilities, including the site suggested earlier by Lanquetin, were considered, the market traders remained the final court of appeal, for the markets could be put only where they were prepared to go.[38] Eventually, the Council retained the 1847 plan, but increased the area of the new Halles from 53,000 to 68,000 square metres. It also decided that old streets should be widened, or new ones built, to link the Halles to the *quais*, the Pont-Neuf, and the Châtelet.[39] Even Lanquetin, who was president of the City Council in 1851, approved the plan for the new Halles on the understanding that it would be carried out in association with a series of street improvements, including the Rue de Rivoli.[40] But the Council put off making a start until 1852. By this time so much pressure had built up on it, partly as a result of Louis-Napoleon's *coup d'état* in December 1851, that it gave final approval both to the plan for the new Halles and for work to begin on the Rue de Rivoli between the Louvre and the Hôtel de Ville. No subsidy could be expected this time, and the City Council agreed to borrow fifty million francs to cover the cost of the works. In return, the Council persuaded the Government to agree to the extension of an *octroi*[41] surcharge on wines until 1870, and the exemption from taxation for twenty years of new houses along the Rue de Rivoli. In March 1852 Louis-Napoleon persuaded the Council to build the Boulevard de Strasbourg, linking

[37] Commission des logements insalubres (Paris), *Rapport général des travaux de la commission pendant l'année 1851* (1852), p. 12.
[38] Merruau, *Souvenirs*, pp. 380–81.   [39] Merruau, p. 387.
[40] He gave his approval in a letter to the *Revue Municipale*, 1851, no. 77, p. 631.
[41] See below, p. 147.

the new Gare de Strasbourg (later Gare de l'Est) to the *grands boulevards*, by offering a subsidy of 1,670,000 francs (£66,800). At the same time, he issued a decree increasing the area of the new Halles. Work also began on the Rue des Ecoles, in what is now the Ve *arrondissement*, for which left bank councillors had campaigned ever since the Council's approval of improvements on the right bank.[42] Yet, in spite of the approval given by Berger and the City Council for Louis-Napoleon's schemes, the Prince-President still found himself baulked by their timidity. He wanted to press quickly on with the extension of the Rue de Rivoli beyond the Hôtel de Ville, and of the Boulevard de Strasbourg across the city to the Châtelet. The results of sales of sites along the Louvre—Hôtel de Ville section of the Rue de Rivoli were encouraging, and to the *Moniteur* they seemed sufficient to justify the undertaking of further improvement schemes in the centre.[43] But Berger refused to float another loan, claiming that the only safe way to proceed was to set aside four million francs each year for public works out of revenue. The Duc de Persigny, Minister of the Interior, tried in vain to prod Berger into action, and in June 1853 Louis-Napoleon, who by now had made himself Emperor, lost patience and dismissed him.[44] Persigny and the Emperor chose as his replacement Georges Haussmann, a Protestant Alsacian career civil servant, who had previously been Prefect of the Gironde, and had carried through some important public works schemes in Bordeaux. The new Prefect took up his functions on 22 June 1853.

It may be appropriate at this stage to analyse what had been achieved by the time Haussmann arrived, and the choices that remained open to him and to his imperial master. What lessons had been learned, what still remained to be done, and how could it best be achieved? Some of the most important lessons had been learned from Rambuteau's work.[45] The Rue de Rambuteau was a failure because it was too narrow, and because not enough land was acquired on each side of it. Many of the houses built along its length were small and inconvenient, owing to the exiguity and irregularity of the cleared sites. The City had acquired as little land as possible, and restricted the width of the

---

[42] Merruau, *Souvenirs*, pp. 420–26, 486, 491.
[43] *Moniteur*, 23 October 1852, p. 1700.
[44] Duc de Persigny, *Mémoires* (1896), pp. 243–4.
[45] For criticism of Rambuteau's improvement schemes, see Merruau, *Souvenirs*, pp. 77–8, 343–9.

street, in order to save expense, but this was a false economy because the resale of building lots along a broad traffic artery could recoup a high proportion of the cost of the operation. The Rue de Rambuteau had also taken too long to build—nine years from the first studies until the completion of the last acquisition. Yet it had been the most ambitious of Rambuteau's projects. Most of his public works investment was in penny packets. Many short stretches of street had been built or widened, but the failure to link them up restricted their effect. Much of this confusion resulted from the lack of an overall improvement plan. Rambuteau generally followed the Artists' Plan, but it was already largely out of date. Above all, it needed modification to take account of the displacement of the business centre to the northwest, and the construction of railway termini on the fringes of the centre. Louis-Napoleon, of course, had his own plan, but it existed only in sketch form. In any case, it included a number of projects, such as the Rue de Rivoli, which had already obtained general consent. Although it enabled Louis-Napoleon to establish an order of priority for the schemes he suggested to the City Council, it was totally inadequate as a basis for a large-scale improvement programme. By 1853 no harm had been done because most of the schemes undertaken were isolated from one another. But without a proper plan there remained a danger that at some stage the new streets would be seen to interlink inadequately, or that no preparation would be made for one new street to cross another by the advance provision of crossroads, thus making necessary the demolition of new buildings. Furthermore, only with a comprehensive plan for large-scale improvement would it be possible to use the methods of financing that had been seen to be necessary.

Most of the City's revenue came from taxes on buildings and lands, and dues paid on consumer goods entering Paris (*octroi*). Even a nominated City Council could be expected to resist any increase in the rates of taxation, so that revenue growth depended on a rise in the numbers and/or wealth of the population, and the construction of new houses to accommodate that population. But of course, as the population grew so did the charges borne by the City, so that no large budget surplus could be expected. This, at any rate, was the argument used to prove that the City could not afford to borrow large sums for public works. It had prevailed until the early 1850s, and the results achieved by public works up to then appeared to confirm it, for little had been achieved, at high cost. The lesson that Berger drew from this experience was that improvement schemes should be prudently financed out of revenue. But Louis-Napoleon arrived at the opposite conclusion. If enough money were borrowed to execute the complete transformation of the city, the number and wealth of the citizens would increase so greatly that adequate extra revenues would be available to repay the debt in later years.[46] But such a transformation would have to be carried out quickly, before the rise in property values and costs which would result from the first improvements slowed down the execution of the rest of the programme. The more land acquired, the better, for its resale would enable the City to recoup some of the betterment value which would result from its investment effort.[47] Similar reasoning dictated the abandonment of street widening in favour of the construction of totally new thoroughfares. Acquisition of properties in existing main streets was very costly, because values were always higher there than in the back streets and there were many commercial interests to compensate. And the final result of widening appeared aesthetically unsatisfactory to contemporaries, because a row of new houses on one side would still be faced by 'displeasing sinuosities and buildings unworthy of occupying a place on a great thoroughfare' on the other.[3] In principle, widening should have been easier because some houses would already have been set back to the improvement line, and the City would have needed to acquire only those that still infringed it. But the results of the improvement line procedure had been disappointing. If anything, it caused landlords to postpone the demolition of old houses, for they would lose part of their site for very little compensation, and in many cases find themselves left with a remnant too small for the construction of a profitable building. Of the area of land which, in 1807, was due to become part of the highway under the improvement line legislation only one-third had actually been removed from private ownership by 1857.[49] Haussmann later wrote, 'At that rate, it would have taken nearly another century to finish the job!' And in the city centre the proportion of land ceded was certainly much less than one-third, especially in the densely constructed main streets. So it was preferable to make a completely fresh start. And when it *was* later necessary to acquire properties in commercial streets, the good sense of the decision to avoid them was made apparent.

---

[46] This contention was proved correct by the sound state of the City's finances, at least until the early 1860s (see 'The finances of the City of Paris, 1858-9', *Journal of the Statistical Society* [of London], vol. 23, 1860, pp. 233-4).

[47] The Metropolitan Board of Works followed a similar reasoning from 1876. See Ralph Turvey, *The Economics of Real Property* (1957), pp. 108ff.

[48] Haussmann, *Mémoires* (1890-3), vol. III, p. 50.

[49] Haussmann, vol. III, p. 52.

In 1859, for instance, the City had to acquire some houses in the Rue Saint-Martin in order to link existing streets to the Boulevard de Sébastopol. One shoe manufacturer received 75,000 francs (£3,000) compensation for the interruption of his lease, which was much more than many indemnities paid for whole properties in the side streets.[50]

It had also been learned, from Berger's period as Prefect, that close control was needed over the City Council. Although its members were nominated and its powers limited, its failure to cooperate with the Prefect was enough to place serious obstacles in the way of any improvement scheme. The councillors would have to be chosen very carefully, and great attention would have to be paid to managing the debates and striking up a partnership with the councillors. In this way, municipal sources of finance could be assured. Equally important, experience had shown that State subsidies could be the deciding factor in persuading councillors to undertake a project. The Prefect would have to maintain good relations with the Government and Parliament, and know what schemes would be likely to appeal to them enough to qualify for subsidy. It could sometimes be argued, as Persigny encouraged Berger to do,[51] that radial road improvements ought to qualify for subsidy because they were extensions of national trunk routes, but the argument that they were essential to the maintenance of public order carried more weight.

Haussmann was very fortunate in that the opportunities to apply these lessons of experience were very good in the early 1850s. Once he had studied the Emperor's sketch plan and obtained his agreement to certain modifications, he knew that he could depend on the backing of Louis-Napoleon, who was then at the height of his prestige, in its general implementation. He was also lucky that the limitations on compulsory purchase of land which partly explain Rambuteau's modest acquisitions for the Rue de Rambuteau were temporarily suspended. Before 1789 expropriation had been a royal prerogative, but it was codified by the law of 16 September 1807, which introduced certain limitations. In particular, the law laid down that all parts of properties acquired which were not needed for the works should be restored to the original owner or attached to adjacent private properties. But in compensation the public authority would have the right to tax betterment values which resulted from the improvement work in neighbouring properties. However, this facility was never upheld by the

---

[50] *Gazette des Tribunaux*, 2 June 1859, p. 533.
[51] Persigny, *Mémoires*, p. 240.

courts. The law of 3 May 1841, which modified expropriation procedure mainly with a view to the rapid construction of railways, made
no mention of taxation of betterment values, but still incorporated
the stipulation that land should be acquired only for the works.
Rambuteau did not object, because the City preferred to acquire too
little land rather than too much,[52] but the application of the law proved
so restrictive that when a decree of public utility was obtained for the
Rue de Rivoli extension in May 1848, the former Prefect's officers
persuaded the temporary, Government-appointed mayor of Paris to
make use of the absolute powers created by the revolution. So a clause
was included which allowed the City to acquire the totality of sites
crossed by the new street and to resell them for as much as the market
would stand.[53] This principle was incorporated in the law of 13 April
1850, on unhealthy dwellings (Loi Melun), and in 1851 it was applied
to the further extension of the Rue de Rivoli. Finally, it was made
applicable to all streetworks in Paris by the decree-law of 26 March,
1852, which allowed the complete expropriation of properties, part of
which was needed for the works, when the remainder was too small
for the erection of 'healthy houses'.[54] This allowed Haussmann to
acquire enough land for the construction of a row of tall houses on
each side of any new street.

Haussmann was also lucky that the Second Republic had created
the City Council that he needed. Its constitution was not modified for
some years under the Second Empire, and even then changes were
very small. So the councillors continued to be nominated by the
Emperor on the Prefect's recommendation. But Haussmann appears
to have taken more care in choosing his councillors than Berger had
done. He always took the Council into his confidence, and paid
attention to its views on the execution of public works. For this reason
he wanted the Council to be as representative as possible, and although
most of the men he chose were Parisian bourgeois notabilities, he tried
to ensure that there were two from each *arrondissement*.[55] And it was
very largely due to the pains he took that there was almost no opposition
to his policies from within the City Council.

State support was more difficult to obtain than municipal harmony.

[52] Merruau, *Souvenirs*, pp. 77–8.   [53] Merruau, pp. 77–8.
[54] A. Bailleux de Marisy, 'La Ville de Paris: ses finances et ses travaux publics depuis
le commencement du siècle', p. 806, *Revue des Deux Mondes*, September-October 1863,
pp. 775–829.
[55] Lucien Lambeau, *L'Hôtel de Ville depuis les origines jusqu'en 1871* (1920), p. 144;
Gérard Lameyre, *Haussmann Préfet de Paris* (1958), p. 80.

But when Haussmann came to the Prefecture in 1853 the chances of obtaining subsidies were still very good. Even before Louis-Napoleon's *coup d'état* the Assembly had been afraid of riots and unrest in Paris and had been eager to accelerate work on the Rue de Rivoli by granting subsidies ⟨*see* plate 18⟩. Such a project could be expected to reduce popular discontent by providing work, and facilitate the entry of troops into the central areas which were often the home of insurrection. And there was an even better chance of obtaining subsidies now that Louis-Napoleon had greatly extended his powers and a Bonapartist majority had been elected to the Assembly in March 1852. But they could be expected only for streets that had a definite strategic importance; that is, broad arteries crossing the poor districts of the centre and east, linking them with barracks and railway termini. Small-scale improvements, or works in the rich western districts, could not expect to qualify.

Although conditions were clearly favourable to the continuance of a street improvement programme, they cannot alone explain why Napoleon III and Haussmann chose to push ahead so forcefully. What, then, were public works intended to achieve?

It would be wrong to try to distinguish a single dominant motive for street improvements in the mid-nineteenth century. At that time, much more than in any other period, street improvements appeared to be a panacea for every urban problem.[56] Although opposition grew up to Haussmann's methods, few objected to his basic aims, which were to modernise Paris and adapt it to the needs of a quickly growing population and economy. And one of the most pressing requirements of any great city is an adequate communication system.

In 1861 Bailleux de Marisy wrote that traffic considerations alone were enough to justify the public works programme.[57] The population of Paris had grown from 547,756 in 1801 to 1,053,262 fifty years later. There was also an increase in the population of the suburbs, which in the 1840s were surrounded by a new ring of fortifications, thus emphasising the anomaly of their administrative separation from the City. But most of the increased population still had to find accommodation in the city centre, which became grossly overcrowded with

[56] For similar thinking in relation to London, see H. J. Dyos, 'Urban transformation: a note on the objects of street improvement in Regency and early Victorian London', *International Review of Social History*, vol. II, 1957, pt. 2, pp. 259–65.

[57] A. Bailleux de Marisy, 'Des sociétés foncières et de leur rôle dans les travaux publics' p. 214, *Revue des Deux Mondes*, July–August 1861, pp. 193–216.

population densities of up to one thousand persons to the hectare in some of the older districts. Traffic congestion became so serious that the development of new residential districts on the outskirts was compromised by the difficulty of reaching the centre, which remained the main source of employment and services. The arrival of the railways in the 1840s made matters worse. A law passed in 1842 laid down that Paris should be linked by rail to all the frontiers, so that Paris became the hub of a radiating system of trunk lines. It was clear to contemporaries that the capital's new accessibility would accelerate immigration and the development of Paris as a commercial and industrial centre. At this time none of the railway companies, except the one using the Gare Saint-Lazare in north-west Paris, was very interested in suburban services,[58] so that little immediate suburban development could be expected. Furthermore, the railways made no contribution to transport within the city. The companies had originally planned to bring their lines into the very centre of Paris, with a number of stops inside the fortifications, but these projects were thwarted by the City and the Government. The termini were finally sited on the fringes of the city centre. Railway omnibuses were operated to transport passengers to the railheads, and to enable through travellers to cross the city centre from one terminal to another. Plans were made for a circular line just inside the fortifications linking up all the radial routes to allow freight to be transferred without crossing the city centre. But work on its construction did not begin until 1851, and the line was not fully operational until 1867.[59] No passenger service was operated until the 1860s, and it remained very slow and inconvenient until the following decade.[60] So the railway stations put an extra strain on the main radial thoroughfares, on or near which they had all been sited. Most of these streets were no more than ten metres wide at their broadest points, and through traffic was continually held up by local traffic having business at the shops and other concerns which were concentrated along them. Even in 1844, before the railways began to have any effect, the Rue Saint-Martin was very difficult to *walk* along before midday owing to the carts, carriages and vendors that thronged it.[61] Most other radial streets were as bad. In 1851 it used to take fifteen minutes to walk from the corner of the Rue Saint-Denis

[58] Pierre Merlin, *Les transports parisiens* (1966), pp. 90–92.
[59] Jean Bastié, *La croissance de la banlieue parisienne* (1964), p. 122.
[60] René Clozier, *La Gare du Nord* (1940), p. 66.
[61] Le Roux de Lincy, 'Rue et Faubourg Saint-Martin', p. 64, in (ed. Louis Lurine), *Les rues de Paris* (1844), vol. II, pp. 41–64.

and the Rue de Rivoli to the Hôtel de Ville.[62] Fortunately, the *grands boulevards* allowed through traffic on the right bank to bypass the centre, but here too congestion was starting to build up. In one traffic census in the 1840s 10,750 horses drawing vehicles were found to have passed through the Boulevard des Italiens in one period of twenty-four hours.[63] The obvious solution was to improve the radial routes, and to provide means of communicating directly from one station to another without crossing the centre. This would remove the commercial activities of the inner districts from the stranglehold of congestion, and encourage the development of new suburbs to house the increased population. As Haussmann said, a system of wide streets could 'give an equal impetus everywhere to building enterprise'.[64] And the provision of new housing would slow down the general increase in rents which could also be a cause of social unrest.[65]

A further big advantage of street improvements was that they were the only practical means of demolishing slum houses in any numbers. As we have seen, the cholera epidemic of 1848, which killed 19,000 people in Paris, revived public interest in health problems. Although there was still considerable controversy about the cause of disease, most doctors had come to agree with the anti-contagionist hypothesis which attributed the propagation of disease to local causes such as dirt, poverty, overcrowding and defective sewers.[66] So the best way of fighting disease seemed to be to demolish as many old houses as possible, or at least to allow air and sunlight to reach them. Powers to acquire and demolish unhealthy houses as a last resort were established by the Melun law of 1850, but their application was limited. Compensation was fixed according to the 1841 law on expropriation, which did not allow for a reduction in the case of insalubrity. So it could cost as much to acquire a slum house compulsorily as one in good condition. Moreover, the site of such a house, once cleared, was worth very little, because it would still be surrounded by similar buildings. Yet the clearance of groups of houses was impossible under the 1850 powers because a state of irremediable insalubrity had to be proved to exist in each property. In contrast, the demolition of large numbers of houses, whatever their condition, was easy when carried out in connection with a street scheme. And as the new streets were usually

[62] *Gazette des Tribunaux*, 6 October 1868.
[63] Louis Réau, etc., *L'oeuvre du baron Haussmann* (1954), p. 32.
[64] Conseil général, *Procès-verbaux*, 1857, Prefect's report, p. 10.
[65] Conseil général, *Procès-verbaux*, 24 November 1856, p. 12.
[66] See David H. Pinkney, *Napoleon III and the Rebuilding of Paris* (1958), p. 23.

routed across poor districts in order to limit compensation costs, most of the houses demolished were slums. Of course, slum houses remained on either side of the new streets, but contemporaries optimistically assumed that the creation of a single corridor of fresh air and sunlight across a crowded area would generate breezes and allow the sun to shine into adjacent streets. Public gardens and squares, which Louis-Napoleon had admired in London, could be laid out at frequent intervals, their greenery serving to renew the vitiated atmosphere. Furthermore, the street works would be accompanied by the construction of new sewers and water ducts. Indeed, the provision of new underground works, although it cannot be discussed here, was an integral part of the Second Empire's improvement policy.[67] Short of demolishing the whole of the centre of Paris (and even this was tried in the Cité) nothing more could be done.

All this expenditure of public money was certain to provide work and stimulate the city's economy, and this was clearly seen as another point in favour of a public works policy. Louis-Napoleon accepted more completely than most of his republican opponents that it was the Government's duty to provide relief for the poor and unemployed. A law of 11 January 1849 had set up the Paris *Assistance Publique* in its modern form, and Haussmann worked hard to organise and improve it. [68] In December 1853, after a poor harvest, he set up the *Caisse de la Boulangerie* to provide cheap food for the working classes.[69] But the prime need was to provide work for the many building and civil engineering labourers in Paris, whose numbers had increased in the 1840s during work on the railways and the new fortifications.[70] Not only would general prosperity be increased by full employment, but street improvements would provide an effective encouragement to the building trade, as the compensation paid to landlords would be invested in new constructions. Commerce would benefit from the provision of modern accommodation. All this activity would provide expanding investment opportunities which, helped by the development of a nationwide banking and credit system, would attract from individual investors large amounts of capital which previously had remained unproductive. As Haussmann proudly told the General Council of the Seine in 1857:

[67] See Pinkney, *Rebuilding of Paris*, chapters V and VI, pp. 105–50.
[68] See Haussmann, *Mémoires*, vol. II, pp. 405–42.
[69] See Haussmann, vol. II, pp. 341–66.
[70] Pierre Riquet, 'Le quartier de l'Opéra et l'évolution du centre d'affaires de Paris', p. 151, in *Urban Core and Inner City* (1967), pp. 141–61.

'Certainly, the main result aimed at by the Emperor's Government in carrying out such improvements was to draw the whole nation into the productive path of confidence and work.'[71]

He claimed that the increase in the number of commercial premises resulted 'to a large extent from the happy influence of public enterprise on private business, from the impulse that all branches of commerce in Paris have received, after the building industry.[72] And Bailleux de Marisy wrote a few years later that the distribution of generous indemnities had created 'a movement of capital which must be considered as the principal cause of the progress of public wealth in Paris.'[73]

A further result of this development of wealth would be to put the City's finances on a firmer footing. Municipal revenues had hardly even kept pace with the increase in population during the first half of the century. Between 1820 and 1840 the City's ordinary revenues rose from twenty-six million to only forty-two million francs.[74] By 1850 they had increased only by a further seven million francs. Although Persigny failed to convince Berger that an energetic improvement programme would produce a business boom from which the City's finances would benefit,[75] Haussmann argued from the first that his public works debts would be serviced and amortised by revenue growth. In 1857 he proudly stated that the interest on the two loans floated since 1851 could be covered by the increase in *octroi* duties on building materials since that date.[76] By 1855 ordinary sources of revenue were producing nearly fifty-eight million francs, and when the City boundaries were extended to the fortifications in 1860 receipts rose to over 100 million francs. In 1869 they totalled nearly 146 million francs. *Octroi* dues alone rose from twenty-six and a half million francs in 1848 to just over 100 millions in 1869.[77]

Mention must also be made of the strategic aspect of the public works programme. Ever since 1789 no Government had been safe from the threat of violent overthrow in the streets of Paris.[78] The traditional tactics of revolutionaries were to take over the centre and

---

[71] Conseil général, *Procès-verbaux*, 1857, Prefect's report, p. 5.
[72] Prefect's report, p. 5.
[73] A. Bailleux de Marisy, 'La Ville de Paris devant le Corps Législatif', p. 444, *Revue des Deux Mondes*, March–April 1870, pp. 419–46.
[74] Henri de Pontich, *Administration de la Ville de Paris* (1884), p. 99.
[75] Persigny, *Mémoires*, p. 245.
[76] Conseil général, *Procès-verbaux*, 1857, Prefect's report, p. 14n.
[77] De Pontich, *Administration de Paris*, pp. 99, 101; C. M. reports, 1895, no. 170, annex 2.
[78] See article by André Morizet, in C.V.P., 29 October 1932, pp. 117–22.

east of the city and seize the Hôtel de Ville, where a free commune could be proclaimed and money and printing presses were available. Barricades had been erected in Paris nine times in the twenty-five years before the Second Empire, and a small number of amateurs could use them in the narrow streets to hold off large numbers of troops, at least for a time. If broad thoroughfares could be driven through these turbulent districts, troops would be able to penetrate quickly to the source of any trouble. They would be too wide to be blocked by barricades (or so it was thought). Barracks could be sited near the new streets, preferably at crossroads to allow the quick despatch of forces in various directions. And if the barracks were linked to the railway stations by broad thoroughfares, it would be possible to bring troops back from the frontier by rail and deploy them swiftly in the capital.

Some commentators have suggested that Haussmann's streets were all broad and straight to allow soldiers a clear field of fire. But rectilinear planning was much more an aspect of the aesthetic objectives of the new streets than a military requirement. And it was not the least advantage of street improvements that, in the eyes of most contemporaries, they added to the beauty of the city. All the streets planned by the Artists in the 1790s had been rectilinear, although strategic considerations had not been taken into account. Napoleon III's ambition was to make Paris 'the most beautiful city in the world',[79] and Haussmann always tried to ensure that new streets were terminated by a large or beautiful building.[80] The ideal of the age was to isolate great buildings by clearing away nearby constructions, and this could easily be combined with street works. In some cases, however, no old monuments were available to provide a focal point at the end of a new avenue, and here Haussmann was often prepared to provide one himself. For instance, he insisted that the new commercial tribunal in the Cité be an imposing edifice with a dome, to provide a monumental termination for the Boulevard de Sébastopol. But aesthetics were always secondary to purely practical considerations; Haussmann told the General Council of the Seine that the main objective of the street improvement programme was to satisfy the needs of a growing population, rather than to beautify the city.[81] Straight and level streets were also desirable from the points of view of traffic flow, provision of attractive building sites, and sewer and conduit con-

[79] Persigny, *Mémoires*, p. 256.
[80] Haussmann, *Mémoires*, vol. III, p. 530.
[81] Conseil général, *Procès-verbaux*, 1857, Prefect's report, p. 13.

struction. No engineer enjoying Haussmann's powers of property acquisition would have dreamed of designing anything else.

All these good reasons for building new streets, when taken together, formed so convincing an argument that Haussmann's improvement policy was really inevitable rather than revolutionary. And each one of them justified the concentration of activity on the city centre. We must now consider how and why improvement projects were prepared there, and how they were carried out.

Haussmann realised that the centre would have a key role to play in an enlarged Paris. But before it could do so, the restriction that it placed on free traffic movement would have to be removed. Only then could the outer districts develop fully:

> 'In order to make the vast spaces at the extremities of the city, which remained unproductive, accessible and inhabitable, the first job was to drive streets right through the city from one side to the other, by tearing open the central districts . . .'[82]

The basis of this operation was the construction of what Haussmann called 'the Paris cross' (*la croisée de Paris*) formed by the north-south and east-west routes, which would 'cut through the middle of the city in the form of a cross, and bring its extreme limits at the four cardinal points into almost direct communication'.[83] Haussmann expected it to transform the centre from 'an immense obstacle to general traffic movement' into 'the link for all the rest'.[84] The logic of this scheme was that the centre should retain and even expand its existing functions as a commercial, service and administrative centre, and abandon part of its residential function. Some contemporaries were even hopeful that street improvements would restore to the older areas of the centre some of the prosperous business activities which by now characterised districts further west.[85] Of course, Haussmann had no control over commerce and industry, except indirectly through the Halles and the retail markets, but he could and did ensure that administrative centralisation was maintained.

A rejuvenated centre would certainly not present the same threat

[82] Haussmann, *Mémoires*, vol. II, p. 33.   [83] Haussmann, vol. III, p. 49.
[84] Conseil général, *Procès-verbaux*, 24 November 1856, pp. 13–14.
[85] See, for instance, Louis Huart, 'Rue des Lombards', pp. 235–6, in (ed. Louis Lurine), *Les rues de Paris* (1844), vol. I, pp. 227–36.

to public order as one that was decaying and overpopulated. But dangers would remain during the transitional period, and the decision to retain the main administrative offices in the centre meant that some local protection would be needed. So although the improvement schemes made it unnecessary to turn the centre into an armed camp, some extra barracks were needed at key points. Haussmann provided them in the Cité, behind the Hôtel de Ville, and in the left bank centre, which also had a long revolutionary tradition. But the main new barracks was built at the Place du Château-d'Eau (now Place de la République), to the north-east of the city centre. It could send troops into the centre if necessary, and it was poised to quell trouble in the eastern industrial *faubourgs*, as well as being close enough to the Gare du Nord and the Gare de l'Est to be quickly reinforced by troops arriving by rail. And the Commune of 1871 proved that the main danger of insurrection no longer came from inside the *grands boulevards*, but from east of the Bastille.[86] So it was yet another advantage of Haussmann's emphasis on good communications that large bodies of troops no longer had to be kept in the city centre, to the encouragement of more peaceful pursuits.

We must now consider the planning of each of the new streets provided in the city centre. Although Haussmann built most of the 'Paris cross', he was not the author of the concept, and work had started on both its main elements before he arrived at the Prefecture. But he was responsible for much of its detailed planning. He resolved arguments about the line that should be taken by the Rue de Rivoli east of the Hôtel de Ville by turning it slightly towards the north so that it ran into the Rue Saint-Antoine several hundred yards west of the Bastille. This section was completed in 1855. The Rue Saint-Antoine was not improved because it was already twenty metres wide, the same as the Rue de Rivoli, and any straightening of its course would have been very costly owing to its great commercial activity. In any case, aesthetic considerations were of less importance in the east of the centre than in the west.

Although Persigny denied that the main objective of the Rue de Rivoli was strategic,[87] Haussmann later called it 'a direct, spacious, monumental and, moreover, strategic communication link'.[88] Léon Faucher, rapporteur of the bill granting the City powers to float a loan of fifty million francs in 1851, said of it:

[86] Georges Duveau, *La vie ouvrière sous le Second Empire* (1946), p. 204.
[87] Persigny, *Mémoires*, p. 242.   [88] Haussmann, *Mémoires*, vol. III, p. 21.

'The interests of public order, not less than those of salubrity, demand that a wide swathe be cut as soon as possible across this district of barricades. . . . An intermediate line will be added to the great strategic lines of the boulevards . . .'[89]

The Government, as we have seen, recognised the strategic importance of the street and provided subsidies varying between one-third and two-thirds of the cost of each section.[90] Of the subsidy granted for the length of new street along the north wall of the Louvre, Haussmann wrote:

'It was only right: the interest of the State in the operations carried out in the first [section] was clearly greater than that of the City.'[91]

But the Rue de Rivoli was also of key importance to the easing of traffic congestion. It bypassed the immediate vicinity of the Halles, which caused severe congestion in the Rue Saint-Honoré, and replaced the totally inadequate Rue de la Verrerie and Rue du Roi-de-Sicile east of the Rue Saint-Denis. Even Ferdinand de Lasteyrie, a critic of many aspects of the public works programme, admitted that the dense traffic in the completed Rue de Rivoli was sufficient justification for its construction.[92] The works also brought about the demolition of a large number of slum houses. Councillor Lanquetin, in the early 1840s, described the Hôtel de Ville district as the city's most unhealthy,[93] but the other areas affected were little better. The compensation amounts incurred by the City were generally very small.

In 1855, the year in which the last section of the Rue de Rivoli was completed, Haussmann finished clearing the site for the new Halles, and the six easternmost market buildings were erected between 1854 and 1858. Although a number of streets had been planned to open up the Halles district,[94] Haussmann gave next priority to the other element of the 'Paris cross', the Boulevard du Centre (finally named

---

[89] Quoted in A. des Cilleuls, *Administration parisienne*, vol. II, p. 192.

[90] C.M. reports, 1897, no. 125, pp. 235–6.

[91] Haussmann, *Mémoires*, vol. III, p. 26. The absence of Government subsidies was largely responsible for the limited scale of street improvements in London. See Dyos, 'Urban transformation', pp. 264–5; William Ashworth, *The Genesis of Modern British Town Planning* (1954), pp. 65ff.

[92] Ferdinand de Lasteyrie, *Les travaux de Paris: examen critique* (1861), p. 58.

[93] Commission des Halles, *Documents*, no. 4, pp. 16–17.

[94] In 1861 Bailleux de Marisy was complaining that access to the Halles still remained difficult ('Des sociétés foncières', p. 215n).

Boulevard de Sébastopol on the right bank and Boulevard Saint-Michel on the left). When Haussmann became Prefect the Boulevard de Strasbourg was already under construction. Although no powers had been obtained to extend it southwards beyond the *grands boulevards*, the possibility of doing so had clearly been foreseen by Louis-Napoleon, and in 1855 Haussmann called the Boulevard du Centre the 'indispensable complement' of the Boulevard de Strasbourg.[95] In fact, the existence of the Boulevard de Strasbourg dictated the line of the Boulevard du Centre, although Haussmann claimed later that he had considered widening the Rue Saint-Denis, but had desisted owing to the inevitably high cost of compensation and the disruptive effect it would have on the city's commercial life.[96] Haussmann's eagerness to build this boulevard was due partly to his desire to link up the outer areas of the city across the centre, and it was for this reason that he accorded it priority over the Boulevard Saint-Germain.[97] Moreover, its great strategic significance held out the promise of a Government subsidy:

'It was to tear open Old Paris, the district of riots and barricades, by a wide, central thoroughfare which would pierce this almost impenetrable labyrinth from one side to the other, and would itself be crossed by transversal streets whose continuation would carry on the work begun by the boulevard.'[98]

In the event, the Government provided a subsidy of one-third, suggesting that it was not considered so important as the Rue de Rivoli, but it had considerable advantages for the city from the point of view of traffic and slum clearance. The destruction of slums was particularly urgent in the Cité, which was crossed by the boulevard. Lanquetin had referred to the residential area on the island as 'without possible contradiction, one of the most deprived of elements of prosperity', while 'its filthy alleys and dead ends are the hideout of the majority of released prisoners, so many of whom come to Paris.'[99] Haussmann combined large-scale clearance with the development of three institutions that were already established in the Cité—the Hôtel-Dieu, the Palais de Justice, and the Préfecture de Police. Pursuing his desire

[95] *Moniteur*, 28 March 1855. A plan for a north-south artery across the city, roughly on the line of the Boulevard de Sébastopol, had been made as early as 1840 (René Clozier, *La Gare du Nord*, p. 42).
[96] Haussmann, *Mémoires*, vol. III, p. 52.   [97] Haussmann, vol. III, pp. 49–50.
[98] Haussmann, vol. III, p. 54.   [99] Commission des Halles, *Documents*, no. 4, p. 17.

to centralise still further, he moved the commercial tribunal, which had previously sat at the Bourse, and the *Conseil des Prud'hommes* to new premises in the Cité. He would even have liked to clear the whole island, and devote it exclusively to law, religion and medicine.[100] The Cité was clearly the best place in the city centre to establish vast new buildings because clearance costs were lower there than elsewhere, but this accentuation of existing centralisation was, as in the case of the Halles, not without its critics. The maintenance of the Palais de Justice on its old site was not questioned, and its extension as recently as 1840[101] made any change of site almost out of the question. But a section of medical opinion was worried by the rebuilding of a large hospital, the Hôtel-Dieu, in the city centre, when it could have been transferred to a healthier site in the suburbs.[102] In fact, a branch hospital had already been set up on the outskirts, in the Rue de Charenton. However, there were strong arguments in favour of a central location from the point of view of ease of transport and visiting, especially as poor people could not afford to lose a day's work by going to see sick relatives in a suburban hospital.[103] And the Cité's open position in the middle of the river made it, when cleared of its slums, the healthiest possible central site.

Haussmann's treatment of the Île Saint-Louis was in complete contrast to the Cité. No great traffic route crossed it, and its houses, which dated from no earlier than the seventeenth century, were in much better condition than those of the neighbouring island. All that Haussmann did there was to complete a route which had been planned by the Artists, and begun on the right bank in the 1830s when the Rue du Pont-Louis-Philippe was built. In 1861–2 Haussmann extended it across the western tip of the Île Saint-Louis to provide direct access, via two bridges, to the eastern end of the Cité. The rest of the island was left untouched.

The 'great cross', which was complete by 1860, was intended to provide the basic framework of a grid system of main streets for the right bank centre. Such a plan fitted existing traffic patterns because most of the older streets ran either parallel or perpendicular to the Seine. The Prefect also recognised the need for some diagonal thoroughfares to shorten journeys in the city centre, and to provide more direct

---

[100] Haussmann, *Mémoires*, vol. III, p. 554.
[101] See *Documents relatifs aux travaux du Palais de Justice* (1858).
[102] See Félix Pigeory, *Monuments de Paris*, p. 400.
[103] Pigeory, pp. 399, 400; Yvan Christ, 'Haussmann et son règne', *Jardin des Arts*, no. 132, November 1965, p. 21; Haussmann, *Mémoires*, vol. III, p. 521.

access to it from the north-west and the north-east.[104] But he was able to carry out very little of this supplementary plan. In 1860 Paris annexed the suburban communes within the fortifications, and responsibility for this new area, which had previously seen no improvements, forced Haussmann to turn some of his attention away from the centre. Moreover, while agreeing to provide a subsidy for the so-called Second Network of new streets in 1858, Parliament made it clear that it was unwilling to sanction further subsidies.[105] The City was to build the Second Network over ten years at a total cost of 180 million francs, fifty millions of which would be provided by the State. Parliament had rejected an earlier draft of the agreement, under which the Government would have paid one-third of the total cost.[106] Most of the streets subsidised were in the zone between the *grands boulevards* and the old city boundary. Haussmann said later that the Government 'had restricted its participation to those works whose completion seemed to be the most imperiously demanded by the public interest'.[107] Only two streets in the right bank centre, the Rue de Turbigo and the Boulevard du Palais (Île de la Cité), were included in the subsidy agreement. The Rue de Turbigo was to run from the Place du Château-d'Eau in the north-east to the Halles. As well as linking the Prince-Eugène barracks to the turbulent Arts-et-Métiers district, it extended the Rue du Faubourg-du-Temple into the city centre, thus providing direct access from the Belleville heights, a developing working-class area which had previously been somewhat inaccessible.[108] This new link was especially important to the development of industry in the north-east, for it joined the centre of the Paris metal industry, the IIIe *arrondissement*, to the growing industrial zones in the Xe, XIe, XIXe and XXe *arrondissements*. Thanks to its inclusion in the subsidy programme, the Rue de Turbigo was completed in 1867. And in the previous year Haussmann built, without subsidy, two more short streets to provide access to the Halles. These were the Rue des Halles and the Rue du Pont-Neuf, both of which improved communications between the Halles and the left bank. However, the remaining thoroughfares planned in the right bank centre were only partially

---

[104] See Henri de Pontich, *Administration de Paris*, p. 268.

[105] For a list of works subsidised, see Alfred des Cilleuls, *Histoire de l'administration parisienne au XIXe siècle* (1900), vol. II, p. 331, note 1182.

[106] See Henri de Pontich, *Administration de Paris*, p. 271; Louis Girard, *La politique des travaux publics sous le Second Empire* (1952), pp. 166–7.

[107] Memorandum to the City Council, in *Moniteur*, 11 December, 1867.

[108] See Ferdinand de Lasteyrie's support for the scheme on utilitarian grounds in *Travaux de Paris*, pp. 81–2.

completed by Haussmann. Some of them were laid out at those points where they crossed the Rue de Rivoli, the Boulevard de Sébastopol, and the Rue de Turbigo. Part of the Rue Etienne-Marcel was constructed in this way, in connection with the Rue de Turbigo project, in 1867. Short sections were built at each end of the Avenue de l'Opéra in 1858 (south) and 1868 (north). But only a few yards were laid out of the other planned diagonal artery, the Boulevard Henri-IV. Two sections of the east-west Rue Réaumur were built in 1860 and 1867, as part of the Boulevard de Sébastopol and Rue de Turbigo schemes. But in 1868 a much longer section of this street, separately christened Rue du Dix-Décembre (now Rue du Quatre-Septembre), was built from the Place de l'Opéra to the Bourse. This thoroughfare was much more useful than the fragments mentioned above because it linked the Bourse directly to the new business districts between the Place de l'Opéra and the Gare Saint-Lazare. But it involved the demolition of much modern property, and was extremely costly. It was the first non-radial route to be built by Haussmann in the right route bank centre, and also his last.

Although Haussmann had planned to rejuvenate the whole of the centre, great areas of it were still untouched by improvements when he was forced to resign in 1870. The largest of these sectors was the Marais, between the Rue de Rivoli and the Rue de Turbigo. This part of the city centre was not crossed by any trunk traffic routes because it lay between the Châtelet and the heights of Belleville, Ménilmontant and Romainville. The main roads from Meaux and Lagny skirt round these hills so that, instead of entering the city in the north-east, they come in from the north and east respectively. Because the area had no traffic problems Haussmann had ignored it, and by creating wide traffic arteries to the north-west and south he had ensured that even less traffic than before would pass through it. Similarly bypassed were the Mail and Bonne-Nouvelle wards in the IIe *arrondissement*. Moreover, of those districts that had been traversed by new streets, few had been completely transformed by the provision of subsidiary streets, open spaces and public buildings. Only the Cité, Arcis ward, and the Halles and Temple market districts had been so fortunate. Elsewhere, the dominant principle was one of linear redevelopment, with old properties remaining intact behind the façades of the new streets. So Haussmann failed in his ambition to transform the centre.

No doubt if Haussmann had been able to proceed with his schemes, the centre would have been totally modernised. But as time went on the completion of his plan became increasingly impracticable, for both economic and political reasons.

Mention has been made of the facility enjoyed by the City of compulsorily acquiring and retaining land lying on either side of a new street and not strictly necessary for its construction. This had allowed Haussmann to recoup much of the cost of his works by selling off building sites. But in December 1858 the *Conseil d'Etat*, France's final administrative court of appeal and a vigilant protector of individual rights, modified the application of the decree of 26 March 1852, to allow landlords to retain lands not incorporated in the public highway.[109] This meant that betterment value, which could not be taxed, was retained by the property owner. In practice, this ruling did not mean that no land at all was acquired outside the improvement lines, for many landlords were prepared to negotiate a sale if the City made a satisfactory offer, which, in the interests of aesthetics and good planning, it was usually prepared to do. But the cost of acquisition was thereby substantially increased. Haussmann complained later that the *Conseil d'Etat's* decision had completely upset his calculations.[110] And it came at a time when compensation evaluations were already beginning to be inflated. They were fixed by a panel (*jury*) of property owners, who were naturally more favourably inclined to the pretensions of landlords than the offers of compensation made by the City. In the 1850s the absence of serious speculation kept compensation within reason, and the City set up special machinery in 1856 to negotiate agreements directly with the landlords.[111] But the success of early improvements, and the revival of the Paris economy and property market, encouraged the panels to increase their adjudications. This process was accelerated, according to Haussmann, by the subsidy agreement with the Government in 1858.[112] The negotiation of compensation became rare after 1860 as landlords realised that the panel's adjudication was unlikely to be less, and probably would be

---

[109] See Girard, *Politique des travaux publics*, p. 167; Haussmann, *Mémoires*, vol. II, pp. 310–11.

[110] Memorandum to City Council, 1868, quoted in De Pontich, *Administration de Paris*, p. 295n. See also Bailleux de Marisy, 'La Ville de Paris: ses finances et ses travaux publics', p. 813. William Tite estimated in 1864 that not more than half the cost of new streets was recouped by sales of sites ('On the Paris street improvements and their cost', *Journal of the Statistical Society*, vol. 27, 1864, pp. 378–87).

[111] Girard, *Politique des travaux publics*, p. 167.

[112] Haussmann, *Mémoires*, vol. II, p. 312.

much more, than the City's final offer.[113] The City's increasing use of concessionaries—civil engineering and development companies which undertook the whole of an improvement scheme including the acquisition of properties—removed landlords' scruples about making exaggerated claims, because it was widely believed that only the amount of the developer's profit was at stake.[114] Compensation for displacement of commercial interests and interruption of lease also increased, especially after the *Cour de Cassation* ruled in 1860 that tenants could claim full compensation from the moment expropriation was pronounced, even if the City intended to allow their leases to expire before eviction.[112]

But much as Haussmann complained about the abuses of the jury system, he was not blind to the fundamental cause of the inflation of compensation. The more improvements carried out, the higher rose the values of the remaining older properties in the city, so that subsequent works became more costly. For example, the acquisition in 1858 of land for the Boulevard de Sébastopol and related improvements cost 866 francs per square metre, whereas expropriations for the nearby Rue de Turbigo in 1866 cost 1,595 francs per square metre.[116] Haussmann tried to overcome this inexorable effect by working as quickly as possible, so that values did not have time to rise too far. But this was really no solution either. The release of large amounts of compensation in a short time was bound to over-activate the property market, and rising values would still halt the improvement programme at some stage, while leaving the City heavily in debt. The advantage of the lightning public works programme over the stealthier approach was that more could be achieved before the final breakdown. But even Haussmann admitted that the unfavourable reaction of public opinion and business to constant inconvenience was bound to limit the speed at which improvements could be carried out.[117]

The corollary of rising costs was a diminishing return in benefits. There was a limit to the number of streets that could be driven across a district, and each extra one would be of less benefit to traffic flow, public health, and security. Yet the public works programme attracted

---

[113] Maurice Halbwachs, *Les expropriations et le prix des terrains à Paris 1860–1900* (1909), p. 34.
[114] For the development of the use of concessionaries, see Ville de Paris, *Résumé des traités de concession relatifs aux grandes opérations de voirie* (1869). For a statement of the argument that a developer should expect to pay compensation out of his own high profits, see *Gazette des Tribunaux*, 19 March 1868.
[115] Louis Réau, etc., *L'oeuvre du baron Haussmann*, p. 47.
[116] De Pontich, *Administration de Paris*, p. 271.   [117] *Moniteur*, 28 March 1855.

thousands of labourers from other parts of the country. It could not be halted without throwing them out of work and, in all probability, onto the streets in protest. Furthermore, it is doubtful whether public works did much to improve public health throughout the city, for, un-accompanied by a public housing programme, they resulted in the overcrowding of surviving areas of cheap accommodation in the centre and the creation of slums on the outskirts.[118] So Haussmann, far from controlling the future of Paris, was himself dominated by the machine that he and his imperial master had created. Even if growing political opposition to the regime and the war with Prussia had not resulted first in his dismissal and then in the fall of Napoleon III, the improve-ment programme would have broken down within a few years. Be-tween 1853 and 1870 the City's debt had risen from 163 million francs to 2,500 millions, and in 1870 debt charges made up 44·14 per cent of the City's budget.[119] The municipal financial structure, thus over-stretched, could not have survived the repercussions of the international depression in the 1870s. Haussmann was fortunate at least in that national political issues forced him out of power, leaving his municipal reputation intact, while others had to clear up the mess he left. On the other hand, he had shown courage and enterprise in applying an erroneous planning concept to Paris, and had achieved some spectac-ular results which went at least part of the way towards making Paris a healthy, convenient and pleasant (though not cheap!) place in which to live.

[118] Railway construction in London had similar results. See H. J. Dyos, 'Railways and housing in Victorian London', *Journal of Transport History*, vol. II, no. 2, November 1955, pp. 11–21, 90–100; 'Some social costs of railway building in London', *Journal of Transport History*, vol. III, no. 1, May 1957, pp. 23–30.

[119] Louis Réau, etc., *L'oeuvre du baron Haussmann*, p. 45; Geneviève Gille, 'Recherches sur l'histoire des emprunts de la Ville de Paris 1814–1875', p. 312 (*Doctorat de IIIe cycle* thesis, Paris, *Lettres*, n.d.). For an early warning of the growing financial danger, see William Tite, 'On the Paris street improvements'.

3

The Struggle to Complete the Imperial Plan

1 ECONOMY AND ENTERPRISE, 1871–6

After the fires of the Commune had died down, Paris looked very different from the splendid days of the Second Empire ⟨*see* plate 20⟩. Many public buildings were in ruins, and hundreds of houses had been destroyed or seriously damaged, first by the Prussian bombardment, and then by the savage battles which had accompanied the death throes of the Communards. The city's industry and business were almost at a standstill. At the time, it must have appeared that the conditions which had encouraged the execution of an ambitious improvement policy could never be recreated. Indeed, it seemed very likely that the imperial street plan would be shelved, at least for the foreseeable future. First priority clearly had to go to replacing the Hôtel de Ville and other important buildings which had been burned down, and the cost of repairing municipal buildings alone was estimated at twenty million francs (£800,000).[1] But the resources to achieve even this object were likely to be hard to come by if the city's economy took several years to recover, as was to be feared. Moreover, the City's debts, which had been big enough in Haussmann's time, now appeared crushing, increased as they were by short-term war debts and by the huge obligation to the *Crédit Foncier* which the previous administration had bequeathed. It took a long time to establish the true extent of the short-term debt, but it was summarily estimated at 887 million francs (£35,480,000), including the debt to the *Crédit Foncier*.[2] The City's

---

[1] Ernest Gay, *Nos édiles 1904–1908* (1906), p. viii.
Gay, p. viii.

43

total obligation, including the long-term debt, had risen to 2,500 million francs (£100 million) by 1870.[3] And although these debts presented a serious enough problem in themselves, there was a danger that the City Council, which the Third Republic made elective, would make political capital out of them and, arguing that Haussmann's debts were the result of a confidence trick played on the public by an undemocratic administration, refuse to borrow any more until the debt charges were considerably reduced. The City Council passed under the control of a strong radical-republican and socialist majority after the elections of 1874, and because it was the agitation of these groups that had helped bring about Haussmann's dismissal, it seemed likely that they would abandon the street improvement scheme as an obsolete relic of bygone days.

On the other hand, there were some very good reasons for completing Haussmann's scheme. Firstly, whatever its political implications, informed opinion did not yet object to his approach to town planning on technical grounds. Criticism of parade architecture and 'the tyranny of the straight line' had come from artists, historians and literary figures. But engineers, architects and local government officials throughout Europe were so impressed by Haussmann's achievement in Paris that they were already carrying out or planning similar improvements in their own countries. No one had yet suggested a practical alternative to new streets as a means of bringing obsolete urban areas up to modern requirements. In any case, Haussmann's team of officials remained in charge of public works despite his departure. One of his lieutenants, Jean Alphand, became director of works, and was soon able to create an authority almost as wide as Haussmann's by taking control of several departments. And he was blindly faithful to his former master's methods. But it would have been almost impossible to change the plan even if doubts had been raised about it, because so much of it had already been built. It would have been lunatic not to complete streets of which some sections were already in use, and the provision of crossroads at various points on the thoroughfares built by Haussmann dictated the lines of those that were planned to intersect them. In many cases, powers of compulsory acquisition had already been obtained,[4] and it was in the City's interests to make use of them, for if they were annulled or allowed to lapse

[3] Louis Réau, etc., *L'oeuvre du baron Haussmann* (1954), p. 45; (after Maurice Félix), *Le régime administratif et financier de la Ville de Paris* (1959), vol. IV, p. 276.
[4] In 1871 there remained in force thirty-five decrees of which no use had been made (Alfred des Cilleuls, *Histoire de l'administration parisienne* [1900], vol. II, p. 334, note 1197).

on economy grounds, the Government might raise objections to a request for renewal at some later date. Besides, the *Conseil d'Etat* usually refused to authorise annulments,[5] and while the decrees were in force, the properties due to be acquired were not subject to ordinary improvement line regulations. Furthermore, the City was not allowed to resell houses acquired by negotiation. But once powers had been obtained it was impossible to introduce substantial variations into the design or line of a street without seeking new powers, and here again the Government looked unfavourably on modifications in a project which had already been given the support of the law. Moreover, it was desirable that the City should carry out approved schemes as early as possible in order to avoid cost increases resulting from speculation. The City could not even forbid new building in the areas to be acquired,[6] and so risked having to pay high compensation for very new buildings. So a reconsideration of the whole policy was not to be expected, at least until the main streets which Haussmann had left partially complete had been carried through. Support for rapid completion also came from the general public, especially in the areas which could expect to benefit from the construction of new streets. It was also argued, just as in 1848, that an ambitious improvement policy could provide work and revive the city's economy. City councillors began urging the Prefect personally to get the street improvement programme moving again as early as December 1871.[7] So it would seem that the arguments in favour of going on were at least as strong as those favouring a period of retrenchment.

What now weighted the balance in favour of a further bout of improvements was that the economic and political situation improved more quickly than it had been possible to hope in the first days after the Commune. Despite its strong radical element, the City Council adopted an objective approach to the problems of Paris, and it had few qualms about adopting Haussmann's policy as its own. The councillors realised that to obtain votes they had to represent the interests of their wards, and when their electorate called for the building of a new street, they had to follow suit. There was no opposition, either, from the Government to an improvement policy because of the dominance of the Assembly by a conservative majority, which was further encouraged by the election of the conservative President

[5] C.M. reports, 1878, no. 33, p. 9.
[6] Henri de Pontich, *Administration de la Ville de Paris* (1884), pp. 278–9.
[7] C.M. minutes, 11 December 1871, p. 76.

Mac-Mahon in 1873. Until his resignation in 1877 the City enjoyed positive Government support for its projects. In particular, the decision to hold an Exposition in Paris in 1878, made in 1876, gave the Government a strong interest in seeing the capital prosperous again in time for the influx of influential foreign visitors, and in making sure that there were some spectacular improvements to show them. Of course, there still remained the City's financial problems, and there was no question of Government subsidies for street works. Fortunately, however, the situation was not as gloomy as had been feared. The City's revenues quickly reached their pre-war level as refugees returned and business recovered. France was not affected so badly as some other countries by the international economic crisis of 1873. The debt to the *Crédit Foncier*, huge though it was, was being paid off in instalments, and it was still hoped that the *Crédit Foncier* would agree to reduce the total amount owed. For all these reasons, therefore, the City Council, the prefectoral administration and the Government found themselves able to agree on the principle and the practicability of pursuing a street improvement policy almost identical to that developed by Haussmann. Yet there was one important difference. Haussmann had largely ignored the outer ring of the city annexed in 1860, despite its expanding industries and population. He had good reasons for concentrating on the centre, and with a nominated City Council he could ignore the demands of the outer areas. But under the Third Republic it was no longer possible to do so. The representatives of the outer *arrondissements* in the new City Council were likely to combine their influence to obtain a fair share of public investment for their own wards. The centre, which had already benefited from so many improvements, could no longer claim special treatment. The Prefect, of course, still held the initiative in planning, and could usually push central schemes through. But, as we shall see, he had to pay increasing attention to the wishes of the outer areas. The days when the needs of the centre could dominate the whole city were now past.

The heavy short-term debts resulting from the war had to be converted as soon as possible, and in 1871 the City floated a loan of 350 million francs (£14 million) repayable over seventy-five years. It was impossible to allocate any of these resources to public works, which would have to be financed out of revenue. In November 1871 the Prefect told the City Council that not only was it impossible to undertake studies for new street improvements, but:

'. . . it is even impossible to carry out those that have already been studied and on which work has started; for they represent an outlay of 700 million francs (£28 million), 384 millions of which is for works for which compulsory purchase powers have already been obtained.'[8]

A month later he told the Council:

'. . . we can consider carrying out only those works which would produce a return sufficient to cover their total cost.'[9]

Although nearly fifteen million francs (£600,000) were devoted to public works in the 1872 budget, the public works committee proposed no schemes in the right bank centre, except for a minor paving operation to allow the reinstallation of the flower market on its site in the Cité.[10] Most of the year's resources went to pay for work already authorised and for exceptionally urgent small-scale improvements.[11] Totally new projects were out of the question; for instance, the City was for two years unable to acquire a site for a new school in Bonne-Nouvelle ward because its financial situation made it hesitate to acquire compulsorily. Even when a sale was negotiated, the City could pay only by giving the owner another site and paying the remainder in six instalments.[12]

In 1875 the City's finances recovered for the first time from the effects of the war and the Commune, and for the following seven years budget surpluses of between twenty and thirty-five million francs were achieved.[13] A strong public demand had built up for the resumption of public works, and to make up for lost time the City floated two long-term loans, of 220 and 120 million francs, in 1875 and 1876. This left enough time to complete the greater part of the improvements in time for the 1878 Exposition. Moreover, the desire to impress visitors to the Exposition dictated that much of these resources should be devoted to the city centre, and particularly to its western areas which were the most frequented by foreign tourists. Two projects in the right bank centre were financed by these loans—the Avenue de l'Opéra and the Boulevard Henri-IV.

---

[8] C.M. minutes, 21 November 1871, p. 18.
[9] C.M. minutes, 1 December 1871, p. 51.
[10] C.M. reports, 1872, no. 44, p. 4.
[11] Prefectoral memorandum, quoted in C.M. reports, 1872, no 44, p. 1.
[12] C.M. reports, 1874, no. 6.
[13] Louis Dausset, *Rapport général . . . sur . . . le projet de budget de la Ville de Paris pour 1909*, p. 40 (C.M. reports, 1908, no. 68).

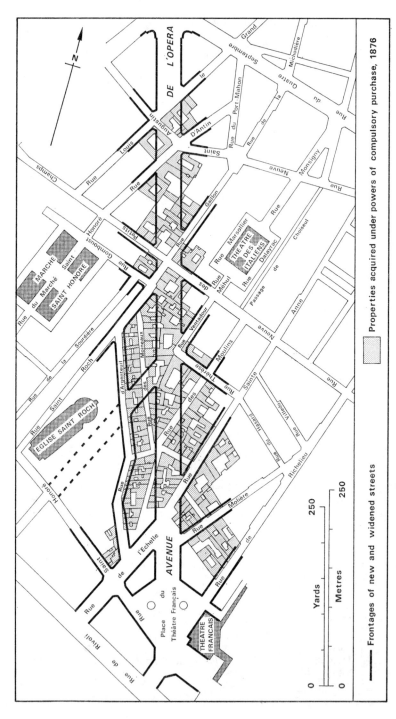

FIG. 2. *The completion of the Avenue de l'Opéra, 1876-7.*

Properties acquired under powers of compulsory purchase, 1876

——— Frontages of new and widened streets

(a) *Avenue de l'Opéra*

The Avenue de l'Opéra ⟨*see* plates 23–25⟩. was the most important diagonal thoroughfare planned in the city centre by Haussmann, but its construction had been put off because diagonal streets were considered to be of secondary importance. Indeed, no powers had been taken to build it, apart from the two short completed sections at each end. But it had been one of the first streets to be planned by Napoleon III in association with Haussmann.[14] It was designed to provide direct access to the city centre from the developing business zone in the north-west and from the Gare Saint-Lazare. And, desirable though it was on grounds of traffic flow alone, it would also serve as a grandiose link between the Louvre and a new opera house which the Emperor was already hoping to site near the Boulevard des Capucines. It was probably for this reason that the Avenue was not included in the streets accepted for subsidy in the Second Network. In the late 1850s the Assembly was resolutely opposed to all extravagant expenditure, and in particular to the rumoured plans for an opera house.[15] Included in the subsidy agreement were two streets, now called the Rue Auber and the Rue Halévy, whose purpose was ostensibly to improve the street system around the Gare Saint-Lazare. But Haussmann had already been indiscreet enough to tell the City Council that a square could be laid out where these two streets converged on the Boulevard des Capucines, to provide a fitting site for a new Opéra. Although he insisted that he was expressing only a personal opinion, the obvious conclusion was that he and the Emperor were in agreement over the site, and this affair was partly responsible for the Assembly's decision to limit the amount of the subsidy, and its determination not to grant further aid in the near future.

After official denials that the building of a new opera house was being considered had failed to satisfy the Assembly, there was no longer any need for dissimulation. In 1860 it was announced that the new structure would be erected on the site mentioned by Haussmann, and the foundation stone was laid in 1862. Preparatory design work on the Avenue was now speeded up.[16] For aesthetic reasons it was

---

[14] According to Charles Merruau, it was one of the streets included by the Emperor in his own private map of desirable improvements (*Souvenirs de l'Hôtel de Ville de Paris 1848–1852* [1875], map).
[15] See *Procès-verbaux des séances du Corps Législatif,* 1858, report no. 273, annex to minutes of 4 May.
[16] See engineer's report on gradients and levels, 25 April 1863, A.S., VO 11, box 2439.

decided that a spectator should be able to see the threshold of the Opéra from any point along the street. This meant digging a shallow cutting through the Butte des Moulins, a slight protruberance which rose to a height of some twenty feet above the surrounding plain. Because ramps were needed to bring existing streets down to the level of the Avenue, a wide area of properties would have to be acquired, but this was both practicable and desirable because the Butte des Moulins district was one of the most depressed in the west of the right bank centre. But for the time being the City hesitated to attack the steepest part of the *butte*, and limited its effort to building the short sections at each end of the street by the late 1860s. Moreover, the expropriation of buildings for the northern section in 1868 proved extremely costly. Nothing more was attempted until Haussmann's resignation in 1870 ruled out further progress.

Although the building of the whole of the Avenue had never been authorised by Government decree, landlords and tenants along the line of the street began to agitate in the early 1870s for its completion, or at least for an official statement of the City's intentions. They complained that they were unable to make firm agreements on leases and rents until they knew exactly when it would be built. One landlord, who had put up a building on the short southern section, sued the City because he claimed that his property would be of little value until the Avenue was extended.[17] The councillors of the Ier and IIe *arrondissements* added their voices in favour of early completion.[18] Of course, they had an eye on the elections of 1874, but there was no insuperable contradiction between the desire to build the Avenue and the need to economise. Because it would link two flourishing commercial streets, the Boulevard des Capucines and the Rue de Rivoli, the Avenue was bound to attract high-class shops and businesses. So the City would be able to recoup much of its outlay by selling building sites at a high price. Yet compensation, at least in the Butte des Moulins district, would be low.

By 1872 the Prefect and the City Council were in complete agreement on the importance of building the Avenue, but the financial situation did not yet allow a big municipal contribution. The Prefect announced hopefully that he was prepared to listen to any proposals for building the Avenue from syndicates of local property owners, but

---

[17] A.S., VO 11, box 2439.
[18] See speech by Councillor Joubert, C.M. minutes, 18 April 1872, p. 3.

the only offers were made by development companies. [19] Cooperation with such agencies was out of the question. Not only was it still impossible for the City to provide the subsidies or financial guarantees which they demanded, but the Council was determined to prevent the speculation and profiteering which had occurred in Haussmann's time as a result of the use of such companies. But without such outside collaboration the City was in an impasse. The public works department produced a scheme for a short extension of the northern section of the Avenue to link it up with several existing streets, but even this was beyond the City's resources.

The Government's announcement that an Exposition would be held in Paris in 1878 came in April 1876. The Prefect and the City Council agreed that the Avenue would have immense prestige value if it could be completed in time for the Exposition. The Prefect immediately suggested floating a loan of 120 million francs (£4,800,000), of which sixty-six millions (£2,640,000) would be allotted to the Avenue.[20] Although the Council was nagged by the feeling that such a sum would be better spent on improving the poorer districts of the city, it was tempted by a prestige project which would glorify republican Paris. The Prefect encouraged the councillors by pointing out that the annual budget surplus was now sufficient to service the debt, and that it would be possible to recoup twenty-one million francs (£840,000) by sale of sites. Cleared sites in a slum area would be worth much less than this. In any case, the Prefect claimed that to build the Avenue was the best way to clear the Butte des Moulins district, which could be regarded as a slum area. Moreover, the project would give positive assistance to the working classes by providing employment and reviving the city's economy. So in May 1876 the Council approved the loan,[21] while strongly defending itself against the implication that it was merely copying Napoleon III. It confirmed that it wanted the City to carry out all the work, instead of letting it out to a private developer. The remaining proceeds of the loan issue were divided between the completion of another big imperial project, the Boulevard Saint-Germain, and the construction of a port and warehouse complex on the banks of the Seine, at the Quai de Bercy.

---

[19] See, for instance, the tender by Boulogne and Lauraney, 13 September 1872, A.S., VO 11, box 2441.
[20] Prefectoral memorandum, 25 April 1876.
[21] C.M. minutes, 13 May 1876.

Compulsory purchase powers were granted by a decree signed by President Mac-Mahon in June 1876. Although only about one landlord in six, and a smaller proportion of tenants, were prepared to negotiate their compensation,[22] the assessment panel proved more judicious than its predecessors under the Second Empire. The average compensation granted for the 168 properties acquired was a mere 225,000 francs (£9,000), and the total was ten million francs (£400,000) less than the City had budgeted for.[23] So it now became possible to consider extending the scheme. In November the Prefect proposed that the Rue des Pyramides should be extended northwards from the Rue Saint-Honoré to meet the new Avenue, as Haussmann had planned fifteen years before.[24] This project was now especially attractive because the Government, who owned the Tuileries gardens, had offered to allow a road to be built across them to link the southern end of the Rue des Pyramides to the *quais* and the Pont-Royal over the Seine. The strong radical-republican majority in the Council was delighted with this plan because it cocked a snook at the Tuileries palace, whose ruins were still standing. In fact, Yves Guyot and other republican councillors had already proposed such a project,[25] mainly with a view to insulting the royalists, whose influence over President Mac-Mahon was causing concern. The Prefect also suggested that more properties should be acquired in the area of the Avenue in order to ease the gradients of the connecting ramps, and that the Rue d'Argenteuil should be widened. Although the City Council recognised the value of these improvements, it had previously obtained a promise from the Prefect that the Avenue de l'Opéra operation would not be extended, so now the public works committee came out strongly against the new proposals on the grounds that it was inequitable to spend so much money on a small area of the city.[26] When their report was debated, some councillors questioned the Prefect's good faith.[27] They insinuated that the big surplus had been rigged so that it could be applied to further operations which the Council would never have approved if full information had been available earlier. These allegations were rebutted by the Prefect, who also pointed out that Government approval would have to be obtained if the money were

[22] Prefectoral memorandum, 8 July 1876.
[23] Calculated from *Gazette des Tribunaux*.
[24] Prefectoral memorandum, 9 November 1876.
[25] Albert Pétrot, *Les conseillers municipaux de Paris* (1876), p. 61.
[26] C.M. reports, 1876, no. 37.
[27] C.M. minutes, 16 November 1876.

to be spent on anything other than the work which had been authorised in the decree giving the City borrowing powers. In the meantime, it would have to be deposited at the Treasury, at 1 per cent interest. So the Council really had no choice but to approve the new proposals, and the public works department was at work on the detailed plans even before the vote was taken. The Council later approved further marginal extensions of the area to be acquired.

Demolition work along the line of the Avenue began in October 1876, and the first new buildings were under construction by the end of the year. The City had made up fifty-five sites, and most of them had been sold by December. The average price paid was nearly 1,000 francs (£40) per square metre. Very few purchasers acquired more than one site, thus perpetuating the traditional fragmentation of property ownership. The deeds required the buyers to construct blocks of apartments, and all façades on the Avenue itself had to be ready in time for the opening of the Exposition in May 1878. Even buildings off the Avenue had to be erected in two years, to prevent speculation on site values.[28]

Although the Avenue had to be of monumental appearance, the City was now more subtle than in Haussmann's time in its methods of ensuring architectural harmony. Instead of preparing a model design for the façades, the City simply wrote into the deeds of sale that all buildings on the Avenue should be of the maximum height authorised by the bye-laws, and that the principal horizontal lines in each block should coincide, which ensured that all the windows would be at the same level. Balconies were obligatory. Owing to the strict stipulations of the Paris building regulations regarding total height, window size, and height of each storey, these simple requirements ensured the aesthetic unity of the Avenue. To provide a clear vista, trees on the existing sections of the street were removed, and all kiosks and public conveniences were banned. The Avenue was officially opened by President Mac-Mahon in September 1877. It was much admired during the Exposition, especially as the Opéra itself, completed in 1875, was already being used for performances. As expected, it immediately became a fashionable shopping street. The total net cost to the City of the Avenue and associated improvements was forty-five million francs (£1,800,000), which, in view of the high value of property in central Paris, was a bargain.

[28] See deeds of sale in A.S., VO 11, box 2442.

(b) Boulevard Henri-IV

The great success of the Avenue de l'Opéra allowed work to proceed rapidly on the Boulevard Saint-Germain and its continuation in the right bank centre, the Boulevard Henri-IV. The object of this scheme was to complete in the south and east the inner ring of streets formed in the north by the *grands boulevards*. Although parts of the Boulevard Saint-Germain had been open before 1870, only a few yards of the Boulevard Henri-IV had been built, owing to disagreement between Haussmann and the Emperor as to whether the bridge should be at right-angles, or diagonal, to the banks of the Seine.[29] But this street presented few problems. The Arsenal ward which it crossed was poor and much less densely populated than most central districts. In any case, a large part of the Boulevard crossed the Célestins barracks, which was due for modernisation and could be rebuilt along the line of the new thoroughfare. When sixteen properties were acquired for the Boulevard in 1876 the average compensation was a mere 141,250 francs (£5,650).[30] Sale of sites was expected to recoup half the cost of acquisition and one-third of the total outlay.[31] Although the Council, here again, was not getting a slum clearance operation, it could at least be happy that the new street and, to a lesser extent, the new barracks, would animate an area which had previously been a quiet backwater.

The total cost of building the Boulevard was estimated at eight million francs (£320,000), of which over two and a half million would be recouped by the resale of sites.[32] Five million francs were allocated to it from the 1875 loan, and the City Council agreed that the difference should be made up out of the surplus achieved in building the Boulevard Saint-Germain.[33] Again, the Council refused to hand the operation over to a private developer, despite a recommendation to do so from its own public works committee.[34] The street scheme, which was completed in 1879, was less costly in the short term than had been expected, because the Célestins barracks was not rebuilt until the 1890s. And then it was financed out of the City's architectural resources, and not out of funds allocated to street improvements as had originally been intended. Needless to say, the Boulevard did not

[29] *Collection Lazare*, vol. 55, p. 466 (A.S., D1Z).
[30] Calculated from *Gazette des Tribunaux*.
[31] C.M. reports, 1875, no. 57, p. 3.
[32] C.M. reports, 1875, no. 57, p. 6.
[33] C.M. minutes, 21 December 1875, pp. 1133–4.
[34] C.M. reports, 1875, no. 57, pp. 3–4, 6.

have the same pretensions to monumental grandeur as the Avenue de l'Opéra, and no aesthetic conditions were imposed on purchasers of sites.

Despite their success, the completion of the Avenue de l'Opéra, Boulevard Saint-Germain, and Boulevard Henri-IV projects marked the end of an era. The happy result of the financial operations associated with the Avenue had been due to the large area of land which the City had been able to acquire, and for which the excuse had been the levelling of the innocuous Butte des Moulins. But the same opportunities did not exist elsewhere in the city centre. The big effort made for the Exposition now produced a reaction in favour of further retrenchment, and the resignation of President Mac-Mahon in December 1877, brought about by a reassertion of the power of Parliament, meant that the Government would look more critically on prestige schemes in Paris.

2 THE YEARS OF PRUDENCE, 1876–9

Although the cost of completing the Avenue de l'Opéra and the two other large schemes was not excessive by the standards of the Second Empire, the work had placed a considerable strain on the City's weakened finances. By 1879 debt charges still made up 40·18 per cent of the City's total expenditure, a proportion which was lower than in Haussmann's time, but none the less a cause of concern.[35] The councillors had agreed to finish these important city centre streets because of the obvious futility of leaving them incomplete, but the demands of those who represented the outer *arrondissements* for similar work in their own wards were now certain to become even stronger. A much more persuasive argument could be made against the completion of other central arteries than had been possible against the Avenue de l'Opéra and the Boulevard Henri-IV. Moreover, councillors were becoming increasingly suspicious of the whole system of financing public works expenditure. The case of those who opposed long-term borrowing was circumstantially strengthened by the negotiations with the *Crédit Foncier* to establish the true extent of the City's indebtedness.

In 1869 Haussmann had floated a loan of 250 million francs (£10 million) to repay part of the debt to the *Crédit Foncier* resulting from the liquidation of the *Caisse des Travaux*, which had advanced loans

[35] Ville de Paris, *Compte général des recettes et des dépenses de l'exercice 1879*, pp. 950–51.

to development companies to carry out street improvements on the City's behalf.[36] At that time the City owed the *Crédit Foncier* some 465 million francs (£18,600,000), which Haussmann hoped could be paid off within ten years out of the normal growth of municipal revenues. But the fall of Haussmann and the war upset these arrangements. Part of the proceeds of the loan had to be directed to other ends, and only about 152 million francs were paid to the *Crédit Foncier*. After the war the City still owed some 313 million francs, and was paying off this debt by annuities of nearly twenty million francs. Because Haussmann had created no extra resources of taxation to cover this charge, and the servicing of the 1869 loan, the City Council had to approve big taxation increases in 1872–4.[37] In 1876 the Council set up a special committee to study the debt and the circumstances in which it had been contracted. Certain irregularities were revealed, but the City Council had to agree in 1879 to pay back 283 million francs, by far the greater part of the sum originally owed.

During these years of uncertainty controversy raged in the City Council over the whole question of public works and finance policy. In 1876 the public works committee advised that new street improvement projects should be examined with great prudence. In 1877 it was asked to draw up a programme of works to be financed out of revenue, as several million francs were available in that year's supplementary budget.[38] Although the committee would have liked to concentrate on one scheme, such as the Rue aux Ours, the Rue Réaumur, or the Boulevard Haussmann, the limited sum available forced it to recommend several smaller projects, all of them outside the right bank centre. Four councillors presented a report strongly attacking this scheme,[39] which had been agreed in private discussions between the committee and the prefectoral administration in the usual way. They argued that to use even budget surpluses for street improvements required serious consideration. If they were to be preferred to an actual reduction of taxation, the City Council would at least have to see the administration's overall plan of future improvement schemes, which had so far remained strictly confidential to reduce the risk of

---

[36] For the City's explanation of the development of this method of financing, see Ville de Paris, *Résumé des traités de concession relatifs aux grandes opérations de voirie* (1869), esp. p. 8.

[37] Louis Daussct, *Rapport général . . . sur . . . le projet de budget de la Ville de Paris pour 1909*, pp. 63–4 (C.M. reports, 1908, no. 68).

[38] C.M. reports, 1877, no. 77.   [39] C.M. reports, 1877, no. 78.

speculation. They went on to attack Jean Alphand, director of works, for his continued application of outdated concepts. The Second Empire's plan, they argued, had been motivated mainly by strategic considerations, and streets had been constructed regardless of expense and the difficulty of creating junctions with existing thoroughfares at different levels. But improvements now had to be justified on purely utilitarian grounds, and even aesthetic factors were of limited importance. Yet the City Council, they complained, had never been consulted on these basic issues.

The four councillors' own positive suggestion, that the surplus should be spent on existing streets by improving pavements and the surroundings of public buildings, was unattractive to the Council. But their attack on rectilinear planning, the first serious criticism to come from within the City Council, was a major factor in the Council's decision to reject the proposed improvement scheme in November 1877. A sum of 5,670,000 francs, which should have been devoted to street works, was consequently transferred to the budget reserve. The following year the administration put forward a modified scheme, involving the expenditure of no more than three million francs, and including only six separate projects instead of nine. Once again, the right bank centre was ignored. The public works committee approved the plan, considering that a sudden end to public works would create a risk of unemployment now that building work for the 1878 Exposition and along the Avenue de l'Opéra was coming to an end.[40] This proposal was accepted by the City Council.

In May 1878 the public works committee reported on the proposals made by the four councillors in 1877, which the Council had referred to it for study.[41] The committee agreed that the City's strictly limited resources made the postponement of some projects inevitable, even though much remained to be done throughout Paris to ease traffic movement. And, in this situation, street widening was to be preferred to the creation of completely new thoroughfares. The Council decided to ask to see an overall plan of improvements, and asked the councillors of each *arrondissement* to classify in order of importance the projects planned in their own areas. A list of improvements scheduled by the administration was made available in 1878.[42] By December 1879 the councillors had completed this examination, and the public works

[40] C.M. reports, 1878, no. 15.   [41] C.M. reports, 1878, no. 33.
[42] See Direction des Travaux, *Projets de voirie 1878* (B.A. 2966).

committee once again put forward an improvement scheme.[43] Unfortunately, it did so at the worst possible psychological moment, for at about the same time the Council had to ratify the City's agreement with the *Crédit Foncier* to repay 283 million francs of the debt run up by Haussmann. Although it took up this burden, the Council passed a resolution to the effect that it would never again finance public works by borrowed money, but would pay for them directly out of budget surpluses.[44] So the public works committee advised the Council to restrict its effort to a few schemes which could be carried out over five or six years and financed out of revenue. Only in special cases, such as the building of a new central post office, could the City expect a Government subsidy. The committee admitted that it had endeavoured to reconcile the needs of the city as a whole with those of each ward. It had also borne in mind the need to facilitate the construction of tram lines, as well as general considerations of traffic flow and sanitary improvement. Consequently, the committee's scheme showed a marked preference for small improvements, which were scattered throughout the city. It included eight right bank centre projects, three each in the Ier and IIe *arrondissements*, and one in each of the IIIe and IVe *arrondissements*. Only two of these, the construction of the Rue Etienne-Marcel and the Rue du Louvre, including the reconstruction of the post office, and the widening of the southern section of the present Rue des Archives, were at all ambitious. The former would cost eighteen million francs (£720,000) including a State subsidy, and the latter, seven million francs (£280,000). None of the other first priority projects in the right bank centre involved an expenditure of more than one million francs, and the widening of the Rue Mondétour (Ier) was classified as of secondary priority because it would cost over two million francs.[45]

As the Council had decided earlier in the year to float no further loans to finance improvement schemes, the public works committee suggested that all the first priority projects could be carried out in a few years if an annual sum were allocated to them out of revenue. Progress would be necessarily slow because at that time only one-fifth was available of the total sum necessary to carry out the first priority projects. The committee suggested that these resources should be expended on an even smaller number of schemes, which included,

[43] C.M. reports, 1879, no. 118.   [44] C.M. reports, 1879, no. 119, p. 1.
[45] C.M. reports, 1879, no. 118.

in the right bank centre, the widening of the Rue de l'Homme-Armé (part of the present Rue des Archives) (IVe) and the extension of the Impasse du Pont-aux-Biches (IIIe).[46]

3 THE PERIOD OF MINOR SCHEMES, 1879–84

Although the City started work immediately on the programme approved in 1879, progress was severely limited by the paucity of the resources available. The first scheme to be tackled in the right bank centre was the extension of the Impasse du Pont-aux-Biches, which had the effect of prolonging the Rue Volta to the north as far as the Rue Meslay. Unfortunately, because of the acute difference in levels, it was possible to provide only pedestrian access between the two streets by means of a stairway. So no contribution was made to the problem of vehicular access to the *grands boulevards* which was particularly serious in that part of the city. Horses and carriages still had to proceed via the Rue Saint-Martin and the Rue de Turbigo, and the IIIe *arrondissement* councillors remained dissatisfied with this relative isolation of the Arts-et-Métiers ward.

In 1882 the part of the present Rue des Archives lying between the Rue de la Verrerie and the Rue des Blancs-Manteaux was widened. This was part of a long-term plan to widen the whole of the southern section of the Rue des Archives as far as the Rue de Rambuteau, which had been approved in 1879. It brought the benefits of an improvement scheme to a part of the city centre which Haussmann had not touched, and which was far from healthy. It would aid traffic flow by linking the Hôtel de Ville to the industrial north-east of the right bank centre, and it would involve the demolition of some of the houses of the rookery in the Rue de Venise district, which was later to become the city's unhealthy area number 1. But considerations of public health were even more predominant in the decision to make a rapid start on an improvement scheme in the IIe *arrondissement*.

(a) Rue des Filles-Dieu[47]

Unlike most street improvement projects, the widening of the Rue des Filles-Dieu (IIe) had only sanitary objectives. In 1879 the public works committee had placed it in the category of secondary urgency, because it considered that the widening would be incomplete without

---

[46] C.M. reports, 1879, no. 119, pp. 3, 9–11.
[47] This street is now called Rue d'Alexandrie.

the building of a new street at right-angles to the Rue des Filles-Dieu to link it to the Boulevard Bonne-Nouvelle.[48] But such a noisy campaign for immediate demolition grew up in the district that the City Council reconsidered its decision.[49] People in the IIe *arrondissement* had been calling for something to be done about the street for twenty years. It had been a traditional centre of prostitution for several centuries, and had become extremely insalubrious. Its existing houses were about two hundred years old. As early as 1877 the City Council had decided in principle to demolish the street, after being assured that sale of sites would cover the cost, but nothing had been done. When the local councillors called once more for the widening to be carried out, in March 1879, they admitted that no contribution would be made to general traffic problems, but the work could be combined with the provision of a new school, of which the area was sorely in need. Although the scheme was estimated to cost three and a half million francs (£140,000), the public works committee hoped that the final cost would be lower as many of the buildings were ruinous and of little value. Nearly three-quarters of the area to be acquired would be disposed of in the form of building sites.[20]

Although the City Council was in general agreement with the acceleration of a start on this project, its very pronounced character of slum clearance resulted in further delay because it was decided to submit the problem for study to the unhealthy dwellings committee.[51] Its report was not submitted to the Council by the Prefect until January 1883. The committee considered that the unhealthiness of the houses had several causes, including the use of the central gutter as an open sewer, and the blockage by rubbish of drains in the nearby Rue Saint-Denis. The façades of the houses were also in bad condition, and although the committee believed that they could be repaired, the most effective way of removing exterior causes of insalubrity would be to widen the whole street.[52] Now there can be no doubt that the street was basically unhealthy, for it was only ten feet wide along most of its length, ran from east to west, and had houses of up to seven storeys. Yet the experts called for total demolition even before seeing what the repair of the drains could achieve. The Rue des Filles-Dieu was by no means the worst street in the city centre, and the taint

[48] C.M. reports, no. 118, p. 7.
[50] C.M. reports, 1881, no. 76.
[52] C.M. reports, 1883, no. 27, p. 3.
[49] *Travaux des commissions d'hygiène*, 1881, p. 32.
[51] See below, chapter 4.

of prostitution probably accounts for the general acceptance of the urgency of its 'improvement'.

The public works committee accepted the arguments of the unhealthy dwellings committee. Its report stated that public health experts and legislators were agreed on the danger to public health and morality which resulted from inadequate dwellings. It was well known that cholera had been particularly lethal in the street, and the improvement would have the additional advantage of displacing a poor and promiscuous population.[53]

Further studies had done nothing to dim the hope that the work could be carried out without loss to the City. By 1883 the estimated cost had risen to four million francs, but it was thought that sale of sites could still cover the outlay. The scheme finally put forward took the form of moving the Rue des Filles-Dieu over by a few metres to absorb an equally unhealthy cul-de-sac. If the street had been widened on one side only there would have been no sites for resale.[54] The City Council agreed to undertake the project with these arrangements and completed it in 1885. But the sale of sites proved a big disappointment until further demolitions were carried out to improve access to the street after 1890,[55] and the City did not recover the total cost of the work. This failure may well have discouraged the City from undertaking similar schemes, and it remained unique in the right bank centre.

(b) Rue de Franche-Comté

It was also in 1885 that the City constructed the Rue de Franche-Comté (IIIe). This was intended to link the Temple market directly to the Boulevard du Temple, and relieve congestion at the eastern end of the market. In view of the chronic lack of access points to the *grands boulevards* from the north-east of the right bank centre, it is not surprising that this particular improvement had long been called for by local inhabitants and market traders.[56] It originally came before the Council in 1877. Like the Rue des Filles-Dieu, the project was so attractive because it offered the chance to purchase an unusually large area of land at a low price. Slum property was not involved this time, but a vast and sprawling mansion, the Hôtel de Marcilly, in the Rue Béranger. Plots on one side of the street would be sold off, and

[53] C.M. reports, 1883, no. 27. p. 4.
[54] C.M. reports, 1883, no. 27, pp. 4–6.
[55] C.M. reports, 1890, no. 25, annex B.
[56] C.M. reports, 1877, no. 49, pp. 3, 10.

on the other side a new school would be built to replace the badly sited girls' school in the Rue du Vert-Bois. This work was to be combined with the use of the site of the old Saint-Martin food market to build a new Central School of Arts and Manufactures. Here, as in the IVe *arrondissement*, local markets were very little used. This particular one had lost many of its customers since the new Halles, and the wide streets radiating from them had been built, and could easily be resited on part of the Temple market. Indeed, it was hoped that the new Central School would provide a bigger boost to the economy of the district than the existing market, and it was partly for this reason that the City was prepared to share in the building costs with the Government. However, the scheme was put off for a few years while the City tried to ensure that the Central School would be free of Government control, and it was not completed until 1884.[57]

(c) The central post office

The old central post office, and the streets leading to it, had long been recognised as inadequate. The accommodation had not been purpose-built, and was a cause of great inconvenience to the postal services. Plans had been made in Haussmann's time to erect a new building at the Place du Châtelet, and an agreement to this effect was signed by the Government and the City in April 1854.[58] The City began to acquire the necessary properties, but the Government soon lost interest, and in 1865 the Assembly refused to authorise the scheme.[59] The Government promised to compensate the City for the loss incurred in acquiring sites, but failed to keep its word. This contributed to the atmosphere of distrust between the two parties that was apparent when the Government again approached the City in the late 1870s, after several plans to move the post office to a new site had fallen through.[60] The Prefect submitted a draft agreement to the City Council in 1879. A tempting carrot was offered to the City; the Government was prepared to cede parts of the site of the present building for the widening of the Rue Jean-Jacques-Rousseau and the building of part of the Rue du Louvre at 1,000 francs (£40) a square metre. It would pay the same price for land taken from the highway and included within the perimeter of the enlarged central post office site, and would also contribute to roadmaking expenses. This meant

[57] C.M. reports, 1878, no. 26, p. 21; Henri Bidou, *Paris* (1937), p. 356.
[58] A.S., VO 2, box 83.
[59] Louis Girard, *La politique des travaux publics du Second Empire* (1952), p. 340.
[60] Prefectoral memorandum, 17 May 1879; C.M. reports, 1879, no. 80.

that the City would have to pay only eighteen million francs (£620,000) towards an improvement scheme which otherwise would have cost thirty millions. In addition to the carrot, the Government brandished a stick which was equally persuasive; if the City refused these terms a new central post office would be built on the Quai d'Orsay, vacant since the *Cour des Comptes* had been burned down in 1871. Such a move would have been logical in view of the concentration of Government offices in the VIIe *arrondissement*, where there was less congestion, but it would have been a serious blow to the expanding business district in the north-west of the right bank centre. The same blackmail techniques were used by the Bank of France to persuade the City to accept the continuous growth of its buildings. In this case, however, the terms of the agreement were not unfavourable to the City, especially at a time when it was actively seeking such arrangements with other interests to facilitate street improvements. Moreover, State participation ensured that there would be no objection from the Assembly to the financial arrangements.

The Rue du Louvre had originally been planned by Haussmann,[61] from the Rue de Rivoli to the Rue Montmartre, to ease traffic flow in the vicinity of the Halles and clean up an insanitary area.[62] Compulsory purchase powers were granted by a decree of 9 June 1860. It was hoped eventually to link it up via a new bridge to the extended Rue de Rennes on the left bank.[63] Although this ambitious scheme seemed highly unlikely to be brought to fruition, the Rue du Louvre had sufficient utility in itself, and the compulsory purchase powers had never been rescinded.

The public works committee gave very full consideration to the financial aspects of the problem. It thought the price of 1,000 francs per square metre to be very fair, in view of the fact that the City could probably resell some of the land surplus to the requirements of the improvement for up to 1,400 francs. Although it thought that the State's contribution should be larger, it approved the agreement as it stood because of the urgent need to improve traffic movement and public health conditions in the area. Moreover, the extension of the Rue aux Ours (Rue Etienne-Marcel) from the Rue Montorgueil to the Place des Victoires would create a big traffic artery reaching, via the Rue de Turbigo, as far as the Place de la République. The committee expected

---

[61] See plan in *Collection Lazare*, vol. 70, p. 2120 (A.S., D1Z).
[62] *Moniteur*, 28 February 1860, p. 247.
[63] *Moniteur*, 26, May 1868, p. 727.

that the scheme would take four years to complete, and no borrowing would be necessary. The City tried once again to persuade the Government to increase its contribution, but after meeting a refusal decided to accept the original agreement in December 1879.[64] The works were completed in 1884 and 1885 at a time when, as we shall see, the City was considering the further southward extension of the Rue du Louvre.

4 THE RETURN TO BORROWING, 1885–90

During the years in which improvements were financed directly out of revenue, a growing number of councillors began to demand a new loans policy. In November 1881 the Prefect suggested that a scheme to improve the vicinity of the Palais-Royal and extend the Bank of France could be financed only by a loan. The City should take the opportunity of borrowing directly from the Bank, which would offer a low rate of interest because of the direct benefit that it would obtain from the scheme. Although the Prefect claimed that such an arrangement would fulfil a desire frequently expressed in the City Council for cheap loans to be obtained from interested parties, the public works committee opposed the plan. It considered that the Bank would get much more advantage from the work than the City, which would have to tolerate the closure of the Rue Radziwill in an area that was already short of thoroughfares.[65] On this occasion the Council ignored its committee's report, and ratified the agreement in August 1882 by thirty-five votes to twenty-nine, although it tried to get the Bank to agree to contribute an extra 1,600,000 francs to the cost of the work. More negotiations followed, in which the Bank refused to increase its offer, and a complicated series of exchanges ended with the City Council again confirming the original agreement in the following year.[66] The scheme would undoubtedly have brought some benefit to the City in the shape of street improvements, and the Bank was prepared to lend at the extremely low rate of 2 per cent. Moreover, the Bank threatened to move to a new site outside the centre if it were not allowed to expand. However, after all this ado the agreement was never put into effect, and when a councillor tried to have it revived in 1890 he was told that it had already lapsed.[67]

This confusion may well have encouraged the Prefect to submit to

---

[64] C.M. reports, 1879, no. 118, p. 5.
[66] C.M. reports, 1883, no. 42.
[65] C.M. reports, 1883, no. 42.
[67] C.M. reports, 1890, no. 13.

the City Council in 1883 a scheme to float a 220 million franc loan, but opposition was still great, even though the public works committee pointed out the problems which the City would face if it ever tried to finance a really big scheme like the Rue Réaumur out of revenue.[68]

Given the continuing financial stringency, it was hardly surprising that a group of councillors should call in 1885 for a regular State subsidy for public works.[69] They argued that the nation as a whole benefited from improvements in Paris, and that as they led to an increase of population and therefore of tax revenue, of which the Government took its share, a subsidy was only fair. Of course, such arguments fell on very deaf ears at the Ministry of Finance. So the persisting economic crisis, and the need to decide on a new public works programme, continued to influence City Council opinion in favour of a new loan. Fortunately, the 1884 elections produced a Council that was less opposed to borrowing than its predecessor, and the rapporteur of the 1885 budget report, Councillor Camille Dreyfus, was a strong supporter of the idea.[70] Although individuals and groups of councillors continued to put forward schemes for financing public works with little or no borrowing,[71] the 1885 depression forced the City to take action to revive the local economy. In April the Prefect communicated a list of improvement schemes which he thought should be undertaken within five or six years after 1886, and a plan for the associated financial arrangements. The Council set up a special loans committee to study his memorandum. It was out of the question to finance the scheme out of revenue because the contents of reserve funds and balances were diminishing each year. The Prefect proposed that the City should make an annual issue of bonds in 1886, 1887 and 1888 up to a total of 150 million francs (£6 million). They would be reimbursed in 1889 or 1890, when the Prefect would seek an authorisation to float a 370 million franc loan in order to fund the short-term bond debt, to amortise completely the ninety million francs that remained of loans floated from 1855 to 1860, and to provide an extra 130 million francs for public works. This would provide a total of 280 million francs (£11,200,000) for improvement schemes, but it could not be achieved without additional taxation.[72]

Although the loans committee reported in favour of the Prefect's

[68] C.M. reports, 1883, no. 27, p. 5; no. 38, p. 2.
[69] C.M. reports, 1885, no. 17.
[70] C.M. reports, 1903, no. 72, pp. 15, 16.
[71] For two such schemes, see C.M. reports, 1885, nos. 20 and 23.
[72] C.M. reports, 1885, no. 71, pp. 1–3.

proposals, with some minor modifications,[73] the City Council declined to authorise tax increases. In August 1885 it rejected the committee's report on the grounds that even an increase in direct taxation would affect not only property owners, but, indirectly, everyone in the city. It was prepared to agree to a loan, but only if it were based on existing revenue resources. It therefore approved the issue of municipal bonds up to a limit of 250 million francs (£10 million) from 1886 to 1896. They would be repayable over a period of seventy-five years from 1887.

The loans committee had also been given the task of suggesting how the borrowed resources should be employed. It had recommended an expenditure of 104 million francs (£4 million) on street improvements, of which nearly twenty-five million francs would be allotted to three schemes in the right bank centre. This sum would be shared between one new project, the building of the Rue Réaumur (fourteen million francs), and two that had already been started, the Rue du Louvre (six millions) and the widening of the Rue des Archives (4·6 millions).[74] Although the Council's August decision reduced the total amount that would be available through borrowing, it decided to maintain street improvement expenditure at 104 million francs. So the main effect of the decision was that this sum would become available over a period of ten years instead of four. Now that the financial arrangements had been defined, the Council had to decide exactly how the resources should be spent. To help it in its choice, the public works committee drew up a list of projects that were either planned, or demanded by councillors and petitioners. The Prefect also drew up a list of schemes recommended by his officers, which was passed to the Council in August 1886. The criteria of choice were similar in each case; the committee considered that the schemes had the double objective of making the city more healthy and creating the thoroughfares necessary to its industrial and commercial development.[75] The Prefect's memorandum emphasised the needs of traffic and public health, and the desirability of encouraging building enterprise.[76] In the right bank centre the Prefect recommended, as had the loans committee, the Rue du Louvre and Rue des Archives schemes, but said nothing of the Rue Réaumur, whose construction was now relegated to the more distant future.

At this stage a new complication reared its head. The Senate

[73] C.M.reports, 1885, no. 71. p. 38.
[75] C.M.reports, 1886, no. 48, pp. 1–2.
[74] C.M. reports, 1885, no. 71. pp. 9–10.
[76] C.M. reports, 1886, no. 96, p. 2.

passed an amendment to the law authorising the City to contract the 250 million franc loan, to the effect that the sum should be spent entirely in accordance with a schedule which the City was required to provide immediately. So in July 1886 the Prefect urged the Council to make up its mind on the schemes which it wanted to see started in that year, so that parliamentary approval could be obtained.[78] At a joint session the public works and finance committees, although highly critical of the Senate's intervention, drew up a list of ten schemes, involving an expediture of 43½ million francs. Only one of them, the widening of the Rue des Archives, was in the right bank centre. The committees gave as their reason for choosing it that it would result in an improvement in traffic movement between the Rue de Rivoli and the Rue de Rambuteau, but they were no doubt influenced as well by the relatively small expenditure required to finish a project that was already near completion. They put back the southward extension of the Rue de Louvre to a later stage because they wanted to see how the financial arrangements worked out for the part of the street that was being built in connection with the new central post office. And they recommended that the City should try to obtain the cooperation of the Government to build a short northern extension of the street, between the Rue d'Argout and the Rue Mont-martre, which would be essential to provide access to the new post office once it was in full operation. The committees had also considered a scheme to extend the Rue aux Ours from the Boulevard de Sébastopol to the Rue Saint-Martin, which would clear away a rookery. Although they decided not to recommend it for immediate execution, they asked for it to be classified as a project of prime urgency.[79]

The City Council approved the committees' recommendations on 7 July 1886,[80] and the schedule of improvements was given parliamentary authorisation by a law of 19 July. Although total expenditure on the ten schemes was reduced at this stage to thirty-seven million francs, the allocation for the Rue des Archives was maintained at 4,600,000 francs (£184,000). It was announced that work would start immediately so that it would be completed in time for the 1889 Exposition. It was also hoped that these improvements would be enough to blow the city's economy out of the doldrums in which it still languished.

[78] Prefectoral memorandum, 1 July 1886; C.M. reports, 1886, no. 96, p. 1.
[79] C.M. reports, 1886, no. 96. pp. 1–7. Work did not begin on the Rue aux Ours extension until 1906.
[80] C.M. *Délibérations*, 1886, pp. 352–3; C.M. reports, 1887, no. 11, p. 1.

(a) Rue du Louvre and the Halles

While the loan was still being discussed, the City had been presented with the opportunity to extend the Rue du Louvre southwards and enlarge the Halles in association with private interests. In 1880 the central committee of the Paris chambers of trade had petitioned the City Council to set up a commercial exchange.[81] Several schemes were subsequently suggested, but the finance committee showed most interest in the one proposed by the Chamber of Commerce which involved the conversion of the circular cornmarket building just to the west of the Halles. All that had prevented firm approval being given to the project was the warning by the director of works, Jean Alphand, that the scheme would give nearby buildings a betterment value which would involve the City in higher compensation payments if it were later decided to extend the Halles and finish the Rue du Louvre. The obvious solution was that put forward by the combined finance, public works and estates committees in 1884, when they suggested that all three schemes be combined at a total cost of twenty-five million francs (£1 million). The Council was assured that the loan of this sum could be obtained through the Chamber of Commerce from the *Crédit Foncier* at a preferential rate. The City would benefit directly from the extra dues charged in the two new market buildings that would be erected, and indirectly from the stimulus of a commercial exchange on business activity in the area.[82] In December 1884 the Prefect announced that he intended to negotiate for the work to be carried out by the inveterate developer Blondel, who had worked on street improvement schemes as a municipal concessionary before 1870, on behalf of the Chamber of Commerce. Perhaps the idea of working with Blondel, whose integrity was not entirely beyond question, as well as borrowing from the *Crédit Foncier*, was too much to swallow for councillors who had so roundly condemned the financial procedures of the Second Empire. At any rate, the committees advised against Blondel's proposal, and declared in favour of putting the scheme out to tender.[83] Their report was accepted by the City Council on 25 March 1885.[84] But further obstacles forced a return to the original plan, and Blondel's company completed the scheme in 1888–9. But after this delay it cost more than had been expected, and an extra five

---

[81] C.M. reports, 1884, no. 33, p. 1.   [82] C.M. reports, 1884, no. 33.
[83] C.M. reports, 1885, no. 18, pp. 23–4.   [84] C.M. *Délibérations*, 1885, pp. 93–7.

million francs had to be attributed to it out of the 110 million francs allocated to street improvements in the 1886 loan.[85] This miscalculation dashed all hopes that the last two pavilions of the Halles could be built in connection with the scheme.[86]

5 FURTHER DIFFICULTIES, 1890–95

In 1890 it became clear that a residue of twenty million francs would be left out of the 110 million francs allocated to street improvements. To satisfy the demands of the different wards, the public works committee divided these resources among thirty-one small schemes, only four of which were in the right bank centre. Although the City Council finally increased the number of these central projects to five, all were of little significance and involved the acquisition of only a handful of buildings.[87] But even these small schemes required parliamentary approval, which was granted by a law of 12 December 1890.

Looking further ahead, the public works committee drew up a list of large projects which still remained to be carried out, but which had to be postponed because of the City's limited resources. In this list of six schemes, five were in the right bank centre. This clearly showed that to share out resources equally over the whole city meant ignoring the problems of the centre. And these problems could never be resolved unless the councillors were prepared to agree to concentrate any future resources on work in the centre. Of course, there was a better chance of reaching an agreement with private interests to carry out schemes in the centre than elsewhere, but this could be no excuse for putting off all action. Each scheme was estimated to cost between thirty and forty million francs. The five in the right bank centre were: the completion of the northern section of the Rue du Louvre, the isolation of the Halles, the extension of the Rue Beaubourg as far as the Hôtel de Ville, the completion of the Rue Réaumur, and the extension of the Rue aux Ours. The sixth project was the extension of the Rue de Rennes northwards to the Seine.[88]

Unfortunately, there seemed to be no possibility of resorting to further borrowing for some years to come. Current taxation was only just sufficient to service the existing long-term debt. Further tax increases were out of the question after the big rise that had been

[85] C.M. reports, 1890, no. 25, annex A, p. 12.
[86] Max Boucard, *La vie de Paris* (1892), p. 103.
[87] C.M. reports, 1890, no. 25; *Délibérations*, 1890, pp. 269–70.
[88] C.M. reports, 1890, no. 25, p. 4.

necessary, despite the Council's strenuous efforts to avoid it, in 1886.[89] One indication of the strength of public feeling against high taxation was the election of the conservative Henri Froment-Meurice in the Madeleine ward in 1890 after campaigning on an economy platform. He told the electors:

> 'As one who lives in the hard-working atmosphere of industry and commerce, I know that wise administration depends on a spirit of economy. I shall do all that is in my power to halt the continual increase of municipal expenditure and to avoid the increased taxation that would be its inevitable result.'[90]

Froment-Meurice was immediately appointed to the finance committee, and appears to have exercised considerable influence there during the 1890s. Meanwhile, the cost of improvements was rising; Councillor Deville and a number of his colleagues estimated that the works which had been recognised as necessary by the Council in 1885 at an estimated cost of 300 million francs would cost 400 millions (£16 million) to carry out in 1890. Deville wanted to see work start again as soon as possible, but he thought that it would be difficult to contract a further loan until 1910, when the debt charges would have diminished considerably. In the meantime, he suggested, the City should negotiate with development companies to make advances for certain schemes, which could be reimbursed by annuities. This short-term debt could be converted when it again became possible to issue stock.[91] Nothing came of this suggestion, nor of that made by a special committee in May 1891 which recommended the conversion of the City's debt by the issue of new stock repayable over eighty-one years.[92] So, with no work at all planned for 1893 onwards, and the loan of 1886 used up,[93] it appeared inevitable in 1891 that the City's improvement programme would soon grind to a halt. Yet 1891 proved to be just the darkest moment before the dawn.

(a) Rue Réaumur

The City Council had already decided that one of the lines of the future *Métropolitain* would follow the planned route of the Rue Réaumur, only short sections of which had been built. As the City's

[89] C.M. reports, 1890, no. 79, p. 2.
[90] Quoted in C.E. Curinier, *Dictionnaire national des contemporains* (n.d., c. 1905).
[91] C.M. reports, 1890, no. 79.
[92] C.M. reports, 1891, no. no. 22; no. 30.
[93] C.M. reports, 1891, no. 10, pp. 12–13.

hopes of being allowed to build its underground railway began to brighten considerably during the early 1890s, pressure built up in the Council for the street scheme to be carried out so that this particular line would not be retarded.[94] Several attempts had been made in the 1880s to persuade the City to build the street, or allow it to be built by private interests. It was claimed that it would take some of the pressure of traffic off the congested *grands boulevards*, especially at points of intersection with radial routes.[95] In 1882 and 1883 the City refused two separate offers by a developer to carry out the work after negotiations in which the indefatigable Blondel had played a leading role.[96] The public works committee considered that the total cost, then estimated at thirty million francs (£1,200,000), was not justified because construction of the street was insufficiently urgent. It also suggested that the developer, a benevolent society on whose behalf Blondel was acting, was eager for the street to be built only because it owned 5,000 square metres of land in the area which could only acquire its full value after the improvement had been carried out. In any case, the financial arrangements proposed by Blondel were somewhat suspect. The committee suggested that the street should be built in sections, having regard to the City's limited resources.[97] In fact, the loans committee wanted to allocate fourteen million francs to this scheme in 1885,[98] but nothing came of the idea.

In 1891 the Prefect told the Council that he was negotiating with the *Crédit Foncier* for a fifty million franc (£2 million) loan to build the Rue Réaumur. The public works committee welcomed this initiative, not only because of its importance to the *Métropolitain*, but also because of its merits as a street scheme. It would also improve an old area of narrow and unhealthy streets, and complete the isolation of the Conservatory of Arts and Crafts (the former abbey of Saint-Martin-des-Champs), thus protecting its precious library and museum collections from the danger of fire. The new street, for which the City had possessed compulsory purchase powers since 1864, would be built as Haussmann had planned it, 'a great, rectilinear thoroughfare'. Resale of sites would produce the unusually high figure of about twelve million francs (£480,000), because of the great area of some of

[94] This new consideration was first brought to the Council's notice by report no. 109 (1891) of the public works committee.

[95] C.M. reports, 1883, no. 38, p. 1.

[96] C.M. minutes, 19 July, 18 November 1882; reports, 1883, no. 38.

[97] C.M. reports, 1883, no. 38, pp. 2–3.   [98] C.M. reports, 1885, no. 71, p. 9.

the properties to be acquired. This would reduce the net cost to only thirty-eight million francs.[99]

With the Prefect already negotiating a loan, the Council found itself in a difficult position. It could not refuse to build the Rue Réaumur because it had been the first to emphasise the need to clear the way for the *Métro* line. But it knew that the inhabitants of other parts of the city would be indignant if the IIe *arrondissement* enjoyed the benefit of the only big improvement scheme in Paris. And elections were coming up again in 1892. So as it seemed likely that favourable terms would be obtained, the Council decided rather hurriedly to invite the Prefect to borrow a total of 120 million francs. It pointed out that in routing a *Métro* line down the Rue Réaumur it had not intended that it should be built to the exclusion of all other improvements. The *Crédit Foncier* agreed to increase the loan to this new amount, yet still offered conditions that were more favourable than the City had ever obtained before. In fact, no new taxation was required. The loan would be serviced during the early years by existing resources, and, after 1898, by the additional centimes currently servicing the 1886 loan, which would be freed in that year.[100]

Although some objections were still raised to the priority given to the Rue Réaumur on the grounds that, like the Rue du Louvre, it might absorb far more than the sum allotted to it at the expense of improvements elsewhere,[101] the City Council approved the 120 million franc loan on 18 January 1892. However, market conditions were now so favourable that it was able to reject the proposed agreement with the *Crédit Foncier* in favour of public subscription. In fact, the City's credit now stood so high[102] that on 27 January the Council approved a further loan of twenty-five million francs as the first instalment of a total of 100 millions for water supply and sewage improvements. This total borrowing of 145 million francs (£5,800,000), which already had the approval of the Prefect and the Minister of the Interior, would be repayable over seventy-five years from 1898 at a rate of 2 per cent.[103] Indeed, the state of the money market remained so favourable that the Council could not resist the temptation to increase the total loan to 200 million francs, on 1 April 1892. But the extra resources provided were to be used for school building, and

[99] C.M. reports, 1891, no. 109, pp. 7–8.   [100] C.M. reports, 1891, no. 109.
[101] C.M. reports, 1891, no. 114.   [102] C.M. reports, 1892, no. 34, p. 1.
[103] C.M. reports, 1892, no. 34, pp. 1, 2, 9.

there was no increase in the street improvement allocation, which remained at 120 million francs.[104]

The City Council decided to fix a schedule of expenditure for the whole sum, to prevent the Rue Réaumur from absorbing more than fifty million francs. The remainder would be divided equally between the left and right banks. The public works committee's choice of projects was determined, as usual, by considerations of traffic and public health. It showed a preference for local schemes which had the effect of complementing past undertakings rather than totally new projects, and its report had a few hard words to say about Haussmann, who had begun a large number of schemes which in many cases had had to wait thirty years before they were completed. In the right bank centre, the committee agreed to the Prefect's suggestion that two sections of the Rue Beaubourg should be included, at a cost of eight million francs (£320,000), and it added a much smaller scheme, the partial widening of the Rue Mondétour (Ier *arrondissement*).[105]

Although the Council remained favourably disposed to borrowing, and voted a further loan of 116 million francs for water and sewers in March 1893, its glowing optimism was proved by the reaction of investors to be unjustified. The new stock was taken up very slowly, and although the eastern half of the Rue Réaumur was completed in 1894, none of the other scheduled schemes had been started by the spring of that year. This was much to the chagrin of the public works committee, which regretted the hardship caused to building workers, and feared that the delays might prejudice the eventual execution of the works.[106] But progress was more satisfactory in the following year, when the western part of the Rue Réaumur and the first section of the Rue Beaubourg were completed. By now, however, the attention of City officials and councillors was switching increasingly to the building of an underground transport system. In many ways, the *Métropolitain* had positive attractions, which we shall discuss in the following chapter. But the change to a new transit policy also reflected a disenchantment with street improvements, the origins of which were mainly financial.

6 CONCLUSION

In the early 1870s a reaction had taken place against the exorbitant compensation awarded by assessment panels under Haussmann. The

104 C.M. reports, 1892, no. 140.
105 C.M. reports, 1892, no. 140. pp. 2, 4, 6–9, 20.
106 C.M. reports, 1894, no. 4, pp. 1–6.

City made it clear that it expected the panels to take a firmer stand against landlords' pretensions, and to apply the letter of the 1841 law, which laid down in particular that when an owner wished to retain part of his site, its value would be taken into consideration in the calculation of compensation.[107] At first, the panels observed the City's recommendations, and it was even possible to let improvement schemes out to concessionaries without the panels taking it upon themselves to cut the developers' profits by increasing indemnities.[108] Most operations, however, were carried out directly by the City, which enabled it more easily to retain the cooperation of the assessment panels. The climate of sweet reasonableness was confirmed by the absence of the speculative fever that had gripped Paris in the 1860s. It was even possible to revive, in 1875, the department originally set up by Haussmann to acquire properties by negotiation.[109] The success of these arrangements helped to achieve a big saving in the Avenue de l'Opéra operation, and even though this work helped to accelerate the revival of the Paris property market, the panels were still moderate in their assessments as late as 1879.[110] But a deterioration soon set in. By 1883 the panels were starting to take advantage of development companies, and the public works committee recommended that no further schemes should be let out to concessionaries.[111] In 1885 the panels began to allow a general inflation of indemnities, and several councillors supported a demand for more precise rules of assessment.[112] But nothing was done, and five years later the public works committee stated that the City's resources were insufficient for a big improvement scheme 'owing to the enormous and scandalously exaggerated compensation which the assessment panels allow themselves to be drawn into agreeing to'.[113] By now, the City had adopted the practice, for widening schemes, of acquiring properties by negotiation over what could be a very long period. Compulsory purchase was kept only for the most intransigent landlords.[114] Compensation was particularly crushing in the city centre, owing to its high concentration of commercial enterprises. In 1879, for instance, indemnities paid to tenants

---

[107] C.M. reports, 1872, no. 44, p. 18.
[108] C.M. reports, 1875, no. 57, p. 4.
[109] De Pontich, *Administration de Paris*, p. 273.
[110] C.M. reports, 1879, no. 76, p. 5.
[111] C.M. reports, 1883, no. 27, p. 6.
[112] C.M. reports, 1885, no. 27, p. 1; no. 28, pp. 1–2; Gustave Jourdan, *Etudes d'hygiène publique* (1893), p. 92.
[113] C.M. reports, 1890, no. 25, p. 4.
[114] C.M. reports, 1890, no. 25, annex B.

made up over half of the total cost of acquisition.[115] Furthermore, they were extremely high in areas where improvements had already been carried out. In 1879 the public works committee was unable to give first priority to the widening of the Rue Mondétour, near the Halles, because of the very high estimated cost of 2,251,000 francs (£90,000). Compensation for the interruption of business leases made up a very large part of this sum, because of the commercialisation of the district since Haussmann had devoted so much attention to it, and had made it the centre of his network of new streets.[116] There might have been some consolation if the City had been allowed to tax betterment values resulting from its public works investment under the law of 1807, but this had not been attempted since 1852,[117] and the courts were now resolutely opposed to it. The public works committee agreed to look at the whole issue once again in 1879, but there was no positive result.[118]

Increasing compensation costs might have been ignored if the City had been in a stronger financial position. But the history of public works in these years is overshadowed by an almost permanent lack of resources. The City did not recover from the war and the Commune until 1875, when there was a budget surplus of sixteen million francs (£640,000).[119] Until 1882 the annual surplus varied between eighteen and thirty-six million francs, and allowed the City to undertake several big street schemes. But from 1883 to 1888 there was a series of deficits, and although the accounts were subsequently balanced until 1896, the financial weakness was concealed rather than cured. The Council staunchly refused repeated demands by the Prefect that it should vote extra additional centimes (direct taxation) after 1889. Between 1876 and 1896 the City's ordinary revenues rose by 35 per cent, and expenditure by 44 per cent.[120] A further burden was laid on the City from the 1880s by educational reforms which obliged it to spend large sums on primary educational provision and vocational training. A big programme of educational building was undertaken from 1886, and the new Sorbonne was built in 1892.[121] Matters were made worse

[115] C.M. reports, 1879, no. 76, p. 4.
[116] C.M. reports, no. 118, p. 6.
[117] Louis Dausset, *Rapport général. . . sur . . . le projet de budget de la Ville de Paris pour 1909*, pp. 194–5 (C.M. reports, 1908, no. 68).
[118] C.M. reports, 1879, no. 76, pp. 6–10.
[119] C.M. reports, 1903, no. 72, pp. 10–14; 1908, no. 68, pp. 39–40, 228–9.
[120] Gaston Cadoux, *Les finances de la Ville de Paris* (1900), p. 155.
[121] Louis Dausset, *Rapport général. . . sur . . . le projet de budget de la Ville de Paris pour 1911*, p. 116 (C.M. reports, 1910, no. 91); Jean Bastié, *La croissance de la banlieue parisienne* (1964), p. 196.

by the fact that the City no longer enjoyed the same flexibility of financial procedure as in Haussmann's time. The *Caisse des Travaux*, which had allowed Haussmann to float concealed loans by guaranteeing advances made to development companies by the *Crédit Foncier*, had been liquidated in 1870 and 1871.[122] In 1878 the Government extended its control over the City by ruling that no resources could be allocated to expenditure not included in the annual budget, that outlay under a given heading could not exceed the sum allocated to it in the budget, and that if expenditure did not reach the amount allocated, the surplus could not be transferred to another heading.[123]

Because of the Council's fixed aversion to taxation increases, the City was forced to adopt improvement policies more subtle than Haussmann's. We have already seen how it attempted to combine street schemes with other useful projects such as the building of schools and colleges, and to associate them with private interests. It also economised, from the 1880s, by acquiring only those properties necessary for the improvement work, and leaving certain old houses standing along new streets like the Rue Réaumur and the Rue des Archives. But this was really a false economy. The sale of large sites helped to produce the big Avenue de l'Opéra surplus which financed further works; but later schemes netted far less from this source, and occasionally ran into deficits when the original estimates were too optimistic. On the other hand, the more prudent borrowing policy undoubtedly had a beneficial effect on the City's finances. In 1893 loan charges were still less than 110 million francs, compared with 106 millions in 1879, and they made up 36·78 per cent of the City's total budget, compared with 40·18 per cent in the earlier year.[124]

While the total resources allocated to street improvements tended to decline, so did the right bank centre's share of them. The improvement in death rates from the 1880s suggested that total clearance of slums was not quite so necessary to public health as had previously been believed. In any case, several of the working class *arrondissements* of the east and south had far higher death rates than the centre. And now that the City Council was democratically elected by full manhood suffrage, with four representatives from each *arrondissement* and a radical-socialist majority, the demand for an equitable apportionment of works among all wards was almost irresistible. This centrifugal

---

[122] De Pontich, *Administration de Paris*, p. 272.
[123] Eugène Raiga and Maurice Félix, *Le régime administratif et financier de la Ville de Paris* (1922), p. 564.
[124] Ville de Paris, *Compte général des recettes et des dépenses de l'exercice 1893*.

effect was accentuated by the growing cost of central improvements, and the area's declining population. Those who advocated the execution of schemes in the city centre could no longer argue that they were essential for the benefit of a dense and needy local population. Instead, they had to argue that it was in the interests of the whole city, and even of the whole country, to enjoy rapid communications in the centre. Street improvements there could also be defended as essential to the extension of mechanical means of traction such as tramways and the *Métropolitain*. But as the central business district moved further west, the right bank centre had increasing difficulty in claiming priority in this respect. Similarly, the departure of the 'dangerous classes' to the east removed the need to carry out improvements in the right bank centre in the interests of public order, even assuming that a radical City Council would have allowed them to be undertaken with this objective.

1895 does not mark the end of the Parisian street improvement strategy, and we shall see that it makes a spectacular though shortlived return to the front of the municipal stage in 1909. But from now on it has to face growing obstacles, not only as a result of the difficulties mentioned in this chapter, but owing to the competition of alternative policies. And it is these policies which we must now begin to consider.

4

The Period of Distractions

Within the financial limitations which it chose to set itself, the City pursued the completion of Haussmann's street plan with singleminded application between 1871 and the early 1890s. Now, its policy becomes more complex. For both financial and technical reasons, it chooses to switch its effort to the building of an underground railway, and for over ten years street improvement work is halted. Then it changes course again, and resumes its street policy with almost frenetic energy. Yet it no longer sees it as a panacea, for it realises that new thoroughfares cannot alone secure the health of the population. From now on, slum clearance must be a separate policy. In this chapter we shall study, firstly, the building of the *Métropolitain*, and secondly, the effort devoted to street works during and after the *Métro* interlude. Lastly, we shall examine the development of a slum clearance policy which was destined to change the whole Parisian public works strategy.

I THE *METRO* INTERLUDE

To understand why there was so much enthusiasm for building the *Métro* in the 1890s, one must go back seventy years to the origins of the Paris public transport system.

The public transport era began in Paris in 1828 when the first omnibus company commenced operations. Others soon followed, but services were irregular and unevenly distributed, because companies refused to route their vehicles through poor or outlying districts.[1] Responsible for coordinating the different services was the Prefect of Police, who in 1854 required the eleven companies that then existed

---

[1] J. Benedetti, 'Le Métropolitain et les transports en commun parisiens', *La conjoncture économique dans le Département*, 1958, IIIème trimestre, p. 494; C.M. reports, 1907, no. 60, pp. 7–8.

to group themselves into one, the General Omnibus Company. In return for this loss of independence, he offered the new company a thirty year concession of twenty-five lines and a complete monopoly of omnibus transport. The Company signed this contract in July 1854 and it was ratified by an imperial decree in February 1855. After the annexation of the suburban communes a new contract was signed, in June 1860, which extended the period of the concession to fifty years. In return, the Company accepted the power of the City to lay down routes and timetables, and it was understood (or so the authorities thought!) that the monopoly involved the obligation of operating routes to certain districts even at a loss.

During the early years the Company's prosperity obscured the inherent defects of this arrangement. Services were improved and the average price of a ticket was reduced to twenty centimes (2d). By 1873 the company was operating thirty-two routes and carrying 111 million passengers a year, compared to thirty-four million in 1854.[2] And a decade later, with its first trams in operation as well as omnibuses, it was carrying nearly twice this figure.[3] However, there were still large areas of the city, not only on the outskirts, which were very badly served. In 1854 the Prefect of Police had pointed out that omnibus transport was greatly hindered by the inadequate street system.[4] Haussmann admitted soon afterwards that although omnibuses ran along all the main thoroughfares, they 'hardly penetrate the areas of narrow streets at all'.[5] When the City tried to encourage the General Omnibus Company to improve its services in such areas, it was usually met by a firm refusal supported by technical and financial arguments. The Company claimed that it was in no position to start new routes, because even those which would return a profit in the long term suffered losses during the first few years. And in 1868 fifteen lines out of thirty-two were still running at a loss.[6] The City was very reluctant to revoke the concession to the Company, because it at least provided a transport system at no cost to the taxpayer, and the Company actually paid a considerable proportion of its profits to the City in parking fees. When the first trams started to run the omnibus routes became even less profitable, and in 1872 the Company asked the Prefect to allow a general reorganisation of the network. The City Council, when

[2] C.M. reports, 1874, no. 5, p. 5; René Clozier, *La Gare du Nord* (1940), p. 53.
[3] Henri de Pontich, *Administration de la Ville de Paris* (1884), p. 399.
[4] De Pontich, p. 394.
[5] Conseil général minutes, 24 November 1856, p. 14.
[6] C.M. reports, 1874, no. 5, pp. 6–7.

consulted, asked for more routes and a general improvement in the services. But it proved impossible to agree on a compromise, and the existing arrangements, which satisfied no one, remained in force.[7]

In 1880 the Company asked for permission to increase its fares, and the City took the chance of considering whether it could be merged with the North and South tramway companies, whose lines linked the suburbs to the city but did not penetrate the city centre. But a special study committee declared against any change in the 1860 agreement because the two other companies were also in a dangerous financial position. It also questioned the accuracy of the Company's own assessment of its difficulties, and the Council, accepting its conclusions, refused permission for the merger.[8] A suggestion by the General Omnibus Company that it should take over the other two companies was refused on the advice of the same committee in 1881,[9] and a counter-demand by the City in 1883 that twelve routes should be created or altered was ignored.[10] In 1888 the public works committee urged that the Company should be required to do as it was told, under the threat of withdrawal of the 1860 concession. If necessary, it thought, the City should operate the services itself.[11] Relations between the City and the Company were now in a parlous state. The Company was taken to court by the City for changing its timetables without permission, and lost its case. It then offered to carry out the changes called for in 1883, but failed to obtain an adequate quid pro quo from the City.[12]

Although the Company was often accused of inefficiency and incompetence,[13] the root of the problem was the clear inferiority of omnibuses to trams.[14] The first tram line was opened in Paris in 1854, but it was only partly successful and was not emulated for many years.[15] But by the early 1870s the success of lines in other cities encouraged the General Council of the Seine to approve the creation of a tram network for the Paris suburbs.[16] The plan was based on a

[7] C.M. reports, 1874, no. 5, pp. 1–2, 7, 18, 25.
[8] C.M. reports, 1880, no. 208; C.M. minutes, 4 May 1881.
[9] C.M. reports, 1881, no. 109.
[10] C.M. reports, 1888, no. 83, pp. 13–14.
[11] C.M. reports, 1888, no. 83, pp. 1, 13–14.
[12] Dr. Chassagne, *Dix-neuf ans du Conseil municipal élu de la Ville de Paris, 1871–1890* (1890), p. 30, 30n.
[13] See, for instance, C.M. reports, 1877, no. 20, p. 28.
[14] Trams were bigger, faster and more comfortable than omnibuses. For a description of the unpleasantness of omnibus travel, see J. K. Huysmans, *Croquis parisiens* (new ed., 1886), pp. 53–6.
[15] De Pontich, *Administration de Paris*, p. 401.
[16] C.M. reports, 1873, no. 8, p. 1.

81

circular line within the city, from which ten radial routes ran into the suburbs. The operation of the circular line was entrusted to the General Omnibus Company, and two new companies, the North and South Tramways, were floated to run the other lines.[17] The General Omnibus Company was worried about competition from the radial lines, and because the City wanted at this time to preserve the Company's monopoly, it approved in 1876 a request by the Company for six new tramways within the city boundaries.[18] New lines were granted almost every year after 1877 to the three companies, but internal routes were always entrusted to the General Omnibus Company.[19]

From the very beginning the trams won the affection of the public and omnibuses were deserted on sections where the two forms of transport were in competition. Although the Company was allowed to abandon omnibus routes or parts of routes when corresponding tramways were built, the omnibus system slipped even further into the red because it was always the best routes that were replaced by trams. The Company avoided making an overall loss until 1901, but thanks only to its tram profits.[20] However, trams also had their disadvantages. They caused traffic jams even in the broad thoroughfares along which they ran,[21] and so could not possibly penetrate the narrow and tortuous streets of the old city. Single track working was inefficient, and was never introduced into the city centre. In the fashionable west of the city centre there was considerable local opposition to trams,[22] just as there was in London at the same period. Even as late as 1888 the only lines in the right bank centre ran along the Boulevard de Sébastopol, the Rues de Turbigo, Baltard and des Halles, and the *quais*. With the exception of the *quais*, all these thoroughfares had been built by Haussmann. The parts of the centre which he had not touched were also deprived of trams. In fact, trams were generally considered to be of most use in linking the city to the suburbs, and they never made any great contribution to transport within the city centre. In any case, they quickly became overcrowded, and by 1883 it was already being said that they were inadequate.[23] The General Omnibus Company's trams, in particular, were cumbrous and antiquated.[24] In the Exposition year of 1889 the public transport system was stretched to its

[17] Benedetti, 'Le Métropolitain', p. 495.
[18] C.M. reports, 1877, no. 20, pp. 3–4.
[19] Benedetti, 'Le Métropolitain'.
[20] C.M. reports, 1907, no. 60, p. 9.
[21] Benedetti, 'Le Métropolitain', p. 498.
[22] C.M. reports, 1878, no. 111, pp. 6, 7.
[23] C.M. reports, 1883, no. 30, p. 10.
[24] Karl Baedeker, *Paris and Environs* (9th ed., 1888), p. 21.

very limit,[25] making a metropolitan railway appear indispensable. Surface transport seemed to be incapable of further expansion without bringing itself to a halt by saturating the street system, especially in the old thoroughfares of the centre.[26] In particular, the east of the right bank centre was hardly served by surface transport, and it was to be hoped that an underground railway would revive just such declining areas. But when the *Métropolitain* came to be built, a very different pattern resulted.

The first section of London's Metropolitan Railway was opened in 1863. In Paris an internal railway system for goods, linking the main termini, had been proposed as early as 1845, but was turned down by the City Council. In 1856 a project was published for a rail link to the new Halles, but again nothing came of it.[27] But from the first years of the Third Republic the City Council showed considerable interest in an underground system. Councillor Léon Say called for one to be built in 1871, and in the following year the General Council of the Seine authorised the Prefect to study a metropolitan railway network to be built under powers contained in the 1865 law on branch lines.[28] But no potential concessionary came forward, and before any detailed scheme was proposed the *Conseil d'Etat* and the Minister of Public Works let it be known that any such network could not be regarded as a branch line, which meant that the City would not have complete control over it. The City carried on with preliminary studies, but in the end the idea had to be dropped.[29] At all costs, the City Council wanted to prevent control slipping into the hands of the Government, for it knew that such authority would merely be delegated to the dreaded railway companies, who would operate and develop the underground system only as a feeder for their own lines.

New hopes were aroused by the law of 11 June 1880, which gave local authorities power to build and operate branch lines within their own boundaries. The Prefect was soon approached by private interests seeking to construct a metropolitan network, and in May 1882 he invited the City Council's views on such a scheme[30] ⟨*see* plate 9⟩. The

---

[25] C.M. reports, 1896, no. 26, p. 2. [26] Benedetti, 'Le Métropolitain', p. 499.
[27] Jean Robert, *Notre Métro* (1967), p. 13.
[28] C.M. reports, 1883, no. 30, p. 2; De Pontich, *Administration de Paris*, p. 407.
[29] De Pontich, p. 407; C.M. reports, 1883, no. 30, pp. 2–3; Clozier, *La Gare du Nord*, p. 61.
[30] C.M. reports, 1882, no. 44, p. 1; 1883, no. 30, p. 1; De Pontich, *Administration de Paris*, p. 408.

Council set up a special committee which reported in April 1883 in favour of an underground system following existing streets, so that preliminary street improvements would not be necessary. It thought the railway essential because of the patent inadequacy of the tram service. It would also encourage the development of suburbs and reduce densities in the centre, thus creating a better life for Parisians. The City Council gave its agreement in principle to the preparation of a scheme on 4 June 1883.[31] But there still remained the legal problem. No confirmation had been received that the 1880 law applied to Paris. The Government still wanted a line to link up the terminal stations, under the railway companies' control, and produced schemes to achieve this end in 1885 and 1886. But Parliament turned both of them down because they involved a State financial guarantee.[32] On the other hand, there was no doubt by now that the lines would have to be built underground, even though a number of engineers and would-be concessionaries were still canvassing for aerial lines.[33] But they would have to follow existing streets because if they took a new route, even at some depth, under private property, there was a risk that the courts would decide that compensation was payable. Indeed, with the *Conseil d'Etat* still pursuing its apparent vendetta against the City, such an unfavourable interpretation of the law seemed extremely likely.

By the time the City Council had approved the Prefect's own detailed plan in 1886 the Government had made it clear that it would not allow the system to be built under branch line legislation.[34] Although the Government and the railway companies continued to put schemes forward, the City was now even less prepared to compromise because its experience with the General Omnibus Company confirmed it in its determination to establish direct authority over any new means of transport. The Government did not show any inclination to review its decision until 1895, when it became concerned that inadequate transport arrangements might detract from the success of the planned 1900 Exposition. In November of that year the Minister of Public Works, Louis Barthou, agreed to recognise all future railways in Paris as branch lines. But there still seemed to be a danger that the Government might allow the railway companies to take over any underground

[31] De Pontich, p. 408; C.M. reports, 1883, no. 30, pp. 9, 10, 12, 19, 32.
[32] Clozier, *La Gare du Nord*, p. 62.
[33] These schemes aroused considerable opposition on aesthetic as well as practical grounds. See *Bulletin de la Société des Amis des Monuments parisiens*, 1886, p. 20.
[34] See C.M. reports, 1886, no. 69.

lines later on, and in March 1896 the Council's special *Métropolitain* committee called for a narrow gauge system which would not extend beyond the boundaries.[35] This would make it impossible for the companies to link their lines to the system and run through trains, and would not give the Government the excuse to take the system over on the grounds that it served a number of local authority areas. The City Council approved this report on 4 December 1896. And although the gauge was later increased to standard width by a decree of 30 March 1898, the loading gauge remained too small to allow the through running of main line rolling stock.

In July 1897 the *Métropolitain* committee reported on the definitive scheme prepared by the administration ⟨*see* plate 10⟩. It had proved possible to plan for drilling tunnels everywhere, so that no trenches or cuttings need be dug. Large scale demolitions would be necessary at two points only, neither of them in the city centre. Because the legal position on compensation was still unclear, it had been decided to keep as far away as possible from private properties, and the lines had had to be routed only along very wide streets.[36] In most cases, these streets dated from the time of Haussmann or later, and some, like the Rue Réaumur, were still being built. The decision to use them ensured that the lines would follow the most important traffic currents, which was what the *Métropolitain* had always been intended to do,[37] but it meant that areas like the Marais would receive no benefit at all. Of course, it would have been possible to introduce a much greater flexibility into the system by building tube lines, as London had been doing since the early 1890s. They could have run at such great depth that little or no compensation would have been payable to landlords, and they could have complemented the existing street system instead of duplicating it. Although it was generally held that the Paris subsoil was unsuitable for deep tunnelling, mainly because of its numerous caverns and galleries, an engineer, J. Berlier, had aroused the City's interest in what he called 'tubular underground tramways' as early as 1888.[38] In 1892 Berlier was offered the chance to build one narrow gauge tube line, but the Government postponed a decision on its approval until 1895. Then its general sanction for a *Métro* network deprived Berlier's scheme, which many councillors had unfairly

---

[35] C.M. reports, 1896, no. 26, p. 9.
[36] C.M. reports, 1897, no. 75, pp. 1, 7, 10. For a discussion of the legal position on compensation, see p. 15.
[37] Benedetti, 'Le Métropolitain', p. 506.   [38] C.M. reports, 1888, no. 54.

called a 'toy railway', of its attraction, and the City revoked the concession of the experimental line.

Powers to build the *Métro* were granted by a law of 30 March 1898. The first line, from the Porte de Vincennes to the Porte Maillot, was partially opened in time for the Exposition in July 1900. Two other lines were opened in the same year, and 120 kilometres were in operation by 1914, by which time the City had spent 620 million francs (£24,800,000) on the work.[39] Yet within a few years of the opening of the first line disenchantment was setting in.

The total number of passengers transported annually by the *Métro* rose from sixteen millions in 1900 to 149 millions in 1905, and 254 millions in 1909.[40] Clearly, the new facilities were encouraging people to move about who otherwise would have stayed where they were. As early as May 1910 the general purposes committee presented a report on congestion which stated that surface traffic was generated not only by the increasing number of motorcars, but also by the underground railway.[41] This conclusion was shared by Louis Dausset, rapporteur of the budget committee:

'When we built the *Métropolitain* and encouraged the development of mechanical trams, we gave our citizens and visitors a taste for moving about. It is axiomatic that in a great conurbation like Paris the demand for transport increases in direct relation to the development of speedy and cheap means of transport. In future the effects of this law will mean that even our most optimistic plans will not be enough. . . . So underground transport does nothing to reduce surface movement in Paris; on the contrary, it multiplies it.'[42]

This disappointment helps to explain why the City did no more after the war than complete the lines that had already been planned, and extend some others into the suburbs, having overcome its fears of a Government takeover. The relative failure of the *Métro*, the unforeseen proliferation of the motorcar, and the growing demand for slum clearance, dictated a return to a policy of surface improvements. So we must now examine how much time had been lost, and what was done to make it up.

[39] Commission d'extension de Paris, *Considérations techniques préliminaires* (1913), p. 31; Maurice Félix and Eugène Raiga, *Le régime administratif et financier du Département de la Seine et de la Ville de Paris* (1922), p. 643n; André Morizet, *Du vieux Paris au Paris moderne* (1932), p. 332; C.M. reports, 1936, no. 95, p. 10.
[40] C.M. reports, 1910, no. 17, p. 23.   [41] C.M. reports, no. 17, 1910, pp. 24-5.
[42] C.M. reports, 1909, no. 128, pp. 269-70.

2 THE DEATH AND REBIRTH OF STREET IMPROVEMENTS

After 1893 budgetary difficulties began again for the City. The Council was prepared to invest in the *Métropolitain* because its anticipated operating profits would cover the loan charges. Equally attractive were gas, electricity, water and drainage works, all of which produced revenue in the form of charges to users or service taxes. But the Council's stolid refusal to increase taxation made it highly unlikely that it would approve further borrowing for street improvements. The City's continuing inability to tax betterment values meant that such works always made a loss, which it was pointless to incur at a time when it seemed likely that the *Métropolitain* alone would reduce surface congestion. There still remained an articulate street improvement lobby in the Council, which argued that public works schemes led to a rise in revenue from taxation which offset the failure to collect betterment value.[43] But this traditional argument was no longer enough. Far more influential was the judgement of the *Métropolitain* committee:

> 'The building of a few new streets will bring about only the partial decongestion of those that are overloaded, and will absorb, as a total write-off for the City, a bigger capital sum than the *Métropolitain*, which will be a productive investment.'[44]

So although the continued decline in interest rates, and the City's improving credit, encouraged the Council to borrow,[45] it concentrated on productive loans of which the *Métro* received the lion's share. In 1896 it floated a loan of forty-four million francs to fund the short-term debt to the *Crédit Foncier*, and in 1898 it borrowed 165 million francs to convert the 1886 loan, and begin work on the *Métro*.[46] For other capital investment projects only forty-four million francs could be made available, and the Council decided to share this sum between four different committees.[47] The portion finally allotted to the public works committee was 24½ million francs (£1 million), six millions of which were allocated by decision of the Council to paving and lighting. The remainder, by a decision of the committee, ratified by the Council, was to be distributed 'as equally as possible between the eighty wards'.[48] This was the best way of achieving nothing. In the right bank centre the public works committee recommended three small widenings in

[43] See, for instance, C.M. reports, 1895, no. 170.
[44] C.M. reports, 1896, no. 26, p. 13.
[45] See the report of the budget committee, C.M. reports, 1896, no. 125, p. 375.
[46] Morizet, *Du vieux Paris*, p. 332.   [47] C.M. minutes, 12 April 1897.
[48] C.M. reports, 1897, no. 69, p. 2.

the Ier and IIe *arrondissements*. In the IIIe *arrondissement* it suggested
the extension of the Rue Beaubourg as far south as possible before the
money ran out, and in the IVe it wanted to see the Rue des Lions-Saint-
Paul extended to the Boulevard Henri-IV because sale of sites could
cover the whole cost. Any surplus could be allocated to the Rue
Beaubourg, on which it might prove possible to spend as much as one
and a half million francs (£60,000), although even this, it was admitted, would produce only modest results.[49]

Matters were not helped by the City's further financial crisis which
began in 1897, when unfavourable national conditions were aggravated
by the abolition of some of the *octroi* dues.[50] A big deficit built up,
and there was no real recovery until 1904. But from this year onwards
circumstances began to combine to force the City Council to recon-
sider its position on non-productive borrowing. New legislation in
1904 and 1905 placed further responsibilities on the City in education
and public assistance.[51] And early faith in the *Métro* as the new panacea
was being shaken, mainly by the councillors' growing awareness that
the slum problem still remained to be dealt with. In November 1904
Prefect De Selves submitted to the General Council of the Seine a
schedule of public works to be financed by a loan of 200 million francs
(£8 million) contracted by the *Département*. It included a number of
schemes within the city, which were approved by the City Council on
14 April 1905. But this arrangement could be only a partial solution.
On 29 December 1904 the City Council had voted firmly against
further issues of municipal stock and had decided that public works
schemes would be financed by the exclusive allocation of resources freed
by the progressive amortisation of previous loans. The chairman of the
budget committee was a strong opponent of borrowing,[52] and Councillor
Ambroise Rendu, although the Council's leading exponent of slum
clearance, agreed with him.[53] Although the floating of the loan by the
Département seemed the best possible compromise, it could not provide enough resources for all the schemes which the City Council had
recognised as necessary in Paris.

Meanwhile, the Council had to make a decision on the allocation
of resources created by the departmental loan. The Prefect asked it

[49] C.M. reports, 1897, no. 69, p. 3.
[50] See Louis Dausset, *Rapport général . . . sur . . . le projet de budget de la Ville de Paris
pour 1909*, pp. 39–40 (C.M. reports, 1908, no. 68).
[51] C.M. reports, 1901, no. 105; 1903, no. 72, pp. 7–9; Dausset, *Rapport général . . .
pour 1909*, pp. 199–213.
[52] See *Rapport général sur le budget de 1905*, pp. 15–30 (C.M. reports, 1904, no. 79).
[53] C.M. minutes, 14 April 1905.

to do so as quickly as possible in order to prevent speculation, and proposed that nearly seventy-four million francs (£2,960,000) be allocated to a list of schemes for immediate execution. The Council approved this schedule, and a further list of projects whose financing was to be arranged later. Nearly a third of the available sum, twenty-three million francs, was to be spent in the right bank centre. The biggest scheme there was the partial isolation of the Halles by the widening of the Rue Coquillière, the Rue des Deux-Ecus, and other streets, at a cost of ten million francs (£400,000). The other projects were much smaller, but three million francs were devoted to building a short section of the Rue du Louvre between the Rue du Mail and the Rue d'Aboukir, and a similar sum was allocated to widening part of the Rue de Bretagne. The Council also approved the extension of the buildings of the Paris history library at a cost of three million francs. No resources were allocated to the Rue Beaubourg, but 850,000 francs were voted for the partial widening of the Rue du Renard. The total sum attributed to the centre was so large because most of the schemes planned there had been placed in the first schedule. The second list, of less important schemes, contained only three very small projects in the right bank centre.[54]

This somewhat tentative return to street improvements was just the thin end of the wedge. Whereas the works approved in 1905 were considered necessary mainly because the *Métro* made no contribution to slum clearance, subsequent pressure for more improvements was strengthened by its failure to solve traffic problems. From 1905 the general purposes committee presented an annual report on traffic and pedestrian movements in the city. Each report emphasised and confirmed that surface movement was increasing, and that the *Métro*, far from checking it, was actually encouraging it. The small improvements approved in 1905 merely served to stress how much remained to be done. The chairman of the public works committee, André Chérioux, a civil engineering contractor, began a campaign for the upward revision of the width standards of all streets. In 1907 he presented a report urging that the minimum width of new streets should be raised from twelve to fifteen metres, and to eighteen metres wherever possible.[55] The Council approved his proposal and referred it to the public works committee for more thorough study.[56] Its report, placed before the Council in March 1908, took the form of a complete

---

[54] C.M. reports, 1905, no. 14, pp. 3, 5, 9.   [55] C.M. reports, 1907, no. 68, pp. 1–2.
[56] C.M. minutes, 25 November 1907.

reappraisal of the traffic problem. The committee suggested that new methods of communication like the *Métro* and the telephone had failed to reduce street congestion because Parisians were acquiring the habit of moving about more often and were spending more time outside their homes. So the City's attention would have to turn once again to easing surface movement by, in particular, the construction of wide streets for vehicles and trams. The ideal minimum width for streets would be twenty-four metres, but the committee recognised that this was out of the question and restricted itself to supporting Chérioux's original norm of fifteen to eighteen metres.[57] The Council approved the report on 2 April 1908.

There were now signs that the Council's resistance to further borrowing was weakening. Councillor Rendu's campaign for the demolition of areas of high tuberculosis mortality was building up to a peak, and it was already being suggested that the revenue resources which would be freed in 1910 by the amortisation of a previous loan could be used to finance a new borrowing rather than to reduce taxation. As early as 1906 Councillor Chautard proposed the conversion of four loans contracted between 1865 and 1876, but this came to nought after objections by the budget committee chairman, Councillor Lefèvre, and the Prefect, to the length of the period of repayment.[58] In September 1908 Councillor Deville called for a long-term loan of 1,000 million francs (£40 million) to balance the budget, liquidate the existing debt, and finance a massive public works programme.[59] Meanwhile, the Prefect was having a schedule of improvements drawn up, and it was placed before the Council in March 1908. Although the difficulties involved, and a series of big strikes by building workers, subsequently made the administration less enthusiastic about its own proposals,[60] many councillors were now convinced that an ambitious programme was essential. In 1908 the budget committee, now chaired by the energetic Councillor Dausset, came out in favour of a large-scale public works policy. It favoured a new loan to be serviced by the 'resources of 1869'—taxes raised for the loan of that year, which would become available in 1910. Not only should current projects be completed, but new ones undertaken 'to ease traffic movement,

[57] C.M. reports, 1908, no. 26, pp. 11–12.
[58] Louis Dausset, *Rapport général . . . sur . . . le projet de budget de la Ville de Paris pour 1911*, p. 122 (C.M. reports, 1910, no. 91).
[59] C.M. reports, 1908, no. 66.
[60] C.M. reports, 1908, no. 68, p. 353; 1909, no. 82, p. 4; Jean Bastié, *La croissance de la banlieue parisienne* (1964), p. 196.

improve public hygiene, allow the great municipal services to keep pace with the growth of population and, finally, to contribute so far as it lies within our power to the embellishment of Paris.' Dausset argued that it was the City's duty to look ahead beyond its current needs, to prepare the future:

'A city like Paris is in a state of permanent and, so to speak, chronic transformation . . . Cities which have not changed are dead cities.'

Paris, said the report, was inferior in transport facilities to all big foreign cities and even to some in France. Two types of improvement were necessary; those which were of general interest, and those relevant only to a particular ward. Great thoroughfares would always be needed, but, at the same time, '. . . every one of our eighty wards requires urgent improvements in sanitation, hygiene, ventilation and streets.' The public might complain of the inconvenience caused by street works, but they were essential if Paris were to maintain pride of place among the world's capitals.[61]

In July 1909 the finance committee suggested that the Prefect should be invited to issue stock to the value of 900 million francs (£36 million), repayable over fifty-six years. Some members, notably Councillor Lampué, protested that until only recently both Council and administration had been resolutely opposed to further borrowing, and chided their colleagues for their inconsistency.[62] But after further talks with the administration, and encouragement by Dausset, the Council declared itself ready to approve a loan of 900 million francs, to be floated in three instalments with 440 million francs (£17,600,000) allocated to street improvements. This was a popular decision with the general public, which had become very worried about congestion, and not even the most inveterate opponents of borrowing dared to vote against it in the end.[63] The loan was authorised by a law of 30 December 1909. Dausset hailed it as the biggest step forward since the Second Empire.[64]

The City Council had drawn up a list of improvements to be financed by the loan in July 1909. The width of all new streets was

---

[61] Louis Dausset, *Rapport général . . . sur . . . le projet de budget de la Ville de Paris pour 1909*, pp. 353–366 (C.M. reports, 1908, no. 68).
[62] C.M. reports, 1909, no. 79.
[63] Louis Dausset, *Rapport général . . . sur . . . le projet de budget de la Ville de Paris pour 1910*, p. 242 (C.M. reports, 1909, no. 128).
[64] Dausset, p. 266.

fixed at a minimum of fifteen metres, in accordance with the 1908 resolution, except where traffic was minimal or where widening was carried out for public health reasons only.[65] Many of the very large number of schemes were simply widenings, but there were some ambitious new projects. In the right bank centre the main objective was to complete the existing network of streets with a width of eighteen metres or more, and so the biggest operations were concentrated in the east, which previously had been somewhat neglected.[66] In the IIIe *arrondissement* the plans included the completion of the Rue Beaubourg, the extension of the Rue Etienne-Marcel from the Rue aux Ours to the Boulevard Bourdonnais, and the widening of the Rue de Bretagne, which would have the effect of extending the Rue Réaumur to the east. In addition, it was planned to extend the Rue Volta to the Boulevard Saint-Martin. In the IVe *arrondissement*, apart from the completion of the Rue Beaubourg and the Rue du Renard, a new street was to be built between the Quai des Célestins and the Rue François-Miron, and others on the site of the Passage Saint-Pierre. But the first two *arrondissements* were by no means excluded. In the Ier *arrondissement* the isolation of the Halles would continue, while in the IIe the Rue du Louvre would be completed, and the Rue Dussoubs extended to the Rue d'Aboukir to create a new thoroughfare from the Rue Etienne-Marcel to the *grands boulevards*. Seen as a whole, the plan of campaign aimed to finish two almost completed north-south thoroughfares, and to extend to the east two streets—the Rue Réaumur and the Rue Etienne-Marcel—which had been built only in the west of the right bank centre. The area to the west of the Palais-Royal, where property values were high and there were no slums, was allotted hardly any improvements. The same was true of the extreme east of the centre. The most favoured area was the central sector between the Rue de Richelieu and the Rue Beaubourg. This concentration was partly the result of the continuing need to improve the area around the Halles. Between 1869 and 1885 nothing had been done to improve the area because it was considered that the scheme should be carried out as a whole.[67] Then, in 1885, the City took the chance to carry out some of the work in connection with the commercial exchange project, but the Rue du Louvre, as we have seen, cost more than expected and took up the whole of the allocation made by the Council. Unfortunately, the

---

[65] See C.M. minutes, 13, 14, 24 July, 1909; C.M. reports, 1910, no. 21, pp. 2, 5–21.
[66] For a plan of the schemes financed by the loan, see Commission d'extension de Paris, *Considérations techniques préliminaires* (1913), plan no. 9.
[67] This account of the Halles case is taken from C.M. reports, 1925, no. 153, pp. 6–10.

City had promised as part of the agreement to provide a network of broad streets around the exchange, and was sued for breach of contract. The *Conseil d'Etat*, acting true to form, decided in favour of the plaintiffs in December 1889. The City was required to carry out the work by December 1892, after which it was to pay annual damages to the commercial exchange so long as the work remained incomplete. For some years the City was able to avoid paying anything, but in May 1906 the *Conseil d'Etat* fixed the damages for 1892 to 1902 at 80,000 francs (£3,200) a year. The City had to agree to pay the same sum for every succeeding year, subject to reductions in respect of partial improvements. This obligation, as well as the growing congestion of the Halles, explains why the City devoted considerable resources to the area in the last years before 1914.

The Rue Beaubourg and Rue du Renard schemes had also been begun some years before. The main objective in building them seems to have been to improve traffic flow,[68] but the slum clearance element became more prominent as it was demonstrated with increasing clarity that the area which they crossed had an extremely high tuberculosis death rate. In the early 1900s this consideration reinforced the campaign that local councillors Brenot and Opportun had been leading for some time to have the streets built. From a traffic point of view, the improvement was designed to provide adequate access to the Hôtel de Ville from the north, and provide a direct link between the Réaumur-Turbigo crossroads and the point of intersection of two new streets on the left bank, the Rue Dante and the Rue Lagrange.[69] It would also allow the construction of the Châtelet-Lilas *Métro* line. The extension of the Rue Etienne-Marcel to the Boulevard Beaumarchais also had advantages for public health, but here again traffic considerations predominated.[70] So did they in the case of the widening of the Rue des Deux-Ponts, in the Île Saint-Louis, which was in the ridiculous position of being approached by two bridges of over fifteen metres in width, when the street itself was only seven metres wide.[71]

The schedule also included lists of complementary projects, mainly widenings or small street construction schemes, although there was one highly significant exception. This was the demolition of a block of houses, in the unhealthy area number 1,[72] bounded by the Rues de Venise, Saint-Martin, des Etuves, and Beaubourg. But, this apart, the

---

[68] See, for instance, C.M. reports, 1891, no. 10, p. 6.
[69] Maurice Halbwachs, *Les expropriations et le prix des terrains à Paris* (1909), p. 252.
[70] C.M. reports, 1907, no. 4, p. 2.   [71] C.M. reports, 1914, no. 27, pp. 4–5.
[72] See below, pp. 109 ff.

most striking feature of the whole schedule was the large number of widenings that it contained. Even the extension of the Rue Etienne-Marcel across the east of the right bank centre was essentially a widening scheme. The City was probably influenced by the fact that many streets had been partially widened by the application of improvement line regulations. Louis Dausset envisaged the construction of several completely new traffic arteries across Paris, but only in the long term.[73] The City could not afford to wait until the remaining houses were demolished voluntarily because the number of demolitions in the centre was decreasing, and the owners of houses which projected beyond improvement lines were even more tenacious than most. Between 1908 and 1911 only thirty-two fractions of sites were ceded to the highway in the right bank centre, compared to 227 in the rest of the city.[74] In theory, the buildings should have fallen down very quickly owing to the ban on structural repairs, but it had in fact become very difficult to enforce.[75] The *Conseil d'Etat* was inconsistent, often requiring the City to follow compulsory purchase procedure when fractions of sites were due to be ceded, and since 1860 properties which infringed the improvement line in their entirety had been exempted. As early as the 1870s the City had begun to enforce improvement line regulations only on buildings whose demolition would result in the widening of a street rather than in a fundamental change in its direction. The *Conseil d'Etat* steadily restricted their application still further, and ruled, for instance, in 1901, that a property should be exempt if more than a quarter of its area were involved, and, in 1902, that the procedure should not apply in cases where the resulting widening would be considerable.[76]

The City Council's next task was to decide what schemes to undertake with the first 235 million franc instalment of the loan. In a memorandum of 7 November 1910, the Prefect proposed to allocate 100 million francs (£4 million) to street improvements to be begun between 1910 and 1913. He believed that as many schemes as possible should be started because acquisition procedure was now so lengthy

[73] *Rapport général . . . sur . . . le projet de budget de la Ville de Paris pour 1912*, pp. 555–7 (C.M. reports, 1911, no. 95).

[74] *Rapport général . . . pour 1912*, pp. 697–8.

[75] See C.V.P., 15 January 1903, pp. 2–3.

[76] Alfred des Cilleuls, *Traité de la législation et de l'administration de la voirie urbaine* (1877), p. 287; Henri de Pontich, *Administration de la Ville de Paris* (1884), p. 278; Emile Henry, *De la servitude de reculement* (1906), pp. 113–14, 124.

that even the small sections financed out of the first instalment would hardly be finished by 1913, when further resources would be available. It would thus be possible to make a start on 100 out of the 200 schemes in the general schedule of the 900 million franc loan.[77] The public works committee agreed that the works should be spread over several years because it wanted to avoid too great an influx of labour, which would lead sooner or later to an unemployment crisis.[78] In the right bank centre all the projects previously approved were split into instalments, except for the Rue Beaubourg and the Rue du Renard. But nearly half the total sum available, forty-five million francs, was allocated to the right bank centre, partly as the result of Parliament's insistence that the whole country should benefit from the work. So the City had to give priority to schemes in the central business and administrative districts.[79] The greater part of these resources was concentrated on a few projects; isolation of the Halles, 3,700,000 francs, the extension of the Rue du Louvre and the widening of the Rue Montmartre, 4,250,000 francs, and completion of the Rue Beaubourg and Rue du Renard, 16,500,000 francs. The other schemes all had allocations of less than two million francs, with the sole exception of the Rue de Bretagne widening (5,200,000 francs).[80]

It had originally been intended to float the second instalment of the loan in 1914, but Dausset had convinced the Council of the need for haste, and it now wanted the second fraction to be issued between 1912 and 1916.[81] The Prefect agreed to this request, and on 30 June 1911 the City Council asked the administration to make proposals for the schemes to be financed by the second instalment. But by November the Prefect had made no reply, and some councillors became worried that not enough real progress was being made, especially in view of the approaching municipal elections in 1912.[82] They were also unhappy about the 'derisory' sums allocated to unhealthy areas and workers' dwellings. Dausset's budget report, which appeared soon after, also declared in favour of the rapid continuation of the works. And it supported a suggestion by the Prefect that the City should use private developers in order to obtain the full value of sites on resale, now that the law of 10 April 1912 had made it easier to acquire parts of sites not required for streetworks.[83]

[77] C.M. reports, 1910, no. 89, pp. 5, 9, 46. [78] C.M. reports, 1910, no. 89, p. 6.
[79] C.M. reports, 1917, no. 2, p. 5. [80] C.M. reports, 1910, no. 89, pp. 9–10.
[81] Louis Dausset, *Rapport général . . . sur . . . le projet de budget de la Ville de Paris pour 1914*, p. 343 (C.M. reports, 1913, no. 120).
[82] C.M. reports, 1911, no. 88, pp. 1–2. [83] C.M. reports, 1912, no. 95, pp. 440–45.

On 25 November 1912 the City Council called on the Prefect to give priority in the schedule of the second instalment of the loan to works which it had not been possible to complete with the resources of the first. The Prefect followed this advice in a schedule placed before the public works committee early in 1913. Only four completely new projects were proposed, and only one of them, the isolation of the Conservatory of Arts and Crafts, was in the right bank centre. The Prefect wanted to allocate nearly twenty-five million francs to thirteen schemes in the right bank centre, compared with forty-five million francs for seventeen schemes in the 1910 schedule. Much of the reduction was the result of the completion of the Rue Beaubourg and Rue du Renard projects. As in 1910, the greater part of the available resources was attributed to a few schemes; 7,850,000 francs for the Rue du Louvre, 5,400,000 for the isolation of the Halles, 2,300,000 francs for the new street between the Quai des Célestins and the Rue François-Miron, and 2,130,100 francs for the widening of the Rue de Bretagne and the Rue Froissart.[84] The lower allocation to the centre led some critics to complain that the City was again sharing out resources equally among all the wards.[85] Although this accusation was unjustified, there was a clear trend away from operations in the right bank centre now that the Halles, Rue du Louvre and Rue Beaubourg schemes were complete or nearly complete. The only other large project there in the general schedule for the loan, the extension of the Rue Etienne-Marcel, was clearly being postponed until much later, and no resources had been allocated to it so far.

In fact, the City seemed to be reaching another turning-point. The Extension of Paris Committee, an assembly of officials, councillors and outside experts set up to take a long-term view of the city's problems, published in 1913 a report which questioned the whole concept of the street improvement policy established by Haussmann and followed ever since:

'The tremendous impulse given before 1870 has been continued by an uninterrupted forty year effort, without bringing us anywhere near reaching our objective.'[86]

The committee stressed the seriousness of the growing street congestion, which was caused mainly by the motorcar. It suggested that the

[84] C.M. reports, 1913, no. 10, pp. 1–5.
[85] See, for instance, Charles Lortsch, *La beauté de Paris et la loi* (1913), pp. 328–9.
[86] Commission d'extension de Paris, *Considérations techniques*, p. 37.

solution was to create new thoroughfares in the centre, but this should be done mainly by widening existing streets.[87] The present network of streets with a width of eighteen metres or more was so tight and coordinated, especially in the centre, that it would be useless to replace it by a new system, even if that were possible. The excessive multiplication of streets made the blocks too small, and caused courts and gardens to disappear. But the committee was against the distribution of resources among a multitude of small schemes; '. . . efforts must be concentrated on a few key traffic streets . . . or else it is to be feared that great sums will be wasted without any appreciable result.'[88] What the committee seemed to be suggesting was the wholesale widening of streets like the Rue de Richelieu, Rue Saint-Honoré, Rue Montmartre, Rue Saint-Denis, Rue Saint-Martin, Rue du Temple and Rue Vieille-du-Temple, all of which were marked on the draft improvement plan[89] ⟨*see* plate 8⟩. These thoroughfares had retained much of their original charm and appearance precisely because Haussmann had chosen to build completely new streets. However, the City Council had no time to discuss the change of policy recommended by the Extension of Paris Committee. Within a few months all works were halted by the declaration of war. The second instalment of the 900 million franc loan was never even floated owing to the financial crisis which began in 1912. And because the City had chosen to start work on as many schemes as possible, most of them were now left incomplete.

3 THE EVOLUTION OF A SLUM CLEARANCE POLICY

During the last few years before the war the City Council had devoted more attention than in the past to housing conditions, and had evolved a distinctive slum clearance policy, even to the extent of including one clearance operation in the schedule of the 900 million franc loan. Although this scheme was not actually started before 1914, it was clear that in future a high proportion of the City's resources would be allocated to the demolition and redevelopment of slums. But why had slum clearance not matured as a distinctive policy during the nineteenth century?

The association between high mortality and bad living conditions was first made clear in 1832, during the cholera epidemic.[90] The

---

[87] *Considérations techniques*, p. 34.   [88] *Considérations techniques*, p. 21.
[89] *Considérations techniques*, plan no. 9.
[90] See *Rapport sur la marche et les effets du choléra-morbus dans Paris et les communes rurales du Département de la Seine* (1834), esp. pp. 188–9.

Government hastily set up a central sanitary committee which re-commended in 1832 that blocks of apartments should be smaller, better built, with adequate water supply and refuse disposal, and efficient water closets. Minimum dimensions should be fixed for rooms.[91] Unfortunately, when cholera did not return in 1833 and the following years, many of these proposals were forgotten. Some pro-gress was made in improving sewers and water supplies, which could be achieved at low cost, but the authorities ignored the recommended higher standards for dwellings, which would have been both difficult and expensive to enforce. Instead, they convinced themselves that it would be enough to remove the external causes of insalubrity. There was also a division of responsibility in Paris between the Prefect of the Seine, who directed such works as water conduit and sewer construction, and the Prefect of Police, who organised more super-ficial sanitary arrangements like street cleansing and inspection of buildings. The Prefect of Police was advised from about 1830 by a sanitary council of doctors and public health experts,[92] but it had no powers to enforce the internal examination of dwellings.

Under the July Monarchy these arrangements were not substantially modified, but immediately after its overthrow the Provisional Govern-ment took the first steps towards reforming French public health administration. An order of 10 August 1848 set up a consultative committee of public hygiene in the Ministry of Agriculture and Commerce, and abolished the old higher council of public health. By December 1848 this new committee had produced a scheme for the establishment of councils of hygiene and salubrity in each *arrondisse-ment* of the Republic. Although there was disagreement between the Minister of Agriculture and Commerce, who wanted the councils to be elected, and the *Conseil d'Etat*, which thought that they should be nominated and directed by the Prefects, it was decided to set them up immediately in the form proposed by the *Conseil d'Etat* in view of the sudden reappearance of cholera in some areas.[93] But Paris, where public health administration was already more sophisticated than elsewhere, had to have special arrangements, and the order of 18

---

[91] Charles Gourlier, *Des voies publiques et des habitations particulières à Paris* (1852), pp. 26, 41.

[92] Vivien, 'Etudes administratives: II, La Préfecture de Police', p. 455, *Revue des Deux Mondes*, vol. IV, 1842, pp. 430–56.

[93] See report by the Minister of Agriculture to the president of the *Conseil des Ministres*, in collection of documents relating to the public health law of 1850, no. 2 (B.M., CT 436).

December 1848, which set up the councils of hygiene and salubrity, did not apply to the city.

So Paris had to face the approaching cholera epidemic under the old arrangements. Before the disease struck the capital, the Prefect of Police issued a set of instructions for the maintenance of healthy conditions in dwellings, on 20 November 1848.[94] Its preamble stated that the various public works carried out by the City should be accompanied by steps to ensure the salubrity of individual dwellings and, in particular, of lodging houses. It laid down vague standards for disposal of liquid sewage, provision of water closets, ventilation, and density of occupation of lodging houses. A separate schedule described how dwellings could be kept healthy by methods such as cleaning and sweeping. But there was no effective means of enforcing many of these recommendations. Meanwhile, the sanitary council was drawing up a more specific statement of precautions to be taken during the epidemic, which was published by the Prefect on 19 January 1849.[95] It urged citizens to keep calm, and suggested that if elementary precautions were taken, the epidemic could be kept under control. This optimism was echoed by the National Academy of Medicine, which published a pamphlet in March urging everyone to take certain simple precautions, and expressing the hope that the sanitary works—street widening, new fresh water outlets, and sewers—undertaken in Paris and other towns since 1832, in conjunction with an efficient medical service, would slow down the spread of the disease.[96] But the course of the epidemic in Paris did not bear out these forecasts. On 15 May 1849 the Prefect of Police had to introduce emergency measures similar to those pioneered in 1832. Sanitary committees were set up in each *arrondissement* of the city to organise local medical posts and relief work. No doubt they helped to some extent to limit the effects of the disease, but the cholera mortality figures do not suggest that Paris was significantly better protected against the epidemic than in 1832, despite Charles Merruau's assertion to the contrary.[97] Then, 18,402 people had died out of a population of 786,000. In 1849, 19,615 died out of just over a million.[98] Moreover, the official report on the epidemic concluded that the incidence of cholera was not significantly

[94] Documents relating to law of 1850, doc. no. 4.
[95] Documents relating to law of 1850, doc. no. 5.
[96] Académie nationale de medecine, *Instruction populaire sur les précautions à prendre contre le choléra-morbus* (1849) (B.M., CT 436, doc. no. 7).
[97] Charles Merruau, *Souvenirs de l'Hôtel de Ville de Paris, 1848–1852* (1875), p. 195.
[98] *Recherches statistiques sur la Ville de Paris et le Département de la Seine*, vol. VI, 1860, pp. vi, vii.

less in areas which had benefited from public works since 1832.[99] However, as in 1832, the poorest and most densely populated districts were the worst affected.

Whatever other conclusions were to be drawn from this experience, it was now clear that it was not enough to improve the external environment of the citizen of Paris. As well as providing more sewers and a pure water supply, the authorities would have to penetrate inside his dwelling and ensure that both he and his landlord maintained healthy standards there. The required powers were enacted very quickly. Under the Melun law of 13 April 1850[100] unhealthy dwellings committees were set up in each local authority area with, on paper, very wide authority. The landlord was made responsible for the sanitary condition of his property, and could be required to carry out such work as was necessary to make it healthy. In cases where no superficial repairs could remedy a house's insanitary condition, the local authority could even place a provisional ban on its occupation, pending a final decision by the Prefecture, and when the causes of insalubrity could be removed only by demolition, the municipality could acquire properties compulsorily under the law of 1841. In Paris, the unhealthy dwellings committee would have twelve members (increased to thirty in 1864) and, like similar committees elsewhere, would visit dwellings whose insanitary condition had been reported to it and decide on what steps to take. Its recommendations would be enforceable on landlords after approval by the City Council. Immediately after the law was passed, the Paris unhealthy dwellings committee was set up by the Council.

Since 1848 no arrangements had been made to set up councils of public hygiene and salubrity in Paris, although they were already in existence elsewhere. Their absence was all the more anomalous now that the unhealthy dwellings committee was at work, and was deprived of the detailed information which the councils could provide. So a decree of 15 December 1851 created committees of hygiene in each *arrondissement* under the direction of the Prefect of Police. The old sanitary council, to which the new committees would report, was retained under the title of council of public hygiene and salubrity of the *département* of the Seine. The local committees were set up in December

[99] Merruau, *Souvenirs*, pp. 199–200.
[100] See Jeanne Hugueney, 'Un centenaire oublié: la première loi française d'urbanisme', *Vie urbaine*, 1950, pp. 241–9. The full text of the law is reprinted in M. G. Jourdan, *Recueil des règlements concernant le service des alignements et la police des constructions* (1900), pp. 175–7.

1852, and among the functions delegated to them by the Prefect of Police were the maintenance of a statistical record of mortality and insalubrity, and the provision of information for the Paris unhealthy dwellings committee.[101]

The City's powers were further extended by the law of 26 March 1852, which gave it the right to intervene generally in matters relating to the sanitary condition of buildings. Builders of houses in streets which possessed sewers were required to ensure that all liquid sewage and rainwater flowed into them. The law also required all existing houses to conform to this standard within ten years. The City was allowed to inspect and control sanitary conditions in those parts of apartment blocks that were in communal use, but in respect of private dwellings it was required to act only through the unhealthy dwellings committee. These powers were incorporated in a new set of regulations issued by the Prefect of Police on 23 November 1853, relating to all factors of insalubrity except those which resulted from the mode of construction of the building.

These various dispositions placed a very heavy load on the unhealthy dwellings committee. But its authority was not commensurate with its responsibilities, and it took a conciliatory line with landlords, partly on the advice of the Ministry of Agriculture and Commerce, and partly because it was excessively sensitive to the weakness of its own position. In its first full report the committee stated:

> 'It [the committee] recognised, above all else, that it had to introduce a spirit of conciliation into the application of a law which created an entirely new system, and could damage many interests and become a vexation and an irritant . . .'[102]

The prime need was 'to appeal to the generous feelings of landlords' rather than to hurt them by 'untimely legal proceedings'.[103] And the committee came up against an even more fundamental obstacle. Although it appeared to accept the contemporary orthodoxy of public health through public works,[104] it vaguely recognised that the root cause of high mortality might lie not so much in superficial factors such as dirt and bad sanitation but in overcrowding and poverty. It lamented

---

[101] Instruction of the Prefect of Police to the members of the committees of hygiene, 23 September 1852 (B.M., CT 436, doc. no. 11).

[102] Commission des logements insalubres, *Rapport général des travaux de la commission pendant l'année 1851* (1852), pp. 3–4.

[103] *Rapport général*, pp. 3–4. [104] *Rapport général*, p. 12.

that it had no powers to reduce overcrowding, although it was 'perhaps the most serious cause' of mortality, when the dwelling was superficially healthy,[105] and it urged that precise rules be drawn up to control the dimensions and manner of construction of new buildings.[106]

The committee was not alone in its interest in better housing. In 1849 a housing trust, the Paris workers' dwellings company, had been set up in the capital and by 1852 had built, or was building, several large blocks of flats.[107] In that year the Government took an interest when Louis-Napoleon allocated ten million francs (£400,000) to the construction of workers' dwellings. In October the Minister of Agriculture and Commerce instructed Prefects to examine what could be done in their big towns to improve housing conditions under the Prince-President's scheme, and suggested that the work should be supported by big subsidies from the municipal councils.[108] But no such local contributions were offered, least of all in Paris, where Haussmann was able to gain credence for his belief that public works alone would provide adequate housing for all classes by stimulating the building industry.

Meanwhile, the unhealthy dwellings committee was expanding its activities. In 1851 it studied a mere 160 cases in Paris, but by 1859 its annual total had reached 641.[109] The annexation of the suburban communes greatly increased its responsibilities, and in 1860 it dealt with 1,656 cases. A peak of 4,160 cases was reached in 1865, after which a steady decline set in. In the 1870s the annual total stabilised at about 2,000. Only a minority of these affairs was submitted to the City Council, suggesting that in most instances the committee dealt only with minor causes of insalubrity which the landlord could be persuaded, and not compelled, to put right. Very few landlords were actually taken to court. In fact, the regulations were very difficult to enforce. The authority provided by the law of 1850 was insufficient, and the causes of insalubrity were nowhere precisely defined. In the absence of clear stipulations, builders and landlords complained about the City's arbitrary authority, while the City feared that it had insufficient powers to require the presence of all the necessary conditions of hygiene.[110] Very few houses were condemned as unfit for human habitation, and compulsory purchases were even rarer because

---

[105] *Rapport général*, p. 5. [106] *Rapport général*, p. 7.
[107] Gourlier, *Des voies publiques*, p. 27.
[108] Circular of Minister of Agriculture, 2 October 1852, no. 87 (B.M., CT 436, doc. no. 10).
[109] *Ann. Stat.*, 1882, p. 617.
[110] M. G. Jourdan, *Études d'hygiène publique* (1893), pp. 72, 76.

of the high cost of acquisition under the 1841 law and the difficulty of reselling isolated sites in slum areas. In fact, houses in really bad condition were usually pulled down by the Prefecture of Police to forestall their collapse into the street, before they were condemned as unfit for sanitary reasons. Similar problems also hamstrung the committees of hygiene in each *arrondissement*, which frequently complained about their limited powers and the City's unwillingness to demolish slum houses in connection with street improvements.[111] At least, the division of powers between the two Prefects was partially remedied by a decree of 10 October 1859, which gave the Prefect of the Seine control over many of the public health functions previously directed by the Prefect of Police.

The public health policies associated with Louis-Napoleon and Haussmann appeared to receive some justification from the general improvement in the death rate in the 1850s and 1860s. The crude death rate fell from 29·5 per thousand living in 1853 to 24·9 in 1862, and in 1872 it dropped as low as 21·4.[112] Epidemics of cholera occurred in 1854 and 1865, but they were much less deadly than those of 1832 and 1849. It was generally assumed that the improvement was mainly the result of public works and improved medical organisation.[113] But the reduction in mortality was more apparent than real. Accurate and detailed statistics of deaths were not kept until after 1865, when the municipal statistical department was set up, and much of the apparent decline before then[114] was due to the inclusion of the less densely populated suburban areas in 1860. William Tite noticed the growth of new forms of disease—intermittent fevers and pulmonary complaints— in the early 1860s.[115] Infant mortality remained extremely high. The death rates seemed to be improving in the early 1870s, although this trend might have been merely the temporary result of the very high mortality in 1870 and 1871 when many lives had been ended prematurely as a result of siege conditions. But the number of deaths began to increase sharply from 1875, and reached 24·4 per thousand in 1876. After stabilising at this level, the rate rose again to a further peak of 28·01 in 1880.[116]

---

[111] See, for instance, *Travaux des commissions d'hygiène*, 1888, p. 71; 1890, p. 26.
[112] W. Tite, 'On the comparative mortality of London and Paris', p. 483, *Journal of the Statistical Society*, vol. 27, 1864, pp. 479–91; *Bulletin de statistique municipale*.
[113] See, for instance, *Gazette des Tribunaux*, 28 April 1865.
[114] Crude death rates: 1858, 27·3; 1859, 28·6; 1860, 25·3; 1861, 25·7; 1862, 24·9 (Tite, 'Comparative mortality', p. 483). [115] Tite, 'Comparative mortality', p. 490.
[116] For mortality figures 1865–79, see *Bulletin de statistique municipale*; for 1880– , see *Ann. Stat.*

High mortality was a serious cause of concern to the City after 1870. It could be explained in part by the replacement of epidemic diseases such as cholera by cancer and heart complaints, which attacked people who in earlier times might never have reached middle age. But the problem was really much more serious. Although cholera had been almost completely checked, the incidence of other infectious diseases, and especially those which attacked young children, was either stable or increasing. And the occasional epidemic of redoubtable diseases like typhoid fever could bring about a sharp increase in the overall death rate in certain years. In fact, zymotic diseases killed 5·78 people each year per thousand living between 1879 and 1883, compared to only 3·10 between 1865 and 1869.[117] However, even if infectious diseases could be brought completely under control, there would be only a marginal improvement in mortality, because they were not, and had never been, the main cause of deaths. The principal killers in Paris were respiratory afflictions. Between 1816 and 1819 pulmonary diseases had killed an average of 4,733 people a year in the city.[118] In the early 1830s the only diseases which *regularly* killed over a thousand people every year were two children's afflictions, enteritis and convulsions, and two respiratory diseases, pulmonary catarrh and phthisis.[119] This was bad enough, but the situation was bound to get worse as certain other diseases were checked. In 1872, for instance, phthisis killed ten times as many people as did typhoid fever. In 1879 diseases of the respiratory system caused 36·046 per cent of all deaths, compared to 17·35 per cent resulting from 'general diseases', a category which included cancer as well as all the epidemic diseases.[120]

Despite their high incidence, little attention had been paid to respiratory afflictions. They were less dramatic than the big epidemic diseases, for they worked slowly and almost imperceptibly. Asthma and bronchitis, of course, carried off many young children, but tuberculosis (phthisis), the core of the respiratory disease group, attacked mainly adults and usually took several years to kill them. The only treatment for it was complete rest, good food and country air, all of which were out of the question for working-class Parisians. Until the end of the century no one knew for certain whether tuberculosis was infectious, or whether it was a spontaneous or inherited condition. So it was

---

[117] C.M. reports, 1886, no. 3, pp. 1, 3; *Ann. Stat.*, 1883, pp. 129–78.
[118] Calculated from vital statistics tables in *Recherches statistiques sur la Ville de Paris et le Département de la Seine*, vol. I, 1821.
[119] *Statistique de la France*, 1837, pp. 230–35.
[120] *Bulletin de statistique municipale*.

accepted as a fact of life, rather like a premature old age. But it was slowly dawning on the authorities that the two main causes of death in Paris, children's and respiratory diseases, were not being affected by the sanitary policies pursued by Haussmann, because they were caused by overcrowding, bad living conditions and inadequate diet, rather than by superficial insalubrity.[121] Until these policies were supplemented by an improvement of housing conditions and/or a rise in living standards, the death rate would remain high. However, in the short term it was clearly essential to finish work on the drainage and water supply systems, especially while infectious diseases were still on the increase.

Superficial sanitary improvements were more important after 1870 than before because of the fall in the rate of demolition of slum houses, and Haussmann's failure to make adequate provision for the new areas on the outskirts of the city. As early as September 1871 the director of water and sewers inaugurated a sewer building programme to achieve the total abolition of cesspits.[122] In 1872 the City floated a loan of seventeen million francs (£680,000) for work on the Vanne fresh water aqueducts.[123] When these improvements failed to stop the increase of epidemic diseases, the prefectoral administration began to consider, from the later 1870s, what further steps to take. In 1880 the estates and watch committee was asked to study the whole question with particular reference to the serious and persisting epidemics of diphtheria and smallpox. The committee made a series of recommendations, which included the disinfection of the dwelling concerned, the isolation of those suspected of carrying a disease, and the use of special vehicles to transport patients to hospital. As for smallpox, the vaccination of infants should be generalised.[124] In June 1880 the City Council approved a new programme of sewer construction, and although ministerial objections to the scheme forced its postponement, the Prefect set up a technical committee which in 1883 confirmed the principles contained in it, including its financing by a special sewer tax on all landlords. The project was approved again by the City Council in November 1883, and this time it was possible to carry it out.[125]

---

[121] See, for instance, introduction by Jacques Bertillon, director of the City statistical department, to the published volume of the 1891 census, in which he argues that overcrowding is an important cause of mortality (*Résultats statistiques du dénombrement de 1891 pour la Ville de Paris et le Département de la Seine* [1894], pp. xxvi-lx).
[122] C.M. reports, 1885, no. 125, p.1.
[123] Morizet, *Du vieux Paris*, p. 332.
[124] C.M. reports, 1880, no. 187, pp. 1, 26–30.
[125] C.M. reports, 1883, no. 128.

However, even though this policy was encouraged by the 1884 cholera epidemic, which struck chiefly in streets that were not equipped with sewers,[126] the Council devoted increasing attention to the development of direct prophylactic measures. In 1886 and 1887 the special sanitary committee and the public assistance committee reported on a suggestion made in 1884 by Councillor Vaillant that all who had contracted infectious diseases should be treated outside Paris. They approved Vaillant's proposals, and recommended further isolation measures. They also called for the creation of municipal ambulance and disinfection services.[127] The City Council approved these reports on 17 June 1887. The disinfection service was set up in 1889, and by the following year the City was in a position to meet all demands made on it by doctors and members of the public. In July 1892 it was incorporated into a new department responsible for the interior hygiene of dwellings.[128] In 1893 the Council decided to float a further water and sewers loan, for work to be carried out between 1894 and 1899.[129] In the same year a revaccination programme was begun in primary schools, and the medical services began to vaccinate smallpox sufferers at their homes during epidemics.[130] The law of 10 July 1894, on sanitation in Paris and the Seine, allowed the City to compel landlords to link their properties to sewers, for the disposal of solid as well as liquid sewage, in streets that were equipped with them. Its application was begun in 1897, but progress was slow because no attempt was made to impose it on all landlords at once. In fact, in 1925 nearly one-third of the city's houses still did not comply with the law.[131]

Big improvements were made after 1870 in street cleansing and rubbish removal. Frontagers had been under an obligation to sweep the streets in front of their own houses, but this was a very ineffective regulation, and the City took over responsibility for sweeping in 1873, when a special tax was established to cover the cost.[132] In 1876 an efficient sweeping machine was perfected,[133] and in 1884 Prefect Poubelle required landlords to purchase lidded dustbins to contain rubbish awaiting collection.[134] The supervision of lodging houses was also tightened up. The Prefecture of Police was responsible for their inspection, but it began to cooperate closely with the unhealthy dwellings

[126] C.M. reports, 1885, no. 125; 1886, no. 76.
[127] C.M. reports, 1886, no. 3; 1897, no. 10.   [128] *A.P.*, 29 July 1892.
[129] C.M. reports, 1894, no. 136, p. 1; Morizet, *Du vieux Paris*, p. 332.
[130] C.M. reports, 1907, no. 20, p. 15.   [131] C.M. reports, 1928, no. 82, p. 3.
[132] Law of 26 March 1873.
[133] Louis Girard, *Le nettoiement de Paris* (1923), p. 18.
[134] *A.P.*, 7 March 1884.

committee, and a new set of regulations was issued between 1878 and 1883. From this latter year the police entrusted the task of inspection to a special architectural staff.[135]

These developments seem to have had a beneficial effect on the death rate, which fell from 24·6 in 1881 to 20·3 in 1894. Epidemic diseases were brought increasingly under control; typhoid fever, for instance, killed only 773 people in 1894, compared to 2,121 in 1881. But the tuberculosis problem remained. The disease killed more and more people as the years went by; 11,023 in 1880, 12,376 in 1894. And now that other, more dramatic, killers were fading away, tuberculosis stood out in its full horror.

As early as 1883 a special committee of the City Council reported strongly in favour of providing cheap dwellings for the working classes.[136] It was convinced that the high death rate in working-class districts was above all the result of unhealthy accommodation rather than, as some had suggested, of excessively long working hours. There was already some evidence that death rates were highest in the most densely constructed areas, and the committee had seen figures showing an increase in death rates among the poorest classes since 1872, despite the construction of a number of new traffic arteries. At this time councillors were more concerned with typhoid fever than with tuberculosis, owing to a serious epidemic of the disease in the early 1880s, which the committee attributed to excessive population density. But the reappearance at City Council level of the theory that overcrowding was inherently dangerous was a significant stage in the recognition of the full extent of the tuberculosis threat. However, in the early 1880s the City still had no detailed information which would allow an accurate interpretation of changes in overall death rates, because vital statistics were not abstracted for smaller units than the municipal ward. So the Council's sanitary committee suggested in 1884 that a census of unhealthy buildings should be carried out by the committees of hygiene in each *arrondissement*. A map could then be drawn up showing which areas or streets were excessively unhealthy, allowing the authorities to concentrate their efforts at those points were action was most urgent.[137] But such a census would have placed a heavy burden on the committees of hygiene, which found it difficult enough to carry out their existing duties, and nothing more was heard of the proposal. In any case, the City's powers to deal with individual unhealthy

[135] *Ann. Stat.*, 1882, pp. 614–16.   [136] C.M. reports, 1883, no. 136.
[137] C.M. reports, 1884, no. 131, p. 7.

dwellings were still very limited. The public assistance committee called in December 1884 for new legislation on unhealthy dwellings,[138] but this appeal went unheeded, and the return to a traditional street improvement policy after 1885 may have made new powers appear less urgent.

The idea of a census of unhealthy dwellings was again put forward in 1893. This time, the City Council voted the necessary finance to set up a special department which would build up a health register of Paris houses. Work began in 1894 and the register was completed by 1900. It provided, for the first time, full details of the incidence of disease in every street and house in the city. Each building was given its own file, containing full details of diseases contracted by its occupants, with particular attention paid to tuberculosis and cancer. It now at last became possible to see clearly that tuberculosis was rife in some streets or groups of streets, yet almost totally absent in others.[139]

When the City abandoned street inprovements towards 1895 there was a clear need for more effective sanitary legislation and enforcement. The Government had introduced a bill as early as 1891 to replace the old public health law of 1850, most of which was still in force, but it was not enacted until 1902. It placed on the Prefect of the Seine and the Prefect of Police the responsibility of drawing up a new set of public health regulations. It also reinforced the authorities' powers to deal with unhealthy houses by allowing them to intervene whenever the condition of a house, or the way in which it was inhabited, endangered the health of its occupants or of those of neighbouring houses.

The provision of new information and powers coincided with a series of research breakthroughs which created a better understanding of the tuberculosis problem. Much of the City's failure to attack the disease before the turn of the century can be attributed to its uncertainty about how best to do so. As late as 1888 the committee of hygiene of the XVIIe *arrondissement* suggested that tuberculosis should be classified as an infectious disease, and the same disinfection measures applied to dwellings, furniture and personal effects as for other diseases. While not turning down the suggestion, the rapporteur of the Seine sanitary council commented that, in his opinion, disinfection

---

[138] C.M. reports, no. 134, p. 5.
[139] C.M. reports, 1896, no. 195; 1907, no. 20; Bernard Lafay, *Problèmes de Paris* (1954), p. 107.

after a case of tuberculosis brought far less satisfactory results than in the case of what he called 'the highly infectious diseases'. He feared that tuberculosis was contracted more as a result of personal receptivity than of infection, which would put it beyond the reach of any action the authorities could take.[140] Such disagreements reflected continuing uncertainty about how tuberculosis was contracted.[141] Laënnec did much useful work on the disease in the early nineteenth century, but he was convinced that it was hereditary. The 'contagionist' controversy produced some who believed that it was infectious, but French medical opinion generally supported Laënnec's views even into the second half of the century. The work of J. A. Villemin, who suggested that the disease was caused by a virus, was either ignored or contradicted. But in 1868 Villemin published a book which pointed out that tuberculosis flourished in places where people lived closely together, such as factories, barracks and slums. Slowly, his ideas gained ground, as Pasteur's discoveries made medical opinion more willing to accept microbes as the cause of certain diseases. Then, in 1882, Robert Koch isolated the tuberculosis virus. Although much work remained to be done, the news of his success gradually began to influence medical opinion throughout Europe. As early as 1890 the rapporteur of the sanitary council of the Seine suggested that Koch's theories should be tested in France.[142] Further experiments by Koch and others confirmed that tuberculosis was transmitted by a bacillus ejected by carriers of the disease, generally by spitting. The bacillus could remain virulent for very long periods in dark and badly ventilated places. In April 1905 the Prefect set up a special committee to study the influence of living conditions on the aetiology and propagation of tuberculosis in Paris, and the measures that could be taken against it.[143] In October of the same year an international tuberculosis congress met in Paris, and reached complete agreement that the main cause of urban tuberculosis was the absence of direct sunlight in inhabited dwellings.[144]

A small number of City councillors, the most active of whom was the Council's only remaining royalist, Ambroise Rendu, now began to campaign for effective anti-tuberculosis measures. In March 1906 Councillor Brenot drew attention to the Sainte-Avoie ward, which had the highest incidence of tuberculosis in the city, and demonstrated

---

[140] *Travaux des commissions d'hygiène du Département de la Seine*, 1888, pp. 22–3.
[141] See Jacques Delarue, *La tuberculose* (1949), pp. 12–15.
[142] *Travaux des commissions d'hygiène*, 1890, p. 43.
[143] *A.P.*, 10 April 1905.   [144] Quoted in C.M. reports, 1906, no. 18, p. 1.

that other infectious diseases were more common there than else-where.[145] At about the same time Councillor Rendu presented a report dealing more directly with tuberculosis. After quoting a recent formal statement by the Academy of Medicine to the effect that the continued spread of tuberculosis was the result of 'the conditions of modern life', Rendu went on to claim that overcrowding was one of the most important factors, if not *the* most important. He rejected the orthodox view that street works were an effective method of slum clearance, because those displaced were unable to pay high rents for accommodation in the new houses. Instead, they had flooded into the neighbouring streets, causing even greater overcrowding:

> 'We need, therefore, to combine the demolition of the con-taminated zones with the reconstruction, on the same site, of cheap dwellings, of which some at least should be allocated to workers . . .'

Rendu added to his report a list of six zones which were particularly unhealthy, two of which, Saint-Merri and Saint-Gervais, were in the right bank centre, in the IVe *arrondissement*.[146] All these districts had long been recognised as insalubrious, and Rendu's colleagues cannot have been surprised to learn that tuberculosis was rife there. But, from now on, tuberculosis mortality becomes the main criterion for delimiting slum areas. According to the *Livre Foncier* of 1911, tuber-culosis mortality '. . . provides in an almost rigorously exact fashion the degree of insalubrity of the dwellings in any district'.[147] This meant that if the number of deaths from tuberculosis increased, the slums would be deemed to have deteriorated still further.

Although the transmission of tuberculosis was now understood, it was still believed that disinfection could not destroy the bacillus. So Rendu campaigned for total clearance. In November 1906 he called on the Council to take immediate action by demolishing the houses of tuberculosis victims before the disease could spread to neighbouring buildings:

> 'So we must destroy the house, when it harbours the disease. Any palliative would be an illusion.'[148]

Rendu's conclusions were reinforced by the committee set up to

---

[145] C.M. reports, 1906, no. 18, pp. 1–2.
[147] *Livre Foncier*, 1911, graph no. 40.
[146] C.M. reports, 1906, no. 7.
[148] C.M. reports, 1906, no. 100.

study the reorganisation of the public health services, which reported in June 1907. It pointed out that the sanitary and medical departments recently established by the City had brought the overall death rate down to the level of foreign cities whose public health organisations Paris had copied. Yet no solution had been found to tuberculosis, whose incidence in Paris had hardly fallen at all since 1886, whereas a much greater reduction had been registered in the other capital cities of Europe.[149] So it seemed that an efficient public health organisation was no more an answer to tuberculosis than were street improvements. The Council had to accept that only one course of action—systematic slum clearance—remained open to them. But what would be the cost?

As early as 1905 the Prefect had suggested that a large part of the City's resources should be devoted to sanitary improvements, but the Council was in the midst of serious financial difficulties and ignored his advice.[150] Not until 1909, when it was decided to borrow 900 million francs for public works, did the Council show any real enthusiasm for slum clearance. Even then, there was still a temptation to combine it with street improvements. In June 1909, for instance, Councillor Le Corbeiller suggested that certain streets in the Saint-Merri and Sainte-Avoie wards could be widened in order to improve traffic conditions, ease access to the Halles, and demolish a number of slum houses. But he also called for the total demolition of one notorious block bounded by the Rue de Venise, Rue Saint-Martin, Rue des Etuves-Saint-Martin, and Rue Beaubourg, just to the east of the Halles.[151] Meanwhile, a proposal by Councillor Landrin for the total demolition, one by one, of all six tubercular zones was turned down on financial grounds.[152]

After the approval in principle of the loan, the administration suggested that fifty million francs (£2 million) should be spent immediately on slum clearance, but by the time the water and sewers committee, chaired by Rendu, had been able to study the proposal, the Prefect had changed his mind and was proposing that only fifteen million francs should be so spent, and another fifteen million on the construction of workers' houses.[153] In his report in July 1909, Rendu strongly resisted any reduction of the original allocation. He pointed out that it was neither desirable nor possible to demolish every area in the city which happened to have a higher than average death rate from tuberculosis.

[149] C.M. reports, 1907, no. 20, pp. 24–5.
[150] C.M. reports, 1906, no. 100, p. 2.
[151] C.M. reports, 1909, no. 64.
[152] C.M. reports, no. 69, p. 3.
[153] C.M. reports, 1909, no. 69, p. 3.

In most districts the improvements or demolition of individual defective houses was an adequate weapon against the disease, and in the last few years the City had carried out some 500 of these operations. Only in the six zones where tuberculosis was particularly strongly rooted was it proposed to carry out wholesale clearance, for the demolition of a few houses here and there would be totally useless.[154]

Although the Council respected Rendu's views, serious difficulties were raised by his approach to the slum problem. To allocate a large proportion of the loan to slum clearance alone might threaten the success of the street programme. Could the two really not be combined, as they had been in the past? In any case, to concentrate on a few small slum areas would violate the Council's unwritten law that each ward should be allocated an equal share of any capital investment. Lastly, there were two inter-related problems. Would existing legislation allow the acquisition of whole areas at low cost, and, if not, would it not become necessary to sell the cleared sites to private landlords in order to break even? It was one thing to prove by statistics that traditional town improvement techniques merely exacerbated the slum problem, but quite another to break out of the financial and conceptual straitjacket that Haussmann had bequeathed to his successors.

In 1910 the administration and the Council reached agreement on the allocation of the new resources. Most of the street improvements proposed by Le Corbeiller were accepted, and so was the total demolition of the block to the east of the Halles, in the Saint-Merri ward.[155] But the temptation to reduce the slum clearance allocation was not strongly resisted. In November 1910 the water and sewers committee called for eighteen million francs for urgent demolitions in the unhealthy areas, excluding those connected with street widening in the Saint-Merri ward, and an additional fund for the acquisition of individual buildings in other areas. It wanted work to start in the two areas in the IVe *arrondissement*, although this clearly laid its proposals open to attack from councillors representing the outer *arrondissements*. Rendu now put the case for total demolition more strongly than ever before, for he feared that the Prefect was about to propose the expenditure of only eight million francs, instead of eighteen. He emphasised, therefore, that factors such as poverty, alcoholism and vice were only secondary in the propagation of tuberculosis; the main cause lay in the buildings themselves.[156] A few days later, the Prefect presented his

[154] C.M. reports, 1909, no. 69, p. 3.   [155] C.M. reports, 1910, no. 21, p. 21.
[156] C.M. reports, 1910, no. 85.

plan of campaign for clearance projects to be financed by the first instalment of the loan. As Rendu had feared, only eight million francs were now available for work to be carried out between 1910 and 1913, and they were not to be concentrated on the two worst zones. The water and sewers committee had little choice but to accept, and the Council approved their report. In the right bank centre, 3,290,000 francs would be spent in the Saint-Merri ward, 880,000 francs in Sainte-Avoie, and 105,000 francs in Notre-Dame, which was not even one of the areas for which Rendu had campaigned.[157] The only hope now was that a more generous allocation would be made from the second instalment of the loan.

In March 1912 the Prefect added insult to injury by asking the water and sewers committee to agree to spend part of the sum of eight million francs on the construction of workers' dwellings. This time the committee held its ground, and insisted that the whole sum should be devoted to demolitions, which were the first priority. It also suggested that nearly twelve million francs should be allocated out of the second fraction of the loan to complete the work of clearance.[158] But Rendu and his supporters could already see that demolition would take much longer than they had hoped, and in 1914 the joint tuberculosis committee, chaired by Rendu, recommended the establishment of twelve special tuberculosis dispensaries and associated medical units throughout the city.[159]

The irony of the situation was that both elected representatives and officials fully recognised that the unhealthy areas should be demolished as soon as possible. The Extension of Paris Committee reported in 1913 in favour of total clearance.[160] Yet by the time war broke out, little or no demolition work had taken place. The delay was due in part to the inadequacy of the resources allocated to slum clearance from the first instalment of the loan. Work had been postponed until the rest of the loan was floated, although, even if the other two instalments had been issued, only twenty-five million francs (£1 million) out of 900 millions would have been allocated to slum clearance.[161] Another reason for postponing a start on the work was that it was hoped that existing compulsory purchase legislation would be amended to reduce compensation costs. The 1902 public health law had been criticised for

---

[157] C.M. reports, 1910, no. 173; Rendu's usual place as rapporteur was taken by another councillor.
[158] C.M. reports, 1911, no. 9.   [159] C.M. reports, 1914, no. 34.
[160] Commission d'extension de Paris, *Considérations techniques*, p. 82.
[161] C.M. reports, 1914, no. 37, p. 6.

5

not reforming compensation procedure. The City maintained that less compensation should be paid for an unhealthy house than for one in good condition. In 1904 Jules Siegfried brought in a bill to regulate the procedure of acquisition for health reasons, but by 1910 it had only just reached the Senate, where it could be expected to stay for several years more. Its main proposal was that the value of a building should be calculated by subtracting from its hypothetical value in good condition the cost of the work that would be needed to remedy its defects.[162] Such a procedure would have allowed the City to compensate only for site value in most cases.

The Government responded to the City's demands and to Siegfried's radical proposals by setting up an interministerial committee to study expropriation in December 1910. Its terms of reference included compensation and the acquisition of fractions of sites lying outside the perimeter of improvement operations. In 1912 a law was passed to facilitate the total acquisition of such sites,[163] but what Rendu and his friends really wanted was legislation to allow the compulsory acquisition of whole zones without having to establish the unhealthy state of each individual building. And although the Government introduced a bill to allow this in 1911, neither it nor the Siegfried bill had become law by the time war broke out.

[162] See C.M. reports, 1910, no. 85, pp. 8, 11; 1912, no. 16, p. 2.
[163] Law of 10 April 1912, modifying the decree-law of 26 March 1852.

5

Building in the Right Bank Centre, 1850-1914

I BUILDING IN PARIS IN THE FIRST HALF OF THE NINETEENTH CENTURY

The extremely rapid growth of the population of Paris in the first half of the nineteenth century was not accompanied by a corresponding expansion of building activity. While the population rose from 547,756 in 1801 to 1,053,262 in 1856, the number of houses within the boundaries increased only from 26,801 in 1817 to 30,770 in 1851, and by 1856 demolitions for public works had actually reduced this total to 30,175.[1] Of course, extra accommodation was provided in many apartment houses by extensions or rebuilding, without increasing the overall number of properties. But, on the other hand, many of the totally new houses built were of only moderate size,[2] and there can be no doubt that the provision of new living space lagged seriously behind population growth, causing the grave overcrowding which so worried contemporaries.[3] Most of the new houses were erected on virgin sites on the outskirts of the built-up area, but many gardens and courtyards in the centre were also built on.[4] Yet even though rents steadily increased,[5] private enterprise was not able to make up the growing accommodation deficiency. It was this failure that

[1] Préfecture de la Seine, *Résultats statistiques du dénombrement de 1886 pour la Ville de Paris et le Département de la Seine* (1887), p. xxviii.
[2] Adeline Daumard, *Maisons de Paris et propriétaires parisiens au XIXe siècle* (1965), pp. 203-4.
[3] See, for instance, Commission des logements insalubres, *Rapport général des travaux de la commission pendant l'année 1851* (1852), p. 5.
[4] Daumard, *Maisons de Paris*, pp. 30-3; A. J. Meindre, *Histoire de Paris et de son influence en Europe* (1854-5), vol. V, p. 332.
[5] Jean Bastié, *La croissance de la banlieue parisienne* (1964), p. 189.

forced Napoleon III and Haussmann to intervene before the Paris housing situation broke down completely. The fault lay partly in the organisation of the building industry and investment in property, and partly in the shortage of suitable sites. Building was particularly sensitive to general economic conditions, and slumps were both regular and frequent after the boom of the early 1820s. The depressions of 1826–7, 1830, 1840 and 1846–8[6] all had a more serious effect on building than on other activities. In 1848, for instance, building activity slumped by 66 per cent compared with a reduction in Parisian industrial activity as a whole of 54 per cent. Only the furniture industry was harder hit than building, with which it was, of course, closely interlinked.[7] Indeed, building was so notoriously vulnerable to unfavourable conditions that the following commonplace was often heard—'when building is going well, everything in Paris is going well.' All aspects of building and property management were organised on a small scale. Many Parisian landlords owned only one house, partly occupied by themselves; very few owned more than a handful of buildings. Mademoiselle Daumard has estimated the number of Paris landlords to be over 14,000, so that the average ownership would be two houses each. They tended to buy houses in their own district, the more easily to keep an eye on them. Most of them had purely parochial interests, but even those whose greater wealth gave them wider horizons did not attempt to buy up blocks of property or whole streets. Indeed, as the century wore on they took advantage of growing opportunities to invest in stocks and shares or provincial property, so that buildings in Paris made up a diminishing proportion of their fortunes.[8] This fragmented ownership was paralleled in the building industry, which was organised in very small units on a craft basis, with each firm geared to producing one building at a time, and then looking round for new work. Such a structure was highly vulnerable to economic fluctuations, especially as there was no firm building credit system.

If the increase in population had not been so rapid, the old organisation might still have been adequate to meet the city's needs, by continuing to fill in available sites in the city centre, and undertaking slow peripheral expansion. But with overcrowding reaching a dangerous level in the centre, what was really needed was the large-scale

[6] Chambre de commerce, *Statistique de l'industrie à Paris 1847–8* (1851), p. 89.
[7] *Statistique de l'industrie 1847–8*, pp. 41, 89.
[8] Daumard, *Maisons de Paris*, pp. 235–64; *La bourgeoisie parisienne de 1815 à 1848* (1963), pp. 479–513.

development of virgin areas on the city's outskirts to take the overflow. According to the Chamber of Commerce, everybody wanted to live in a more modern house in a less densely populated area.[9] Yet this was precisely the solution that the existing structure was least able to provide. Capital and enterprise were equally insufficient to take the risk of massive development some distance outside the city centre when road communications into the central industrial and business areas were so congested. Industry, it is true, was already moving to the outskirts and even beyond the city boundaries, but the great majority of firms were still in the central areas in mid-century. And the amount of tertiary sector employment in the centre was increasing as Paris began to make up lost ground as a commercial and financial centre.

2 BUILDING UNDER THE SECOND EMPIRE

As we have seen, Louis-Napoleon was aware of the need to provide dwellings for the working classes, but he failed to obtain financial support from local authorities. Furthermore, the revival of the economy in the early 1850s encouraged the hope that enough accommodation could be provided by the operation of a free market. Haussmann believed that the requirements of even the poorest classes could be satisfied in this way:

> '. . . in such a case it is best to leave to speculation, stimulated by competition, the task of recognising the people's real needs and of satisfying them.'[10]

It could also be hoped that developing public health legislation and building regulations would ensure adequate standards in new buildings and bring about improvements in old ones. So Government attention switched from direct intervention in the provision of accommodation to the creation of favourable conditions for a private building boom. In Paris this was to be achieved 'by the only effective means open to the authorities—an intelligent street building programme.'[11] But street improvements alone would have achieved only a partial success without the economic expansion which was encouraged by political stability after 1852, and the development of a credit system which allowed hitherto untapped investment resources to be channelled first of all into railways and then into building. However, the main benefit did not come until the late 1850s. The rapid growth of the economy

[9] *Statistique de l'industrie à Paris 1847–8*, p. 89.
[10] Conseil général minutes, 1857, p. 13.   [11] Conseil général minutes, 1857, p. 13.

from 1852 resulted in a steady increase in the bank rate, which in 1857 reached 6·40 per cent. Although the Paris building industry at first joined in this expansion, the greater attraction of other forms of investment started to deprive it of capital by the mid-1850s, and a check on its growth in 1856 was followed by a slump in 1857.[12] But from then onwards the expansion of the urban public works programmes in Paris and other cities,[13] and the end of the railway mania, caused capital to be transferred into building.[14] Although this was not enough to pull the Paris building industry immediately out of the depression in which it languished from 1859 to 1862, rocketing rents and compensation payments induced another massive boom in 1863 which lasted until 1869.

The Government's far-sighted effort to improve the credit system began in the early 1850s. After a decree of February 1852 authorising the foundation of building societies, a decree of December 1852 set up the *Crédit Foncier*, with a capital of sixty million francs (£2,400,000), to make short or long term mortgage loans. Although it was originally intended to provide credit for rural improvements rather than urban building, it soon lost this bias and by the early 1860s it was being hailed as the biggest and most active of the various credit organisations.[15] In 1853 the *Crédit Foncier* made 218 loans in the *département* of the Seine, and 235 in 1854. Then there was a sharp drop to a mere twenty-seven loans in 1856, but a steady improvement after 1857 allowed the 1854 figure to be reached again in 1859. There then followed a massive expansion of *Crédit Foncier* activities, at a time when building was most in need of it, so that in 1863 no less than 1,068 loans were made. And they continued to be made at a rate of nearly 1,000 a year until the collapse of 1870.[16]

The *Crédit Foncier* worked closely with the *Sous-comptoir des entrepreneurs*, set up by a decree of July 1848, which was also authorised to make loans. At first this agency acted as an intermediary between individual borrowers and the *Comptoir national d'escompte pour Paris*, set up by a decree of March 1848, but in 1860 the *Sous-comptoir* was placed under State control, and the collaboration of the *Comptoir* was

[12] Conseil général minutes, 1857, pp. 14, 15; Louis Girard, *La politique des travaux publics du Second Empire* (1952), p. 397.
[13] See, for instance, C. M. Leonard, *Lyon Transformed: Public Works of the Second Empire 1853–1864* (1961).
[14] Girard, *Politique des travaux publics*, pp. 261, 397.
[15] Bailleux de Marisy, 'Des sociétés foncières et de leur rôle dans les travaux publics', *Revue des Deux Mondes*, July–August 1861, p. 208.
[16] See list of loans made each year from 1853 in *Ann. Stat.*, 1882, p. 364.

replaced by that of the *Crédit Foncier*. The two bodies complemented each other. The *Crédit Foncier* made advances only on the security of completed buildings, and so could help only big contractors and development companies. The *Sous-comptoir*, on the other hand, helped the individual speculative builder by offering loans on the security of the value of the site and the building to be erected. It was therefore possible for a borrower to reimburse a short-term loan from the *Sous-comptoir* by a long-term borrowing from the *Crédit Foncier* on the security of his newly completed building.[17] The banks also extended their role as providers of credit, and several new banks were set up. In 1859, for instance, the *Société Générale de Crédit Industriel et Commercial* was founded, and the *Crédit Lyonnais*, set up in 1863, opened a Paris branch the following year. 1864 also saw the establishment of the *Société Générale*.

The aim of all these credit agencies in relation to building was, as Bailleux de Marisy put it, 'to democratise real estate, to associate even the smallest sources of capital in the construction and ownership of houses.'[18] But, paradoxically, they also did much to destroy the old individualistic organisation of building and property management in Paris.[19] Now that the law allowed the creation of *sociétés anonymes* a number of development companies were formed on the pattern of the Péreire brothers' *Immobilière*, which had undertaken the construction of houses along the Rue de Rivoli in the early 1850s under the name of *Société des Immeubles Rivoli*.[20] The Second Empire strengthened the the protection that was available to such concerns. A law of 1863 created a limited liability formula for companies, and in 1867 the foundation of *sociétés anonymes* was made a right instead of a privilege granted by the Government. Only large concerns could fulfil the City's requirement of the construction of lofty houses along new streets, and take full advantage of favourable conditions to expand production in the 1860s.[21] And although ownership by individual landlords still remained very fragmented, a proportion of new buildings were bought as investments by insurance companies and similar concerns.

[17] *Statistique de l'industrie à Paris 1847–8*, p. 90; Girard, *Politique des travaux publics*, p. 262; Emile Fender, *La crise du bâtiment dans la région parisienne* (1936), pp. 128–9.
[18] Bailleux de Marisy, 'Des societés fonciéres', p. 213.
[19] For similar developments in London, see H. J. Dyos, 'The speculative builders and developers of Victorian London', *Victorian Studies*, vol. XI, summer 1968, pp. 641–90.
[20] Its name was changed to *l'Immobilière* in 1858. Some idea of the numbers of these building and development companies can be obtained from the list of those that had dealings with the City, in Ville de Paris, *Résumé des traités de concession relatifs aux grandes opérations de voirie* (1869).
[21] *Résumé des traités*, p. 5; Daumard, *Maisons de Paris*, p. 204.

Important though these changes in investment and organisation were, they could not alone have stimulated a building boom in Paris. The catalyst was the imperial public works policy, which at last made external sites quickly accessible from the city centre, and cleared many new building plots in the central areas. And although Haussmann rued the over-generous compensation granted for compulsory purchase, large sums were released in this way for reinvestment by landlords in new building.[22]

We can now examine more closely building trends in Paris during the 1850s and 1860s.[23] Very little building was carried on from the 1848 slump until 1851, and an improvement in 1852 proved to be only temporary. No considerable progress was made until 1854, when the number of buildings and additions to buildings completed rose to 1,400 from 600 in the previous year. From then on, although the totals fluctuated from year to year, building tended to expand, reaching a peak of 1,600 new buildings and additions in 1858. But this progress was checked in 1859 by the beginning of the building depression, which lasted until 1862. To some extent this unsteady performance reflected the continuing difficulties of building inside the city boundaries, where the land shortage was becoming worse. Considerably more building was being done outside the boundaries, and the number of houses in the Seine as a whole rose from 62,400 in 1846 to 81,540 in 1861.[24] It seems likely that when the boundaries were extended in 1860 as far as Thiers' fortifications, twice as many houses were being built in the annexed ring as in the old city area. One of the attractions of building outside the city had been to escape the high Paris property taxes and *octroi* dues, and the closing of this loophole may help to explain the decline of building in the enlarged city area until 1862. But from 1863 onwards building began to expand at a rate never realised before 1860 in the old Paris area, and in 1869 the peak 1860 figure was exceeded, when well over 4,500 houses and additions were built. But in the following year declining confidence in the Empire and the war with Prussia greatly reduced the amount of new building.

The influence on the building rate of compulsory acquisition of properties was clearly much greater in the old Paris area than in the post-1860 city, owing to the shortage of virgin sites there. Yet there

[22] Girard, *Politique des travaux publics*, p. 119.

[23] For building and demolition statistics, see note on sources, pp. 338–41. Annual variations in building and demolition figures in Paris, the right bank centre, and each of the first four *arrondissements*, may be followed on the graphs and diagrams at the end of this volume.

[24] *Résultats statistiques du dénombrement de 1866*, p. xxviii.

still seems to have been a number of vacant plots in the old city area, at least until the later 1850s, for the building rate was able to rise even when the demolition rate was steady and the annual compulsory acquisition figure was falling. Towards the end of the decade, however, it would seem that most of the available sites had been used up, and an increase in the total of demolitions, stimulated by an expansion of acquisitions for public works, could not prevent a fall in the building rate in 1859. Public works seem to have acted as the decisive catalyst in getting building moving in the early 1850s, but they were less decisive subsequently as momentum was built up. Although Haussmann said proudly in 1856 that without his public works demolitions 'the majority of the new houses would not have been started',[25] his own figures do not completely bear him out. Whereas in 1853 fifteen new buildings or additions were built for every ten buildings expropriated, the ratio increased later in the decade, and rose as high as 125:10 in 1858.

After 1860, in the enlarged Paris, the relation of public works to new building was quite different. The number of compulsory acquisitions fell until 1863, and there was no considerable increase until 1865. However, the building slump of 1861 and 1862 clearly had many other causes in addition to the decline in public works, since most new building was in the annexed zone, which so far had seen no improvements at all. Although a sharp increase in the number of expropriations in 1865–7 coincided with a period of rapid building expansion, fluctuations in the number of compulsory acquisitions in other years do not appear to have had much effect on the building rate. In spite of the annexation most public works schemes carried out after 1860 were still in the former city area, so that their influence on building in the annexed zone could be only indirect. So for Paris as a whole after 1860 compulsory acquisitions and demolitions were but one factor among many encouraging an expansion of building, whereas within the old boundaries they were perhaps an even more predominant influence than they had been in the 1850s. We shall return to this point when we come to study the right bank centre in detail.

3 BUILDING UNDER THE THIRD REPUBLIC

In spite of the chaos caused by the war and the Commune, building did not entirely cease, and even in 1871 2,500 buildings and additions were erected. But many of these may have really been war damage repairs, and it subsequently took the sensitive building industry some

[25] Conseil général minutes, 24 November 1856, p. 13.

time to return to normal. After a slight improvement in 1872 the annual total fell each year until 1875, when only 2,200 new buildings and additions were completed. Then, two years of spectacular expansion, 1876 and 1877, were followed by a further slump in 1878, but from 1879 until 1883 the total increased considerably each year, reaching a peak of 4,500. Although a decline set in in 1884, it can fairly be said that the years 1881–4 represented a boom period in the Paris building industry comparable to the last years of the Second Empire. The subsequent slump was equally spectacular, and the annual total dropped every year until 1888, when it was again about 2,500. A recovery in 1889 proved only temporary, and by 1892 the total had again fallen to near the 1888 level, where it stabilised until 1895. But from now on a slow downward trend is apparent, with two exceptionally sharp slumps in 1896 and 1900. The decline of partial building operations was much more pronounced than that of totally new constructions, but even the latter were being erected in the 1890s and early 1900s at about half the rate achieved in the peak years of 1882–3. From 1908 there are signs of a recovery when the number of building permits issued begins to increase, but after 1912 unfavourable economic conditions resulted in a decline in building, and the declaration of war in 1914 brought it almost to a halt.

The fundamental reason for the continuing high building rate after 1870 was the unremitting growth in the population of the city. This resulted from continued immigration, as the capital's industries and commerce expanded, and a declining death rate brought about by sanitary and medical improvements, better diet, and higher living standards. Although new building still did not keep pace with the population increase,[26] and overcrowding remained a serious problem, the Second Empire had created conditions which were at least more favourable for developers and builders than those which would otherwise have existed. So although investors were attracted more and more to colonial and foreign ventures, and less to building,[27] the general prosperity of building enterprise was not seriously compromised before 1914, except, as we shall see, in the field of working-class housing. Many large property and development companies were founded during these years.[28] The steady rise in rents, and the enhanced capital value of rented property which resulted from it, ensured that property remained an attractive as well as a safe investment. Overall rent

[26] Bastié, *Croissance de la banlieue*, p. 189.
[27] Bastié, p. 189.   [28] Bastié, p. 189.

increases for inhabited dwellings have been estimated as follows: 1852–62, 42 per cent; 1862–76, 9 per cent; 1876–1900, 13 per cent; 1900–1908, 3·5 per cent. The average value in capital of apartment houses rose 3·25 times between 1840 and 1914, while the cost of living remained generally stable.[29] Building, however, remained extremely sensitive to economic changes, and catalysts were still often necessary to pull it out of the doldrums. One very effective catalyst was the universal Exposition, which was held regularly after 1870. The approach of an Exposition was enough to revive building in the year or two before it opened, because it had an invigorating effect on all business enterprise. The building booms of 1876–7, 1889 and 1897–9 resulted partly from this temporary encouragement afforded by the Expositions of 1878, 1889 and 1900. But building usually fell to its old level during and after the Exposition year, and if these events had been held more often their beneficial effect on business would have been attenuated. So public works remained the only really effective motor of the Paris building industry, as the City Council well recognised. As before 1870, compulsory acquisition of property for street improvements revived building enterprise by freeing capital for reinvestment, and clearing sites for building in areas which might otherwise have stagnated. The 1881–3 boom, and the smaller boom of 1901–5, were apparently not initiated in this way, and they seem to have taken the form of a spontaneous expansion of building on available virgin sites. On the other hand, the booms of 1876–7, 1889–90, 1897–9 and 1909–13 were clearly activated to a greater or a lesser extent by municipal improvement programmes. Of course, the building rate generally fell sharply once the works were completed, and the Council's failure to provide a regular investment programme like Haussmann's probably accentuated the difference between the troughs and peaks of the building cycle. Yet it was also the Council which had to face up to the problems of the depressed years, which were all the bleaker because the many workers who had been drawn to Paris during the booms now added to the clamouring ranks of the unemployed.

The pronounced cycles which affected building in Paris were partly the result of external factors, such as the general economic crisis of

---

[29] Jean Bastié, 'Capital immobilier et marché immobilier parisiens', *Annales de géographie*, no. 373, May-June 1960, p. 237. For an estimate of annual changes in property values during these years, see G. Duon, 'Evolution de la valeur vénale des immeubles', *Journal de la Société de Statistique de Paris*, 1940, nos. 9–10, pp. 169–92. Duon's figures show that periods of increase in property values usually coincide with intense building activity.

the mid-1880s.[30] But the highly speculative character of new building meant that temporary overproduction, which could affect the rent market, often led to a rapid withdrawal of capital and a brutal slump. Low production in the following few years, and the increase in demand for accommodation, would bring about rent increases which would encourage another round of speculative investment. Even the biggest development companies were not free from the threat of sudden bankruptcy. The depression of the mid-1880s was particularly lethal, leading first the mighty *Union Générale* and then several other big companies to liquidation from 1882 onwards.[31]

Although availability of sites did not constitute a serious problem, at least in the peripheral areas, before 1914, pressure on remaining virgin and under-used plots grew continually. Land values rose almost continuously throughout the period, and the average price of a square metre increased from five francs in 1830 to 150 francs in 1900. The City was paying an average of ninety francs per square metre in the late 1880s for land acquired for street widening; by 1908–10 this figure had risen to 277 francs.[32] The ratio of prior demolitions to new constructions tended to increase, especially after 1885. Such considerations were not enough to discourage building at those rare times when the net return on capital invested in property was higher than the average return from stocks and shares, as was the case after about 1905.[33] Even in more normal circumstances, when the return from property was somewhat lower than that obtainable elsewhere, the security it offered was usually enough to attract the investor. But there was a growing danger, masked by the pre-1914 boom, that the conditions governing the attractiveness of property for the investor were becoming less favourable. Already by 1914 building for the working classes had ceased to be an economic proposition.[34] Rising costs had outstripped the workers' capacity to pay an economic rent for new accommodation. Further discouragements were increasingly stringent building regulations, and rising property taxation. In 1910 taxes on

[30] For a discussion of building cycles, see Clarence D. Long, *Building Cycles and the Theory of Investment* (1940), esp. p. 173. Also, with particular reference to Paris, Lucien Flaus, 'Les fluctuations de la construction d'habitations urbaines', *Journal de la Société de Statistique de Paris*, nos. 5–6, May–June 1949, pp. 185–221.

[31] Fender, *Crise du bâtiment*, p. 153; Bastié, *Croissance de la banlieue*, p. 189.

[32] Louis Dausset, *Rapport général . . . sur . . . le projet de budget de la Ville de Paris pour 1912*, p. 442 (C.M. reports, 1911, no. 95); Bastié, 'Capital immobilier', p. 237.

[33] In 1910 Dausset estimated the net return from property in Paris at 4·3 per cent, compared with 3 per cent from stocks and shares (*Rapport général . . . sur . . . le projet de budget de la Ville de Paris pour 1911*, pp. 51–2 [C.M. reports, 1910, no. 91]).

[34] Bastié, *Croissance de la banlieue*, p. 189.

property were estimated to amount to 9·40 per cent of the annual rentable value. Taxation reduced the average gross revenue of 6·61 per cent to a net revenue of 4·25 per cent.[35] This return was more than enough to attract investors at a time when stocks and shares produced a return of only 3 per cent but such a situation could not be expected to last. In the central districts, these unfavourable influences, and, in particular, shortage of sites, were restricting new building long before 1914. But after the war, with the additional discouragements of rent control and public housing, they were to undermine the foundations of building enterprise throughout the city.

4 THE RIGHT BANK CENTRE

We must now examine how building in the right bank centre compares with that in the city as a whole. Before 1860, when the present boundaries were established, it is impossible to arrive at a total for the right bank centre owing to total lack of correspondence in the ward boundaries. An examination of all the central wards in 1846 and of a sample of central wards from 1852[36] suggests that very little new building was being done in the 1840s and 1850s in the closely built areas near the Châtelet. On the fringes of the right bank centre, in the west, north-west and east, builders were more active. In the outer ring of wards outside the *grands boulevards*, and on the left bank, rather less building was being done, except in the west and north-west. In the dense central core the only wards which showed any extensive building activity in 1844–6 were those affected by street improvements. Twenty-one houses were demolished in the Cité in connection with the widening of the Rue de la Cité, and twenty-five in Sainte-Avoie for the Rue de Rambuteau. The new houses which replaced them would certainly not have been built had demolition not been enforced by the authorities. Only for the wards on the fringes of, or outside, the right bank centre were more than a handful of demolitions, both entire and partial, recorded in 1846. Also, the ratio of new buildings to demolitions was very high in these areas, suggesting a great availability of virgin sites. The relatively large number of demolitions would be explained by the gross under-use of many sites by existing constructions. Within the right bank centre itself, more vacant and under-used sites were available in the east than in the west, and wards such as Marais and Mont-de-Piété saw much new building.

---

[35] Société de Statistique de Paris, *Notes sur Paris* (1909), p. 46.
[36] Based on building and demolition returns held by A.S. at D7P2.

In the 1850s the situation in the central areas was little different. Only demolitions for public works could stimulate building activity in the dense central core. In Saint-Eustache, for instance, just to the north of the Halles, about thirty houses were demolished in 1851–3 to widen the Rue Montmartre. Nineteen new houses were built in these years, most of them on or near the widened section of the street, at a time when building in Paris as a whole was depressed. But in the next four years, when there were no street improvements, only one house was totally demolished in the ward and only one completely new house built—on the cleared site. Even additions and alterations to buildings, which are normally quite numerous in the records, were very rare in Saint-Eustache, where only thirteen were noted in 1850–60. Of course, although public works stimulated building, the areas which they touched were left with fewer houses—albeit more commodious ones—than they had before. Saint-Eustache saw thirty-three total and nine partial demolitions in the 1850s, for which it was compensated by only twenty-five new houses and thirteen additions. Even worse off was the Arcis ward, which had the misfortune to lie on a slight rise on the line of the Rue de Rivoli. Haussmann decided to level the whole area and lay out a public garden around the Saint-Jacques tower. Between 1852 and 1855 the ward lost 293 houses totally demolished. By 1857 they had been replaced by a mere thirty-seven new houses. For the 1850s as a whole the records show 311 total and ten partial demolitions in Arcis, and only forty-six new buildings and fourteen additions. On the other hand, in areas where improvements were more limited in scale, building could be encouraged without causing a net loss of buildings. In Palais-Royal, where a few houses were compulsorily acquired and demolished in 1854, the number of additions and alterations to properties increased, and the construction of new houses continued steadily at two or three a year. For the whole decade eleven total and ten partial demolitions are recorded, and they were replaced by seventeen new buildings and twenty-three additions. This was not a spectacular rate of change by any means, but it shows that the occasional vacant or under-used site could still be found. Of course, Palais-Royal was still a prosperous ward, lying in a slightly eccentric position, and was not as closely built as wards like Arcis. Montmartre,[37] a ward lying slightly further from the Châtelet, to the north-west, shows a similar credit balance, although the absence of demolitions

[37] Not to be confused with the village of Montmartre which, before 1860, was not even part of Paris. The city ward was named after the Rue Montmartre, which ran through it.

for public works seems to have depressed the proportion of completely new houses built. Eleven total and eleven partial demolitions were recorded during the decade, with eight new houses built and thirty additions. And the Montmartre returns, which are more informative than most, make it clear in several instances that new buildings or wings were erected in gardens or courtyards. The proportion of building operations to demolitions is two to one, the same as in Palais-Royal. But it was east of the Boulevard de Sébastopol that builders found the most space. The number of demolitions was not low, but this was because existing buildings there were often much smaller and flimsier than in the west, and invited demolition. It was also more difficult to build extra storeys or abutting wings because of their weak foundations and walls, so that the proportion of partial to complete building operations is lower than in the west.[38] In Marais fifty-five total and twenty-four partial demolitions are recorded for the decade, all of them voluntary. But the ward benefited by the construction of 110 completely new buildings and ninety-four additions. The proportion of five building operations to two demolitions is not greatly higher than in Palais-Royal and Montmartre, but this results from the relatively low number of additions and alterations in Marais. If we compare the ratio of total demolitions to completely new buildings, we find that it is one to two in Marais, but two to three in Palais-Royal. Moreover, the actual volume of building in Marais is much greater than in Montmartre and Palais-Royal.

The returns suggest that the pressure on land and existing buildings increased as time went on. Much of the demand was for commercial and industrial premises, and there were many cases in the 1850s where courtyards were roofed over, or filled with sheds, to provide workshops and storage space. As middle-class residents left some of the larger houses the old stables would sometimes be pulled down or converted to other uses. Often, too, the coach entry would be replaced by shops. But the main pressure was still that of population, and the more old houses Haussmann pulled down in the centre, the greater would the problem become, for few working people could move to the outskirts if they wished to continue working in the centre, where most jobs were still to be found.

The special problems of the right bank centre become clearer in the

---

[38] For a discussion of the tendency to build with poor materials in the less prosperous districts, so preventing later extensions and improvements, see *Résultats statistiques du dénombrement de 1886*, p. xxx.

1860s, when it is possible to compare building trends there with the whole city. The right bank centre represented just over 7 per cent of the city's area, and in 1861 it contained over 22 per cent of the population. But in no year during the 1860s, despite the massive concentration of public works schemes in the centre, did the proportion of building in the right bank centre compared to the whole city rise higher than 6·7 per cent. And this figure was achieved in a totally exceptional year—1864. In 1860, 1865 and 1869 the proportion sank below 4 per cent. Nearly one-quarter of the houses compulsorily acquired between 1860 and 1869 were in the right bank centre. But less than 5 per cent of all new houses were constructed there. The total number of demolitions is higher in the right bank centre than that of new buildings, whereas in the city as a whole the latter total is twice and often three times greater. Spontaneous demolitions are much rarer in the centre. Between 1860 and 1869, 15,373 houses were totally or partially demolished in Paris, 4,028 of them (26 per cent) as a result of compulsory acquisition. But in the right bank centre 900 of the 1,720 houses demolished totally or in part had been expropriated—a proportion of 52 per cent. Moreover, the proportion of total demolitions caused by compulsory acquisition—and most properties so purchased were completely demolished—was about 60 per cent. However, this high proportion of involuntary demolitions, and the high overall demolition figure in relation to new houses built, resulted partly from the very scale of the improvement schemes in the 1860s. When an area was crossed by a new street, building tended to concentrate on the newly cleared sites along or near the street, which had acquired a greatly enhanced value, and the development of more distant sites was postponed. Although this phenomenon was sometimes reproduced after 1870, it was less pronounced because of the generally smaller scale of improvement schemes in the central areas.

After 1870 the annual building figures in the right bank centre remained relatively stable, but were still independent of fluctuations in the city building rate, just as they had been during the 1860s. Activity tended to stabilise at around ninety entire and partial building operations per year, except when extensive public works schemes were in progress. The Parisian building boom of the early 1880s did not touch the centre at all, and building fell off much more rapidly there after 1885 than in Paris as a whole. Even the impulse given to building by public works seems to weaken as time goes on. In 1880 sixty houses were demolished by the City, and the number of houses built in 1881 increased by the same number, but although the City pulled down fifty houses in 1884 the number of new ones erected rose by only fifteen in the following year. Then the City acquired seventy-five buildings for improvements in 1887, but the building rate actually fell in 1888. And although building revived momentarily in 1891, the general decline in right bank centre building which had set in after about 1885 continued until the mid-1890s.

In one important respect, building in the right bank centre after 1870 differed greatly from the last decade of the Second Empire—far less building was done. Between 1860 and 1869 there was an annual average of 149·6 new buildings and additions. During the years 1872–88 the average figure was only two-thirds of this, and it subsequently fell even further. As roughly half these operations were only partial, one can best express the deceleration of the rate of building by saying that only ten completely new houses were being built annually for each *arrondissement* in the right bank centre. At that rate, it would take 200 years to replace all the houses of the centre by modern constructions. In fact, the building rate in the Ier *arrondissement* was so low that it would have taken four hundred years before all its buildings were renewed.

After 1895 right bank centre building continued its slow decline, although there were considerable fluctuations from year to year. Building there recovered sharply from 1895 to 1898, encouraged partly by public works and partly by the general upturn in building throughout the city. But the expansion was not so rapid as in the city as a whole, and the recession of 1900 was very much more serious in the centre. Although the building rate subsequently recovered, slowly and with many hesitations, until 1912, the annual figure of totally new houses built never regained its 1899 level in the centre. Yet in the city as a whole the peak of 1898 was exceeded in 1910–13. Despite numerous demolitions for public works from 1906 onwards, building in the centre shows little of the sturdy expansionist trend of Paris building after that year. Nevertheless, it seems to have been highly dependent on enforced demolitions, and a fall in the number of expropriations after 1906 produced a sharp drop in the number of permits issued for new houses after 1909, at a time when the building rate in the whole city was rocketing. The big increase of 1912 seems to have been caused almost entirely by the massive number of buildings demolished by the City in that year.

Quite simply, fewer and fewer new houses were being built in the right bank centre, and their number would have been even smaller had it not been for the numerous demolitions carried out by the City. In 1895, 3·8 per cent of the completely new buildings for which permits were issued were in the right bank centre. In 1899 the proportion was 3·7 per cent but in 1912 it had fallen to 2·3 per cent. In bad years it could drop much lower; in 1903 it was 1·6 per cent. It seems probable that without the municipal improvement schemes after 1906, nearly all new building in the centre would have ceased before 1914, despite an economic situation that was extremely favourable to the industry.

An examination of trends in each *arrondissement* can throw further light on this general decline of building in the centre. From mid-century, and even before, there appeared a fundamental cleavage between east and west. The westward movement of the city during several centuries had resulted in much denser building in the west of the right bank centre than in the east. Then, in the late eighteenth and early nineteenth centuries the prosperous suburbs of the west of the city were counterbalanced by the growth of new concentrations of industrial population in the east.[39] As a result, the east of the right bank centre was changed from being a suburb of a city whose centre lay to the west to become once more an integral part of the centre of an enlarged, concentric agglomeration. Pressure on land there increased. But the present IIIe and IVe *arrondissements*, bordering as they did on some of the poorest and most industrial of the new areas, could never aspire to the commercial prosperity of the west of the centre, which lay close to the city's most prosperous and aristocratic residential districts. So the dichotomy between east and west remained and was even enforced, except that the east was now called on to share the west's land shortage and residential overcrowding.

In the 1860s the cleavage between east and west from the point of view of new building is already clear. In the Ier and IIe *arrondissements* about 560 building operations, complete and partial, were carried out between 1860 and 1869, compared with a total of about 950 in the two eastern areas. This difference can be explained only partly by the higher number of demolitions for public works in the east, because a high proportion of the some 500 compulsory acquisitions there were

---

[39] See maps showing the growth of the Paris built-up area, in Jacqueline Beaujeu-Garnier and Jean Bastié, *Atlas de Paris et de la région parisienne* (1967), vol. II, maps 31–1, 2, 3.

in the Cité, where hardly any private rebuilding took place. The building of the Rue de Turbigo in 1867 undoutedly stimulated building in the north of the IIIe *arrondissement*, but the west of the centre was by no means deprived of improvement schemes. Indeed, rather more buildings were expropriated in the Ier *arrondissement* than in the IVe, yet nearly twice as many houses were built in the latter area. The Ier *arrondissement* actually had more demolitions, yet fewer new building operations, than any other in the right bank centre. Although over half the demolitions there were voluntary, a higher proportion than elsewhere, the number of new building operations was actually lower than that of voluntary demolitions, suggesting that existing constructions were extremely densely packed. The IIe *arrondissement* does not show quite the same signs of chronic congestion, and the number of building operations there actually exceeds the total of demolitions, both compulsory and spontaneous. But the building rate there is almost as low as in the Ier, probably because so few public works demolitions were carried out.

Unlike the two western *arrondissements*, so different from each other, the IIIe and IVe *arrondissements* appear at first sight to have very similar building and demolition characteristics in the 1860s. Each saw nearly 500 building operations, and a similar number of demolitions. The number of compulsory demolitions was only slightly higher in the IIIe than in the IVe *arrondissement*, but the difference between the two lies in the fact that nearly all the expropriations in the IVe were in the Cité, where large sites were being cleared for open spaces or public buildings. So the proportion of spontaneous building operations—that is, those not preceded by prior enforced demolitions—must have been much higher in the IVe than in the IIIe. The conclusion that there was more space there for building than in the IIIe *arrondissement* can also be supported by other evidence, even though it might seem strange that the situation is the opposite of that in the west of the centre, where the *arrondissement* nearer the river and the Cité was the more closely built. The IVe *arrondissement* had considerably more great mansions than the IIIe, which, although it included part of the formerly aristocratic Marais district within its boundaries, was more populous and industrialised overall than its southern neighbour. In 1861 the IIIe had a density of 854 persons to the hectare, compared with 693 in the IVe. The large gardens and courtyards of the mansions provided extensive building sites. Moreover, the IVe *arrondissement* had one ward, Arsenal, which was the least densely populated of the whole of the right bank centre. In 1861 this ward had a density of only 353 persons per hectare. It had remained very ill-drained until the 1840s, when the Île Louviers, to the east of the Île Saint-Louis, was joined to the northern bank of the Seine and a new embankment was built. Much of the new building of the 1860s was in this ward, which had a higher proportion of vacant land than any other in the right bank centre.

There is no fundamental change in the picture after 1870. Almost twice as much new building was done in the east as in the west in the 1870s and early 1880s, although by the end of that decade the east's supremacy was becoming much less pronounced. At first, too, each *arrondissement* retained the same relation to the others from the point of view of new building as in the 1860s. The Ier, with only about 250 building operations between 1872 and 1888, remained the least active of the four, even though it saw considerably more public works demolitions than the others. Indeed, the number of enforced demolitions is higher during these years than the total of new buildings and additions. Half the demolitions were carried out by the City, a proportion which had been the norm throughout the right bank centre in the 1860s, but which now was much higher than that in any other of the central *arrondissements*. Between 1877, when it first becomes possible to distinguish entire from partial operations, and 1888, nearly all the demolitions were of entire buildings, as were over half the building operations. This predominance of total operations is much more marked than in the IIe *arrondissement*, and considerably more so than in the east of the centre. It confirms that the Ier presented a much smaller number of building opportunities than any other, owing to its few vacant sites and high proportion of tall buildings. Without public improvement schemes, which fortunately continued on a large scale into the 1880s, new building would practically have ceased by the late 1870s. Indeed, in one ward, Saint-Germain-l'Auxerrois, complete building stagnation set in at this time, and between 1882 and 1894 no building permits at all were delivered there. The two western wards, too, were relatively unattractive to builders, who concentrated their efforts, as they had done before 1870, on the Halles ward, where the Rue du Louvre and the Rue Etienne-Marcel were being built. Building was stimulated in Palais-Royal and to a lesser extent in Place-Vendôme by the construction of the Avenue de l'Opéra in the late 1870s, but returned to its previous low level in the 1880s when no further street schemes were undertaken.

The IIe *arrondissement* was still some way from the building crisis that had developed in its southern neighbour. Although far fewer buildings were demolished there, more building operations were carried out. Only one demolition in four, up to 1888, was by the City. In fact, some vacant sites seem to have been still available, for the number of building operations in 1872–88 actually exceeds, though only very slightly, the number of demolitions. More important, there seem to have been more under-used sites there than in the Ier *arrondissement*, for the proportion of partial to total building operations— about one to two—is much higher in the IIe, and similar to that in the east of the centre. Another similarity to the east is the relative independence of building from public works schemes. Although compulsory acquisitions and demolitions certainly encouraged building in the IIe *arrondissement*, they did not dominate it. Indeed, building trends here follow those of the whole city. The 1880–83 boom in the city did not pass the IIe *arrondissement* by, in spite of the almost complete lack of public works demolitions during those years. As in the Ier, building tended to concentrate in the east of the area, in the Mail and Bonne-Nouvelle wards, where big street improvements were carried out, but the distribution between the four wards was much less irregular.

In the east the situation remained, at least until the 1890s, very different from the west. The IIIe *arrondissement*, with almost no buildings compulsorily acquired and fewer demolitions than any other in the centre, showed a much higher building figure between 1872 and 1888 than the IIe. The proportion of vacant or under-used sites was still much higher than in the west, and the number of building operations is 40 per cent higher than that of demolitions. The proportion of total demolitions is much lower than in the IIe *arrondissement*, while the proportion of total to partial building operations is only slightly less. Being free of the influence of public works, building trends follow those of Paris as a whole, although somewhat less closely than in the IIe *arrondissement*. However, an ominous note was sounded from the mid-1880s by the increasing coincidence between the annual totals of constructions and demolitions. By about 1890 it seems that a demolition was necessary prior to every building operation, as in the IIe *arrondissement*, and that the reserves of vacant sites had at last been used up. In fact, the building rate here shows a marked decline after 1881, and from then until the mid-1890s it is only slightly higher than in the IIe *arrondissement*. And this was in spite of the fact that building was being encouraged around 1890 by improvement schemes which, although they involved almost no compulsory acquisitions, resulted in the clearance of a number of new building sites. But when there were no public works, building remained much more regularly distributed between the four wards than in the IIe *arrondissement*.

If the IIIe *arrondissement* is coming more and more to resemble the IIe by the early 1890s, the IVe follows a path that is entirely its own. For the first two decades of the Third Republic it retained and even strengthened its position as leader of the right bank centre in new building. It showed every sign of having an even greater availability of vacant and under-used sites than the IIIe *arrondissement*. More buildings were demolished there than in the IIIe, probably because of the higher number of compulsory acquisitions, and the relation of building operations to demolitions is about the same. But the proportion of entirely new buildings in the aggregate construction figure is greater, and the number of entirely new buildings erected here between 1877 and 1888 is roughly twice as high as in any of the other three *arrondissements*. Demolitions for public works were not numerous enough to provide more than a partial explanation of this high figure. Building here did not follow the pattern of the city as a whole. In 1884–6, for instance, more building was done than at any time since 1870, even though the industry overall was in a period of recession. But then, from 1887, building in the IVe *arrondissement* went into a steep decline. In 1888 fewer operations were completed even than in 1873, which previously had been the worst year since 1870. Although this decline was reversed in 1889, the improvement was ephemeral, and in the 1890s new building declined even further. It would appear that the extended boom of 1884–6 had used up most of the remaining easily available sites. From now on it would be no easier to build there than anywhere else in the right bank centre. Notre-Dame ward, consisting of the Île Saint-Louis and part of the Cité, had seen little new building since 1870, but now the two wards nearest the centre, Saint-Merri and Saint-Gervais, seemed likely to join Notre-Dame as wards which, barring public intervention, would no longer spontaneously renew their own buildings.

After 1895 the Ier *arrondissement* continued to see less building than any other in the right bank centre. Only 113 permits for entire buildings were issued there between 1895 and 1914, and 39 per cent of the total of operations authorised were vertical extensions of existing buildings, a much higher proportion than elsewhere. The annual total of operations tended to fall, except in 1909–10, when the big increase in the number of permits was due to numerous demolitions for public works schemes. On the other hand, building in this *arrondissement* was more active after 1895 than in the 1882–94 period when only about fifty-five permits for whole buildings were issued there. Furthermore, the main area of new building had shifted from the Halles ward, which in 1882–94 had seen more building operations than the whole of the rest of the *arrondissement*, to Palais-Royal and, to a lesser extent, Place-Vendôme. After 1895 Halles sank to third place.

This westward movement was not repeated in the IIe *arrondissement*. As in previous years, it saw much more new building than the Ier with 177 entire buildings authorised there after 1895. Like the Ier *arrondissement*, however, the IIe recorded an increase of building activity after 1895, and the relative expansion compared to 1882–94 was of a similar order to that in its southern neighbour. But the greater availability of sites than in the Ier *arrondissement* is indicated by the slightly lower proportion of vertical extensions (31 per cent). Public works, therefore, were slightly less influential than in the Ier *arrondissement*, and although they appear to have encouraged building from 1896 to 1899, the increase in the number of constructions in 1901–4 took place at a time when no improvement schemes were being undertaken. As in the Ier *arrondissement*, over half the new buildings were concentrated in one ward, Mail, probably as a result of the completion of the northern section of the Rue du Louvre and the western part of the Rue Réaumur. Bonne-Nouvelle, which was the second most important ward for new building, benefited from the northward extension of the Rue Dussoubs. Yet although these two wards account for most of the increased building in the *arrondissement*, compared to 1882–94, Vivienne also saw more activity. But Gaillon remained almost completely stagnant.

While this welcome expansion of new building was going on in the west, the east was losing its former predominance, mainly as the result of a spectacular decline in building in the IVe *arrondissement*. In the IIIe more building was done than in the 1882–94 period, but the expansion there was relatively smaller than in the west, and the total of permits issued between 1895 and 1914 is only slightly higher than in the IIe. The proportion of vertical extensions tends to increase as time goes on, suggesting a growing shortage of sites. In fact, there is every indication that the building figures for the period were higher than those for 1882–94 only because the IIIe *arrondissement* was benefiting for the first time from the execution of large-scale improvement schemes. This impression is reinforced by the concentration of more than half the permits issued in Archives ward, where most of the demolitions were carried out, in connection with the Rue de Bretagne widening. Sainte-Avoie, where work was proceeding on the Rue Beaubourg, although it had considerably less new building than Archives, was in turn well ahead of the two northern wards, Arts-et-Métiers and Enfants-Rouges, which were hardly touched by improvements. This was a far cry from the 1882–94 period, when half the new building in the *arrondissement* had been in the two northern wards.

A steep decline of building in two wards out of four is also a characteristic of the IVe *arrondissement*, though it was considerably more serious than in the IIIe. The IVe *arrondissement* was the only one in the right bank centre to show an actual decline in the rate of new building compared with the previous period. With only 141 permits for entire buildings issued between 1895 and 1914 it fell from first to third place, behind the IIIe and IIe *arrondissements*. As in the IIIe, the building rate was high during the first few years, in spite of only very slight encouragement from street schemes. But a decline set in from 1902, and it required extremely numerous expropriations by the City to bring about an improvement in 1909 and 1912–13. The overall reduction was caused mainly by a drastic fall in construction in the two western wards. New building was more irregularly distributed in the IVe than in any other *arrondissement*, with over three-quarters of the permits issued being for Arsenal ward, which was not only the least densely built, but also the most favoured by improvement schemes. The islands (Notre-Dame ward) also maintained their building rate of the previous period, low though it had been.

To conclude, it would seem that the building congestion which by 1850 afflicted mainly the central core of wards in the right bank centre had spread by 1914 throughout the whole area. Nearly the whole of the right bank centre had become dependent on street improvements to stimulate building. How had this congestion developed?

Haussmann had hoped that if the right conditions were created for building, free enterprise could provide sufficient accommodation for the very poor, and allow rents to stabilise. But by driving new streets through the centre he did the opposite. Although he pointed out that the new buildings contained more dwellings than those that the City was demolishing,[40] he conveniently ignored the fact that much of the land acquired was not available for building after improvement, because it was incorporated in streets or open spaces. He also forgot that the older buildings were often let and sub-let room by room,[41] whereas the new houses in the centre were divided into relatively spacious apartments and were, in any case, rarely occupied by the working classes.[42] However, many workers needed to live near the centre to be near their place of employment, or near the points of assembly where they could find work. Building workers, for instance, were taken on at the Place Baudoyer, near the Hôtel de Ville. Tailors and other workers in the clothing trades assembled at the Place du Caire (IIe).[43] Because improvement schemes swept away the poorest houses, the tenants they displaced were the least able to find adequate new accommodation because of the higher rents they would be required to pay. So these people sought to live in surviving old houses nearby, where the landlord would be prepared to offset the low rents that his tenants could afford by allowing their number to increase. For instance, one contemporary observer noted that many people displaced by demolitions in the Cité moved into the Rue de l'Hôtel-de-Ville, which became more densely populated than before.[44] The same writer also stated that high rents in the new streets near the Halles had caused some workers to move out into the suburbs, but that more had moved just to the east, to the Arts-et-Métiers and Sainte-Avoie wards, which had not yet been disturbed by street improvements.[45] Arts-et-Métiers was bisected a few years later by the Rue de Turbigo; Sainte-Avoie and the Rue de l'Hôtel-de-Ville area remained untouched, but within a few decades both these areas had to be designated as clearance zones because of their high tuberculosis mortality. The displacements of population were so sudden and so immense that sufficient vacant accommodation could not possibly have been provided for all those made homeless; in 1854, for instance, it was estimated that

---

[40] Conseil général minutes, 8 December 1864, p. 15.
[41] See Louis Chevalier, *Classes laborieuses et classes dangereuses à Paris pendant la première moitié du XIXe siècle* (1958), p. 300.
[42] See Edouard Fournier, 'Promenades dans Paris', p. 55, in *Paris dans sa splendeur* (1861), vol. II, pp. 1–76.
[43] These two examples are given by Dr. Chassagne, *Dix-neuf ans du Conseil municipal* (1890), p. 14.
[44] Fournier, 'Promenades dans Paris', p. 59.
[45] Fournier, p. 55.

demolitions for the new Halles and the extension of the Rue de Rivoli would displace 12,000 people.[46]

The inevitable result of this new pressure on central accommodation was a rise in rents in the old houses of the centre. Haussmann himself stated in 1856 that rents had more than doubled in the centre since 1851, although he claimed that only well-to-do districts had been affected.[47] But a year later he also admitted that rents had risen in poor areas too.[48] The return from a property could be further increased by turning it into a lodging house for itinerant workers. Many houses were converted in this way under the Second Empire, and it was estimated in 1864 that as many as 200,000 people lived in them.[49] They were especially numerous in the city centre, and, according to Councillor Lanquetin, they were almost the only economic activity of Hôtel-de-Ville ward.[50]

Another important cause of the increase in rents was the growing number of premises used for commerce or industry. They could command higher rents than dwellings, and their rents increased more quickly than housing rents under the Second Empire.[51] Although Haussmann once claimed, with a degree of optimism that was unusual even for him, that conversions of dwellings to business use would lead to a decline in general rent levels, he stated in the following year that high rents in the Ier, IIe, IIIe, VIIIe and IXe *arrondissements*, the central business district, were due mainly to the extension of business and commerce there.[52]

In such an inflationary situation the demolition of existing buildings, as long as they did not grossly under-use their sites, in order to replace them with something slightly bigger, was often not an attractive proposition. At least a year of revenue would be lost, while the landlord might have to compensate tenants for the interruption of their leases. And the return on the investment might not be very much higher than on the old building. Mademoiselle Daumard has shown that the rents of old houses generally increased more quickly than those of new ones under the Second Empire.[53] Indeed, in the early

---

[46] *Moniteur*, 18 August 1854, p. 2403.

[47] Conseil général minutes, 26 November 1856, pp. 12–13n.

[48] Conseil général minutes, 1857, Prefect's report, p. 11. For confirmation of the tendency for rents to rise rapidly even in the oldest houses, see Adeline Daumard, *Maisons de Paris*, pp. 147, 150.

[49] Conseil général minutes, 9 December 1861, p. 11; 8 December 1864, p. 17.

[50] Commission des Halles, *Documents*, no. 4, p. 16.

[51] Daumard, *Maisons de Paris*, p. 139.

[52] Conseil général minutes, 8 December 1864, p. 17; 27 November 1865, p. 7.

[53] Daumard, *Maisons de Paris*, pp. 225–6.

1850s, before the housing shortage became really acute, the rents of new houses were generally lower than those of older properties, because of the difficulty of attracting tenants to accommodation that was often affected by damp.[54] Older buildings were generally solidly built, often of stone, a result, it was said, of the freehold land tenure system which encouraged the developer to build to last.[55] A municipal improvement scheme, of course, could clear and redefine sites for new building, but as its effect would also be to revalorise those properties which faced onto the new street or stood nearby,[56] the prospect of further, spontaneous demolitions was often diminished. Moreover, when landlords anticipated disturbance by a street scheme, they postponed any improvement or replacement plans that they might have had for their properties, because they could expect to receive rather more in compensation than they were really worth. Because of the general uncertainty under Haussmann as to which properties would be affected—and this uncertainty was encouraged by the City to limit speculation—many old houses must have been retained that might otherwise have disappeared. Mademoiselle Daumard has pointed out a fall in the number of sales of property after 1850, which would indicate that landlords were preferring to hold on to their buildings.[57] And as many central street schemes were not carried out for twenty to forty years after the fall of the Second Empire, many houses probably survived even longer than their owners had originally expected.

After 1870, when the atmosphere of speculation was somewhat attenuated, there was even less reason to demolish older buildings. With fewer street improvement schemes, new building tended at first to scatter throughout the central zone, instead of concentrating in areas where public works were being carried out. However, the most readily accessible vacant and under-used sites were soon built on, so that nearly all building operations had to be preceded by the demolition of substantial older buildings. This point seems to have been reached rather earlier in the west of the right bank centre than in the east. By the mid-1880s 91 per cent or more of houses had four or more storeys in five of the eight western wards, and two more had over

---

[54] Commission des logements insalubres, *Rapport général des travaux de la commission pendant l'année 1851* (1852), p. 6.
[55] Charles Gourlier, *Des voies publiques et des habitations particulières à Paris* (1852), p. 10. Some support for this view is provided by D. F. Medhurst and J. Parry Lewis, *Urban Decay* (1969), pp. 62–4.
[56] Daumard, *Maisons de Paris*, p. 220.   [57] Daumard, p. 45.

86 per cent.[58] In the whole of the Ier *arrondissement* 91 per cent or more houses were of four or more storeys, and one ward, Saint-Germain-l'Auxerrois, had a proportion of 97 per cent. But in the east only three wards had more than 91 per cent, and three had less than 85 per cent. One ward, Arsenal, had only 71 per cent. Even as late as 1913 this discrepancy survived. The average height of buildings was then 16·5 metres in the Ier *arrondissement* and 16·2 metres in the IIe, while the two eastern *arrondissements* each had an average of 14·4 metres.[59] Gardens and courtyards also were still more numerous in the east by 1900.[60] To some extent, the relatively greater spaciousness of the east reflected the lower land prices there, which made it less urgent to build up to the maximum height allowed. It was estimated in 1883 that a square metre was worth only 554 and 297 francs in the IIIe and IVe *arrondissements*, compared to 719 francs in the Ier *arrondissement* and 956 francs in the IIe.[61] It also resulted partly from the lower proportion of very wide streets in the east, which had seen fewer public works than the west, so that there were fewer sites on which construction to the maximum height allowed in Paris could be authorised. However, the available figures make it clear that the east was only slightly better off than the west, and that the whole of the central zone was to all intents and purposes completely built up by the turn of the century.

We must now consider more closely the height factor, which came to dominate the process of spontaneous reconstruction as the number of virgin sites dwindled to nothing. When a demolition was a prerequisite of building, the relative sizes of the old building and the new were an essential consideration. Of course the new building would be better appointed, but even the oldest buildings were usually structurally sound. For instance, out of 193 houses compulsorily acquired to build the Avenue de l'Opéra, in what was claimed by the City to be a slum district, only ten were adjudged by the City's own valuers to be in 'bad' or 'very bad' structural condition.[62] And new buildings had certain disadvantages. If the new house was not going to be much

---

[58] These figures are published in *Guide Foncier 1866–7*, p. 10; or *Résultats statistiques du dénombrement de 1886*, pp. xxviii, xxix. The number of storeys does not include the ground floor, but entresols and attic roofs each count as one storey. For further height statistics, see *Résultats statistiques du dénombrement de 1891* (1894), pp. xxvi, xxvii.

[59] Commission d'extension de Paris, *Considérations techniques préliminaires* (1913), plate 21.

[60] Number of gardens in each *arrondissement*: Ier, 35; IIe, 17; IIIe, 35; IVe, 55. Number of courtyards: Ier, 1,357; IIe, 1,662; IIIe, 2,316; IVe, 2,207 (*Livre Foncier*, second part [1902], table IV).   [61] C.M. reports, 1883, no. 8, p. 13.

[62] Calculated from valuers' reports, A.S., VO11, box nos. 2446–51.

bigger than the old, then why demolish at all? Particularly if it was in a working-class area where high rents could not be asked for the new house. This question became more and more apposite as the smallest houses were replaced by tall blocks, and the average height of existing buildings increased, while the average height of new houses declined owing to the growing shortage of plots on which the regulations would allow very high constructions. The building permit statistics show that building was most active in areas where it was possible to build high, and that the general decline in new building during the Third Republic is accompanied by a fall in the average height of new constructions. On the other hand, in those areas where the existing buildings are relatively low, restrictions on the height of new buildings do not create so great an obstacle to construction as in those wards which are already built up with very high houses. Information on the height of new houses first becomes available in 1882. At that time, new buildings were somewhat higher in the west, with an average over the 1882–94 period of 6·8 storeys in the Ier *arrondissement* and 6·1 in the IIe. The relatively spacious IVe *arrondissement* also saw many high buildings, with an average of 6·1 storeys, but the IIIe was much lower, with 5·6 storeys. Clearly, in the Ier *arrondissement*, where land values were among the highest in Paris, and existing buildings were higher than in any other in the right bank centre, only extremely high new houses could be envisaged. Many sites for such buildings were cleared in Halles by street improvements, which helps to explain why more than half the new building in the *arrondissement* was done there, at an average height of 6·6 storeys. Palais-Royal and Place-Vendôme had equally lofty new buildings—6·8 and 6·4 storeys respectively—but many fewer of them. And in Saint-Germain-l'Auxerrois, the most congested ward of the right bank centre from the point of view of height of existing buildings, there are no new constructions at all. The IIe *arrondissement* shows a similar pattern. Nearly all building is done in the Mail and Bonne-Nouvelle wards, where public works cleared large and convenient sites. The more active ward of the two, Mail, averages 6·9 storeys for new buildings, and the other, 5·9 storeys. The two almost stagnant western wards of the *arrondissement* show only 5·6 and 5·7 storeys. These wards were not particularly congested, but they were still middle-class areas and their existing buildings were in very good condition, while they had few very wide streets. These factors help to explain why a high proportion of building activity there was devoted to vertical extensions of existing structures.

In the eastern *arrondissements*, where pressure on sites was not yet so great, the distinctions were not so clear, but it is noticeable that the most active eastern ward, Arsenal, was easily the least congested of the right bank centre, and new houses there averaged 6·2 storeys. And rather more building was done in the IVe *arrondissement* at an average height of 6·1 storeys than in the IIIe with 5·6 storeys.

Between 1895 and 1914 the picture changed, with a fall in the average height of new buildings in all four *arrondissements*, and a sharp rise in the proportion of vertical extensions. This helps to confirm the assumption that has already been made, that the best sites had already gone, and that builders now had to turn to plots which did not allow such high constructions. Yet in the city as a whole the tendency was to build even higher than before. Height restrictions were relaxed in 1902, and the development of efficient lifts enhanced the value of upper floors. As Joseph Bouvard, director of the City's architectural department, said in 1909:

> 'In the past people did not want to build high . . . today, on the contrary, upper floors are in demand and we have to act to stop excessively high building.'[63]

That more building was done in the west of the right bank centre than during the preceding period was due to the more favourable economic climate, the extension of street improvements, and the expansion of business activities in some wards. Information on the proportion of new buildings used for business is hard to obtain before 1914, but of new premises built in 1913, 92 per cent were used for commerce or industry in the Ier *arrondissement* and 84 per cent in the IIe. But the proportions in the IIIe and IVe *arrondissements* were only 34 per cent and 23 per cent respectively.[64] So the east, with its low property values, declining commerce and industry, and increasingly working-class population, no longer attracted the builder now that the shortage of sites was almost as severe as in the west. The increasing severity of building regulations further reduced the attractiveness of construction, especially in the case of lower-rented dwellings. The fact that by the turn of the century the provision of working-class housing was no longer an economic proposition was one of the main causes of the decline of building in the east, which in turn accelerated its degeneration into a slum area.

[63] C.V.P., 3 April 1909, p. 52.
[64] Louis Dausset, *Rapport général . . . sur . . . le projet de budget de la Ville de Paris pour 1914*, p. 46 (C.M. reports, 1913, no. 120).

Building in the Right Bank Centre, 1850–1914

The relative revival of building in the west of the right bank centre in the last two decades before 1914 must not obscure the fact that the rate of building was extremely low throughout the centre, and, even with the beneficial influence of public works, was tending to fall. The survival there of great numbers of old buildings was in complete contrast to the City of London, much of which was completely rebuilt by private initiative during the second half of the nineteenth century. If the right bank centre had been the financial and business centre of Paris, the same rebuilding would probably have taken place there as in the City. But it was not. Why it was not, and what exactly it was, is what we must now examine.

1 New streets built in Paris 1850–1913. [Commission d'extension de Paris, *Considérations techniques préliminaires* (1913).]

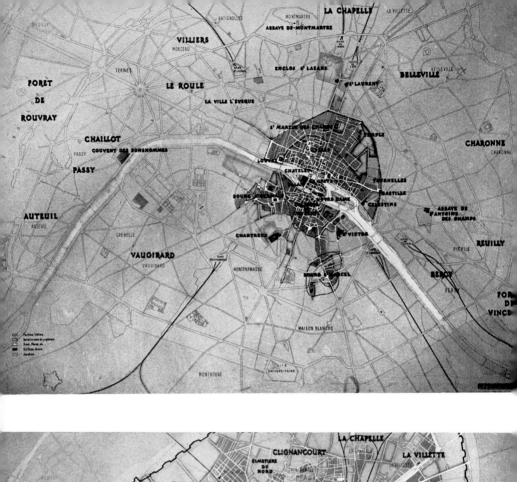

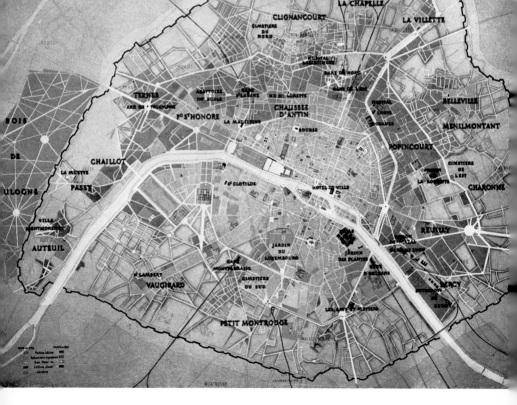

The growth of Paris. Evolution of the built-up area, in relation to major features of the modern city:

2 (*above*, *opposite*) Paris in the later middle ages, still tightly encircled by the fortifications of Philip Augustus and Charles V.

3 (*above*) Paris in the late eighteenth century, encircled by the *octroi* wall.

4 (*below*, *opposite*) Paris in 1850. The newly-fortified area still retains extensive open spaces inside Thiers' earthworks.

5, 6 Changing styles in Parisian domestic architecture: the 1850s (*above*) and the early 1900s (*opposite*). [*The Builder*, 6 March 1858 and 27 February 1904.] The art nouveau design, which won an award in the City of Paris architectural competition in 1904, was made possible only by the relaxed regulations of the 1902 building act. But what emerges above all is the basic similarity between the two designs, which is an indication of the inherent conservatism of Parisian domestic architecture. Building bye-laws and the lack of adventure shown by architects and clients were jointly responsible for this absence of change.

PROPRIETE DE M. CONSTANT

MAISON DE RAPPORT

38ᵇⁱˢ Rue Fabert

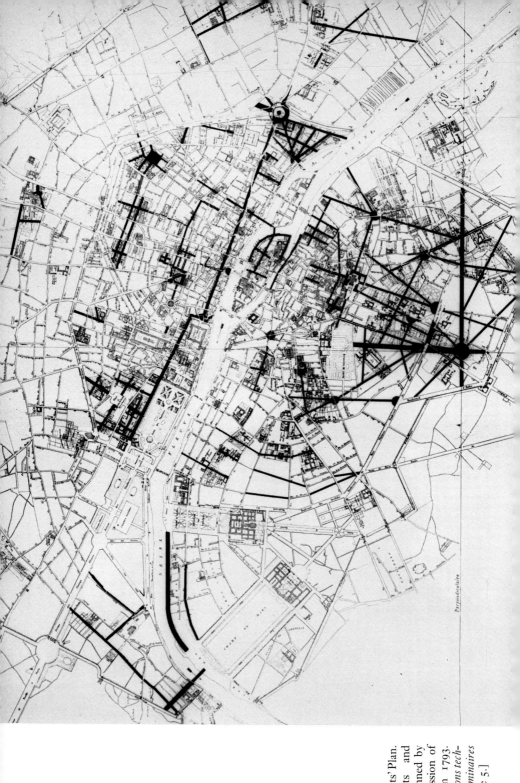

7 The Artists' Plan. New streets and squares planned by the Commission of Artists from 1793. [*Considérations techniques préliminaires* (1913), plate 5.]

8 Long-term plan
of street improve-
ments recommend-
ed by the Extension
of Paris Committee
in 1913. Most were
widening schemes.
[*Considérations tech-
niques préliminaires*
(1913), plate 9.]

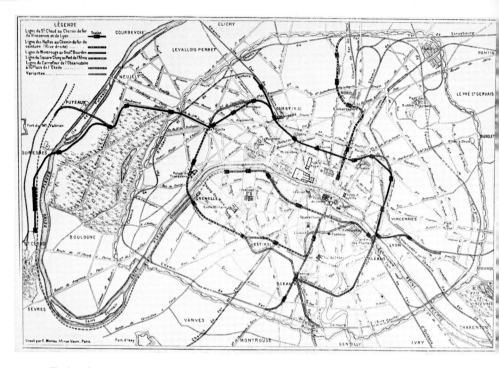

9 Early scheme for the *Métropolitain*, discussed by the City Council in 1882. [*L'Illustration*, no. 2044, 29 April 1882, p. 287.]

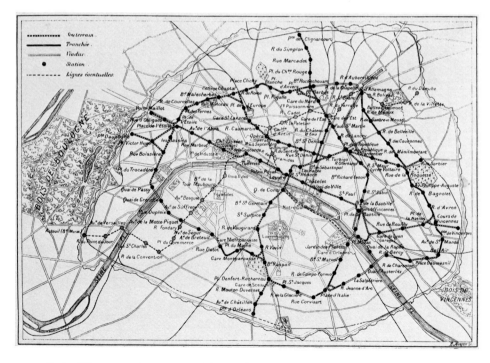

10 Paris *Métro* network as approved by the City Council. [*L'Illustration*, no. 2837, 10 July 1897, p. 23.]

6

The Indian Summer of
Central Paris

A recent public opinion survey asked Parisians to name the spot which they considered to be the centre of Paris. 64 per cent of the sample picked the Opéra, the Champs-Elysées, or the Etoile. Only 25 per cent chose the Cité, or the Châtelet.[1] If the same question had been asked in 1850, the majority of the answers would almost certainly have been very different. Some, perhaps, might even then have chosen the Boulevard des Italiens, near the present Opéra, where theatres and other entertainments, and fine shops, attracted many of the Parisians who had the time to seek such amusement and the money to buy it. But even more still sought such pleasures in the area of the Palais-Royal, which for them would have been the true centre of the city. For businessmen, the Bourse or the Bank of France would have been the city centre. The rich trader would probably have thought of the southern part of the Rue Saint-Denis, while for many thousands of housewives the centre would have been close at hand, at the old Halles. Some older people might even have plumped for the Cité itself, where density of buildings at least gave an impression of centrality. In 1850 the right bank centre, the old fortified area, still housed one-third of the city's population and accommodated one-third of its industry. The best shops, and most business houses, were in the right bank centre. Yet, as we shall see, its predominance was already crumbling away.

[1] Préfecture de la Seine, *Contribution aux études sur l'avenir du centre de Paris* (c. 1965), p. 14.

For many centuries the prosperity of Paris resulted very largely from its position as the administrative capital. If Hugh Capet had never taken the throne of France and the capital had been fixed at Tours, Paris would probably never have developed beyond a large-sized provincial town. Although its site and accessibility would have assured it regional predominance, it did not enjoy the same natural advantages as London, which became capital mainly as a result of the size and prosperity it had already attained. The rich agricultural areas which surrounded Paris could support a large population, but they produced no raw materials beyond the stone, wood and plaster needed to house that population. The industries that grew up in the city produced mainly consumer goods to satisfy local demand, and there was a strong bias towards finishing trades. The presence of aristocratic and administrative classes encouraged the development of luxury industries such as perfumery and jewellery. Products such as combs, hairbrushes and handmirrors were so closely associated with the capital that they came to be known collectively as 'articles of Paris'. Clothing manufacture also grew to prominence as a result of the stimulus of local demand. The steadily growing population maintained very large building and furniture-making sectors. The presence of many government offices and an important university engendered prosperous printing and publishing trades. As time went on, some of the city's products acquired a national and even an international reputation, and an increasing proportion of them were exported from Paris. But if in 1700 the consumers of the Paris area had suddenly moved elsewhere, the city's industry would have ground to a halt.

Although the history of the industrial evolution of Paris is still shrouded in mystery, it would appear that the first stage in the city's development into an industrial and commercial, as well as a political, capital began in the eighteenth century.[2] This development had two facets. Firstly, the growing sophistication of financial transactions allowed them to be centralised, and the developing association of bourgeois financiers with an impecunious monarchy dictated the choice of that central point. Of course, there had long been a concentration of financial activity in Paris, but it was reinforced by John Law's attempt to shore up the royal finances in the early years of the eighteenth century, and his establishment in 1719 of a bank in the Rue Quincampoix, which became the focal point of the hectic events of the following year. Then, in 1724, the Bourse was founded, and, in 1776, the *Caisse*

[2] *Paris: fonctions d'une capitale* (1962), pp. 139–40.

d'Escompte.[3] The second facet of the change was the acceleration of industrial innovation during the eighteenth century. Although France lagged well behind England, the capital's position as a distribution centre, and as a source of skilled labour, made it an attractive production location. After 1800, as France strove to overcome her industrial backwardness, Paris expanded rapidly as an industrial centre. Growth was encouraged by the Bank of France, founded in 1799, which offered credit at low rates, restricted until 1835 to Parisians only. Even before the railways were built the city was also developing as a redistribution centre, and there was an increase in the number of various sorts of middlemen.[4] And, not least, the rapid growth of population was a constant stimulus to industrial expansion. The railways, of course, accelerated all these trends when they started to link Paris to the raw materials and markets of the provinces in the 1840s and 1850s.[5] The law of 1842, which laid down that the prime objective of the main lines was to link Paris to the frontiers, ensured that no provincial centre would ever be able to challenge the commercial predominance of the capital.

Although most of the commercial expansion in the first half of the nineteenth century took place within the city boundaries,[6] most of the new industrial development was sited outside the city. The *octroi*—customs dues levied on all consumer commodities and raw materials entering the city—was an unwelcome burden on any concern whose marketing horizons extended beyond Paris.[7] Furthermore, taxation on property values was lower outside the city, there were fewer public health restrictions on industry, and greater space and low land prices made expansion much easier.[8] When the Paris Chamber of Commerce undertook the first exhaustive industrial survey of the city, in 1847–8, it was revealed that activities within the city itself were mostly on a

[3] *Paris: fonctions d'une capitale*, pp. 140–41.
[4] Mademoiselle Daumard believes that Paris was already tending under the July Monarchy to become one of the most important centres, if not *the* most important, of commercial and financial activity in France (*Maisons de Paris*, pp. 87–8).
[5] Mademoiselle Daumard suggests that a study of the evolution of rents indicates a rapid expansion of some sectors of the Paris economy from the early 1840s (*Maisons de Paris*, p. 139).
[6] See plans indicating an increase in economic activity in all *arrondissements* except one between 1815 and 1848, in A. Daumard, *La bourgeoisie parisienne de 1815 à 1848* (1963), pp. 422–3.
[7] The *octroi* had been abolished at the Revolution, but was reestablished in 1799. Contemporaries blamed it for the departure of a number of industries from the city (see, for instance, Max Boucard, *La vie de Paris* [1892], p. 60).
[8] For a detailed survey of the spread of industry into the suburbs, see Jean Bastié, *La croissance de la banlieue parisienne* (1964).

small scale, satisfying mainly local needs. Less than 10 per cent of Paris industrial production in 1847 was exported from the city.[9] Most concerns were shown to be very small, extremely specialised, and highly interdependent. As the authors explained:

> 'The industries which flourish in big cities are those whose processes can be divided among a large number of small factors and craftsmen.'[10]

In fact, many concerns could not have remained competitive without putting work out to craftsmen working at home. This meant that the industries which could remain in the city were those that had always been there—the labour-intensive skilled trades using little or no machinery. Fragmentation and interdependence were naturally even more pronounced in the right bank centre, except in the north-eastern metalworking sector. In the old IVe *arrondissement*, which covered roughly the eastern half of the present Ier *arrondissement*, only one manufacturer in fourteen employed more than ten workers in 1847–8, and as few as one in twenty did so in the old IXe *arrondissement*, which corresponded to the southern half of the present IVe. Only the VIIe *arrondissement*, which covered part of the present IIIe, where one manufacturer in seven employed more than ten hands, exceeded the Paris average of one in nine.[11] The VIIe *arrondissement* also had a high concentration of production units, with seventy-eight to the hectare, while the IXe had only thirty-six. The IVe *arrondissement* had almost as great a density of units as the VIIe, with seventy-five to the hectare, but they were much smaller. The VIIe was clearly the most industrialised of the three.

The greater industrialisation of the north-east, as compared to the rest of the right bank centre, is confirmed by other sources. The most predominantly right bank central of the city's industries was clothing manufacture, which flourished throughout the area.[12] In particular, the districts east of the Hôtel de Ville were renowned for cotton and

---

[9] Chambre de Commerce, *Statistique de l'industrie à Paris 1847–8* (1851), p. 38. Moreover, the authors believed that a proportion of the exported goods were in fact re-exports, because of the city's developing role as a redistribution centre.

[10] *Statistique de l'industrie*, p. 11. For studies of the very similar industrial structure of London at this time, see François Bédarida, 'Londres au milieu du XIXe siècle', *Annales*, vol. 23, no. 2, March–April 1968, pp. 268–95; Peter G. Hall, *The Industries of London Since 1861* (1962).

[11] *Statistique de l'industrie à Paris 1847–8*, p. 36, table 1.

[12] The main source of this description is Chambre de Commerce, *Statistique de l'industrie à Paris 1860*, pp. xvii–xx.

silk goods, while the Mail and Montmartre wards, north of the Halles, specialised in making shawls and other heavy garments. Associated with clothing were the textile finishing trades, which were concentrated in what is now the IIe *arrondissement*. Metalwork centred on the north-east, in the present IIIe *arrondissement* and in the neighbouring XIe outside the right bank centre; but, of the two, the IIIe possessed the smaller production units in this trade. The IIIe was also the centre of the Paris precious metalworking industry, and in 1860, 1,778 out of 3,199 industrial establishments there were engaged in it. The other *arrondissements* of the right bank centre did not have anything like this concentration, but they, and the present XIe *arrondissement*, had more precious metalworking concerns than any other. The IIIe and IXe *arrondissements* were also the main centre of the furniture industry, and the IIIe had the biggest concentration of the group of 'diverse' industries, which was made up of the precision, musical, leather, coachbuilding, brush, and articles of Paris trades. But article-of-Paris manufacture was spread widely across the east of the right bank centre, and also in the north, near the Porte Saint-Denis. 'Diverse' industries were also well represented in the present IIe, Ve, IVe, XIe and Ier *arrondissements*. The IVe *arrondissement*, which was not an important industrial area, was however the main Parisian centre of the food industries, of which there was another important concentration near the Halles, together with distilleries, soapworks, candle manufacturers and other industries which obtained their raw materials from the markets. Another very important industry in the right bank centre was printing and stationery, although the biggest concentration of these trades was to be found on the left bank, in the Ve and VIe *arrondissements*. The largest group of printing firms in the right bank centre was in the IIe, in the Rue du Croissant area, where the main newspaper editorial offices were situated.

One can generalise by saying that the east of the right bank centre was much more industrial than the west, but that only the north-east had the same pronounced industrial character as the neighbouring XIe *arrondissement*. Apart from the clothing and articles of Paris trades in the east of the present IIe *arrondissement*, and the various industries connected with the markets in the east of the Ier, the west of the right bank centre was not notably an industrial area. The only industries to flourish in its westernmost districts were luxury trades such as confectionery, coachbuilding and saddlemaking, and these were located mainly near the Boulevard de la Madeleine. Industry was sparse in the west because it had developed as an aristocratic and middle-class residential area after the Marais had begun to lose its attraction in the sixteenth and seventeenth centuries, but later, in the eighteenth and early nineteenth centuries, commercial and financial undertakings began to set up there. Unlike most manufacturing concerns, they needed a central location in order to be accessible to as many people as possible, and to be close to such institutions as the Bank of France and the Bourse. The growing links between Paris financial and commercial enterprise and provincial industry helped to create a new type of merchant, whose primary interests were no longer his dealings with local industry.[13] A growing number of large industrial and trading concerns sited their head offices in Paris, and foreign firms opened branches there.[14] All required special accommodation, separate from that of purely industrial undertakings. As the new business functions proliferated, they caused a general rise in rents which acted as a further discouragement to industry, especially in the west central area.

This expansion of business in the nineteenth century greatly accelerated the evolution of the right bank centre. The left bank had very little industry or commerce,[15] and the right bank centre was to all intents and purposes the central business district of Paris, at least until the early nineteenth century. A glance at any directory will show that at the turn of the century the very great majority of merchants and tradesmen still lived and worked between the Seine and the *grands boulevards*.[16] The same source shows that most of the notables had already moved from this hive of activity to quieter areas such as the Faubourg Saint-Honoré and, on the left bank, the Faubourg Saint-Germain. This flight of the leisured classes to the west was accelerated after 1800 as business activities expanded in the centre and caused increasing congestion there. They were followed by the new business classes, whose social aspirations and more sophisticated working methods encouraged and allowed them to move away from the industrial areas. The old merchants of the Rue Saint-Denis area had such close contacts with local trades and industries that they usually

[13] Daumard, *Maisons de Paris*, p. 86.
[14] *Statistique de l'industrie à Paris 1847–8*, p. 17.
[15] See, for instance, A. Audiganne, 'Industrie et commerce', p. 7, in *Paris dans sa splendeur* (1861), vol. II, section VIII. In 1847 the business turnover of left bank concerns was only one-sixth of that of the right bank (A. J. Meindre, *Histoire de Paris et de son influence en Europe* [1854–5], vol. V, p. 474).
[16] See, for instance, *Almanach de Paris . . . pour l'année 1788*, Paris, Lesclapart, 1788, pp. 240.

lived in the same districts and even in the same houses as the artisans themselves.[17] But the new businessmen and financiers needed to be near the new temples of capitalism, the Bourse and the Bank of France, both of which had become fixed in the west of the right bank centre. At its foundation in 1799 the Bank of France was installed in a mansion at the corner of the Place des Victoires and the Rue des Fossés-Montmartre, a few hundred yards to the north-west of the Halles. In 1811 it was transferred a short distance to the Hôtel de la Vrillière, Rue de la Vrillière, which had been occupied since 1793 by the Government printing works. Subsequent growth took place around this site.[18] The Bourse had occupied various sites in the west of the right bank centre, the last of them being the Palais-Royal, but it was finally fixed slightly to the north of the Bank, on the site of the Filles-Saint-Thomas convent (now IIe *arrondissement*), which had been made national property at the Revolution. Work started on the new building in 1808, and it was inaugurated in 1826.[19] From the late eighteenth century financiers started to build their houses in the Chaussée-d'Antin area, just outside the *grands boulevards*, north-west and north of the old city centre, and even some of the high nobility joined them.[20] Under the Restoration the banker Laffitte, one of the richest residents of Chaussée-d'Antin, and other financiers developed the whole of the area north-west from the *grands boulevards* to the city boundaries for middle-class residence.[21] And whereas the old Paris merchants had to live on top of their work, the new businessmen took their work home with them.[22] The migration of many better-off people to the west and north-west of the city also had the effect of attracting to the west of the centre those high-class shops and businesses which depended on their patronage.[23] Enter-

[17] Daumard, *Maisons de Paris*, p. 86.   [18] Meindre, *Histoire de Paris*, vol. V, p. 405.
[19] Meindre, p. 401; [Louis Lurine, ed.], *Les rues de Paris* (1844), vol. II, p. 113.
[20] Edouard Fournier, 'Promenades dans Paris', p. 14, in *Paris dans sa splendeur*, vol. II, ch. III.
[21] Paul Léon suggests that rich traders left the east of the city in the nineteenth century for the west because they feared the popular disorders which multiplied after 1789 (*Paris: histoire de la rue* [1947], p. 126). One such refugee was the wallpaper manufacturer, Réveillon, who moved to the corner of the Rue de la Paix and the Rue des Capucines after his house in the Faubourg Saint-Antoine was burned by rioters in the 1790s (Fournier, 'Promenades dans Paris', p. 25).
[22] According to Amédée Achard, the Rue de la Chaussée-d'Antin began to fill with moneychangers, stockbrokers, tradesmen and shops after 1815, and more quickly after 1830. By 1844 it had become just as commercial a street as the Rue de Vivienne and the Rue des Lombards ('Rue de la Chaussée-d'Antin', p. 45, in *Les rues de Paris*, vol. I, pp. 39-48).
[23] For plans showing this increase in the number of commercial and industrial enterprises in the west of the city centre, see A. Daumard, *La bourgeoisie parisienne*, pp. 422-3. Although the taxation returns do not distinguish between industrial and other enterprises, it can be assumed that most of the growth in the west was commercial and financial, and that elsewhere it was largely industrial.

tainment also began to migrate to the north-west. The Opéra, like the Bourse, had had several homes, and after 1794 it was in the Rue de Richelieu, opposite the *Bibliothèque Nationale*. But in 1820, after the assassination of the Duc de Berry just outside the theatre, it was closed down and a new operahouse was built in the Rue Lepeletier, near the Boulevard des Italiens. This move accelerated the existing tendency of the *grands boulevards* to become the city's entertainment centre. By the 1840s they had replaced the Palais-Royal area, whose decline was accelerated by the suppression of some of the more notorious activities of those who frequented the Palais-Royal itself during Louis-Philippe's reign.[24] Louis Lurine wrote in 1844:

> 'What used to be said about the Palais-Royal can today be applied, with greater justification, to the *boulevards* of Paris . . .'[25]

In fact, so great was the commercial expansion of the *grands boulevards* that by 1850 they had lost their original attraction as a quiet and leisurely promenade. Those who wanted peace and fresh air were already going to the Champs-Elysées.[26]

This development of the *grands boulevards* did not mean that the west of the right bank centre was being deserted. Rather did it mean that the main business and shopping area was slowly expanding to the west and north-west, while its southern and eastern fringes enjoyed rather less prosperity than in the past. Before 1850 the main economic growth occurred in what are now the Ier and IIe *arrondissements*. When, in 1838, the first building in Paris to have shopping accommodation on the first as well as the ground floor was opened, it was at the northern end of the Rue de Richelieu, in what is now the IIe *arrondissement*.[27] When the Rue Saint-Denis lost its position as the centre of Paris merchant enterprise, as it began to do from the beginning of the century, its role was taken over by the Mail and Bourse wards. By 1850 the majority of houses in the area of the Rue du Croissant, the Rue du Sentier, and the Rue des Jeûneurs were occupied by business activities. These areas were still conveniently close to the old centre, but their larger buildings were more suitable to the new forms of

[24] Roger Boutet de Monvel, *Eminent English Men and Women in Paris* (1912), p. 320. Prostitution also tended to expand in this north-western sector, at the expense of Palais-Royal, but to an even greater extent of the traditional prostitution areas near the Hôtel de Ville and in the Cité (see A. J. B. Parent-Duchatelet, *De la prostitution dans la ville de Paris* [3rd ed., 1857], vol. I, pp. 323–4).
[25] 'Les Boulevarts', p. 363, in *Les rues de Paris*, pp. 341–64.
[26] Félix Pigeory, *Les monuments de Paris au dix-neuvième siècle* (1849), pp. 634–5.
[27] *Moniteur*, 2 and 21 February 1838, pp. 197, 361.

business, and their bigger plots offered better opportunities for extensions than in the Rue Saint-Denis.[28] The move from the Rue Saint-Denis was reflected in a deceleration of the rate of increase of rents in that area after 1830.[29]

Although most city wards still retained a large working-class population, and the bourgeois were present nearly everywhere, the movement of many wealthy people to the west, and the expulsion from the western area of poorer people by rising residential and commercial rents, were accentuating class differentiation between districts, and between east and west.[30] Some pockets of relative poverty remained in generally wealthy areas, and middle-class enclaves, like the Marais, survived in districts that were predominantly working class. But, seen as a whole, the right bank centre was coming to reflect within itself the distinction between east and west that was developing in the totality of the city. To the west of the Rue Saint-Denis, big business and middle-class residence. To the east, small-scale industry and working-class dwellings.

2 THE RIGHT BANK CENTRE DURING THE SECOND EMPIRE

In his prophetic report on the problem of the Halles,[31] Councillor Lanquetin blamed the relative decline of the central and eastern wards of the right bank centre on congestion and inadequate communications with the new centre of activity in the north-west. Although the Second Empire did not move the Halles, as Lanquetin would have wished, so that one of the main generators of traffic remained in the centre, it set about improving communications within the central area on a scale far larger than Lanquetin could have expected. At first this policy accelerated the commercial development of the right bank centre and diminished the importance of its residential function. Until mid-century the population of all parts of the right bank centre had expanded or at least, in the most congested central wards, remained stable. But after the mid-1850s the population started to fall almost everywhere, except in the extreme west and east. Much of the loss resulted from demolitions for street improvements, but other residential accommodation was taken over by commerce, especially in the west. Haussmann blamed the rise in rents in the Ier, IIe, IIIe, VIIIe

[28] Daumard, *Maisons de Paris*, pp. 86, 94–6, 139. The Rue du Sentier and the Rue des Jeûneurs formed the centre of the wholesale textile business.
[29] Daumard, *Maisons de Paris*, p. 141.
[30] See Daumard, *La bourgeoisie parisienne*, pp. 181–211.
[31] Commission des Halles, *Documents*, no. 4 (B.A. 2122).

and IXe *arrondissements* on the opening of new shops, and the annexation by commercial activities of the upper floors of houses.[32] This commercial expansion was only to be expected now that the centre was being made more accessible to the rapidly growing population of Paris. Even within the central areas people were encouraged to move about further and more often, and this accentuated the concentration of different types of services in certain districts, instead of their being spread more evenly throughout the city.[33] And the growth of potential clienteles allowed larger units to develop. Department stores appeared for the first time. The earliest of them, most appropriately, was sited on the first big street to be completed in the Second Empire, the Rue de Rivoli extension. This, the *Louvre* department store, opened in 1855,[34] was followed by the *Samaritaine*, at the northern end of the Pont-Neuf, in 1866,[35] and the *Magasins Réunis*, at the Place du Château-d'Eau (now Place de la République) in 1867. The *Belle Jardinière*, over the road from the *Samaritaine*, opened in 1868, and even the left bank had its own department store, the *Bon Marché*. Many of these concerns had very small beginnings. Félix Potin, for instance, opened a shop in the Rue du Rocher in 1850. In 1858 he moved to new premises in the Boulevard de Sébastopol where within eight years his turnover grew from 400,000 francs to six millions, and he went on to develop a chain of department stores.[36] Great hotels also appeared to cater for the tourists and businessmen brought to Paris by the new railways. Here again, the first, the Grand Hôtel du Louvre, which opened in 1855, was in the Rue de Rivoli. Built by the Péreire brothers' *Société des Immeubles Rivoli*, it had nearly 700 bedrooms. A few years later the same company built the slightly larger Grand Hôtel, in the Boulevard des Capucines, and these two remained the biggest hotels in Paris in the 1860s.[37] They were later joined by the Hôtel Continental, which was also in the Rue de Rivoli, at the corner of the Rue Castiglione, and which had over 600 rooms.[38] The Second Empire

---

[32] Conseil général minutes, 27 November 1865, p. 7.

[33] A. Audiganne wrote in 1861 that commercial and business establishments of the same type where tending to group together just as in industry ('Industrie et commerce', p. 7, in *Paris dans sa splendeur*, vol. II, ch. VIII).

[34] At first the store occupied part of the ground floor of the hotel of the same name, but it gradually took over other ground floor shops until by 1874 it occupied the whole area and part of the first floor (Harold Clunn, *The Face of Paris* [1933], p. 61).

[35] The site faced onto the recently completed Rue du Pont-Neuf (Yvan Christ, *Les métamorphoses de Paris* [1967], p. 184).

[36] René Clozier, *La Gare du Nord* (1940), p. 53.

[37] *Chamber's Handy Guide to Paris* (1863), p. 13.

[38] Karl Baedeker, *Paris and Environs* (9th ed., 1888), p. 3.

also saw the development of the big cafe and the big restaurant, especially on or close to the *grands boulevards* near the site of the new Opéra.

One notices that most of these new, large service establishments were sited in the west of the right bank centre, or in one of the new, wide streets. More often than not, they were in both. The new thorough-fares attracted traders because they were lined with large building sites on which commodious and convenient premises could be built, and because they were frequented by so many vehicles and pedestrians. As early as 1852 the *Moniteur* announced that the new accommodation along the Rue de Rivoli was being let to merchants who wanted to leave the narrow and tortuous streets to seek air and light.[39] The parallel Rue Saint-Honoré suffered severely from the competition of the Rue de Rivoli, and contemporaries blamed the relative decline of the commerce of the Rue Saint-Denis on the building of the Boule-vard de Sébastopol.[40] But because the new thoroughfares attracted commerce from neighbouring streets, their prosperity depended on the level of economic activity in the area which they crossed. The zenith of prosperity was reached in those wards of the west and north-west of the right bank centre which had already been described by Lanquetin as the new centre of activity in 1842. Because Haussmann's new streets were not blind pencillings on a map, but carefully designed routes intended to ease existing traffic flows, they inevitably had the effect of improving access to the main focus of those flows—the area near the new Opéra. The very choice of a site for the Opéra, on the *grands boulevards* and at the head of a new avenue running from the Louvre, and linked by new streets to the Gare Saint-Lazare and the Bourse, consecrated the development of the area and encouraged the further growth of its prosperity. The Gare Saint-Lazare, terminus of the big-gest and busiest suburban network, serving the richest segment of the Paris region, was used by a growing number of commuters and shoppers who could find employment and services within easy reach of the station. By 1869 the Gare Saint-Lazare was handling 13,254,000 passengers a year. Five-sixths of this total was suburban traffic. The other six Paris termini handled between them no more than 21,417,000 passengers.[41] The development of vast new middle-class areas in the west greatly increased the number of those who could best be served

[39] *Moniteur*, 23 October 1852, p. 1700.
[40] Robert Hénard, *La Rue Saint-Honoré* (1908, 9), vol. II, p. 542; Daumard, *Maisons de Paris*, p. 95; Ferdinand de Lasteyrie, *Les travaux de Paris* (1861), p. 50.
[41] Clozier, *La Gare du Nord*, p. 53; Audiganne, 'Industrie et commerce', p. 19.

by shopping and services on the western fringes of the city centre. The *grands boulevards* now reached an apogee of prosperity unequalled by any of Haussmann's new streets. English tourists were directed to the section between the Boulevard des Italiens and the Rue de la Paix to see the most brilliant shops and the most aristocratic loungers in Paris.[42] Significantly, the *Théâtre de Vaudeville*, opposite the Bourse, demolished for the building of the Rue du Dix-Décembre (now Rue du Quatre-Septembre), was reopened in 1867 in a new building at the corner of the Rue de la Chaussée-d'Antin and the Boulevard des Capucines.[43] The presence of a rich clientele attracted, as well as entertainments, the big deposit banks, several of which opened on the *grands boulevards*.[44] But the expansion of big business and finance was not limited to this small corner of the centre. Some of it was already taking place outside the right bank centre, in the VIIIe and IXe *arrondissements*. Yet although this growth showed the shape of things to come, the predominance of the right bank centre was not yet threatened. By 1865, one dwelling in eight in the IIe *arrondissement*, and one in nine in the Ier, was being used exclusively for commercial or industrial purposes, compared with one in twenty-one in the VIIIe *arrondissement*, and one in seventeen in the IXe.[45] The corresponding ratios in the IIIe and IVe *arrondissements* were one in thirteen, and one in twenty-five. Although separate figures are not available for commercial premises only, it is clear from the Chamber of Commerce figures of industrial establishments in 1860 that the predominance of the west resulted from its great commercial and financial activity; the Ier and IIe *arrondissements* each had between six and seven thousand manufacturing concerns, while the IIIe had 11,647. The IVe had roughly the same number as the two western *arrondissements*.[46]

On the other hand, the Chamber of Commerce figures show that industry was still flourishing in the west, despite the growth of its commercial function. What then was the state of industry in the right bank centre during the Second Empire? In fact, the city's manufacturing was still concentrated there to a surprising extent. In 1860 34,471 concerns out of a total of 101,171 (34·08 per cent) were located in the right bank centre. Their rentable value represented an even

[42] *Chambers's Handy Guide to Paris* (1863), p. 31.
[43] Clunn, *The Face of Paris*, p. 68. The theatre was later converted into the Paramount cinema.
[44] Pierre Riquet, 'Le quartier de l'Opéra et l'évolution du centre d'affaires de Paris', p. 149, in *Urban Core and Inner City* (1967), pp. 141–61.
[45] Conseil général minutes, 27 November 1865, p. 8.
[46] *Statistique de l'industrie à Paris 1860*, p. xvii.

higher proportion of the city total—43·45 per cent.[47] A similar picture emerges from Haussmann's figures; although only one-fifth of the city's dwellings were in the right bank centre, that area had 37·81 per cent of the dwellings used exclusively for commerce or industry.[48] According to the Chamber of Commerce, the industries which were prepared to pay high rents to obtain a central location were those producing commodities for domestic consumption.[49] Such concerns often handled, or were at least closely connected with, the retail distribution of their products, and needed 'to establish their business in the centre of the capital in the luxurious and elegant surroundings demanded by our present customs and habits'.[50] Examples of such firms were the coachbuilders and confectioners that clustered in the north-west of the right bank centre. Consequently, industrial premises in the west were very much more valuable than in the east. The Ier and IIe *arrondissements* made up 12·55 per cent and 14·05 per cent respectively of the total rentable value of industrial premises in Paris. The IIIe *arrondissement*, despite the vastly greater number of its premises, represented only 10·04 per cent, and the poor IVe, only 6·81 per cent. In fact, the IVe was surpassed in this respect by the IXe (8·11 per cent) the XIe (7·48 per cent) and the Xe (7·44 per cent).[51] The higher rents of the west were weeding out the smaller concerns which might still flourish, with lower overheads, in the east.[52] Firms in the IIIe and IVe *arrondissements* employed an average of 4·3 and 3·0 hands respectively in 1860. In the Ier *arrondissement* the average labour force was 4·6, and in its northern neighbour, 6·0. The proportions of firms employing more than ten workers were as follows: Ier, one in ten; IIe, one in six; IIIe, one in eleven; IVe, one in seventeen.[53]

The extent to which rent levels were generally higher in the west becomes clear from the tabulations prepared by the City from taxation returns. Although each *arrondissement* had roughly the same number of buildings—the totals varied between 2,380 and 2,615—the total rentable value of private buildings in the western *arrondissements* was nearly twice as high as in the east in 1862. The total values in the Ier and IIe *arrondissements* were forty and forty-five million francs

---

[47] *Statistique de l'industrie à Paris 1860*, pp. xvii, xxix.
[48] Conseil général minutes, 27 November 1865, p. 8.
[49] *Statistique de l'industrie à Paris 1860*, p. xxxi.
[50] *Statistique de l'industrie à Paris 1860*, p. xxxi.
[51] *Statistique de l'industrie à Paris 1860*, p. xxix.
[52] In the early 1860s Ferdinand de Lasteyrie was writing of 'the accumulation of innumerable industries in the poorest streets' (*Les travaux de Paris*, p. 104n).
[53] *Statistique de l'industrie à Paris 1860*, p. xxxi.

respectively, and in the IIIe and IVe, only twenty-seven and twenty-two million francs.[54] The average value per building in all the western wards except Bonne-Nouvelle exceeded that of *any* eastern ward. But the most striking feature of the situation in 1862 was the predominance of average property values in four western and north-western wards—Place-Vendôme, Gaillon, Vivienne and Mail. Three wards—Bonne-Nouvelle, Saint-Germain-l'Auxerrois, and Halles—registered values similar to those in the IIIe *arrondissement*, which was significantly the better-off of the two eastern *arrondissements*. Palais-Royal had higher values than Saint-Germain-l'Auxerrois, but it was still well below the lowest of the top four wards, Mail. Significantly, the ward which included one side of the most prosperous section of the *grands boulevards*, Vivienne, had easily the highest average values of the right bank centre. The lowest were in Notre-Dame (IVe). As one would expect, low average property values coincided with a high population density. Five wards definitely exceeded 1,000 people to the hectare; they were Halles, Bonne-Nouvelle, Arts-et-Métiers, Enfants-Rouges and Saint-Gervais. And the net residential density of Saint-Germain-l'Auxerrois, excluding the area of the Louvre and its gardens, would almost certainly have been as high. So population was densest in the central core of wards along the Seine, and along the central spine formed by the Rue Saint-Denis and the Rue Saint-Martin.

Variations in site values within the right bank centre in the 1860s tell the same story.[55] Prices were highest in the north-west, near the *grands boulevards*, where they could go as high as 1,500 francs (£60) per square metre on the *boulevards* themselves or in newly-built wide streets nearby like the Rue du Dix-Décembre. Land was only slightly cheaper in the west of the Ier *arrondissement*, and sites around the Place du Théâtre-Français sold at 1,200 francs. Further east prices were much lower, and even in new streets like the Rue des Halles and the Rue du Pont-Neuf sites did not fetch more than 800 francs. But large sites very close to the Halles could go as high as 1,200 francs. On the other hand, prices could sink as low as 350 francs in the older streets. Even in the Rue Saint-Denis no site sold or valued in the 1860s fetched more than 650 francs per square metre. In the east of the right

---

[54] Commission des contributions directes, *Les propriétés bâties de la Ville de Paris en 1889 et en 1890* (1890), retrospective tables. Factories are included in the total.

[55] The following site value figures have been taken from *Le Guide Foncier: cours de la propriété foncière 1866–1885*, and from the *Gazette des Tribunaux*, which often gives the adjudicated value per square metre of land ceded to the highway under improvement line regulations.

bank centre price levels were even lower. Sites on the Boulevard Saint-Martin and the Boulevard du Temple, which enjoyed a certain commercial prosperity, were worth between 700 and 900 francs, and around the Place du Château-d'Eau they went as high as 1,200 francs, but further east, in the Boulevard Beaumarchais, land fetched only 340 francs. Even in new streets like the Rue de Turbigo land was worth only 700 francs, and prices tended to diminish the further one went east. To the west of the Rue du Temple, prices in the old streets varied between 250 and 500 francs, but to the east most sites were sold for 150–275 francs. Prices were generally lower in the IVe than in the IIIe *arrondissement*, and even in the Rue Saint-Antoine they did not exceed 380 francs. In the Cité, newly cleared sites were worth between 370 and 450 francs. Generally, land prices in old streets in any area were about half those current in new streets nearby. They confirm that Haussmann's new thoroughfares tended to eclipse the older streets.

3 THE RIGHT BANK CENTRE, 1870–1914

(a) The first two decades

After the disastrous events of the Commune the Paris economy was slow to recover, but in the second half of the 1870s business picked up well. There was a further extended recession in the mid-1880s, but a boom followed in the last years of the decade. We can best gauge the effect of this period of mixed fortunes on the right bank centre by examining changes in property values.

Total rentable values had increased since 1862 in all four *arrondissements*, and not significantly faster in the west than in the east.[56] In 1889 total values in the Ier *arrondissement* were 28 per cent higher than in 1862, and the rate of increase was the same in the IIe. The IVe *arrondissement* figure was slightly lower at 25 per cent, but that of the IIIe was slightly higher (30 per cent). These increases reflected to a very great extent the erection of new buildings, although the assessments of older buildings were regularly revised. So even with a building rate nearly twice as high as in the west, and in spite of lower demolition rates, the two eastern *arrondissements* were unable to catch up on their two western neighbours in terms of aggregate property values. In 1889 the total rentable value of properties in the IIIe and IVe *arrondissements* combined was only slightly higher than in the IIe *arrondissement* alone.

[56] The following figures have been calculated from *Les propriétés bâties de la Ville de Paris en 1889 et en 1890*.

The most spectacular increase in values was in the extreme west of the right bank centre. The aggregate of Place-Vendôme rose by 41 per cent, and that of Gaillon even more, by 50 per cent. The increase was not quite so marked in Palais-Royal, and Vivienne showed hardly any growth at all, but Halles and Saint-Germain-l'Auxerrois were even less favoured. On the other hand, in Mail and Bonne-Nouvelle values grew almost as fast as in Gaillon. In the east steady progress was made by all wards and only the one nearest the Châtelet, Sainte-Avoie, had less than a 25 per cent rate of increase. Appropriately, the fastest growing values were in the ward furthest away from the Châtelet, Enfants-Rouges. On the other hand, no ward had made really striking progress in the IVe *arrondissement* except Arsenal, which recorded a 70 per cent increase.

The ward figures help to confirm that new building was having a considerable influence on the development of aggregate values. However, houses built in connection with street improvements were always bigger and more luxurious than those erected in older streets, and this was another advantage for the west. The most striking example of the effect that a street scheme could have is afforded by Palais-Royal ward, where aggregate values appear to have risen only slightly between 1862 and 1878, but then increased by about 30 per cent between 1878 and 1889 after the construction of the Avenue de l'Opéra. The building of many new houses helps to explain the increase in values in Mail and Bonne-Nouvelle. On the other hand, it can only be a partial explanation of the big rise in Gaillon, where little new building was done. In fact, changes in the average value per property confirm that buildings in the extreme west and north-west were very much more valuable than those elsewhere, and were tending to become even more valuable. But they also suggest that extensive street improvements, at least in the west, resulted in a big increase of average values. In Palais-Royal the average value per property had nearly doubled by 1889, and in Gaillon the increase was 60 per cent. Both of these wards were affected by the Avenue de l'Opéra. A 58 per cent increase in Halles appears to have resulted almost entirely from public works. Place-Vendôme, with fewer improvements, enjoyed an increase of just over 40 per cent, the same as Bonne-Nouvelle. In the other wards of the west the percentage increase was slightly lower, varying between 25 and 35 per cent. In the eastern wards of the right bank centre the increase was sometimes as high as this or even higher; Arsenal, in particular, registered a rise of two-thirds. But as their values had been very low in 1862, these rates of increase were not enough to challenge the pre-eminence of the extreme western sector, composed of Palais-Royal, Place-Vendôme, Gaillon, Vivienne and Mail. In these wards, property values were very much higher in 1889 than anywhere else in the right bank centre.[57] This cannot be explained away by public works alone. Halles had been transformed more than any other ward by improvements, but its buildings still remained of relatively small value compared with its western neighbours. Indeed, Saint-Germain-l'Auxerrois, Halles and Bonne-Nouvelle were, as in 1862, little better off than the wards of the east, even though they had all benefited from public works during the Second Empire. At the same time, those eastern wards which had been lucky enough to see some improvements had undoubtedly drawn some benefit from them, and this is reflected in the increase in values in Arts-et-Métiers and Enfants-Rouges (Rue de Turbigo), and Arsenal and Notre-Dame (Boulevard Henri-IV, and clearance work in the Cité).[58]

The growing distinction between east and west in the right bank centre is also reflected in population changes. In Haussmann's time public works had brought about depopulation almost everywhere in the centre. The rate of depopulation between the censuses of 1861 and 1872 was greater in the two western *arrondissements* than in the eastern pair, but not very much greater. After 1870, however, depopulation was halted and even reversed in the east until the 1880s. The population of the IIIe *arrondissement* in 1872 was 89,687. By 1881 it had risen to 96,006, after which it began to fall slightly, declining to 87,617 in 1896. The IVe *arrondissement* showed this same slight decline in the 1880s, after reaching 103,260 in 1881 compared to 95,003 in 1872. By 1886 its population had fallen to 100,929, and ten years later it was 97,674. In contrast, the Ier *arrondissement* showed a steady decline from 74,286 in 1872 to 66,133 in 1896. But its northern neighbour had rather more in common with the east, for its population rose from 73,578 in 1872 to 77,442 in 1881, before starting a decline which left it with 67,167 inhabitants in 1896. The greatest population growth was in the poorer areas. The early increase in the IIe *arrondissement*, for instance, took place almost entirely in Bonne-Nouvelle, although

---

[57] Their pre-eminence is emphasised even more strongly by a table of average capital values per property, based on sales in 1888 and 1889, in *Les propriétés bâties de la Ville de Paris en 1889 et en 1890*, table iv.

[58] In 1888 the finance committee pointed out that rent increases in recent years had been sharpest in those areas where new streets had been constructed (C.M. reports, 1888, no. 38, p. 26).

the rich residential and business wards of Vivienne and Place-Vendôme show relatively large increases before 1881. But although the west follows the east in the 1870s, with growth in all wards except Palais-Royal (decimated by the Avenue de l'Opéra) and Gaillon before 1881, the decline of population in the richer wards of the west in the 1880s is very much more marked than in the east. By 1896 the populations of the Ier and IIe *arrondissements* had declined by 26·1 and 17·7 per cent since 1861, while the populations of the two eastern *arrondissements* had fallen by only 11·6 (IIIe) and 10·0 per cent (IVe).

Depopulation in the west was accompanied by growing commercialisation. The *Louvre* department store, for instance, began an extension programme after 1871.[59] In 1890 it employed 1,289 people, by which time it and other stores were beginning to have an adverse effect on long-established retail markets like that of the Temple.[60] The City Council became worried in the 1880s about the development of large industrial and commercial units which were squeezing out small concerns.[61] One such unit which hardly stopped growing was the *Crédit Lyonnais*, in the north-west of the right bank centre. In 1878 it built an office at the corner of the Rue de Choiseul and the Boulevard des Italiens. In 1882 more buildings were constructed, to make the whole complex three times bigger than in 1878. Further extensions in 1895, 1901, 1902 and 1913 resulted in the bank's occupation of a whole block, covering one hectare, compared with 600 square metres in 1878.[62]

Although figures are available to show the extent of occupation by commerce and industry after 1870, they cannot be directly correlated with those of the Second Empire.[63] However, like Haussmann's statistics, they do not distinguish purely industrial from purely commercial premises. But they clearly confirm the predominance of the west of the right bank centre as a business district. In 1889, 27·3 per cent of all premises were used for commerce or industry in the IIe *arrondissement*, and 25·1 per cent in the Ier. The IIIe *arrondissement* was less specialised, with 20·2 per cent, and the IVe registered only 14·3 per cent. The figures for factories, despite the very wide definition of the term, indicate that the east had more mechanised

---

[59] Hénard, *Rue Saint-Honoré*, vol II, p. 542n.

[60] Dr. Chassagne, *Dix-neuf ans du Conseil municipal* (1893), p. 38.

[61] C.M. reports, 1883, no. 8, p. 13. Baedeker stated that department stores were gradually superseding smaller shops because of their greater choice of goods (*Paris and Environs* [9th ed., 1888], p. 38).

[62] C.V.P., 23 February 1918, pp. 52–6.

[63] See note on sources, pp. 341–4.

industry. In 1890 there were twenty-seven factories in the IVe *arron-dissement*, and forty in the IIIe. The Ier *arrondissement* was relatively industrial, with as many as thirty-two factories, although only four of these were in the two western wards, and there were only twelve factories in the IIe *arrondissement*, nine of them in Bonne–Nouvelle. But not even the IIIe *arrondissement* could compare with the XIe, which had 147 factories. Moreover, a higher proportion of the premises in the XIe (25·7 per cent) were used for commerce or industry than in the IIIe. Although it is impossible to know whether industrial premises in buildings other than factories were similarly distributed, the evidence of contemporary observers suggests that it was still commerce and business, and not manufacturing, which gave most employment in the north-west of the right bank centre. The IIIe still seems to be the most industrial *arrondissement* of the four, and some manufacturing still goes on in the east of the Ier *arrondissement*. But the IVe *arrondissement* seems to have very little commerce *or* industry. The census returns, which provide figures for place of residence only, indicate that in 1886 fewer non-manual workers, such as clerks and shop assistants (*employés*) and more manual workers (*ouvriers*) lived in the IIIe than in any other right bank central *arrondissement*. In all its wards just over half of those exercising a remunerative activity were manual workers. Saint-Merri (IVe) also had just over 50 per cent manual workers, and Saint-Gervais (IVe) and Bonne-Nouvelle (IIe) had 49·5 and 48·4 per cent respectively. Saint-Germain-l'Auxerrois (Ier), Mail (IIe), and Notre-Dame (IVe) had over 40 per cent. Of the wards with between 30 and 40 per cent, only one, Arsenal, was in the east. The only ward with less than 30 per cent was Gaillon (21·4 per cent). The IIIe *arrondissement* was similar to those in the outer ring, all of which, except the XVIe and XVIIe, had more than 50 per cent manual workers. All the wards of the IIIe *arrondissement* had 20 per cent or less *employés*, while all the other wards of the right bank centre had between 20 and 30 per cent.[64] Finally, we must glance briefly at the two *arrondissements* which are already coming to rival the west of the right bank centre as a business district. The IXe, to the north-west, which contained Chaussée-d'Antin and the Gare Saint-Lazare, was already as commercialised as the Ier and IIe *arron-dissements*, with 26·9 per cent of its premises used for commerce or industry. But to the west, the VIIIe *arrondissement*, which included the Champs-Elysées, still had relatively few activities, with only

[64] *Résultats statistiques du dénombrement de 1886 pour la Ville de Paris*, pp. lv, lvi.

15·5 per cent of its premises having some business use. From now on, however, we shall have to pay increasing attention to these two areas in tracing the growth of the central business district of Paris.

Within each *arrondissement* of the right bank centre the distribution of activities in the 1880s is similar to that in Haussmann's time, although the westward movement within the Ier and IIe *arrondissements* seems accentuated, partly because of the building of the Avenue de l'Opéra, and partly because of the growth of the business centre near the Opéra, straddling the borders of the right bank centre, which was eclipsing the eastern wards of the two *arrondissements*. The movement of business and commerce out of the right bank centre altogether might well have been faster if the Avenue de l'Opéra had not been built. This thoroughfare became almost immediately the main shopping street of the interior of the right bank centre, and rivalled the *grands boulevards*. It clearly encouraged activity in Palais-Royal, transformed Gaillon, and its effect on Vivienne cannot have been inimical. In 1890 between 30 and 35 per cent of the premises in all these wards were used for commerce or industry. Compared to this diagonal axis of activity the rest of the west was relatively residential, with only 29·0 and 22·1 per cent of premises used for commerce or industry in Mail and Bonne-Nouvelle, and only 20·0 per cent in Place-Vendôme. Even Halles had only 24·8, and Saint-Germain-l'Auxerrois only 22·8 per cent. In the east of the right bank centre, only two wards, Arts-et-Métiers and Archives, had a higher proportion of commercial and industrial premises than Place-Vendôme, the most residential of the western wards. Arts-et-Métiers had 23·5 per cent, and Archives, 21·6 per cent. Enfants-Rouges was not far behind, with 19·2 per cent. But none of the other eastern wards had more than 17·5, and Notre-Dame had as little as 10·2 per cent.

As one might expect, commercial and industrial premises were most valuable in the areas of greatest concentration. Their average rentable value in 1890 was 2,307 francs in the IIe *arrondissement* and 2,183 in the Ier. The east was much worse off, with an average value of 1,235 francs in the IIIe and only 945 in the IVe *arrondissement*. The highest business rents in the right bank centre were in Gaillon, which registered an average rentable value of 4,085 francs, but in other western wards average values rose nowhere above about 2,800 francs. In the highly commercialised wards the value of business premises was much higher than that of residential accommodation. The most extreme case was again Gaillon, where the average rentable value of dwellings was

1,502 francs, compared to 4,085 francs for business premises. Yet the wards of the extreme west had much higher residential rentable values than elsewhere. Place-Vendôme (1,585 francs), Gaillon (1,502 francs) and Palais-Royal (1,134 francs) were the only wards of the right bank centre where the average value of a dwelling exceeded 1,000 francs.

Another index of economic activity is provided by traffic movements. Exhaustive traffic censuses were rare, and the only figures that are available for this period are those obtained by the public works department in 1881 and 1882.[65] They show that the greatest concentration of traffic was to be found in the new streets, and in those few older thoroughfares, like the *grands boulevards*, that were of adequate width. However, right bank central traffic was much denser to the west of the Boulevard de Sébastopol, while the proportion of goods vehicles was much higher in the east, and around the Halles. In all the eastern streets covered by the census, 50 per cent or more of vehicles were carrying goods. The most frequented street was the Avenue de l'Opéra, with 36,200 units of traffic in twenty-four hours. The Boulevard des Italiens had only 23,700 units, but this was more than in any other central street except the access roads to the Halles.[66] Taken as a whole, the *grands boulevards* had more traffic than most streets inside the right bank centre, and they had an extremely low proportion of goods traffic. The most frequented streets, both inside and outside the right bank centre, were those which led to or crossed the area of the Opéra. In contrast, the Rue de Rivoli had an average of only 11,400 traffic units, 30 per cent of which were goods vehicles. The Boulevard de Sébastopol, although it led to two railway termini, had only 9,600 units, half of them being goods traffic. But these figures were high compared to most eastern streets, with only a few exceptions, namely the eastern *grands boulevards*, the Rue de Turbigo, the Rue de Rivoli–Saint-Antoine, and the Quai de l'Hôtel-de-Ville, which had up to 11,000 traffic units. The older streets had between 2–4,000 units, the majority of which were goods vehicles. The Rue Saint-Denis and the Rue Saint-Martin between them carried less traffic than the parallel Boulevard de Sébastopol.

[65] Commission d'extension de Paris, *Considérations techniques préliminaires* (1913), plate 96. A full explanation is given of the method of the census. The unit used was the 'collier', which was one horse attached to a vehicle. A vehicle drawn by two horses counted as two units.

[66] One foreigner on a visit to Paris in 1878 took three-quarters of an hour to pass through the Boulevard Saint-Denis in his carriage (Edmondo de Amicis, *Ricordi di Parigi* [Milan, 1928], pp. 8–9).

We must now begin to look at the right bank centre in the context of the city as a whole. It was already declining somewhat from the pre-eminent position which it had maintained and even enhanced under Haussmann. Just as it housed a decreasing proportion of the population the centre also represented a declining proportion of total property values, despite the expansion of commerce there. In 1862 the rentable value of houses and factories in the right bank centre had been 32 per cent of the Paris total. By 1889 this proportion had fallen to 22 per cent. Of course, this was largely the result of new building on the outskirts where land was readily available. But the expansion of business in the wealthy residential areas of the north-west of the right bank centre inevitably displaced part of the well-to-do population. This was an ominous trend for the right bank centre, for there was a danger that business might once again follow the rich into the new wealthy residential districts, and leave the central area altogether. By the late 1880s the wealthiest sector of Paris from the point of view of residence was composed of all the VIIIe *arrondissement*, Chaussée-d'Antin (IXe), Plaine-Monceau (XVIIe), Porte-Dauphine and Les-Bassins (XVIe), Invalides and Saint-Thomas-d'Aquin (VIIe), and Place-Vendôme (Ier).[68] The movement of the most select residential area across the city was like a carpet unrolling at one end while being rolled up at the other. The taxable value of dwellings on the western and north-western fringes of the right bank centre was everywhere lower than in neighbouring wards outside the *grands boulevards*. This difference was greatest in the west; in the north-west and north it was far smaller, and in the east of the right bank centre the wards outside the *grands boulevards* had lower average values than their neighbours inside the right bank centre.

The census returns confirm this general picture. In 1886 only twelve Paris wards had 400 or more female servants for every 1,000 households of two or more persons. Only two of these, Place-Vendôme and Gaillon, were in the right bank centre, while the others were in the VIIe, VIIIe, IXe and XVIe *arrondissements*. The VIIIe was the only *arrondissement* all of whose wards were in this category, which the census authorities designated as a 'luxury' area. Only three right bank central wards were in the next category, designated as 'rich', with between 300 and 399 female servants. They were Palais-Royal, Vivienne and Halles. Two were 'very well-off', with 200-299 servants—

---

[68] These wards had the highest average taxable value of dwellings in Paris (C.M. reports, 1888, no. 38, annex 7).

Saint-Germain-l'Auxerrois and Arsenal. Finally, Bonne-Nouvelle and the whole of the east of the right bank centre except Arsenal, were 'well-off', with between 100 and 199 female servants.[69] Servants were numerous in the west of the right bank centre because the class of employers (*patrons*) was so well represented there. Just over half (50·6 per cent) of individuals living in Gaillon and exercising some remunerative activity were employers. Palais-Royal, Place-Vendôme and Vivienne had over 40 per cent employers. No ward in the west of the right bank centre had less than 30 per cent, except Bonne-Nouvelle (29·2 per cent), while in the east only two, Archives and Arsenal, had more than 30 per cent. On the other hand, Gaillon's proportion of 50·6 per cent was exceeded in Odéon (VIe), three wards in the VIIe, all the VIIIe, and Porte-Dauphine (XVIe).

(b) Developments after 1890

After the 1880s the increase of property values in the right bank centre slowed down, except in the extreme west and north-west. In the east, the beginnings of a decline in values set in. Between 1889 and 1910 the total rentable values of buildings in the Ier *arrondissement* increased by 8·5 per cent, in the IIe by 4·3 per cent, and in the IVe by 4·5 per cent. Values in the IIIe *arrondissement fell* by 2·8 per cent. These changes must be contrasted with rises in all four *arrondissements* of between 25 and 30 per cent in the 1862–89 period. The fall in the IIIe *arrondissement* took place between 1889 and 1900, after which its rentable values again began to rise slowly. Largely to blame for this general deceleration was the lower construction rate, which in turn resulted from the smaller number of street improvement schemes carried out. There was less speculation on property after the 1880s, and the average capital value of Paris buildings stabilised until about 1910, when renewed speculation brought about a further increase.[70] In the city as a whole, where more new building was going on, rentable values rose by 32 per cent between 1889 and 1910. So in 1910 the total rentable value of the right bank centre was only 17 per cent of that of the whole city, compared with 22 per cent in 1889, and 32 per cent in 1862. The amount of new building, however, was not the only factor affecting these changes in values. Also influential was the slower economic development of the centre, as we shall see later.

[69] *Résultats statistiques du dénombrement de 1886 pour la Ville de Paris*, p. lviii.
[70] G. Duon, 'Evolution de la valeur vénale des immeubles de rapport', *Journal de la Société de Statistique de Paris*, 1940, nos. 9–10, p. 180.

Only in the extreme west and in the south-east of the right bank centre did values continue to increase rapidly. By 1910 Place-Vendôme had registered a 23 per cent increase in the aggregate value of its buildings since 1889, the highest of the whole right bank centre. Place-Vendôme now overtook Palais-Royal, where the growth in values which resulted from the building of the Avenue de l'Opéra had not persisted. Even Halles and Saint-Germain-l'Auxerrois, with 7 and 5 per cent growth respectively, did better than Palais-Royal, although these increases appear to have reflected mainly the demolition of some of the wards' older buildings in street improvement schemes and their replacement by a few new houses. In the IIe *arrondissement* Gaillon did well, with 17 per cent growth, but in its other wards values stabilised or, in the case of Bonne-Nouvelle, declined. So after 1889 Place-Vendôme took the place of Gaillon as the fastest developing ward, from the point of view of total rentable values, in the right bank centre. But Gaillon still led in terms of growth of average rentable value per building, with a 29 per cent increase since 1889, compared with 25 per cent in Place-Vendôme. The number of units of accommodation in Place-Vendôme had risen more sharply than in any other right bank central ward since 1889, mainly as a result of extensive hotel development there, while Gaillon had registered a reduction. Moreover, the number of commercial and industrial premises had stabilised in Gaillon, but in Place-Vendôme it had increased by nearly one-quarter. However, owing once again to the building of a number of hotels, each of whose rooms was counted as one unit of accommodation, the proportion of industrial and commercial premises in Place-Vendôme dropped from 20·0 per cent in 1889 to 18·6 per cent in 1911. In Gaillon, partly as a result of the decline in the total of units of accommodation, the proportion of industrial and commercial premises had risen to 34·8 per cent from 30·9 in 1889. The growth of values in Place-Vendôme reflects the rapid commercialisation of a ward which had previously seemed to be somewhat isolated from the development of the north-west central business district. For the causes of this phenomenon it is again necessary to look outside the right bank centre.

We have seen how in the first half of the century the more prosperous classes tended to move north and north-west into areas beyond the *grands boulevards* like Chaussée-d'Antin, and that they were followed by luxury commerce and sophisticated business activities. But as early as the 1840s the growing commercialisation of these districts was depriving them of their attraction as a place of residence. Although

Chaussée-d'Antin could still be described as an 'aristocratic' district, it was now considered inferior to the Faubourg Saint-Honoré, in the VIIIe *arrondissement*. The two embassies of Naples and Belgium, which had helped give the district its cachet, had already moved elsewhere.[71] Expanding business was causing congestion in the streets. The area which benefited most from Chaussée-d'Antin's fall from favour was that of the Champs-Elysées and the Faubourg Saint-Honoré, between the Place de la Concorde and the Etoile, to the west of the old city centre.[72] And it attracted aristocratic and well-to-do residents not only from Chaussée-d'Antin, but also from the declining aristocratic district of the Faubourg Saint-Germain to the south, on the left bank of the Seine.[73] Unlike the Faubourg Saint-Germain it was conveniently close to the new north-western business district and to the traditional centre of activities around the Halles and the Bank of France. The leafy glades of the Champs-Elysées themselves, which the City had purchased from the State in 1828,[74] offered a calm and sylvan charm which had long since been lost on the *grands boulevards*. Although by 1845 there were still only four aristocratic mansions in the Champs-Elysées, many more were soon to be built there.[75] In the 1860s English tourists were told that the Champs-Elysées and the Faubourg Saint-Honoré were, together with the Faubourg Saint-Germain, the most aristocratic residential districts in Paris, although Chaussée-d'Antin remained the favourite quarter of the great capitalists.[76] Under the Second Empire the creation of a star-shaped network of streets around the Etoile, which was linked to the Gare Saint-Lazare, the Opéra and the *grands boulevards* by the Avenue de Friedland— Boulevard Haussmann artery, greatly encouraged the development of the western end of the Champs-Elysées as a residential district. The well-to-do, encouraged by the imperial improvement policy, even began to move south-west from the Etoile into the XVIe *arrondissement*, towards the Bois de Boulogne, which Haussmann developed as Paris's Hyde Park. The Champs-Elysées now took the place of the Rue de la Chaussée-d'Antin as the residential axis of well-to-do Paris. By 1903, seventy-four mansions had been built along it.[77] Although

[71] Achard, 'Rue de la Chaussée-d' Antin', pp. 45–6.
[72] For a geographical study of the development of the Champs-Elysées, see Klaus D. Wiek, *Kurfürstendamm und Champs-Elysées: geographischer Vergleich zweier Weltstrassen-Gebiete* (1967).
[73] Daumard, *Maisons de Paris*, p. 146.
[74] Wiek, *Kurfürstendamm und Champs-Elysées*, p. 16.   [75] Wiek, p. 16.
[76] *Chambers's Handy Guide to Paris* (1863), pp. 31, 52.
[77] Wiek, *Kurfürstendamm und Champs-Elysées*, p. 16.

Chaussée-d'Antin and nearby areas did not lose their predominantly residential character for some years,[78] they had become much more suitable for the expansion of business than of residence. On the other hand, the Champs-Elysées could not remain a purely residential area. The proximity of a wealthy clientele soon began to attract luxury commerce, just as it had in Chaussée-d'Antin in the first half of the century. Theatres were opened, and some mansions were converted to commercial purposes.[79] Increasing traffic congestion to the east and north-east, and the introduction of the automobile, helped to make the Champs-Elysées the centre of the bourgeois life of the capital by 1914.[80] The number of mansions used for residence began to fall after 1903, and the last private house to be sited on the Champs-Elysées was built just before the Great War.[81] By 1913, 131 businesses or commercial activities were being carried on along the Champs-Elysées.[82] This development made the area an increasingly attractive site for the erection of hotels, and apartments there were among the most expensive in Paris at the turn of the century.[83] It was largely as a result of growth in this area that the proportion of premises used for business in the VIIIe *arrondissement* rose from 15·50 per cent in 1889 to 22·65 per cent in 1900, and to 25·73 per cent in 1911.

Within the right bank centre Place-Vendôme was the ward best situated to take advantages of this shift in the equilibrium of middle-class residence towards the west. Luxury commerce no longer wished to locate itself on the Boulevard des Italiens or the Avenue de l'Opéra, which were much less accessible from the Champs-Elysées and the west than from the north-west. Nor had a location on the Champs-Elysées themselves become decisively attractive before 1914, because while the Opéra district remained prosperous, it was dangerous to move too far away.[84] So the most sought-after locations were those that were easily

---

[78] As late as 1888 Baedeker describes the Rue Laffitte, Rue Taitbout and Rue de la Chaussée-d'Antin as chiefly inhabited by moneyed men and wealthy bankers (*Paris and Environs* [9th ed., 1888], p. 75).

[79] Jules Bertaut, *Paris 1870–1935* (English ed., 1936), pp. 216–17.

[80] Riquet, 'Le quartier de l'Opéra', p. 153. For an appraisal of the depressive effect of traffic congestion on business in central areas, see D. F. Medhurst and J. Parry Lewis, *Urban Decay* (1969), p. 75.

[81] Wiek, *Kurfürstendamm und Champs-Elysées*, p. 16; Paul Cohen-Portheim, *The Spirit of Paris* (1937), p. 25.

[82] Wiek, p. 121.

[83] Karl Baedeker, *Paris and Environs* [16th ed., 1907], p. 3; An English Officer, *Society Recollections in Paris and Vienna 1879–1904* (1907), p. 57.

[84] Baedeker warned that although the hotels in and near the Champs-Elysées were pleasant, they were rather far from the centre of attractions—although this inconvenience was mitigated by the construction of the *Métro* (*Paris and Environs* [16th ed., 1907], p. 3.)

accessible from both, in the Rue Royale, the Rue de la Paix, and the Place-Vendôme. The movement of fashionable commerce to these new locations began in the 1880s. New hotels began to open, and the number of hotel and boarding-house rooms in Place-Vendôme ward rose from 1,288 in 1889 to 3,281 in 1901. The Place-Vendôme itself became the centre of a group of exclusive hotels after the Ritz opened there. Maxim's and the Café Weber helped to raise the tone of the Rue Royale.[85] By the early 1900s Place-Vendôme had become the centre of the Paris fashion trade, with shops selling all the essentials of feminine elegance. By 1909 the Place Vendôme was occupied mainly by luxurious hotels and insurance companies.[86] Between 1901 and 1910 the rentable value of the twenty-four buildings in the square rose by 53 per cent, and in four of them the increase was of 160 per cent.[87] Gaillon also benefited greatly from the new trend, just as it had from the previous expansion of commerce towards the north-west, but the rest of the right bank centre was not so lucky. Even so recently prosperous a ward as Palais-Royal now found itself on the fringes of the new fashionable district, although there was some growth in the hotel trade there. In 1884 the famous Café de la Rotonde in the Palais-Royal had to close its doors, and it was demolished before the end of the decade.[88] The shops in the Palais-Royal were deserted, and the whole ward suffered.[89] Shops in the Avenue de l'Opéra could no longer attract a high-class clientele, and were forced to lower their prices and the quality of their wares. The ward's City councillor, F. Levée, elected in 1898, regretted that so many traders had moved from his ward to the Rue de la Paix and the Rue Royale, because it was 'not easily accessible to members of elegant society who travel in carriages and even in motorcars'.[90] He called for extensive street improvements to revive the ward's economic activity.

The effect of this westward trend was to destroy the homogeneity

---

[85] Bertaut, *Paris*, p. 216.

[86] Georges Cain, *Walks in Paris* (1909), pp. 301, 313. According to Baedeker the hotels in or near the Place-Vendôme were the most fashionable in Paris (*Paris and Environs* [16th ed., 1907], p. 3).

[87] Louis Dausset, *Rapport général . . . sur . . . le projet de budget de la Ville de Paris pour 1911*, p. 44 (C.M. reports, 1910, no. 91). By 1910 all the floors of all the houses in the square were occupied by business activities.

[88] Baedeker, [9th ed., 1888], p. 57.

[89] In 1910 shops in the Palais-Royal could hardly command rents of more than 1,000–1,500 francs, whereas they had once been as high as 5,000 francs (Dausset, *Rapport général . . . pour 1911*, p. 44).

[90] Ernest Gay, *Nos édiles* (1911), p. 46. The ward had become notoriously congested, partly owing to the proximity of the Halles, which in themselves must have been a serious embarrassment to high-class traders (see C.M. reports, 1882, no. 62, p. 2; 1890, no. 13).

of the group of five western wards all of whose property values were developing rapidly up to 1889, and which appeared then to form a cohesive centre of activity. Changes in the average value per building show that whereas Gaillon and Place-Vendôme were developing almost as quickly as before 1889, the rate of increase had slowed in Mail, while values remained stable in Palais-Royal and Vivienne. Vivienne, the ward of the Bourse, had been eclipsed by 1910. In 1862 its average rentable value had been by far the highest in the IIe *arrondissement* and the whole of the right bank centre. In 1910 it had been overtaken by Gaillon and Place-Vendôme, and Palais-Royal and Mail had almost caught up with it. Such wards as Vivienne, whose commercial development had begun very early in the century, ran the risk as a result of their long prosperity of becoming completely built up. Only big companies and public bodies, such as the *Crédit Lyonnais* and the Bank of France, had the resources or the powers to extend their existing buildings. Other expanding concerns were forced to leave the central wards. In any case, offices no longer needed to be concentrated in certain areas after the introduction of new means of communication such as pneumatic letter delivery and the telephone. And building land was more expensive inside the right bank centre, no doubt owing to the great shortage of virgin sites, even than in the newly prosperous wards of the VIIIe and IXe *arrondissements*. In 1901 a square metre of land was worth 702 francs in Place-Vendôme and 1,041 francs in Gaillon, compared to 617 and 813 francs in the corresponding neighbouring wards outside the *grands boulevards*.

Between 1900 and 1910 average capital values of properties in Place-Vendôme and Gaillon increased so fast that they overtook their neighbours outside the *grands boulevards*, Madeleine and Chaussée-d'Antin. In fact, in 1910 the average capital value of Gaillon's properties was the highest in Paris, followed closely by Chaussée-d'Antin, with Place-Vendôme in third place. The only other right bank central ward to show a similar rate of increase was Saint-Germain-l'Auxerrois. Values were stable or only slightly increased in the other wards with the exception of Halles, Vivienne, Bonne-Nouvelle and Archives, where the average capital value fell.[91] This stagnation of most of the west of the right bank centre, as well as the east, reflects its declining commercial importance, which can best be judged from the published returns of the business tax (*patentes*).[92] In 1873 26·73 per cent of the total

[91] *Livre Foncier*, 1900–1902, 2nd part, graph no. 2; *Livre Foncier*, 1911, graph no. 13.
[92] *Ann. Stat.*

product of the tax came from businesses in the first two *arrondisse-ments* alone, while those of the IXe *arrondissement* provided only 4·94 per cent, and the VIIIe even less, 2·29 per cent. But as early as 1880 the IXe *arrondissement* was providing 13·48 per cent of the total return from the tax, and its share continued to rise until in 1910 it was 19·83 per cent. In the VIIIe *arrondissement* business expansion was not so rapid, but by 1910 the *patentes* return there was 7·48 per cent of the Paris total. In the meantime, the shares of the Ier and IIe *arrondissements* had fallen to 10·97 and 12·36 per cent respectively. Their eclipse is just as striking when expressed in absolute terms. In the IIe *arrondissement* 12,674 businesses paid 7,273,199 francs in tax in 1873; in 1910, 11,769 businesses paid no more than 8,778,679 francs.[93] But in the IXe *arrondissement*, 10,838 businesses paid 2,249,107 francs in 1873; in 1910, 16,849 of them paid 14,085,045 francs. Admittedly, the return rose slightly more in the Ier than in the IIe *arrondissement*; and in the VIIIe *arrondissement* it did not rise as quickly as in the IXe, until the war. And the areas of the VIIIe and IXe *arrondissements* were much greater than those of their two right bank central neighbours. But these trends do not reflect a mere expansion of an existing business centre whose roots remained firmly fixed. There is a definite shift in the centre of gravity towards the west and north-west, and the five-fold increases of the *patentes* return in the VIIIe *arrondissement*, and the six-fold increase in the IXe, occurred during a period when the total product in the city as a whole rose by less than half.

The east of the right bank centre, even further removed from the new residential areas, was at an even greater disadvantage than in the past, especially now that its building rate was slowing down. In the IIIe *arrondissement* total rentable values were stable between 1889 and 1910 in three wards out of four, and fell in Sainte-Avoie. The IVe *arrondissement* was slightly better off because although values were stable in Saint-Merri and Saint-Gervais, they rose by nearly 10 per cent in Arsenal and nearly 20 per cent in Notre-Dame. New building was still going on apace in Arsenal, and in Notre-Dame, although few houses were built, the Île Saint-Louis was again attracting middle-class residents who were improving and enlarging the houses along the *quais*. In fact, the most striking feature of the years after 1889 is the stagnation of property values in the central core of wards in the right bank centre, except in the Ier *arrondissement*. This meant

93 The rate of taxation remained the same throughout this period.

that the oldest and most closely built wards of the centre were no longer benefiting from a general rise in values as had been the case under Haussmann and in the early years of the Third Republic. This phenomenon was clearly observed by contemporaries. Louis Dausset wrote in 1910 that rent increases were most marked in new houses, and that the old houses of the centre, which did not conform to modern standards, would soon be completely deserted if it were not for the housing shortage.[94] The motorcar and the *Métro* made the outskirts more attractive to the middle classes, and apartments there competed more and more fiercely for tenants with central accommodation.[95] So the old houses of the centre were abandoned to the working classes and an accelerated degradation.

The population of these poorer areas stabilised or even began to increase. That of the IIIe *arrondissement* rose from 85,062 in 1886 to 88,680 in 1891, and although it subsequently declined, it still had a higher population in 1911 (85,763) than in 1886. In the IVe *arrondissement* the population rose from 98,644 to 100,408 between 1891 and 1911. There was no expansion of business to drive out residents, as in some of the western wards. In the IIIe *arrondissement* the proportion of premises used for commerce or industry, excluding premises in factories, fell from 20·2 per cent in 1889 to 19·5 per cent in 1911. In the IVe it fell from 14·3 per cent to 13·1. All the wards of the east shared in this reduction. The number of businesses paying the *patentes* tax fell from 12,059 to 10,244 in the IIIe *arrondissement* between 1880 and 1910, and in the IVe from 7,611 to 6,932. And this was clearly not the result of any expansion or concentration of units, for the product of the tax remained stable in the IVe *arrondissement* and actually fell in the IIIe from just over three million francs in 1880 to just over two and a half million in 1910. Of course, these figures do not distinguish between commercial and industrial uses, but the separate statistics for factories suggest a considerable flight of industry from the east. In 1911 the IIIe *arrondissement* retained only eighteen of the forty factories working there in 1889, and the IVe's total had fallen from twenty-seven to twenty-two. Of course, pressure on industry in the east did not result, as in the west, from the competition of commercial users prepared to pay higher rents, but there was a more limited form of pressure in the shape of stable or rising residential rents in the east of the right bank centre, at a time when they were declining in the west.

[94] Louis Dausset, *Rapport général . . . pour 1911*, p. 44.
[95] Commission d'extension de Paris, *Considérations techniques préliminaires* (1913), p. 85n.

Between 1889 and 1911 the average rentable value of dwellings in the Ier *arrondissement* fell from 916 to 787 francs, and from 671 to 578 francs in the IIe. During the same period the average rentable value in the IIIe *arrondissement* fell by only fifteen francs to 460 francs, and in the IVe it increased from 450 to 466 francs.[96] Shortage of space for expansion or for the installation of machinery was perhaps an even more important factor in driving out the more prosperous concerns, now that almost all vacant sites had been built on. And the City of Paris was becoming more and more stringent in its attitude to unhealthy industries, which were discouraged in densely populated districts. Building regulations were also tightened up; the rules governing the construction of flues inside houses, for instance, were made increasingly strict between the 1870s and the 1890s, and must have prevented many conversions of houses into workshops.[97] And while industry declined, lodging houses grew rapidly in numbers. In the IIIe *arrondissement* there were 369 of them in 1913 compared to 296 in 1890, and in the IVe they had increased from 578 to 628. Yet during this period the total of lodging houses remained stable in the IIe *arrondissement*, and fell slightly in the Ier.[98] The poverty of the residents of the east, compared to those of the west, emerges clearly from an estimate of the average annual income of households in each ward made in 1902 on the basis of the rentable value of dwellings.[99] The poorest central ward was Saint-Gervais, with an estimated average income of 1,910 francs (£76 8s. od.). This ward also had the biggest concentration of lodging houses in the centre—316 of them in 1900. Seven wards had estimated average incomes of between 2,000 and 3,000 francs; all of them, with the exception of Bonne-Nouvelle and Mail, were in the east. Three wards averaged between 3,000 and 4,000. Two of them, Arsenal and Notre-Dame, were in the east, and the other was Halles. The remaining five wards, all of them in the west, averaged over 4,000 francs, and Gaillon and Place-Vendôme stood out, with average household incomes of over 10,000 francs. Figures for the numbers of lifts tell the same story. In 1900 the Ier and IIe *arrondissements* had 152 and 105 lifts respectively but there were only twenty-one in the IVe and eleven in the IIIe *arrondissement*.[100] So the extreme west still

[96] *Les propriétés bâties de la Ville de Paris*, 1890, graph no. 4; *Livre Foncier*, 1911, graph no. 9.
[97] *A.P.s*, 8 August 1874; 15 January 1881; 25 November 1897.
[98] *Ann. Stat.*, annual tables of lodging houses inspected by the police.
[99] *Livre Foncier*, 1900, 1902, 2nd part, table VI. No equivalent figures appear in the edition of 1911.
[100] *Livre Foncier*, 1900, 1902, 2nd part, table V.

had the most prosperous residents as well as the most prosperous activities.

But it was not clear how long this state of affairs would last, for the richer residents of the west were moving slowly out. Unlike that of the east, the west's population continued to fall. Between 1891 and 1911 that of the Ier *arrondissement* fell from 66,133 to 58,751, and in the IIe *arrondissement* it fell from 67,167 to 59,594. And the accompanying fall in the average rentable values indicates that it was the poorer resident who was staying behind. This depopulation resulted, as we have seen, partly from the pressure of commercial expansion, which was particularly strong in such rich residential areas as Place-Vendôme, and partly from the growing ease of access to the outskirts coupled with the obsolescence and inconvenience of the older buildings of the centre, fewer and fewer of which were being replaced by new buildings as time went on. Commercialisation seems to have been the dominant influence on population in the Ier *arrondissement*, where the proportion of premises used for commerce, industry, and hotels rose from 38 per cent in 1889 to 44 per cent in 1911, mainly as a result of an increase from 36 to 59 per cent in Place-Vendôme. It was apparently less influential in the IIe *arrondissement*, where the proportion of such premises remained stable.

From 1900 the right bank centre was affected increasingly by the operation of the *Métro*. It appears to have accelerated existing trends rather than to have modified them. Contemporaries noticed that after the first lines were built, the depopulation and commercialisation of the centre were more pronounced, and that congestion there was increased.[101] But the *Métro* accentuated the growing dichotomy between west and east in the centre, for the biggest concentration of lines and stations was created in the existing central business district around the Opéra. The east of the right bank centre, relatively badly served, was now at an even greater disadvantage than before. At first, Gaillon and Place-Vendôme benefited from this accentuation of business functions in the central business district of which they were still an important part. But in the long term, as the *Métro* became congested and began to create its own congestion on the streets above, the wards on the south-east fringes of the central business district were

[101] See, for instance, C.M. reports, 1912, no. 95, pp. 378, 384. The single price ticket encouraged Parisians to travel even long distances into the centre.

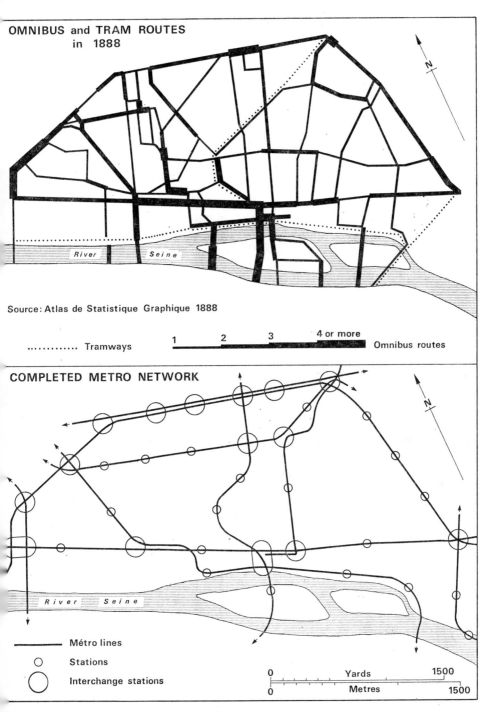

OMNIBUS and TRAM ROUTES
in 1888

River Seine

Source: Atlas de Statistique Graphique 1888

.... Tramways

1   2   3   4 or more

Omnibus routes

COMPLETED METRO NETWORK

River Seine

——— Métro lines

○ Stations

⭕ Interchange stations

0   Yards   1500

0   Metres   1500

FIG. 3. *Public transport in the right bank centre.*

7

bound to suffer more than those which lay nearer the Gare Saint-Lazare. As the population of the conurbation grew, more and more people came in to work, shop and do business from outside the city boundaries. Most of them had to travel by rail, because the *Métro* hardly penetrated at all into the suburbs. So it was in the interest of shops and businesses to move closer to the railway termini, to spare employees and customers a further uncomfortable journey in the *Métro*. And of course, the Gare Saint-Lazare, with its teeming suburban network, was the biggest pole of attraction.

The deceleration or decline of commercialisation everywhere except in the extreme west was a depressing augury for the future of the right bank centre. But the immediate problem area was the central core and the east. As the number of dwellings in the centre declined, pressure on the remaining accommodation increased. Cheap accommodation for the working classes was especially in demand, because street improvements had always swept away many more working-class than middle-class dwellings, and because private building enterprise was increasingly unable to supply new accommodation at low rents anywhere in the city, and certainly not in the centre. Low rent districts consequently became even more densely populated, and the degradation of their buildings was accelerated. This process was particularly advanced in the wards of Saint-Merri, Sainte-Avoie and Saint-Gervais, which contained the only two unhealthy areas designated in the right bank centre, but there was clearly a danger that, as commerce, industry and better-off residents moved elsewhere, this same blight would spread throughout the entire area. But suddenly war intervened. And from it emerged a totally new situation, which was to have a profound influence on the development of the right bank centre.

7

The Battle for Preservation,
1850-1914

Just as the demand for improvements which was met by Napoleon III and Haussmann was the result of years of inaction in the face of growing problems, so was it perhaps to be expected that the demolition of many hundreds of old houses and the loss of familiar scenes would produce a reaction by a section of informed opinion in favour of conservation. This reaction was still very weak before 1870, but it grew greatly in strength under the Third Republic. By 1914 it had led to the establishment of a number of preservation societies and had influenced the policies of both the City of Paris and the Government. It is the aim of this chapter to study the evolution of this reaction, and its effect on the planning of Paris.

During the Second Empire the call for preservation was muted. Although personalities like Chateaubriand, Montalembert and Victor Hugo had been attacking vandalism for some years, and the Government had accepted responsibility for the protection of ancient monuments since the 1830s, the evident need to modernise Paris was enough to drown what protests there were. Moreover, Haussmann's approach to planning was comprehensive enough to allow him to meet these critics on their own ground. If they objected to the loss of beautiful buildings and streets, he could put forward a conception of urban aesthetics which would justify his actions. He replied to those who attacked him for destroying historical evidence by encouraging historical research so that full details could be kept of all that was lost, and by developing a Paris museum. And however deficient his policies may have been in both these respects, the disarray of his opponents ensured that he was protected from effective criticism during the period of his administration.

The irony of the situation was that although Napoleon III and Haussmann wanted to make Paris the most beautiful city in the world, they were both singularly deprived of artistic talent. Haussmann was often annoyed by the Emperor's failure to appreciate the pains he took:

> 'The Emperor, who so often revealed such good taste, used to complain that I put too much art into planning. He said that I did too much to get the lines of streets just right, and that I tried too hard to find focal points to justify the direction they took.'[1]

But Haussmann's art did not go beyond geometrical layouts and rigid symmetry. In private he was prepared to admit to being totally ignorant in all artistic matters.[2] Yet, however regrettable his insensitivity to the charm of variegated, symmetrical townscapes may have appeared to his critics, it enabled him to proceed with sublime confidence in imposing a rectilinear aesthetic on Paris ⟨*see* plates 24, 25⟩.

The principles of regularity and symmetry had been applied to all planned new development in Paris since the Renaissance,[3] but until the Second Empire almost all this development took place outside, or on the fringes of, the built-up area. Haussmann now applied rectilinear planning to the very oldest areas in the city. He was not aware of any serious problems here. He respected all the city's large monuments because they provided focal points for his new streets. But he was not interested in undistinguished domestic architecture, however ancient, which he considered fit only to be demolished, or, if this were impossible, to be hidden away behind the regular façades of his new thoroughfares. He once told Achille Fould, Minister of Finance:

> 'I am no more of an enthusiast for old masonry than you are, if it has no breath of art to bring it to life.'[4]

But if Haussmann thought that a monument could play an effective

---

[1] Haussmann, *Mémoires*, vol. II, p. 523.
[2] See letter from Prosper Mérimée to Madame Lenormant, 6 June 1867, in *Lettres à Viollet-le-Duc*, ed. P. Trahard (1927), p. 211.
[3] See *Paris: croissance d'une capitale* (1961), p. 108; Pierre Lavedan, *Histoire de l'urbanisme*, vol. II (1959) and vol. III (1952). For the influence of French geometrical planning abroad, see, for instance, Elbert Peets, 'L'Enfant's Washington', *Town Planning Review*, vol. XV, no. 3, May 1933, pp. 155–64.
[4] Haussmann, *Mémoires*, vol. III, p. 501.

visual role in his new Paris, attention would be lavished on it. It would be restored, isolated by the demolition of surrounding buildings, and made visible from great distances along the new avenues. Other old buildings, which he considered unworthy of such exaltation, would have to take their chance. Haussmann did not even consider such erections to be monuments at all, and so could honestly write in answer to later detractors:

> 'But, my good fellows—you who seem to have seen nothing beyond the gloom of your libraries—name me just one ancient monument of interest, just one building of artistic value, destroyed by my administration!'[5]

On the contrary, claimed Haussmann, he had never interfered with an interesting monument 'except in order to isolate it, enhance its value, and provide as beautiful a view of it as possible'.[6] Of course, the facts contradict him. Because he insisted on rectilinear thoroughfares, the choice of existing large buildings as terminal points placed everything else in the vicinity at risk. Even churches could not command greater flexibility. The choir of the church of Saint-Leu was cut off by the Boulevard de Sébastopol, when a slight inflection would have avoided it completely. Several churches were demolished in the name of total clearance in the Cité, including the eleventh-century church of Sainte-Marine.[7] But on the whole Haussmann showed greater respect for churches than for secular buildings. His public works inevitably destroyed numerous mansions, medieval houses, and archaeological remains. However, most criticisms of Haussmann on this score were retrospective. At the time, his own confidence in his policies was confirmed by official opinion. The isolation of monuments, which deprived them of surroundings which later generations have considered to be an essential part of their charm, was supported by the Historic Monuments Office on both aesthetic and practical grounds.[8] The thorough restoration and reconstruction to which monuments were usually subjected to fit them for their new role as focal points had been pioneered by Viollet-le-Duc and his school, under the aegis of the Historic Monuments Commission, long before Haussmann arrived at the Prefecture. Support for his actions, and in particular for his

[5] Haussmann, vol. II, p. 28.
[6] Haussmann, vol. II, p. 28.
[7] Georges Pillement, *Destruction de Paris* (1941), p. 25.
[8] Paul Léon, *La vie des monuments français* (1951), pp. 327–8. Isolation removed the risk of damage by fire in adjoining buildings.

isolation policy, also came from the City Council and informed public opinion.[9]

Although Haussmann was contemptuous of those who wanted to retain old buildings for their antiquity alone, he did not ignore the past. He came to Paris at a time when interest in the history of the city was already very lively. The first half of the nineteenth century had seen a rapid growth of interest in history, and particularly in historical studies based on primary evidence. Little was published on the history of Paris between about 1780 and 1820, but then a flood of books began to appear.[10] Interest was further quickened by public works under the July Monarchy.[11] The City even employed two full-time historians, the Lazare brothers, to act as chroniclers and historical advisers. Their researches into previous policies, laws, regulations and agreements were of great practical assistance to the City.[12] Much work was done on the history of the city's buildings, not so much because of their intrinsic interest, but because of their value as primary historical evidence; as Montalembert had once said, 'The monuments of the past are essential auxiliaries of historical studies.'[13] This interest did not lead directly to a demand for their preservation, but it brought home the need to keep full details of everything that disappeared. Popular histories often drew attention to buildings by relating events associated with them. Louis Lurine's *Les rues de Paris: Paris ancien et moderne*, published in 1844, aimed to provide a vivid account of the history of Paris through the relating of events and anecdotes associated with individual streets and buildings. A similar technique was used by Fanny Richomme in her *Paris monumental et historique* (1850).

The public works of the Second Empire further increased this interest in the past, and for the first time effective encouragement was given by the City. Haussmann may have been genuinely interested in the history of Paris, or he may, as at least one critic suggested, have

---

[9] See, for instance a memorandum by the President of the City Council in Préfecture de la Seine, *Documents administratifs* (B.A. 21522), 14 December 1860, document no. 11; Théophile Gautier, article in *Moniteur*, 21 January 1854.

[10] Marius Barroux, *Le Département de la Seine et la Ville de Paris: notions générales et bibliographiques pour en étudier l'histoire* (1910), p. 59.

[11] See, for instance, Félix and Louis Lazare, *Dictionnaire administratif et historique* (1844), p. vii.

[12] See Louis Lazare, *Paris: son administration ancienne et moderne* (1856), pp. 1-2.

[13] Quoted in Ernest Pariset, *Les monuments historiques* (1891), p. 4. For later expressions of this view, see M. F. de Guilhermy, *Itinéraire archéologique de Paris* (1855), p. iii; Eugène de la Gournerie, in *Paris dans sa splendeur* (1861), vol. I, p. 1.

hoped to make demolitions more acceptable to the public thereby.[14] Whatever his motives, he injected unprecedented resources into the City's flagging patronage of historical research, which had previously produced only one work.[15] In 1865 the Prefect founded the 'General History of Paris' series, directed by a committee of councillors and scholars. He set up an archaeological and historical department at the Hôtel de Ville, and historical research was carried on in close association with municipal excavations. New techniques of photography and reproduction were developed.[16] The City also made grants towards the research of independent scholars, as well as meeting the cost of publication, without which some could not have continued.[17] Encouragement was also given to the study of old maps, and to attempts to reconstruct the city's topographical structure in previous centuries. In 1849 Albert Lenoir, who was then directing the compilation of the *Statistique monumentale de Paris*, asked Adolphe Berty to prepare an archaeological plan to accompany it. Such reconstitutions had been attempted before, but Berty soon discovered that existing plans and books were not enough, and so decided to use the archives to reconstitute the properties in each block. Later, he had to supplement the plan with an explanatory text based on the same sources.[18] Several more maps by other scholars appeared in the 1860s, after their work had been accelerated by the City's encouragement.[19] They all represented the combined efforts of the paleographer, the historian, and the architect-archaeologist; a cooperation which had not previously been achieved, and which resulted largely from the interest taken by the City.

The foundation of museum collections was a natural extension of the compilation of information about the city's past. Here, the State led the way. In 1844 the Government took over the collection of an antiquary, Alexandre du Sommerard, who had died in 1842, together with the mansion in which it was housed—the Hôtel de Cluny on the left bank. Although the collection was not considered outstanding, and the Government's action was prompted mainly by a desire to

---

[14] 'Ferragus', in *Le Figaro*, 5 June 1868.

[15] This was the *Monographie de l'Hôtel de Ville* (1846) (see C.M. reports, 1871-2, no. 34, p. 1).

[16] See, for instance, the description of reproduction methods in Eugène Belgrand, *La Seine, I: le bassin parisien aux âges anté-historiques* (1869), vol. I, p. viii.

[17] Adolphe Berty, *Topographie historique du Vieux Paris* (1866), vol. I, p. iii.

[18] Berty, vol. I, pp. ix-x.

[19] See list of archaeological plans and conjectural reconstructions in *Atlas des anciens plans de Paris* (1880), pp. 17-19.

protect the building,[20] the museum prospered. It specialised in medieval relics. The foundation of a Paris historical museum had to wait until the Second Empire. The aim of this initiative was to extend the benefits of a knowledge of the past to those who had no time to read books, or money to buy them.[21] Baron Poisson, one of the originators of the idea and a close friend of Haussmann, explained that his plan was 'to create, alongside written history, a material history composed of objects of all kinds . . . intended to throw light on the capital's past.'[22] The other main supporter of this scheme was Charles Read, departmental head at the Hôtel de Ville, who assumed responsibility for the museum after its foundation in 1866. To house the collection the City bought the Hôtel de Carnavalet, Rue de Sevigné, which was being used as a boarding house, and carried out some restoration work.[23] Unfortunately, the premises had not been made ready by the time of the Commune, and a large part of the collection was destroyed by fire at the Hôtel de Ville, where it had been stored. The main practical benefit which the museum conferred on Haussmann was to make demolitions of ancient houses more tolerable, as interesting details could be preserved in what the *Gazette des Tribunaux*, an opponent of general conservation, called 'really practical conditions'.[24] Yet, as we shall now see, the museums, the historical works, the engravings and the maps whose production Haussmann did so much to encourage, were to help in slowly turning public opinion against him.

Although there was no sudden change in the public attitude towards old buildings after the Second Empire fell, the preservationist case was growing steadily stronger. Under Haussmann, objections to demolitions were made either by antiquaries and scholars of no great influence, or by political opponents of the régime who were clearly out to gain some tactical advantage. Prominent among the critics of the demolition of individual buildings of artistic interest were men like Victor Hugo, Baudelaire, the Marquis de Laborde, Ferdinand de

[20] See Roger de Beauvoir, 'Rue de la Harpe', p. 103, in (ed. Louis Lurine), *Les rues de Paris* (1844), vol. I, pp. 93–104. Balzac referred to Du Sommerard as the 'prince du bric-à-brac' in *Le Cousin Pons*.
[21] Henri de Pontich, *Administration de la Ville de Paris et du Département de la Seine* (1884), p. 549.
[22] Quoted in De Pontich, p. 549.
[23] C.M. reports, 1903, no. 40, p. 10n; Gérard Lameyre, *Haussmann: Préfet de Paris* (1958), p. 209; *Bulletin*, 1886, p. 204; Yvan Christ, *Le Marais* (1964), p. 227; C.M., *Arrêtés de convocation*, 2 August 1867.
[24] 5 September 1866.

Lasteyrie, and M. F. de Guilhermy. De Guilhermy even produced a scholarly work, *Itinéraire archéologique du Vieux Paris*, at short notice in time for the 1855 Exposition, 'in order to show France's guests what still remains of Old Paris, after so many vicissitudes, and in some way to place the monuments of our past which deserve eternal respect under the protection of the whole of Europe.'[25] But most criticisms of the destructions were more half-hearted. Edouard Fournier, for instance, wrote that he greatly regretted what was being lost, but he was prepared to look on the bright side, assuring his readers that something was always left to catch the attention and awaken memories.[26] None of these attacks provided a formidable challenge, and with the support of a nominated City Council and an authoritarian régime Haussmann could ignore them. Strong opposition was aroused only when demolitions were carried out in middle-class districts, as occurred in the late 1860s, when numerous properties were acquired in the area of the new Opéra. But nearly all these houses were modern, whereas most of the city's older constructions were in central districts which had been deserted by better-off residents. Now that they no longer lived there, the middle class could easily dismiss ancient houses as 'hovels' and take no interest in their fate. The one exception to this generalisation resulted from the clearance of most of the Cité in the early 1860s. Here, the unprecedented scale of the demolitions, combined with the great antiquity of many of the buildings in what had been the heart of medieval Paris, aroused some misgivings. But at the time the demolitions were carried out, criticisms were lightly dismissed by the City, and much was made of the unhealthy condition of many of the houses in the area.[27] It was not until later in the 1860s, as political opposition to the régime grew and the seriousness of housing conditions in the old Cité was forgotten, that the demolitions there were cited as an example of Haussmann's vandalism. In 1866, *L'Opinion nationale*, one of the first newspapers to attack Haussmann, argued that the Cité could have been made healthy without wholesale demolitions, and should have been preserved as a relic of the past in the midst of the modern city.[28] This view was expressed even more strongly by 'Ferragus' in *Le Figaro* in 1868.[29]

[25] *Itinéraire archéologique de Paris* (1855), p. i.
[26] Edouard Fournier, 'Promenades dans Paris', p. 25, in *Paris dans sa splendeur* (1861), vol. II, pp. 1–76.
[27] See, for instance, an article ridiculing the enthusiasm of 'the so-called friends of the picturesque' for such 'hovels' in *Moniteur*, 7 August 1861, p. 1195.
[28] Article reprinted in *Gazette des Tribunaux*, 24 August 1866.
[29] *Le Figaro*, 5 June 1868.

Although this renewed debate over the Cité was only of academic interest, it reflected a greater sensitivity towards demolitions at the end of the decade, and which developed rapidly after 1870. The loss of the Cité might perhaps have been dismissed as an isolated excess, but it was followed by other examples of wanton destruction, official and unofficial. One of Haussmann's last acts was to authorise the destruction of part of the newly discovered Roman arena on the left bank for the building of the Rue Monge in 1869–70. More would certainly have been heard of this vandalism if the war with Prussia had not resulted in far more horrifying destruction wrought by enemy bombardment. Then, the last days of the Commune which followed the end of the war were accompanied by an orgy of destruction in which the Tuileries, the Hôtel de Ville and the Cour des Comptes were among the buildings burned down. Fortunately, this frenzy of destruction was not maintained. The public works projects of the late 1870s seemed to herald a further period of destruction but they themselves affected relatively few interesting buildings, and did not cut right across the historic centre as some of Haussmann's streets had done. And this period of activity was very short. In the 1880s the City Council returned to a policy of economy, allowing a breathing space free from public demolitions. For the first time in three decades the public was able to experience a period of several years without street diversions, dusty or muddy pavements, noise, and general inconvenience, which it had accepted in the name of progress, and had come to regard as normal.

This short lull coincided with a further development of opposition to demolitions. Now that frenetic modernisation, accompanied by the inevitable municipal justifications which brooked no contradiction, was no longer the order of the day, the stiller, calmer voices of the preservationists began to be heard more clearly. The previous thirty years could now be viewed like a battlefield after the contending armies have moved on, allowing the extent of the losses suffered by Paris to be gauged objectively. Certain types of buildings, such as late-medieval and Renaissance turrets on mansions, all medieval military architecture, and gable ends on humbler houses, were seen to have become very rare, and a strong demand grew up for the preservation of those that remained. But, even more important, the criteria which were considered by educated opinion to make a building worthy of preservation became more liberal after 1870. Under the July Monarchy and the Second Empire definitions had been very restrictive. Moreover, there was no consensus of opinion, even among antiquarians and scholars, as to what was worth preserving. There was even disagreement over the value of certain types of medieval building. Haussmann and the Emperor were not the only ones to confuse size and quality. The very wealth of the city's architectural heritagecon demned many small constructions, such as the churches in the Cité, to obscurity. Classical architecture was even less respected, partly because the medieval revival had temporarily driven it out of favour, and because the city had a positive glut of classical mansions and churches. For most scholars, interest increased with age.[30] De Guilhermy, for instance, excluded all buildings dating from later than the first half of the seventeenth century from his *Itinéraire archéologique de Paris*. And Adolphe Berty made 1610 the terminal date for his study of historical topography.[31] The materials used also influenced some opinions; for G. Touchard-Lafosse monuments of interest were built of stone, and Félix Pigeory had a low opinion of brick. Roger de Beauvoir, a lover of gothic, hated the use of plaster.[32] On the other hand, Pigeory and others like him, who were more concerned with the history of buildings than with their aesthetic aspects, were prepared to give their attention to any old construction, whatever its appearance. Pigeory wrote:

'What is more, leaving the question of art on one side, a monument forces itself upon us solely by virtue of the fact that it has come down through the centuries, however inferior it may be.'[33]

This view was at complete variance, not only with that of Haussmann, but also of the Historic Monuments Commission, which was prepared to list only buildings of exceptional artistic quality.

This disarray of scholars and preservationists made it easy for Haussmann to ignore and ridicule them during his period in power. But after 1870 they grew more catholic in their interests, which consequently tended to coincide more and more, creating a united front. The Historic Monuments Commission led the way when its revised list of protected monuments, published in 1873, stated for the first time that a building need not mark the origin or the full development

[30] A rare exception was Félix Pigeory; see his *Les monuments de Paris au dix-neuvième siècle: histoire architectonique de Paris ancien et moderne* (1849).
[31] Adolphe Berty, *Topographie historique*, vol. II, p. xxiii.
[32] Louis Lurine (ed.), *Rues de Paris*, vol. I, pp. 103, 130; Félix Pigeory, *Monuments de Paris*, p. 618.
[33] Pigeory, p. 74.

of a school of architecture to qualify. However, the Commission still refused to list buildings for their historical associations alone. The City, on the other hand, was prepared to go further, believing that historical importance could be set alongside architectural merit as a factor justifying preservation. Among the constructions which it included in this category were the surviving traces of medieval fortifications, the question of whose preservation came to the fore in the 1880s. It took particular interest in the tower of John the Fearless, near the Rue Réaumur, and the few surviving towers of the wall of Philip Augustus. But interest in the middle ages no longer obscured the architecture of later periods, and for the first time the mansions of the Marais began to attract the attention of informed opinion. Yet, for the time being, the idea that whole groups of old houses could be interesting, not for any architectural merit of their individual elements, but for their overall visual effect, made little progress. The view of Charles Delon, a writer interested in architecture and archaeology, remained typical:

> 'The word "picturesque" means something like "making a beauti-
> ful picture". That is excellent—in painting! But in real life?
> The streets of old Paris may be interesting to visit, but it is no
> pleasure to live in them!'[34]

There were still disagreements among scholars, but they revolved increasingly around methods of restoration rather than the principle of conservation. After 1870 public opinion, influenced by the more cautious teachings of men like Ruskin and William Morris, began to react against the radical reconstructions of Viollet-le-Duc and his school. But many architects persisted in their old ways. In 1884, for instance, an acrimonious dispute blew up when the City's archaeological department wanted to add a conjectural set of battlements to one of the towers of Philip Augustus' wall, which was enclosed in the build-ings of the Mont-de-Piété (municipal pawnbrokers). The Historic Monuments Commission took violent exception to this plan, and called for the careful reconstruction of existing remains, without any hypo-thetical additions. Eventually the City Council intervened in support of the Commission, which had its way.[35] But complaints continued about public and private restoration projects, and even the Commission was later attacked for over-enthusiastic reconstructions.[36]

[34] Charles Delon, *Notre capitale Paris* (1888), p. 254.
[35] C.M. reports, 1885, no. 39.
[36] Ernest Pariset, *Monuments historiques*, p. 15; *Bulletin*, vol. VI (1892), pp. 117–18.

Although growing public interest in an increasing range of buildings need not necessarily have led to stronger demands for preservation, it coincided from the 1880s with declining death rates and a greater mastery of epidemic diseases. This progress undermined the arguments of those who claimed that demolitions were necessary to protect public health, at least until tuberculosis began to frighten public opinion in the late 1890s. Romanticised engravings and descriptions of Old Paris before Haussmann's demolitions began to come into their own as better sewerage and cleansing methods brought about a superficial improvement in the older streets. As time passed, fewer people remembered the old slums, and many began to assume that artists like Charles Méryon had painted a true picture of Paris before 1850. But Méryon himself, whose work, significantly, had met total public indifference during the Second Empire, admitted that his drawings were often factually inaccurate.[37] He aimed to create an effect. Indeed, one could expect nothing else from romantic artists, and their idealised pictures made a sharp contrast with the more prosaic efforts of early photographers[38] ⟨*see* plate 22⟩. But engravings were much easier to reproduce than photographs, so until the 1890s the public saw pre-Haussmannic Paris through the eyes of artists like Méryon and Thomas Shotter Boys.[39] It was in vain that Haussmann fulminated from his retirement against those who admired a Paris that they knew only through collections of etchings:

> 'That the narrow and tortuous streets, especially those of the centre, were almost impenetrable to traffic, filthy, stinking, unhealthy—they do not worry about this!'[40]

Although the number of municipal demolitions declined sharply in the 1880s, there was no slackening of the growth of public interest in the fate of old buildings. Whereas the City's schemes could not easily be criticised, because they were carried out in the name of the community, demolitions by private landlords could be attacked without misgivings, as it was assumed that they were executed purely

---

[37] See Martin Hardie, *Charles Méryon and his eaux-fortes sur Paris* (1931), p. 12; *Old Paris: Twenty Etchings by Charles Méryon with an Essay on the Author by Philip Gilbert Hamerton* (1914).

[38] A convenient selection of early photographs of Paris is to be found in Yvan Christ, *Les métamorphoses de Paris* (1967).

[39] See Thomas Shotter Boys, *Picturesque Architecture in Paris, Ghent, Antwerp, Rouen, etc.* (1839), and reprinted 1928 with an introduction by E. B. Chancellor; Hugh Stokes, 'Thomas Shotter Boys', *Walker's Quarterly*, no. 18, 1925.

[40] Haussmann, *Mémoires*, vol. III, p. 28.

for profit. The preservationists were often able to arouse public indignation against 'the black band of speculators'[41] more easily than against the City, even though, over the years, it destroyed many more old buildings than did private enterprise. In fact, although increasing sensitivity to demolitions, caused by nostalgia, made it appear to enthusiasts like Charles Normand that vandalism was on the increase,[42] the rate of demolition was far less than in Haussmann's time. What was really happening as time went on was that Parisians were again becoming used to lack of change, in contrast to the frenzied modernisation of the Second Empire, and finding that they liked it. They were now returning to that state of conservatism from which only Haussmann had been able to drag them.

It was in the late 1880s that a new movement of opinion, more constructive than the nostalgia aroused by old etchings, began to strengthen the growing reaction against what Haussmann had done. This was the development of a more flexible, artistic approach to the aesthetics of town planning. As we have seen, Haussmann favoured rectilinear, symmetrical layouts using large buildings as focal points. Because this technique was totally in accordance with French urban planning traditions, it had at first aroused little unfavourable comment. Haussmann was even able to revive the old practice of ipmosing standard façade designs on private builders to ensure regularity in key streets and squares.[43] M. F. de Guilhermy and Edouard Fournier criticised the monotony of the new streets,[44] and Viollet-le-Duc and Bailleux de Marisy attacked Haussmann's rigid approach on grounds of cost as well as of the unnecessary destruction of old buildings which it caused.[45] There were also some complaints from landlords who resented restrictions on their freedom to build what they liked.[46] But most people admired Haussmann's boulevards, because at first they made a welcome change from the twisting, tortuous maze of streets which had previously characterised central Paris. Even in the 1870s, when some of Haussmann's uncompleted thoroughfares were carried through without modification of his plans, there were few protests.

[41] *Bulletin*, vol. I, p. 36.
[42] *Bulletin*, vol. I, p. 8.
[43] See M. L. Taxil, *Recueil d'actes administratifs et de conventions relatifs aux servitudes spéciales d'architecture* (1905).
[44] M. F. de Guilhermy, *Itinéraire archéologique*, p. iii; Edouard Fournier, in *Paris dans sa splendeur*, vol. II, p. 61.
[45] *Bulletin*, vol. III, 1889, p. 107; Bailleux de Marisy, 'La Ville de Paris: ses finances et ses travaux publics depuis le commencement du siècle', *Revue des Deux Mondes*, September-October 1863, p. 817.
[46] See, for instance, 'J.B.', *Arcades de la rue de Rivoli* (1852).

Indeed, the Avenue de l'Opéra represented the apotheosis of the Haussmannic street, and deserved the wide praise it received. But with a City Council bent on economy, similar aesthetic attentions could not be lavished on every new street, and the Boulevard Henri-IV and the Boulevard Saint-Germain were given little artistic distinction. A further deterioration set in in the 1880s when shortage of money and legal difficulties forced the City to restrict to a minimum its acquisition of properties for new streets, thus allowing unsightly blocks of old property to break into the regular lines of the new façades. Moreover, when public works slowed down in the 1880s architects and writers enjoyed a breathing space in which they could assess the value of what had been achieved over the previous thirty years, free from the distortion caused by constant change. And whereas most people had been won over by the novelty of wide, straight streets under the Second Empire, so many had been built by the 1880s that they had begun to cloy. Because some were now nearly thirty years old, symmetry was no longer synonymous with modernity, and people began to find it boring. This reaction against Haussmann's techniques was even more influential than that of the preservationists, because it often characterised eminent architects and engineers, whose views could not be dismissed as easily as those of obscure scholars. One such respected voice was that of Charles Garnier, architect of the new Opéra and by no means an extreme preservationist, who wrote in 1885:

> 'We do not want boredom to be the dominant factor in our new, healthy city; we want original views which are incompatible with the odious abuse of the straight line.'[47]

This spontaneous, Parisian reaction to the planning principles applied by Haussmann was reinforced in the 1890s by changes in national and international opinion. Haussmann's influence abroad had resulted in the copying of his techniques in many cities, where the subsequent reaction against them was often much stronger than in France. In particular, Belgium and Germany produced counter-influences which began to filter back into France during the last years of the century. Charles Buls, mayor of Brussels from 1881 to 1899, managed to secure the preservation of the Grand-Place and its immediate surroundings,[48] and the obvious success of his initiative was used

[47] *Bulletin*, vol. I, p. 29. For other criticisms of Haussmannic planning see J. K. Huysmans, *Croquis parisiens* (1886), p. 94; Henry Maret, 'L'haussmannisme', *La Ville*, 16 April 1892, p. 4.
[48] Pierre Lavedan, *Histoire de l'urbanisme*, vol. III, p. 125.

increasingly as an argument by French preservationists in the 1890s. In Vienna, Camillo Sitte was developing his artistic theories of town planning which achieved international prominence soon after the publication of his *Der Städtebau nach seinen künstlerischen Grundsätzen* in 1889.[49] Although Sitte's book was not translated into French until 1912, its teachings, which stressed the great importance of visual appeal in the planning of cities, soon filtered into the consciousness of French architects and engineers through periodicals and the proceedings of international conferences. In 1890, for instance, the International Congress of Public Art passed the following resolution:

'In future municipalities will not regard it as one of their main concerns to establish geometrical street lines, for the preservation of public edifices or houses of artistic interest will be enough to justify irregularities in the direction and width of certain streets.'[50]

These influences helped to produce a new generation of architects and planners, very different from the school of Haussmann and Alphand, both of whom, incidentally, died in the early 1890s. Men like Eugène Hénard and Marcel Poëte, who came to prominence in the early 1900s, brought new skills to town planning. Hénard, a young architect, produced a series of planning studies for Paris[51] which showed great respect for the past, and endeavoured to accommodate the needs of convenience, aesthetic appeal, and preservation of interesting buildings. Marcel Poëte, on the other hand, came to town planning from the starting point of urban history. His pioneering work in urban studies and planning made him the dominant figure in the development of a new approach to the planning of Paris in the last years before the Great War.[52] In 1903 he was appointed to the Paris Historical Museum, where he held a seminar on the history of the city. In 1907 he organised an influential exhibition, 'Evolution of Paris and Urban Art', and he later published his *Art Urbain*. Although his interests developed increasingly in town planning teaching, of which

[49] English translation by Charles T. Stewart, *The Art of Building Cities* (New York, 1945). For the significance of Sitte's work, see George R. and Christiane C. Collins, *Camillo Sitte and the Birth of Modern City Planning* (1965).
[50] Quoted in C.V.P., 11 November 1905, pp. 163–6.
[51] Eugène Hénard, *Études sur les transformations de Paris*, 8 vols (1903–9). However, the more ambitious of these schemes would have involved considerable destruction. But for a strongly preservationist statement by Hénard, see his 'Rapports à la Commission des perspectives monumentales de la Ville de Paris', *L'Architecture*, March–April, 1911.
[52] See below. p. 219ff.

he was virtually the founder in France, his knowledge of the historical evolution of cities enabled him to stress that planning should work with and not against natural growth. And Poëte's eminence as a planning theorist now allowed conservation to gain respect as a worthy object of urban improvement.[53]

The growth of Sitte's influence in France in the 1890s coincided with the development of new architectural forms originating mainly from Belgium, which had come into close contact with English proto-Art Nouveau in the 1880s.[54] The work of Victor Horta and his school in Brussels quickly attracted international attention, and its influence soon spread to Paris. Hector Guimard, who was later to design the well-known Art Nouveau entrances to the *Métropolitain*, adopted the style for his Castel Béranger, Rue de la Fontaine, as early as 1894. Although French Art Nouveau architecture rarely matched that of Belgium, and lacked the fantastic imagination of Gaudi's work in Barcelona, it influenced the style of a whole generation of architects. As we shall see, the asymmetry and unusual proportions of many Art Nouveau buildings came into direct conflict with the Paris building regulations, which were eventually modified to accommodate the new movement. And once irregularity had been accepted by officialdom and by public opinion as a feature of new building, its presence in older constructions became more tolerable. Furthermore, perhaps because Art Nouveau was to some extent a derivative, neo-Baroque style, its exponents showed a new respect for the architecture of the past. This is not to say that all Art Nouveau architects were preservationists, although some of them certainly were. But their demands for greater freedom of architectural expression enabled them to make common cause with those who were seeking the right for old buildings, however irregular in design and layout, to exist in a modern city. Both groups were linked by a common love of the picturesque.

So it was that in the 1890s the City and the Government began to take an interest, almost for the first time, in aesthetics. Although they were concerned primarily with design standards in new buildings rather than with the protection of old townscapes, it soon became clear that the two could not be separated. From about the time of Alphand's death, which was followed by considerable reorganisation

[53] Robert Auzelle, 'Marcel Poëte', *Town Planning Review*, vol. 21, 1950, pp. 158–9.
[54] See S. Tschudi Madsen, *Art Nouveau* (1967), pp. 101ff; Nikolaus Pevsner, *Pioneers of Modern Design* (1960), pp. 96ff.

and rethinking at the Hôtel de Ville, great pressure was placed on the City to alter its building regulations and tolerate a more irregular street pattern. Existing building regulations limited the flights of fancy of Art Nouveau architects by limiting the depth of projections jutting out over the street from the façades of buildings. In 1896 the Prefect set up a mixed committee of councillors, engineers and architects to consider modifying the highly restrictive 1882 regulations.[55] As it would inevitably be some years before changes could be made, the City decided to give immediate encouragement to good design by inaugurating a competition for the best facades, first of all in the new Rue Réaumur, and later in Paris as a whole. In 1897 the City Council approved the Rue Réaumur competition, and the annual competition for houses built anywhere in the city began in 1898[56] ⟨*see* plates 5, 6⟩. The City also encouraged builders to place the date of construction and the name of the architect on all new buildings. But the main product of the deliberations of the special committee was the new building regulations of 13 August 1902, which modified those of 1882 with regard to heights and projections. As the first building bye-laws to take aesthetic considerations into account, they appeared to mark the triumph of the new architectural movement. In theory, they should have enabled the modern buildings of Paris to rival those of Brussels and Barcelona. But, paradoxically, within a few years they had almost stifled architectural innovation, and given the Parisian preservation movement one of the biggest boosts that it had ever received. How did this result come about?

The 1902 regulations were drawn up mainly in response to pressure from avant-garde architects who wanted to be free to vary the rooflines of their buildings and introduce variety into the façades by creating substantial projections above the ground floor. They hoped that when the bye-laws were modified the great mass of architects would be encouraged to experiment with similar innovations. But they reckoned without the Parisian property owner, whose philistinism belied the Gallic reputation for good taste, and who could be relied upon to use any loophole to put the last possible cubic centimetre of occupiable space on his site. Moreover, the new regulations were badly drafted, for although they were easy to twist in the interests of profit, they were not liberal enough to allow the emulation of the more daring

---

[55] Charles Magny, *La beauté de Paris: conservation des aspects artistiques* (1911), p. 61.
[56] C.M. reports, 1897, no. 119, pp. 1–3. See also Fernand Bournon, *La voie publique et son décor* (1909), p. 75.

Art Nouveau styles. And they perpetuated the Parisian tradition of façade architecture. Most houses built between 1902 and 1914 merely included some half-hearted changes in the decoration of their façades and the only buildings to stand out were those distinguished, as Parisians soon began to realise, by their size alone. Instead of designing artistic projections, architects added bays, known as 'bow-windows', to the façades of apartment blocks in order to increase their floor area. Instead of using the new latitude in the maximum height of roofs to add turrets and cupolas, they filled the whole of the extra space with two and sometimes three storeys of attics. Parisians were particularly horrified by the addition of extra attic storeys to existing buildings in the Rue de Rivoli, despite the architectural ordinances forbidding changes, and the construction of a massive hotel over-shadowing the Arc de Triomphe. Such abuses convinced the general public of the need to preserve existing townscapes from the intrusion of out-of-scale constructions.

After a few years, when the results of the 1902 regulations had become clear to all, numerous criticisms began to be heard. Indignation was by no means restricted to a small minority of aesthetes and preservationists. Georges Cain's complaints in the Old Paris Committee[57] about 'the ceaseless attacks' on the beauty of Paris[58] were echoed in the City Council by Councillor Massard, who called for the 1902 bye-laws to be completely recast. He condemned the construction of 'skyscrapers' in Paris, and urged that existing regulations and ordinances should be enforced.[59] His proposals received considerable support in the press as well as in artistic and literary circles. In April 1909 the City conceded something to this movement of opinion by making a number of modifications in the 1902 regulations. The old method of fixing the maximum height of roof was reintroduced, so that it was no longer related to the depth of the building.[60] This was not enough for the fanatical preservationist, André Hallays, who wanted even stricter regulations for areas of architectural interest.[61] Paul Léon and Charles Magny continued to call for the complete reform of the 1902 bye-laws,[62] but the City hesitated to make further concessions. When Charles Normand raised the matter again in 1911 he was told

---

[57] See below, pp. 208ff. [58] C.V.P., 14 March 1908, p. 43.
[59] Paul Léon, 'La beauté de Paris', in *Revue de Paris*, 15 August 1910, p. 847; C.M. reports, 1909, no. 7, p. 33; no. 37, p. 1.
[60] C.V.P., 3 April 1909, pp. 50–53. [61] C.V.P., 3 April 1909, p. 51.
[62] Paul Léon, in *Revue de Paris*, 15 November 1909, pp. 297–301; 15 August 1910, pp. 847–64; Charles Magny, *Beauté de Paris*, p. 1.

by the City Architect, Louis Bonnier, that the existing regulations were enough to prevent the erection of buildings of excessive height.[63] This uncompromising attitude led Charles Lortsch and André Hallays to launch a more violent attack in 1913, in which they criticised not only the regulations but the men who enforced them. By their laxity and incompetence, raged Hallays, men like Prefect De Selves and Joseph-Antoine Bouvard, the former City Architect, had injured the beauty of the city by allowing an 'invasion of exotic styles'.[64]

Exaggerated though these criticisms were, they contributed to a more general recognition of the role that questions of aesthetics had to play in town planning and urban building. Louis Bonnier, whose own designs had come under Art Nouveau influences in the 1890s, was quoted as having said '. . . beauty is not a luxury for a people, but a need and a right just as is hygiene.'[65] The City Council reflected public opinion by taking a more active interest in aesthetic matters, particularly after the Prefect encouraged it to do so in June 1909.[66] One of its first initiatives was to call on the Senate to modify a bill passed by the Chamber of Deputies in March 1910 amending the 1841 law on compulsory purchase, so that the City could have powers to acquire backland when it was insufficient for the erection of buildings that would be in harmony with the appearance of the area.[67] Senate agreed, and by the law of 10 April 1912 the City was empowered to purchase compulsorily backland which did not allow the building of 'constructions suitable to the importance or appearance of the thoroughfare.' And shortly before this law was passed, article 118 of the finance law of 13 July 1911 gave the City power to refuse building permits for constructions which would damage perspective views and townscapes. The Prefect had previously been unable to refuse permission for a building on aesthetic grounds alone, as the result of a decision by the *Conseil d'Etat* in 1859. However, refusals to grant building permits under the 1911 powers were still subject to appeal to the *Conseil d'Etat*.

The reaction against geometrical street planning became even stronger after the turn of the century than it had been in the 1890s. Emile Magne attacked the creation of symmetry at all costs, and Auguste Rodin condemned the 'stupid barbarism' of the straight

[63] C.V.P., 8 March 1911, pp. 68–70.
[64] Charles Lortsch, *La beauté de Paris et la loi* (1913), preface by André Hallays, pp. xi, xii.
[65] Quoted in Lortsch, p. 11.
[66] Paul Léon, in *Revue de Paris*, 15 November 1909, p. 280.
[67] C.M. reports, 1910, no. 49.

line.[68] In 1909 Louis Bonnier called for the complete reform of the City's policy. He wanted to see a special committee set up to modify existing improvement lines, in order to preserve the city's architectural heritage and avoid 'blind street planning'.[69] But the battle for conservation had by no means been won, even among the supporters of higher aesthetic standards. Councillor B. Robaglia, for instance, called in almost the same breath for the establishment of a civic embellishment bureau, and the demolition of 'these ugly gable ends and even façades, too many of which are still with us, standing back from the improvement lines.'[70] No action was taken on Bonnier's proposals, even though they were passed on to the City Council by the Prefect,[71] and a number of previously planned streets were built in the city centre as part of the 900 million franc loan programme. In the Rue Beaubourg and the Rue du Renard a number of old houses standing behind the improvement lines were not demolished, but this was only because financial and legal difficulties precluded their acquisition, just as they had when the Rue Réaumur was built in 1895. Although informed opinion had been growing more favourable to the conservation of groups of old houses, the revelation of the effect of bad housing conditions on tuberculosis mortality in the late 1890s led to a revulsion of feeling against them. Protests against slum clearance proposals became rare even in the Old Paris Committee after about 1905, and preservationists took care to show respect for medical opinion. Emile Magne, for instance, called for discrimination in the assessment of the value of old buildings so that 'superfluous fetishism' might be avoided. Blocks of old houses should not be allowed to remain the home of 'foul odours and plagues' merely so that their original appearance could be preserved.[72] Another threat to old houses lay in the fact that there was still plenty of support for the view that important monuments should be isolated. The 1913 law on historic monuments clearly established the power of compulsory purchase for this purpose, and Councillor Robaglia urged that they should be freed of the 'sordid hovels' surrounding them.[73] But men like André Hallays, Robert Hénard, Emile Magne and even Louis Bonnier were of the contrary opinion,[74] which eventually prevailed, mainly because limited

[68] Emile Magne, *L'esthétique des villes* (1908), pp. 14–15; *Les Amis de Paris*, January 1913, p. 492.
[69] Magny, *Beauté de Paris*, pp. 158–9.
[70] C.M. reports, 1913, no. 130, pp. 9–10.
[71] Magny, *Beauté de Paris*, pp. 158–9.
[72] Magne, *Esthétique des villes*, pp. 9, 11.
[73] C.M. reports, 1913, no. 130, pp. 9–10.
[74] C.V.P., 3 April 1909. p. 52; *Les Amis de Paris*, 1 May 1911, p. 52; Magne, *Esthétique des villes*, pp. 9–10; C.V.P., 8 February 1913, p. 9.

financial resources made isolation increasingly impracticable. And the same applied to slum clearance. Although the City had proudly announced its intention to demolish a number of tubercular areas, nothing was done before 1914. While these old houses were still standing, under sentence of death, public interest in them was bound to increase. Baedeker's Paris guides first began to mention the interest of the Rue de Venise district, which had the highest death rate from tuberculosis in the city, in the early 1900s.[75] Interest also began to grow in the Marais and the Île Saint-Louis, partly as a result of the growing rarity of certain types of construction,[76] and partly owing to increased interest in styles of architecture which had not previously been valued. The first protests against the degradation of the Marais were made in the early years of this century, but because conservation was essentially a middle-class movement, the time was not yet ripe for a serious campaign in support of the preservation of a central area. On the other hand, a strong movement of opinion built up just before the war in favour of the integral preservation of Montmartre. This part of the city, sited on the crest of a steep hill, had no health problems, and among its population lived a large number of artists and men of letters, who had been attracted by its cheap accommodation and un-spoilt, semi-rural appearance. When the City carried out a series of street improvements which made the hill more accessible, and vacant building sites in more central and low-lying parts of the city became rare, developers began to build towering apartment blocks on the slopes of Montmartre, arousing the ire of residents who appreciated the calm and charm of the place. Between 1911 and 1914 the campaign to save Montmartre, 'the last hamlet', took up as much space in pre-servationist periodicals like *Les Amis de Paris* as those hardy annuals, the 1902 building regulations and street advertising. This movement was clearly a reaction against the excessive urbanisation and over-population of Paris. Its importance for the right bank centre lies in the fact that certain campaign techniques perfected in the defence of Montmartre were to be used later to protect the historic central areas and, in particular, the Marais.

The growth of public interest in the conservation of whole areas

[75] The interest of blocks of old houses was also pointed out by Fernand Bournon in *La voie publique*, p. 93.
[76] See, for instance, Lucien Lambeau's use of this argument in C.V.P., 14 March 1908, p. 44, and Georges Cain, *Walks in Paris* (English edition, 1909), p. 266.

was of very great significance for the future, when central improvement schemes would grind to a halt, and preservation would become the only feasible town planning policy for the city centre. But in the meantime preservation, to most people, meant the protection of architectural gems. Here, too, expert opinion was becoming much more liberal, allowing an increasing number of buildings to be classified as monuments. One effect of the growing interest in the appearance of cities was that the historical aspect of preservation became less important. The Old Paris Committee came out clearly in favour of the preservation of buildings of architectural merit, even when they had no particular historical associations or were of comparatively recent construction. Some members were in favour of excluding anything built within the previous fifty years, but no formal decision was made. Certainly, the Committee took an interest when buildings erected during the first half of the nineteenth century were threatened with destruction or modification, and a suggestion that the Committee should limit its attention to the period before 1789 was unanimously rejected. But it was easy to talk; and the main responsibility for the actual preservation of monuments lay not with the City and its Old Paris Committee, but with the State.

Although the Government set up the Historic Monuments Commission as early as 1837 its activity remained very limited for some time. Its role in Paris was even more restricted than in the nation as a whole. At first it had powers to list only masterpieces, and even then it was difficult to ensure their protection. Powers of compulsory acquisition were provided by the 1841 law, but they were rarely used because of the Commission's limited resources, which in any case had to be shared out as fairly as possible throughout the country.[77] No such compulsory purchase was made in Paris during the Second Empire, and in effect the City was alone responsible for the preservation of monuments, with the exception of those which already belonged to the State. It was easy to list churches, but as most of them already belonged to the City they were in no great danger. On the other hand, the demolition of the late-medieval Hôtel de la Trémoille was unopposed in 1841 because it was unlisted, and the City did not have the funds to acquire it.[78] Most of the mansions in the Marais remained unlisted not only because they were private property, but because of the general lack of interest in classical architecture. By

---

[77] Paul Léon, *La vie des monuments français* (1951), p. 131.
[78] Léon, pp. 131–2.

1875 only about six of them had been listed.[79] In fact, before the Commission's powers were extended in 1887 nearly all the buildings listed in Paris already belonged to the City or the State, and only three private properties were listed in the right bank centre during the Second Empire.[80] Between 1871 and 1887 the Commission listed only five buildings there, all of them belonging to the City. Some hope for the future was aroused by the new law of 1887. It resulted largely from the patriotic euphoria and heightened awareness of international competition which dominated the last decades of the nineteenth century. It was based on the philosophy that the nation's riches could be augmented, not only by founding colonies across the seas, but by developing home resources. Art treasures of all kinds were not excluded. Charles Normand typified the mood of the time when he accused owners of historic buildings who refused to sell them at reasonable prices of lack of patriotism; '. . . patriotism consists of memories as well as hopes.'[81] Ernest Pariset saw the protection of monuments as 'a patriotic activity'; '. . . in this whole question the national interest is predominant.'[82] But patriotic urgency did not distinguish the voting of new powers to the Commission. The Marquis of Chennevières presented a bill in 1874 to give the Historic Monuments Commission authority to ensure the protection of listed buildings, but local authorities protested that this would weaken their own powers, and among the bill's strongest critics was the Prefect of the Seine.[83] Preparation of a new bill began in 1875, and it was read in the Chamber in 1878. After study by the *Conseil d'Etat* it came back to the Chamber in 1882, and was finally passed in 1885. It eventually became law in 1887, and its regulating decree was published in 1889.

The result of this long period of gestation was to weaken the bill rather than strengthen it. The *Conseil d'Etat* was advised by its rapporteur, Jean Courcelle-Seneuil, that any new legislation should protect only a very few monuments of outstanding interest.[84] As a result, the act became law with a first article stating that it dealt only with buildings having 'a national interest from the point of view of art or history'. It even abolished the power of arbitrary listing which

[79] Yvan Christ, *Le Marais* (1964), p. 25.
[80] See *Liste des immeubles protégés au titre de la législation sur les monuments historiques et sur les sites dans le Département de la Seine* (1956).
[81] *Bulletin*, vol. I, pp. 26-7.
[82] Ernest Pariset, *Monuments historiques*, pp. 8, 217.
[83] *Bulletin*, vol. I, pp. 134-7.
[84] Louis Tétreau, *Législation relative aux monumnets et objets d'art dont la conservation présente un intérêt national au point de vue de l'histoire ou de l'art* (1896), p. 24.

had been embodied in previous legislation. Henceforth, if the owner was opposed to the listing, the only recourse would be to compulsory acquisition. Yet, even though it was now more necessary than ever to encourage the goodwill and cooperation of the owners, the regulating decree of 3 January 1889 stated that to list a building did not necessarily imply that the State would share in the cost of restoration, repair or maintenance, and that the amount of any subsidy would depend on the 'sacrifices' made by the owner.

Although Ernest Pariset considered that the new powers were adequate, the committee of the Friends of Paris Monuments was disappointed, and turned to the City of Paris to ensure preservation.[85] Experience proved Pariset to have been over-optimistic, for the powers of compulsory purchase were used only very rarely, on financial grounds.[86] Although the Historic Monuments Commission's annual budget rose from 1,100,000 francs (£44,000) in the last years of the Second Empire to 1,630,000 francs in 1882, it was subsequently reduced by Parliament until 1897.[87] The City of Paris found it hard to obtain any grants at all, especially as the decree of 1889 laid down that any public body asking for a subsidy should provide documentary evidence of its financial situation—and many local authorities were worse off than Paris. When a grant was made, it was usually to ensure the authority of the Historic Monuments Commission over the City's architectural department, for the two were still in a state of rivalry.[88] On the other hand, the Commission managed to consolidate its control over listed buildings owned by Government departments after 1887. But the overall results of the act of 1887 were distinctly disappointing. Although the number of listings increased after 1887, the problem of the private property was still not tackled. Nine listings were made in the right bank centre between 1887 and 1895, but only one, the Hôtel d'Albret, was a private property, and its owner-occupiers, an old bourgeois family, were clearly in full agreement.

The Commission's responsibilities were increased further by the law of 19 December 1905, which disestablished the French Church. As a result, the tutelage of the Minister of Religious Worship over church buildings, which the Historic Monuments Commission had always criticised, was abolished, but it meant that the entire responsibility now fell on itself. Many churches risked being deprived of all

[85] Pariset, *Monuments historiques*, p. 216; *Bulletin*, vol. V, p. 15.
[86] C.V.P., 7 November 1908, p. 141. [87] Léon, *Vie des Monuments*, p. 166.
[88] For an account of this struggle, see Léon, pp. 220–21.

financial help, because the Commission could give subsidies only to listed buildings, but the law modified the listing regulations in respect of churches in order to forestall this danger. Henceforth, a church might be listed if it were of general historic or artistic interest. It was no longer required to be of national importance.[89]

It seemed likely that the effect of these changes in Paris would be to put many old religious buildings in danger, as a result of sales of properties by religious orders. But it soon transpired that hardly any of the threatened buildings were of interest, and the Old Paris Committee let the matter drop.[90] The Historic Monuments Commission faced up to this new challenge, and 1,862 buildings were added to the national protected list between 1905 and 1909. In 1914 the Government decided to create a special fund for historic monuments.[91]

These new responsibilities encouraged Parliament to take a new look at preservation legislation. Once again, its debates emphasised the national importance of safeguarding the French architectural heritage. Guillaume Chastenet, opposing the growing ugliness of Paris in the Chamber of Deputies in 1908, said: 'A great city can be a work of art . . . [but] Paris . . . is the very synthesis of the life of our nation.'[92] The Chamber passed a resolution supporting Chastenet, and on 24 June 1909, after another of his speeches, it called on the Government urgently to draw up measures to safeguard the city's beauty. In July 1909 the Government set up a mixed inter-ministerial committee of deputies, officials, architects and scholars to centralise the activities of the various departments responsible for the protection of Parisian monumental perspectives. It aimed to coordinate the actions of Government and City, and the ministries of the Interior, Finance and Fine Arts were represented on it. It soon added its voice to criticisms of the 1902 building regulations whose abuse had been largely responsible for its establishment.[93]

After passing a law on the protection of natural beauty spots (21 April 1906), Parliament turned its attention to the reform of legislation on historic monuments. The first practical result was the passing of a law in 1910 forbidding billposting in the vicinity of listed monuments.[94]

[89] Léon, pp. 141–2.   [90] C.V.P., 10 March 1906, p. 43; 7 April 1906, p. 62.
[91] Léon, *Vie des monuments*, pp. 141, 177; *Revue de Paris*, 15 November 1909, p. 289. The fund was not established until 1921.
[92] Session of 11 November 1908.
[93] Magny, *Beauté de Paris*, p. 166, 166n; *Revue de Paris*, 15 November 1909, p. 280; C.M. reports, 1909, no. 37, p. 2; C.V.P., 8 March 1911, p. 68. The committee was sometimes referred to as the Paris Monumental Perspectives Committee.
[94] Law of 22 April 1910.

A new law on historic monuments was finally enacted, after many amendments, on 31 December 1913. It authorised the arbitrary listing of private properties, subject to the payment of compensation. Any building could henceforth be listed as long as it was of 'public interest'. The law also established a provisional listing procedure without compensation, which made it possible to prohibit all structural modifications during a period of two weeks while the possibility of a definitive listing was examined.

Although the 1913 act was of great importance nationally, it did little to strengthen the Historic Monuments Commission's powers to defend Old Paris. Its national responsibilities still prevented it from giving adequate attention to Parisian interests, and in 1913 Charles Lortsch was already calling for a 'municipal protected list' to safeguard the many buildings whose conservation was desirable, but whose interest was Parisian rather than national.[95] In fact, the Friends of Paris Monuments had drafted a list of such buildings in 1898, and the Old Paris Committee had immediately taken a direct interest in the enterprise.[96] Of course, it was easy to draw up lists, but very difficult to persuade the only other possible preservation body apart from the Historic Monuments Commission, the City of Paris, to take action. Although the Ministry of Fine Arts was empowered from 1910 to make maintenance and repair grants to local authorities for historic monuments, Paris had to take its place in the national queue, and received little benefit.

Because of the prolonged weakness of the national preservation machinery, effective responsibility had long been borne, whether it liked it or not, by the City of Paris. To some extent it accepted this burden. As we have seen, its main effort during the Second Empire was devoted to the encouragement of research, but its purchase of the Hôtel de Carnavalet created an important precedent. After 1870 financial difficulties at first forced it to reduce the amount spent on historical studies,[97] but after a few years it was again able to subsidise the publication of works on Paris. In the 1871 reorganisation of the City Council a new Fine Arts Committee was set up with control over museums and historical studies. From 1877 the fine arts department issued various volumes of a general inventory of art

[95] Lortsch, *La beauté de Paris et la loi*, p. 272.
[96] C.V.P., 8 December 1898, pp. 9–11; 19 January 1899, pp. 15–17.
[97] C.M. reports, 1872, no. 34, p. 4.

treasures in Paris and the Seine.[98] In 1880 it published the *Atlas des anciens plans de Paris* after organising a display of old maps at the 1878 Exposition.[99] Subsidies were granted, in particular, for the publication of more of Hoffbauer's engravings of Paris through the ages.[100] And in 1887 the City Council sponsored the publication of a series of documents relating to Paris and the Revolution in time for the centenary in 1889.[101]

Despite the loss of much of its collection in 1871, the Council approved in 1872 the necessary expenditure to install the historical museum and library in the Hôtel de Carnavalet. The library was opened in 1875 and the museum itself in 1880. Then, in 1894, the City decided to acquire the adjoining Hôtel Lepeletier de Saint-Fargeau to house the library, leaving more room in the Hôtel de Carnavalet for the expanding museum section.[102]

In 1879 the City set up an Inscriptions Committee, composed of councillors, administrators and scholars, whose job was to place plaques on the walls of buildings to recall historical events.[103] In 1881 the principle of a mixed committee was extended to historical studies in general when the Prefect replaced the single Fine Arts Committee set up ten years earlier by two separate bodies. One continued to deal with fine arts administration, while the other was given the task of directing 'activities concerning the general history of Paris'. It included a number of men, such as Léopold Delisle, Albert Lenoir and Jules Cousin, who were actively interested in the preservation of the city's beauty, and several of its members were later invited to join the Old Paris Committee.[104]

Although the City acquired a number of interesting buildings after 1870, it usually did so on purely practical grounds. The tower of John the Fearless happened to be standing on a site acquired for a new school, and a tower of Philip Augustus' wall was acquired when the Mont-de-Piété was extended.[105] Other buildings were converted to new uses, like the Hôtel de Montrésor, Rue de Turenne, bought in

---

[98] *Inventaire général des richesses artistiques de la Ville de Paris et du Département de la Seine* (1877–). Nine volumes had appeared by 1901.
[99] For an account of the preparation of this collection, see *Atlas des anciens plans de Paris* (1880), pp. 5–6.
[100] Dr. Chassagne, *Dix-neuf ans du Conseil municipal élu de la Ville de Paris 1871–1890* (1890), p. 90.
[101] Max Boucard, *La vie de Paris* (1892), p. 100.
[102] C.M. reports, 1895, no. 46, p. 1.
[103] De Pontich, *Administration de Paris*, p. 549.
[104] *A.P.*, 12 February 1881, in *R.A.A.*, pp. 368–70, 408.
[105] C.M. reports, 1885, no. 39, pp. 1, 7; Pariset, *Monuments historiques*, p. 10.

1880 to house a primary school. Some purists criticised the use of monuments for other than their original purposes, but most preservationists were grateful to the City, and the Friends of Paris Monuments called on it to acquire and convert even more old buildings.[106] In fact, the preservationists were often very critical of the City. Charles Normand, for instance, blamed most destructions on the philistinism of property owners, but he thought that the City should intervene more often to restrain their excesses.[107] Attacks on its policy became especially strong towards 1890 when the City declined to act to prevent the demolition of the Hotel des Prévôts, near the Rue Saint-Antoine. Much of this criticism was unfair, for the City had shown its willingness to act whenever possible, but was afraid to go as far as acquiring a property compulsorily, which would place it at the mercy of the evaluation panel. But it was clear that no public authority was willing or able to act effectively to prevent vandalism, and the preservationists began to feel that they could achieve their ends only through organisation.

Public interest in history and antiquarian studies continued to develop during the Third Republic, thus providing a wide base of potential support for the preservation movement. New editions were published, for example, of the Abbé Lebeuf's classic study of the city and diocese of Paris in order to 'make an indispensable work available to all those who are interested in the antiquities of our history, and whose numbers increase daily'.[108] New works of great scholarship, such as Edouard Fournier's *Paris à travers les âges* (1875–82), continued to appear, but the number of popularisations increased even faster. Indeed, after 1880 most of the books published on Paris were aimed at the general reader.[109] Many writers, like Fernand Bournon,[110] continued to teach the history of the city though its streets and buildings and so helped to arouse public interest in their preservation. This widened public interest now created favourable conditions for the foundation of historical and preservation societies, and the publication of related periodicals.

---

[106] *Bulletin*, vol IV (1890), p. 70. For a criticism of conversions, see Pariset, *Monuments historiques*, p. 10.
[107] *Bulletin*, vol. I, pp. 8, 36n; vol. V, p. 42.
[108] Lebeuf, *Histoire de la Ville et de tout le diocèse de Paris* (new edition, 1883), vol. I, p. iv. It was necessary to publish a further edition in 1890.
[109] Marius Barroux, *Le Département de la Seine et la Ville de Paris*, p. 63.
[110] See his *Paris* (1888), p. v.

An attempt to set up a Paris Archaeological and Historical Society failed in the mid-1860s,[111] but in 1874 the Society of the History of Paris and the Île-de-France was successfully founded. The Society of Parisians of Paris, whose membership was limited to those who had been born in the city, was founded in 1890, and the magazine *La Ville* was first published in 1892, 'to defend the rights and interests of Paris'.[112] These and older institutions, such as the Academy of Inscriptions, acted indirectly in the cause of preservation. But much more directly involved in the preservation movement was the unprecedented Society of Friends of Paris Monuments, founded by the antiquarian Charles Normand in 1884. This was the first attempt to obtain mass support for preservation in order to create an influential climate of opinion, and it achieved immediate success. From the late 1880s there was a further development, the foundation of local societies. In 1886 the Old Montmartre Society was formed. Then followed, outside the right bank centre, the Auteuil and Passy historical society (1892), the *Montagne Sainte-Geneviève* (1895), the historical society of the VIe and XIVe *arrondissements* (1898), the historical and archaeological society of the VIIIe and XVIIe *arrondissements* (1899), and, finally, the historical society of the VIIe and XVe *arrondissements* (1903). In the right bank centre the most important society was *La Cité*, set up in 1901 at the suggestion of Georges Fabre, mayor of the IVe *arrondissement*.[113] In 1909 it extended its area of interest to take in the IIIe *arrondissement*, and it also formed a federation of all local history societies. It published a regular bulletin, *La Cité*, fifty numbers of which had appeared by 1923. The Ier and IIe *arrondissements* had to wait a little longer, as perhaps befitted their more limited historic interest, but they were covered in 1912 by the foundation of the *Centre de Paris* society. A number of more specialised groups were also formed, like the Society of Friends of the Louvre (c. 1898) and the 'Tuileries Committee', which added its voice in 1911 to the protests against the excessive height of modern buildings.[114]

The societies described so far directed their appeal to the educated middle classes, and were supported mainly by leisured or professional people. Although they were consequently very different from the older specialised societies supported only by antiquarians and other

[111] Barroux, *Le Département de la Seine et la Ville de Paris*, p. 101.
[112] *La Ville*, 19 March 1892, p. 1.
[113] C.V.P., 5 April 1900, p. 113. The account of other local societies is based on C.V.P., 27 January 1923, pp. 24–30.
[114] *Les Amis de Paris*, September-October 1911, p. 120.

scholars, they were still too esoteric to appeal to the generality of the middle class, not to speak of the working class. One serious weakness was that they did not attract the landlords who owned the buildings they wanted to preserve, nor the artisans, traders and poor tenants who worked and lived in them. But their great initial success encouraged the belief that support could be sought from a much wider social range. The result was the foundation of the Association of Friends of Paris in 1911. The stated aims of its organisers were very confused, but they wanted both to popularise the work of the historical societies and to encourage tourism.[115] The Association was at first spectacularly successful, and it soon attracted several thousand members. But its membership was too disparate and undistinguished, and its policies too vague, to gain much influence over the City's planning and preservation policies. After a few years it lost its momentum, and by 1923 it had progressed from moribundity to total collapse. But even the Friends of Paris Monuments did not enjoy a better fate, for it began to fade away after the turn of the century as its leading members put most of their energies into the Old Paris Committee. But most of the local societies have carried on, although they have never regained the enthusiasm of their early years, and the average age of their members, to judge from attendances at their meetings, must now be well over sixty.

However abject the eventual failure of the big societies, their phenomenal popularity before 1914 helped to bring about a change in the City's attitude towards preservation. Both City Council and officials began to provide frequent indications of their interest around the turn of the century. Prefect De Selves told the Old Paris Committee in 1900 that the City was convinced that improvements and a greater respect for the past were not incompatible.[116] The City Council decided a year later that photographs should be taken of all buildings acquired for demolition, and in 1903 it inaugurated an annual Paris photographic exhibition.[117] Some councillors, notably Councillor Massard, urged the Council to take more positive action.[118] In March 1909, he asked it to request the administration to enforce laws and architectural ordinances relating to the appearance of Paris, and to ratify the resolution passed by the Chamber of Deputies on 11 November

[115] *Les Amis de Paris*, February 1912, p. 233.
[117] C.M. reports, 1903, no. 40, p. 20.
[116] C.V.P., 19 July 1900, p. 124.
[118] Magny, *Beauté de Paris*, p. 3.

1908 against the city's increasing ugliness.[119] In May he called for the City Council to be represented on the new interministerial monumental perspectives committee.[120] In 1911 the City Council, shocked by the demolition of what was said to be the original Moulin de la Galette at Montmartre, demanded full details of buildings worth conserving that were threatened by public works operations.[121] And it always indignantly rejected accusations that it was itself responsible for acts of vandalism.

Yet, in spite of this flood of goodwill, the extent of the City's positive activity in favour of preservation was still limited. Although it bought several old mansions,[122] as the Old Paris Committee wanted, its resources were insufficient for it to have a methodical purchasing programme. In fact, its main contribution was indirect, in that it set up a number of bodies which were to become, under its aegis, a force for conservation. The first such body was the Technical and Aesthetic Committee, set up by Prefect De Selves in August 1896, mainly to study the various proposed changes in building regulations that were eventually codified in 1902. Its members were officials, engineers, architects, and a large number of individuals with general artistic interests. It faded away after a few years, but was re-established in 1909 at the request of the City Council, when it was instructed to give an opinion on the technical and aesthetic aspects of public works schemes submitted to it by the Prefect, who generally used it as a defence against exaggerated criticisms.[123]

Much more significant was the Old Paris Committee, the most important organism of preservation to be created by the City before 1914. It was set up by Prefect De Selves in December 1897 after Councillor Alfred Lamouroux and many of his colleagues had spoken in the City Council of the need for such a committee.[124] During its early years the Committee's influence was strengthened by the personal interest of De Selves, who chaired seventy-one out of a total of ninety-nine meetings held between 1898 and 1911. But the Committee soon came up against difficulties and frustrations, and was easily controlled or out-manoeuvred by the administration and the City Council. Its preservationist members, realising that extreme views would be

---

[119] C.M. reports, 1909, no. 7, pp. 2, 33.   [120] C.M. reports, 1909, no. 37, p. 43.
[121] C.V.P., 23 December 1911, pp. 183–8.
[122] Notably the Hôtel de Lauzun (1900, resold under a protection order in 1906), and the Hôtel de Sens (1911).
[123] Magny, *Beauté de Paris*, pp. 119–20; C.M. reports, 1911, no. 22, p. 3.
[124] Magny, *Beauté de Paris*, p. 122; C.V.P., 28 January 1898, pp. 1–2.

ignored by the City, usually remained moderate in their attitudes in order to retain what influence they could. André Hallays, who was not willing to dissemble, suffered constant frustration. But those lay members who were prepared to accept the basic necessity of public works schemes, and discuss issues objectively, were able to achieve an effective working relationship with the officials and councillors who sat with them.

A similar course of development was followed by the Sites Committee. In 1898 the Ministry of Fine Arts issued a circular recommending local authorities to pay more attention to the protection of beauty spots.[125] A number of bills were subsequently considered, and the one passed by the Chamber in February 1905 finally became law in April 1906.[126] It established a procedure for listing beautyspots and 'natural monuments', with compulsory purchase powers, and allowed for the establishment of a committee in each *département* to supervise the enforcement of the law. After some prodding by the Old Paris Committee, the Prefect set up a Sites Committee for the Seine in May 1907.[127] It was another mixed committee, but it had even less direct authority than the Old Paris Committee, and it achieved very little influence over the City's policies. After 1910 it almost ceased to meet. The City agreed to list only three areas as natural beauty spots, none of them in the city centre. In any case, all three already belonged to the municipality and were in no danger. Although the Prefect clearly considered the application of the 1906 act to be irrelevant in Paris, the City showed great enthusiasm in enforcing lapsed architectural ordinances like those of the Rue de Rivoli. In 1899 the Old Paris Committee persuaded the City to demand the removal of trade signs from the Place-Vendôme, whose appearance was governed by an ordinance, and it was decided to enforce the other ordinances wherever possible to prevent structural changes.[128] The City Council, encouraged by the Old Paris Committee, decided in 1904 to draw up a detailed list of all existing ordinances, and the result was the 'Taxil collection', published in 1905.[129] In 1911 the City required a landlord in the Place des Victoires to rebuild his demolished house in the style laid down by an ordinance, and in 1912 it modified the improvement line on one side of the Place des Vosges to prevent the mutilation of

[125] Magny, *Beauté de Paris*, p. 104.   [126] Law of 21 April 1906.
[127] C.V.P., 20 April 1907, p. 203; *A.P.*, 6 May 1907, *R.A.A.* (P.P.), pp. 90–91.
[128] C.V.P., 12 October 1899, pp. 239–42.
[129] M. L. Taxil, *Recueil d'actes administratifs et de conventions relatifs aux servitudes spéciales d'architecture* (1905).

the square.[130] In the case of the Rue de Rivoli, the courts delivered a ruling favourable to the City in 1913, and landlords had to remove the offending vertical extensions.[131]

Although fanatical preservationists like André Hallays were far from satisfied with the City, and suspected the committees which it had founded, these bodies, for all their faults and weaknesses, represented a true compromise between the interests of modernisation and preservation. They enabled each side to see the other's point of view. But this was not the only way in which the gulf between the scholar and the man of affairs was being narrowed. The city's commercial classes were now beginning to see that beauty could pay. Paris had always attracted foreigners, but the success of its regular international exhibitions and improvements in international transport were making it an increasingly important tourist centre. From the 1890s Paris hoteliers, aware that their accommodation did not match standards abroad, made considerable efforts to catch up.[132] By 1913 Paris was welcoming 300,000 tourists a year, and the views of writers like Charles Lortsch, who believed that the preservation of the beauty and interest of Paris would increase the figure still further, made sound commercial sense.[133] The support of all sections of the press also helped to make preservation respectable. Most newspapers were not strongly committed to the cause, but any controversy in which individuals opposed blind administrative or financial forces made good copy. It gave the Old Paris Committee, and councillors like Massard who presented reports on the appearance of the city, almost unanimous support.[134] With increasing attention being paid to their views, the preservationists moderated their more extreme prejudices against change. Emile Magne's views were typical. Although admitting that urban improvement often created ugliness, he attacked those scholars who stubbornly opposed all changes. He believed that preservation could be achieved only in cooperation with authority, and not by the scribbling of 'miserable protesting quills'. And although he considered that a commemorative plaque often sufficed to compensate for the loss of a building, he loved the past and praised the harmonious appearance of

[130] C.V.P., 26 March 1938, section 6.
[131] C.V.P., 14 June 1913, pp. 144–7; 5 December 1913, pp. 268–9.
[132] *Les Amis de Paris*, January 1913, p. 488.
[133] Lortsch, *La beauté de Paris et la loi*, p. 21n.
[134] See expressions of gratitude to the press in C.V.P., 19 July 1900, p. 129; C.M. reports, 1909, no. 37, p. 1; André Billy, *Paris vieux et neuf: la rive droite* (1909), p. 198.

the old districts of Paris.[135] Paul Léon wrote of the double task of conserving the works of the past, and planning the building of the contemporary city.[136] Charles Normand recognised the need for new streets, as long as their route was designed to avoid interesting buildings.[137] This compromise was maintained, from the administrative side, in the reports of the Paris Extension Committee which appeared in 1913. Indeed, the appointment to the Committee of the urban historian, Marcel Poëte, who had a considerable influence on its work, was itself a sign of the City's confidence in the validity of the compromise. The Committee's conciliatory approach was epitomised by its call for the preservation and isolation of monuments in unhealthy areas, and the widening of existing streets while protecting 'the glorious past of Paris', despite the problems involved. It opposed any alteration in the city's aesthetic character, and called on the authorities to spare 'old buildings whose historic character and beauty should make them inviolate'.[138]

It is the development of this compromise which makes the last two decades before the First World War the most interesting period in the history of conscious preservation in Paris. During these years the movements of conservation and modernisation reached their apogee at the same time. So some arrangement between them was desirable, and perhaps inevitable. After 1918 the preservationists were to become much more intransigent, but the forces working for the transformation of Paris are weaker, so that the contest becomes one-sided. But it was because the City had already gone a long way towards accepting a conservationist role in the city centre before 1914 that it could tolerate the virtual moratorium on improvement schemes there that was forced on it after the war. Because it had already admitted that preservation of the city's character and appearance was desirable, it was later able to disguise stagnation and ossification as municipal planning policy. Moreover, the power of private interests to modernise the city centre was also limited in later years as a result of decisions taken before 1914. The year 1902 saw the last attempt to modify the building regulations applying to the city centre in order to allow the larger constructions which the introduction of steel and concrete framing had made possible. If there had been no opposition, height restrictions

[135] Magne, *Esthétique des Villes*, pp. 7, 8, 9, 10n, 18.
[136] *Revue de Paris*, 15 November 1909, p. 281.
[137] C.V.P., 3 February 1912, p. 18.
[138] Commission d'extension de Paris, *Considérations techniques préliminaires* (1913), pp. 56, 83.

might later have been relaxed still further. But the success of a movement of public opinion in resisting these small changes meant that a building ceiling which had been established in the eighteenth century would continue to apply in central Paris. This, as much as any other factor, ensured that the buildings of central Paris would remain virtually undisturbed for many decades to come.

8

The Abandonment of the Grand Design, 1915-70

The City's efforts to transform central Paris before 1914 were marked by an abundance of energetic improvement activity but a lack of adequate town planning, except in the very restricted sense of the forward planning of street schemes. After 1914 there is a clear contrast. While actual achievement is greatly restricted, town planning techniques are developed and applied with increasing sophistication. And whereas improvement activity before the First World War had been concentrated predominantly on the city centre, attention subsequently switched more and more to the outskirts where the main growth in population was taking place. Only in the field of slum clearance did work continue on any more than a small scale in the city centre. It is the aim of this chapter to study, firstly, the fading effort to apply the traditional strategy based on street improvements, secondly, the development of new town planning policies, and, thirdly, the slum clearance programme which had originally evolved from Haussmann's plan, but was incorporated in the new schemes after 1945.

I THE ABANDONMENT OF THE GRAND DESIGN

The declaration of war and the rapid German advance in the summer of 1914 brought all public works to an abrupt halt. Early hopes that the interrupted schemes, and many more, could be completed after the war were soon destroyed by the rapid rise in the City's short-term war debt. As early as 1916 the rapporteur of the budget committee, Louis Dausset,[1] a firm supporter of improvement, had reluctantly to propose the cancellation of all schemes in the schedule

---

[1] See below, p. 221.

of the 900 million franc loan to consolidate the floating debt. Several of his colleagues opposed this suggestion, but the Council as a whole was prepared to face facts. Councillor Louis Rollin referred to the 900 million franc loan in March 1917 as a 'deceptive and dangerous mirage for those who, in spite of the realities and the inevitable consequences of the war, still insist on seeing it in terms of its original conception and promises!'[2] As the war dragged on, the Council had to approve further consolidating loans and taxation increases. Even after peace was signed further borrowings were necessary for this purpose, and also to cover budget deficits in 1920 and 1921. No capital funds could be allocated to public works until 1921, when part of an emergency loan of 1,800 million francs (£36 million) was set aside for works and the construction of workers' dwellings. And the total allotted to street improvements was a mere 150 million francs (£3 million).[3]

In these circumstances the adjournment of most pre-war projects was inevitable. To complete the 1909 schedule would have cost 261 million francs (£10½ million) at pre-war values, and costs had more than quadrupled since 1914. Yet the public works committee was opposed to the complete renunciation of pre-war plans because of the danger of fragmentation if available resources were devoted only to surfacing and the purchase of occasional properties for widening. It wanted to proceed on the basis of the 1909 schedule, reduced to more manageable proportions.[4] But by the time the Council came to discuss the matter the resources available had been reduced to 125½ million francs, over half of which had to be allocated to schemes for which contracts had been let some time before. Three of these interrupted operations were in the right bank centre, including the isolation of the Halles and the Conservatory of Arts and Crafts in the Rue Réaumur. The public works committee approved the Prefect's schedule for the remaining fifty-seven and a half million francs, which included five small schemes in the right bank centre. It was hoped that work would begin on these projects, all of which had appeared in the 1909 programme, in 1922.[5]

Although the financial outlook remained bleak, the City's powers of compulsory purchase had been greatly extended by new legislation in 1915, 1918 and 1921. On the other hand, the housing shortage,

[2] C.M. reports, 1917, no. 9, p. 2.
[3] André Morizet, *Du vieux Paris au Paris moderne* (1931), p. 332.
[4] C.M. reports, 1921, no. 159, p. 2.
[5] C.M. reports, 1921, no. 159, pp. 4–8.

which had become increasingly serious since the beginning of the war, placed a new restriction on the City. As early as 1921 the public works committee promised:

> 'Naturally enough, we shall evict tenants only if it is possible to do so. It is not our intention to run the risk of aggravating the rent crisis.'[6]

A further discouragement was the continuing impossibility of taxing betterment values. Although the Council expressed its concern in 1912, 1917, 1923 and 1935,[7] none of the laws on compulsory purchase during this time improved the legal situation, and the *Conseil d'Etat* remained resolutely opposed to such taxation. And in the meantime new legislation on property rights was greatly increasing the cost of expropriation. The law of commercial property, passed on 30 June 1926 and modified by several subsequent enactments, established that commercial establishments existed separately from the premises in which they were situated. This meant that compensation for compulsory purchase was no longer related to the length of lease still to run, but to the total turnover. A series of rulings extended this interpretation to premises such as offices and workshops, even though they were not normally visited by customers.[8] Previously the City had postponed its compulsory acquisitions until commercial leases were about to expire, and the extra cost of acquisition after 1926 was an additional serious obstacle to street schemes, especially in the city centre.[9]

Although Councillor Chérioux revived his pre-war campaign for the building of wide streets throughout the city, for both traffic and public health reasons,[10] most councillors were prepared to seek alternative solutions. Some were in favour of underground roads, which could be built without aggravating the housing shortage, though at unprecedented cost.[11] A more practical suggestion, made by the Prefect and approved by the Council in 1929, was for the building of car parks under the streets.[12] One councillor suggested that the *quais* should be cantilevered on both banks of the Seine to provide riverside

[6] C.M. reports, 1921, no. 159, p. 7.
[7] C.M. reports, 1917, no. 58; 1923, no. 55; 1935, no. 22.
[8] Emile-Xavier Fender, *La crise du bâtiment dans la région parisienne* (1936), pp. 240–43.
[9] C.M. reports, 1936, no. 95, p. 10.
[10] C.M. reports, 1924, no. 5; 1929, no. 62.
[11] See, for instance, C.M. reports, 1928, no. 132, p. 4.
[12] See C.M. reports, 1929, no. 144, p. 12.

highways.[13] Another proposed a general revision of improvement lines.[14] But none of these ideas was actually taken up by the Council. Even the reform of improvement lines was not undertaken, although the need for *Conseil d'Etat* approval was rescinded in 1926.[15] However, the almost complete halt of new building in the centre[16] made the occasions on which improvement lines could be enforced extremely rare.

To save expense, the City acquired properties only when they came on the market, even though improvements such as the widening of the Rue des Deux-Ponts (Île Saint-Louis) and the isolation of the Halles were held up while it waited for the last few buildings needed to come up for sale. Positive results seemed so distant that one councillor even called in 1925 for the cancellation of certain schemes and the resale of properties acquired in connection with them so that the remaining works could be financed out of the proceeds.[17] However, in the mid- and late 1920s an improvement in the financial situation raised new hopes. The City was able to scrape together sufficient resources to build the last few metres of the Boulevard Haussmann, whose incomplete state had long been a music-hall joke, in 1926. The stabilisation of the franc and the consequent reduction in interest rates allowed the City to return to a tentative loans policy.[18] But street improvements were not given priority. The 350 million franc (£3 million) loan approved in 1928 was allocated to the completion of the *Métro* network and the construction of workers' dwellings. A much bigger loan of 2,300 million francs (£18½ million) floated in 1929 was to convert several loans contracted at high interest rates in the early 1920s, and to provide 100 million francs for clearance work in the unhealthy areas. Street improvement was no longer considered to be as effective a public health measure as in the past, and had to be justified on traffic grounds alone. And as enormous expenditure would have been necessary to produce any appreciable improvement the City preferred to concentrate on slum clearance and housing, which it believed would do most to promote public well-being.

Contemporaries themselves now recognised that the age of great street improvements was over.[19] Even when public works were

---

[13] C.M. reports, 1924, no. 117, p. 5.   [14] C.M. reports, 1924, no. 127.
[15] (after Maurice Félix), *Le régime administratif et financier de la Ville de Paris* (1957–8) vol. I, p. 24.
[16] See below, chapter 9.   [17] C.M. reports, 1925, no. 64.
[18] See C.M. reports, 1927, no. 70.
[19] See, for instance, Albert Guérard, *L'avenir de Paris* (1929), p. 116, and Morizet, *Du vieux Paris*, pp. 330–31.

revived after 1930 to provide employment, available resources were concentrated on housing and slum clearance. And once again financial problems were a big obstacle, even though the *Département* of the Seine was now ready to make a much bigger contribution to schemes within the city than had previously been usual, out of the proceeds of a loan of 700 million francs (£7 million) floated in 1931. Even greater hopes were raised in 1934 by the Government's unprecedented offer of generous subsidies under the Marquet plan of national re-equipment. A plan of improvements was approved for the Paris region involving the expenditure of 4,500 million francs (£60 million) over five years.[20] The City drew up, as one element of this plan, a schedule of street improvements to be financed by a loan of 525 million francs (£7 million). But this loan was not taken up, and in June 1936 it had to be reduced to 120 million francs. Although the City received a further grant of 110 million francs from the 1931 Departmental loan in December 1936, and a number of street schemes were undertaken, the only one on a large scale in the city centre was associated with the long-delayed isolation of the Halles.[21] The City blamed this slow progress on the Government, which had so far failed to provide any appreciable financial aid.[22] But worse was to come. From 1937 the Government refused to allow the City to contract any more loans, and the steadily increasing budget deficit precluded the financing of any schemes out of revenue.[23]

In such unfavourable circumstances it was inevitable that the centre, where property values were so high, should suffer more than the outskirts. Even the few schemes completed there between 1918 and 1939 were made possible only by the fortuitous purchase of individual properties, or by cooperation with private interests. A number of concerns were slowly buying up nearby properties in order to extend their premises, and were happy to negotiate exchanges of lands with the City. Such agreements were made with the *Magasins du Louvre*, in 1915, for the widening of part of the Rue Croix-des-Petits-Champs, and with the *Samaritaine*, in 1924, to allow a considerable widening of the Quai du Louvre.[24] And the western section of the Rue du Colonel-Driant was built in 1921 in connection with the extension of the

[20] C.M. reports, 1934, no. 47, p. 124; Jean Bastié, *La croissance de la banlieue parisienne* (1964), p. 328.
[21] C.M. reports, 1937, no. 48, p. 6.
[22] See, for instance, C.M. reports, 1936, no. 95, p. 107.
[23] C.M. reports, 1937, no. 56, pp. 1, 2.
[24] See C.M. reports, 1924, no. 170.

Bank of France, which had been planned since the 1880s.[25] In contrast, the short eastward extension of this street to the Rue du Louvre, which was decided by the City Council in 1930, but which depended on the purchase of individual properties, was not carried out until after 1936.

Some progress was made on street schemes that had been approved before 1914. Several streets in the IIIe *arrondissement* were widened to twenty metres as part of the Rue Etienne-Marcel extension scheme, but a number of very narrow sections still remained in 1939. More immediately useful was the widening of the northern section of the Rue des Deux-Ponts in 1931. And a successful windfall operation was the widening of the Quai de l'Hôtel-de-Ville between 1921 and 1925 in connection with the building of a *Métro* line. On the other hand, some old schemes had been sunk without trace by 1939. The plan to build a street from the Quai des Célestins to the Rue François-Miron, which had been approved before 1914 and confirmed in 1921, was forgotten even though it would have helped to clear part of the unhealthy area number 16.[26] Another abortive scheme was the westward extension of the Rue du Colonel-Driant across the Palais-Royal to link the Opéra to the Halles. The City Council approved it in 1930, and, despite protests against this intrusion into the calm of the gardens of the Palais-Royal, called on the Prefect to proceed with the work in 1937. But by the time a definitive scheme had been prepared the Government ban on borrowing had made its execution out of the question.[27] In any case by the late 1930s it was generally accepted by councillors and officials that new traffic streets, to be any real use, would have to be at least forty metres wide, which was out of the question.[28] So it is hardly surprising that the City diverted its precious resources to more rewarding schemes, and endeavoured to provide a partial remedy for congestion by introducing more sophisticated measures of traffic control. Automatic traffic signals, for instance, were used from 1923.[29] But the most significant diversion of attention was not from one type of city centre improvement to another, or even from the centre to the outskirts. It was from the municipal city of Paris to the conurbation as a whole. Paris was now full, and future plans would be made in the context of the *département* of the Seine

[25] The exchange of lands was agreed by the City Council on 27 March 1912.
[26] See below, pp. 239ff.
[27] C.V.P., 29 January 1938, section 5; C.M. minutes, 1 January 1938.
[28] Henry Bidou, *Paris* (1937), p. 409.
[29] Philip John Stead, *The Police of Paris* (1957), p. 194.

and even of the whole Paris region. And it is to the development of these wider planning policies that we must now turn.

2 THE NEW POLICIES

As we have seen, until the turn of the century the Government and the City authorities were happy to work steadily towards the completion of the Second Empire's Paris plan. The assumptions on which it was based were rarely questioned. Of course, it was not a town plan in the modern sense of the term, but a plan of campaign designed to remedy the worst defects of uncontrolled growth. It did not attempt to direct the future development of the capital. Even the street improvement grid, which influenced the city's evolution to some extent, looked back rather than forward. Improvements were concentrated in the central districts where the population was in decline, and by linking the centre more closely with the outskirts they helped to accelerate the growth of problems there without providing any solutions. So by about 1900 the authorities were having to shift their attention from the problems of the centre to those of the outer ring, on both sides of the city boundary.

The decision to build the *Métropolitain* did not in itself constitute a radically new approach to the city's problems. By conforming to the Haussmannic street pattern, and declining to penetrate beyond the city boundaries, the *Métro* lines accentuated the existing distinction between privileged and under-privileged districts. But the sudden switch from street improvements to an underground public transport system began a process by which Haussmann's whole concept of urban planning was undermined. It made it necessary to formulate a slum clearance policy separate from street schemes, and when the failure of the *Métro* forced the City to turn once again to street improvements, the motorcar had arrived in such large numbers that Haussmann's scheme was no longer adequate to deal even with traffic congestion. It was with this double problem—the growing irrelevance of the imperial plan to the centre's problems, and the total absence of any plan for the outer areas, that the authorities now began to be concerned.

Although Paris had set an example to the whole of Europe in mid-century, the apparent success of Haussmann's methods had strangled further positive thinking on town planning in France. It was left to Germany and Britain to replace the planning of the engineer and the civil servant by a more positive form better adapted to the changing needs of cities. The writings of Camillo Sitte and his school won a more important place for the architect in the town planning process. More refined techniques of statistical analysis were developed, and they resulted in a better understanding of cities and their problems. The steady extension of building and sanitary regulations, and of public powers to carry out improvements, made it easier to envisage the achievement of complete control over the urban environment, in which private enterprise would be required to conform to an overall plan. Finally, the continued growth of urban areas led to boundary extensions and the merging of administrative units, which created areas large enough for this overall planning to be carried out.

In the 1890s Paris at last began to realise that its former primacy in urban planning had been lost. The death of the much-respected director of works, Jean Alphand, in 1892, came none too soon, for he had established over all public works departments a grip almost as tight as that of Haussmann himself, and had remained blindly faithful to his former master's methods. After his death the departments were again split up, and separate chief officers were appointed.[30] This reform allowed several highly qualified specialists, such as the architects Joseph-Antoine Bouvard and Louis Bonnier, to move forward into positions where they could influence overall policy. But to promote technicians to key positions was only part of the answer. Independent professional opinion had to be associated with the administration in studying urban problems. In this respect the appointment of Justin de Selves as Prefect of the Seine in 1896 is very significant, for he was a firm believer in the merits of the mixed committee of municipal officers and outside experts.

Another very important cause of change in these years was the nationalist landslide in the 1900 Paris municipal elections. Although the defeat of the radical-socialist-republican axis which had dominated the Council since 1874 reflected a purely national controversy, and the nationalist councillors had no distinctive municipal policy,[31] it brought an unusually large number of new men onto the Council. Many of them remained long after the Dreyfus controversy had died down, and the Council's relations with De Selves had again become cordial. It was this partnership between a dynamic Prefect and a renewed and forward-looking City Council that made possible an energetic return to street improvements after the *Métro* disappointment, and the

---

[30] Léon Martin (ed.), *Encyclopédie municipale de la Ville de Paris* (1902), p. 781.
[31] See, for instance, the election address of J. Caron, successful nationalist candidate for Bonne-Nouvelle ward in 1900, in Ernest Gay, *Nos édiles* (1901), p. 58.

development of a more original approach to the capital's problems. One of the most influential of the nationalist newcomers was Louis Dausset, who defeated the republican-socialist president of the Council, Louis Lucipia, in 1900, and was himself elected president in 1901–2. Even in these stormy years of political struggle he took an interest in the problems of his ward. Gradually he built up an encyclopaedic knowledge of his adoptive city, and in 1909 he became rapporteur of the budget committee. On his own initiative he developed the annual budget report into a wide-ranging survey of the administration, economy and society of Paris, in which he continually emphasised the need for detailed study of urban problems, and foresight and enterprise in dealing with them. Dausset was to a large extent responsible for convincing the Council of the need for heavy public works investment from 1909 onwards.

It was only to be expected that the schemes financed by the 900 million franc loan would be essentially conservative, for it was logical to complete the basic network of Haussmann's street system before formulating a new policy. But councillors and officials were by no means closing their eyes to the future. The climate of informed opinion was becoming increasingly favourable to a new approach. Urban studies and town planning established themselves as disciplines in France in the early 1900s. The word 'urbanisme' was first coined in about 1910, and the *Société Française des Urbanistes* was founded in 1911.[32] So when Louis Dausset urged that Paris should have a development plan like other big European cities, and received some support from City officials, Prefect De Selves acted fast.[33] In 1910 he set up one of his mixed committees, the Extension of Paris Committee, with a membership of councillors, officers and outside experts. Its reports, which appeared in 1913, were written largely by two of the most influential members, Marcel Poëte[34] and Louis Bonnier.[35] Although the Committee's deliberations, brusquely interrupted by the war, were of a purely exploratory nature, it recommended that the eventual development plan should cover the whole of the Seine *département*.[36] A tentative plan was suggested, but it was limited at this early stage to the provision of adequate roads and open spaces in the outer

[32] Jean Bastié, *Croissance de la banlieue*, p. 196.
[33] Louis Dausset, *Rapport général . . . sur . . . le projet de budget de la Ville de Paris pour 1911* (C.M. reports, 1910, no. 91), p. 192; Bastié, *Croissance de la banlieue*, p. 197.
[34] See above, chapter 7.   [35] Bastié, *Croissance de la banlieue*, p. 197.
[36] Commission d'extension de Paris, *Considérations techniques préliminaires* (1913), p. 47.

suburbs.[37] With regard to the municipal city the Committee was less original. It proposed a large number of street improvements, most of which involved the widening of existing thoroughfares,[38] and by recommending that widening should be carried out over a long period by the application of improvement lines the Committee returned to a strategy which Haussmann had abandoned.

Unfortunately, progress towards the comprehensive planning of the conurbation was not maintained after the war. The law of 14 March 1919, modified and reinforced by that of 19 July 1924, required all towns of more than 10,000 inhabitants to draw up a development plan and submit it for approval to the prefectoral administration. This included the City of Paris and all the communes of the Seine.[39] At first Paris seemed to be giving a lead to the rest of the country by making its plan the subject of a public competition, and Parisians were given to understand that the prize-winning entry had been adopted by the *Département*.[40] But the plan, which was considered incapable of realisation in the short term, was quietly pigeon-holed and forgotten. The effect of inflation and economic uncertainty in the 1920s was to postpone all positive consideration of a Paris development plan and of administrative changes that would take account of the rapid spread of the built-up area outside the city boundaries. The communes outside the city boundary were equally slow in producing local development plans. In theory, the control exercised by the Prefect of the Seine over the ring of suburbs and the fact that Paris city councillors also belonged to the General Council of the *Département* should have ensured that a coherent planning policy was applied to the whole of Greater Paris. But it did not. The uncontrolled suburban sprawl of the 1920s and 1930s, so graphically described by Jean Bastié, caught the prefectoral authorities napping. As though it were not enough that the problems of old Paris should be as serious as ever, an entirely new crisis was allowed to develop outside the city boundaries. Tuberculosis mortality, for instance, rose higher in many suburban communes than in the poor *arrondissements* of central Paris.[41] By 1928 it was clear that the preparation of a development plan for Greater Paris could be delayed no longer, and the Government took a hand by setting up the Superior Committee of Planning and General Organisation of the Paris Region. The drafting of a plan for the Paris region was authorised by a law of

---

[37] *Considérations techniques*, plate 8.   [38] *Considérations techniques*, plate 9.
[39] See Pierre Lavedan, *Géographie des villes* (1936), p. 154.
[40] Henri Sellier and A. Bruggeman, *Le problème du logement* (n.d.), p. 143.
[41] Sellier and Bruggeman, p. 93.

May 1932, and a working party was set up under the direction of the architect Henri Prost. The first draft of the 'Prost plan' appeared in 1934, and it was finally approved in 1939. By 1944, however, it was no longer relevant, and the Prefect ordered its revision.[42] In any case, the new plan did not attempt to deal with the administrative city of Paris. Not until December 1936 did the City Council approve the preparation of a development plan for Paris itself.

In the field of town planning as in so many others the collapse of 1940 induced a mood of positive self-criticism. The Vichy Government determined to give town planning a big part to play in the creation of a new France, and in the exceptional conditions of wartime it had no difficulty in passing legislation to establish a town planning code. This was the law of 15 June 1943. It re-enacted that every town should have a development plan, based on street and zoning maps, and it laid down a complicated approval procedure involving several ministries.[43] It placed a specific obligation on Paris to prepare such a plan. Of course, owing to the interruption of all public works in the city outside the unhealthy areas there was plenty of time for reflection and study. Perhaps there was even too much, for although preparatory work started immediately it went ahead in a somewhat leisurely fashion. Even after the Liberation no urgency was instilled into the preparations, because the City's limited resources prevented it from returning to a public improvement policy. Moreover, the drafting of the development plans of the City and of the rest of the conurbation remained separate, even though they could have been coordinated more closely under the supervision of the Prefect of the Seine.

Although the work was by no means rapid, more progress was made in the late 1940s and the early 1950s in preparing the Paris plan than in revising that of the conurbation. The first draft was presented in 1950, and in December the City Council approved its general proposals for zoning, land use, and building regulations. The study of its more controversial elements was delegated to a mixed committee of councillors and officials. One of its vice-presidents, Councillor André Thirion, presented the committee's report to the Council in December 1951.[44] Its proposals were primarily concerned with ensuring the easy movement of wheeled vehicles over the next hundred years.[45] Because they could be carried out only over a very long period,

---

[42] Bastié, *Croissance de la banlieue*, pp. 31, 374.
[43] For a discussion of this law, see Bernard Lafay, *Problèmes de Paris* (1954), pp. 5–7, 53–5, 59–67.
[44] C.M. reports, 1951, no. 2 ('Rapport Thirion').   [45] 'Rapport Thirion', p. 15.

the committee merely sketched out the main lines of communication to be provided, without providing detailed working plans. Three north-south arteries were proposed, one of which would cross the right bank centre by widening the Rue Saint-Denis to fifty or sixty metres and drilling a tunnel from the Rue de Rambuteau to the Boulevard Saint-Germain, with a subsidiary widening of the Rue Montmartre. The committee suggested that this operation was one of prime urgency.[46] Other fundamental elements of the plan were the reconstruction of the Halles on the same site, and the creation of a business zone to the north of the right bank centre in a triangular sector bounded by the Gare Saint-Lazare, the Gare du Nord, and the Place de la République. Otherwise, the right bank centre was little affected. The other street improvements foreseen there were of only local importance and, with one exception, involved the widening of existing streets. The artistic importance of the Marais was recognised. No street improvements were planned for the IVe *arrondissement* which, it was suggested, should receive special treatment with a view to preserving its old houses. Although the Ier *arrondissement* was allotted eleven street schemes, all were connected with the proposal to reconstruct the Halles. Even the proposed new urban renewal operations did not affect the right bank centre.

Strong objections were raised to the 'Thirion plan' in the City Council. The finance committee was in favour of its approval, but only as an advance project. It was against the committal of financial resources and the creation of planning restrictions for such a vague scheme, and suggested that a few urgent works should be selected to form the planning scheme proper.[47] But other councillors objected to the fundamental planning principles embodied in the plan, and in May 1952 the Council voted its reference back. Its main criticism was that the plan envisaged a large number of demolitions without providing new buildings to replace them.[48] But the Thirion proposals were clearly out of the question in any case, because they were too ambitious, and were unlikely to make a major contribution to the solution of the traffic problem within the foreseeable future, if ever. Their rejection foreshadowed, and made necessary, the formulation of a totally new approach to the city's planning problems.

In 1952 several councillors presented a carefully studied report

---

[46] 'Rapport Thirion' pp. 12, 61-3.
[47] C.M. reports, 1952, no. 1, annex pp. 20-21.
[48] Lafay, *Problèmes de Paris*, p. 59.

calling for the improvement of traffic flow by the decongestion of the centre.[49] They wanted to see parking restrictions imposed, car parks and pedestrian subways built, the railway termini moved to the outskirts, express *Métro* lines constructed, and the Halles decentralised to the suburbs. The City authorities were already thinking along similar lines. Apart from palliatives such as street widening at the expense of pavements and central reservations[50] the only alternative to the Thirion proposals was to limit as far as possible the circulation of wheeled traffic. In March 1953 the City Council approved the second part of the development plan, which included a revised street scheme of much more modest ambitions than that of the Thirion plan. But this decision was still of mainly academic interest, because considerable delay was expected before the Government approved the plan, and the financial resources to carry any of it out were still lacking. Meanwhile, the City and the Government were slowly perfecting two new basic strategies, designed to reduce pressure on the city instead of attempting to meet ever-increasing demands. The one strategy, for the centre, was based on the decentralisation of the Halles to the outskirts. And the other, for the conurbation as a whole, revolved round the decentralisation of employment to the provinces.

(a) The decentralisation of the Halles

Ever since the First World War the City had been fighting a losing battle to adapt the Halles to increasing pressure on their facilities. In 1921 the general purposes committee called on the Prefect to prepare a plan for the transformation of the markets and the erection of the two pavilions which should have been financed by the 900 million franc loan.[51] But only a derisory thirteen million francs (£260,000) were allocated to the isolation of the Halles from the 1921 loan,[52] and by 1925 nothing had been done towards the building of the two pavilions. In fact, most of the resources allocated had been diverted to other purposes. By the time Councillor Quentin exposed this situation and called for work to start,[33] the general purposes committee had reversed its previous position. It now pointed out that the scheme would provide only a mediocre return for the expenditure of up to thirty million francs (£300,000) that would be involved. The committee thought

---

[49] C.M. reports, 1952, no. 2.
[50] This procedure was recommended by the Prefect in 1952 (see Lafay, *Problèmes de Paris*, p. 200).
[51] C.M. reports, 1921, no. 33.   [52] C.M. reports, 1921, no. 159, p. 4.
[53] See C.M. reports, 1925, no. 153.

that the ultimate solution would be to move the Halles outside the city centre altogether, but this seemed 'unlikely, whatever happens, to be carried out immediately, or even in the near future.'[54] The controversy revived again in 1929,[55] by which time the committee had again changed its mind, favouring the extension of the Halles on their present site and the utilisation of basements in existing buildings. To move the Halles, it now reported, would be 'to abandon a policy with which the City has associated itself, and to which we can even say it has chained itself.'[56] This time work actually went ahead, and the new market buildings were completed in the early 1930s. But they were already insufficient to compensate for the extra load imposed on the Halles by the growing consumption of the Paris area. The City Council and even the Chamber of Deputies maintained a steady demand that the Halles should be modernised and enlarged.[57] Before 1939 the majority of proposals involved reorganisation on the same site, but once it became clear after 1945 that public investment on communications within the city would remain minimal, informed opinion swung in favour of decentralisation. The arguments put forward were much the same as those of Lanquetin in the 1840s, namely that extensive street improvements would be unnecessary if the Halles were moved. Although this hypothesis was even less well founded than it had been a century before, the absence of other feasible schemes in the centre resulted in desperate over-optimism about the effect that the departure of the Halles would have on the whole of the right bank central area.

Until 1949 the possibility of rebuilding on the same site was not definitely ruled out, but detailed studies begun in that year clearly revealed that such a solution was out of the question.[58] The time and effort wasted in using the Halles were evaluated at several billion francs a year, and there was already a tendency for the bigger wholesale traders to move their businesses to the suburbs.[59] On the other hand, the leases of many traders occupying space in the Halles still had some years to run, so that no immediate move was possible. So from 1953 the Government passed a series of acts, with the agreement of the City

[54] C.M. reports, 1925, no. 166. [55] See C.M. reports, 1929, nos. 51, 59.
[56] C.M. reports, 1930, no. 17, pp. 48, 80–81.
[57] For a list of debates and motions concerning the Halles, see *Les Halles Centrales de Paris*, an inquiry by the Institut Français d'Opinion publique, published by the Préfecture de la Seine in May 1958, pp. 112–16.
[58] See *Les Halles Centrales de Paris* (Etudes et Travaux du Conseil Economique, no. 1, 1949).
[59] 'Paris, Rungis, La Villette: transfert des Halles Centrales', special number of *Techniques et Architecture*, December 1964, pp. 43–4.

Council, to establish control over the activities of the Halles, and prepare for an eventual radical solution.[60] To overcome immediate congestion problems it was decided to establish an annex for wholesale fruit and vegetable sales on the Seine at Bercy, just to the east of the city centre, and the City proceeded with the modernisation of two of the existing pavilions that had been decided in 1950. Finally, in July 1957, the Government's permanent study committee for markets of national importance decided to investigate all possibilities of building a new wholesale market in the suburbs. The Prefect of the Seine undertook a survey of the present use of the Halles, and found that although most market traders expressing an opinion were in favour of keeping the Halles on the old site, the proportion of Paris retailers obtaining supplies directly from there was only 63 per cent, and declining. And this proportion was as low as 30–40 per cent among suburban traders.[61] If the Halles had served Paris alone the arguments for moving them would have been weak. But a central location was becoming less and less necessary to markets whose function was increasingly to serve a growing urban region, and had even become a positive hindrance. The recognition of this fact coincided with the emergence of an effective regional planning organisation, which alone could coordinate a successful move. In May 1960 the interministerial planning committee for the Paris region, which had been set up only three months before, decided in principle on the transfer of all the activities of the Halles to two suburban sites. Fruit and vegetables would go to a completely new complex to be built on over 200 hectares at Rungis, five miles to the south of the city boundary. Wholesale meat and related trading would be carried on in a new market to be built near the existing abattoirs at La Villette, just inside the city boundary to the north-east of the centre.[62] Finally, a decree of 13 July 1962 classified the Rungis project as a market of national importance. In November 1963 the City Council agreed to give its full support and cooperation to the transfer which, it was hoped, would be completed within five years. The story of the creation of the new market complex does not concern us here. But as the great day of the final liberation of the Halles, postponed until March 1969, approached, a decision on the future of the site and the surrounding area, now

---

[60] For a list of legislation relating to the Halles 1953–63, see *Halles Centrales de Paris* (1963), published by the *Journal Officiel*.

[61] Préfecture de la Seine, *Les Halles Centrales de Paris* (1958), pp. 15, 89, 96, 98.

[62] *Techniques et Architecture*, December 1964, pp. 44–5. The decision to create a meat market at La Villette had been taken in 1959.

deprived of its main economic activity, became increasingly urgent. We shall return to this question in chapter 10.

(b) The decentralisation of employment

After the Liberation public investment was directed to areas and cities, such as Caen and Rouen, which had been severely damaged or degraded in the war. Paris was not one of these areas. But it seemed likely that when normal conditions were restored Paris would resume its pre-war position as a magnet for both public and private investment. Provincial jealousy of the capital had been very strong for centuries, but in the post-Liberation atmosphere of reappraisal it gained a new respectability. In 1947 Jean-François Gravier published his influential *Paris et le désert français*, a violent assault on the primacy of Paris which, he claimed, had bled the provinces white. For the first time, the Government and the City authorities were prepared to listen to such arguments. Just as in Britain, the 1930s had emphasised the problem of depressed areas of declining or underdeveloped industries, and the war had helped produce the will and the powers to direct the location of industry. Inter-war experience had made the City Council and the General Council of the Seine aware of the problems which result from rapid industrialisation and immigration without adequate public investment. In 1948 the Paris region planning committee, set up at the Liberation, passed a resolution opposing the extension of the industrial potential of the conurbation.[63] From 1949 the Government began to make grants to encourage industrial movement to the provinces. In 1955 restrictions were placed on new industrial developments in the Paris region, and were extended to offices in 1958.[64]

The effect of these policies on the growth in the number of jobs in the Paris area has been limited—the majority of proposed developments have been approved, and most of the firms that have moved have established their production within easy reach of the capital. But their effect on public investment planning was more far-reaching. Because it was believed that improvement schemes in the Paris conurbation would strengthen its attraction of population and activities, the Government declined to encourage or subsidise them. The elected representatives of Paris and the Seine were prepared to accept this situation because their finances were still in a sorry state after the war and they were afraid to impose fresh burdens of taxation. Although a steady improvement in the financial situation from the mid-1950s

[63] Bastié, *Croissance de la banlieue*, p. 367. [64] See below, chapter 9.

allowed increasing investment, it was still totally insufficient to meet the conurbation's needs. Only massive Government subsidies could provide the necessary finance, but to grant them would have compromised the decentralisation strategy.[65]

So it was in an atmosphere of approved investment inactivity that the preparation of the Paris development plan was carried forward. Not surprisingly, it was a slow and often infuriatingly academic process in the 1950s, during which the City Council occasionally lost its patience.[66] After the first part of the Paris development plan was approved by the City Council in 1950 the Government submitted it to the Paris region planning committee, which suggested a number of modifications. In October 1952 the Minister of Reconstruction asked the Prefect to incorporate a number of these suggestions in a new draft of the plan. After a period of study the Prefect replied in July 1954 that he still held to most of the criticised points.[67] Further negotiations followed, as a result of which the City Council approved some changes in this part of the plan in July 1956 and April 1957. But Government approval did not ensue, and the prefectoral administration had to undertake a new study in 1958.[68] The second part of the plan, including the street improvement scheme, was voted by the City Council in 1953 but had still not received Government approval in 1959. By this time its proposals needed complete revision owing to their inadequacy and the failure of the improvement line strategy to produce results.[69]

What was clearly needed at the end of the 1950s was a new look at the whole plan. Population and job opportunities had continued to grow—and so had public indignation against inadequate housing and amenities. This mood of reappraisal influenced the preparation of two ten year interim plans—the *PADOG*, covering the whole of the Paris region, and a new plan for the city alone to be integrated with the *PADOG*.

(c) The PADOG

It was decided in 1944 to revise the Paris regional development

---

[65] For a study of the development of the expenditure of the City up to 1958, see (after Maurice Félix), *Le régime administratif et financier de la Ville de Paris* (1959), vol. IV, pp. 5–8. See also 'La Préfecture de la Seine 1967', *B.M.O.*, special number, March 1967, pp. 141–2.
[66] See, for instance, Lafay, *Problèmes de Paris*, p. 67.   [67] Lafay, pp. 66–7.
[68] *Mémoire préfectoral*, 1959, no. 2, p. 4.   [69] *Mémoire préfectoral*, 1959, no. 2, p. 10.

plan which had been approved in 1939. But no progress was made until an order of January 1956 laid down that a new plan should be presented to a public inquiry, with the 1939 plan remaining in force in the interim. The plan was prepared by the Paris regional town planning department, which was somewhat embarrassed by the fact that official policy was still at the time opposed to the growth of the city, whereas most of the problems that had to be dealt with in the plan were problems of growth. The outline plan (*Plan d'aménagement et d'organisation générale—PADOG*) was approved by a decree of 6 August 1960, as an interim plan for 1960–70, and various detailed plans were published at intervals over the next few years. Its aim was to revitalise the suburbs by creating four new main 'urban nodes' and eight or nine secondary nodes a few miles outside the city boundaries.[70] New towns were rejected because they might add to the attraction of the Paris region, but plans were made for the expansion of some existing towns lying between twenty and sixty miles from the capital.[71] However, most of the planned population growth was to be accommodated within the existing conurbation. The new nodes would provide supplementary centres of employment in order to limit congestion in the city centre and restrict the growth of jobs there. In fact, work had already started on an office complex at La Défense, which lay to the north-west of the city, and was the closest of the nodes designated by *PADOG* to the existing business centre. An essential feature of the plan was the provision of an adequate transport system, based on a radiating network of motorways, with an outer ring running several miles outside the city and an intermediate ring on the line of the city boundaries. An express *Métro* system linking with existing railway lines outside the city would provide rapid transit throughout the conurbation, and revitalise some of the more distant suburbs. Extensive car parking facilities would be provided.

(d) The Paris interim development plan

In 1958 it was decided to draw up a ten year interim development plan for the city that could be integrated with the *PADOG*.[72] The City Council was able to approve the draft in October 1959 and it was published by the Government in its final form in July 1961. The City

---

[70] Bastié, *Croissance de la banlieue*, pp. 374–6. For a diagram of the urban node principle in *PADOG*, see Bastié, *Paris en l'an 2000* (1964), p. 196.
[71] Peter Hall, *The World Cities* (1966), pp. 69–71.
[72] *Schéma directeur d'aménagement et d'urbanisme de la Ville de Paris* (1968), p. 10.

Council and the prefectoral administration had both declared that Paris should maintain its existing level of population,[73] and the new plan was basically conservative, with what was claimed to be a supple zoning system adapted to the needs of a historic city. Paris was divided into 'functional zones', categorised as residence, artisanal activity and warehousing, industry, business, administration and higher education, and 'protected zones', including the city's historic core, where special regulations would be applied to all new and existing buildings. A plot ratio would be fixed for each of these zones—the first time that the principle of plot ratios had been applied in Paris. Also included in the plan was a series of dispositions relating to urban renewal zones and the modernisation of degraded street blocks, thoroughfares and court-yards. The fundamental strategy of the plan was to comprehend and confirm the status quo in Paris, in the hope of establishing some control over its future evolution. It consecrated the business vocation of the west-central district by zoning for primary commercial functions a large sector centred on the Opéra area. Similarly, the planned administrative zone was centred on the VIIe *arrondissement* and the university zone on the Ve *arrondissement*. The plan aimed to concentrate expansion of business activity either in the existing central business district or in new office complexes at La Défense, and at Maine-Montparnasse on the left bank. This would prevent the un-controlled movement of business to the perimeter where it might create new problems.[74] Through traffic would be allowed to bypass the centre by the construction of a motorway box roughly linking the main terminal stations and a north-south artery to the east of the city centre on the line of the Canal Saint-Martin.

Taken together, these two plans represented a policy of restriction of growth combined with the greatest possible measure of improvement of services, equipment and accommodation for those who would continue to live and work in the conurbation. If there was a contradiction in this policy, the Government was at this stage not prepared to recognise it. The Ministry of Construction's official brochure on the *PADOG* stressed that there was a double task of reestablishing a balance between the provinces and Paris in order to prevent migration to the capital as far as possible, and of improving conditions inside the Paris region. This echoed the remark of the prime minister, Michel

[73] Bastié, *Croissance de la banlieue*, p. 377.   [74] *Schéma directeur* (Paris), pp. 62–5.

Debré, in a speech to the Assembly in December 1960, that the organisation of the Paris region was a problem of national importance.[75] But this official policy, now clearly formulated for the first time, was attacked from two sides. Some argued that it underestimated the growth rates of population and employment, and that much stronger restrictions were necessary. Newly available data tended to bear out this view; for example, the 1962 census figures showed that the *PADOG* housing target of 75,000 new dwellings a year was hopelessly inadequate.[76] On the other hand, many believed that an expanding capital was inevitable and even desirable, and that by refusing to face this fact the Government was preparing future chaos. Georges Pilliet, in his *L'avenir de Paris* (1961), called for the vigorous development of Paris as a potential European capital and as a key element of a prosperous national economy, and his views were strongly supported by Alain Griotteray in his *L'Etat contre Paris*, published in 1962. Furthermore, the two plans disappointed numerous architects and planners who had been hoping for a more adventurous approach, and many were already drafting and canvassing for alternative schemes. The most imaginative of these projects was for a 'parallel Paris', published by a group of architects early in 1960. It examined and rejected in turn the solutions of peripheral growth, satellite towns, underground development and decentralisation to the provinces, and proposed the creation of a completely new city twenty or thirty kilometres from Paris to take some of its functions and population. Other architects were disappointed by the authorities' conservative approach to the design of buildings within Paris, and Michel Holley, for instance, called for a relaxation of height restrictions.

The largely unfavourable reaction of informed opinion against the plans coincided with the Government's conversion to a more liberal attitude towards the growth of Paris. This change had been brought about by two fundamental changes in the national politico-economic situation since 1958. France's participation in the Common Market gave a fillip to its economy and a north-eastward orientation to its industry. Paris, it seemed, could not only grasp the role of capital of Europe to which it had long laid claim, but would benefit directly from its proximity to the centre of gravity of the Common Market, the industrial areas of Belgium and northern Germany.[77] And secondly,

[75] Ministère de la Construction, *Le plan d'aménagement et d'organisation générale de la région parisienne* (1962), pp. iii, 18–19.
[76] Peter Hall, *World Cities*, p. 77.
[77] *Paris: présent et avenir d'une capitale* (1964), p. 66.

the election to the presidency of Charles de Gaulle provided the political stability in which the economy could grow rapidly, and put in power a man whose desire to enhance the grandeur of France was reflected in his ambition to make of Paris a city worthy to assume the rank of European capital in terms of both prestige and efficiency. These two changes accelerated the recognition of the limited results of the negative planning policies of the previous decade. Moreover, the Government now began to set up an administrative machine which would allow it to direct the replanning of the whole of the Paris region.[78] By a law of 2 August 1961 it set up the *District de la région de Paris*, which brought the whole of the Paris area under a single planning authority. Also established, in 1960, was the Institute of Town Planning and Urban Studies of the Paris Region, a multi-disciplinary body of great potential.[79] Although the powers of the *District* were limited until administrative boundaries could be changed to conform to it, the Government granted it increasing financial resources and encouraged it to coordinate the efforts of existing local authorities. The President chose as his special delegate to the *District* Paul Delouvrier, a civil servant who had distinguished himself during the Algerian troubles and had a reputation for solving tough problems. Delouvrier was soon convinced that an expansionist policy was the only realistic one. In a statement published in 1963, popularly known as the *Livre Blanc*,[80] he called for the allocation of more land for development in the Paris area. He countered the 'Paris and the French desert' hypothesis by demonstrating that, outside the capital itself, the Paris region was generally less well equipped than the provinces. But his dominating aim was to give Paris a fair chance of becoming the capital of Europe by taking full advantage of its favourable position as a productive and distributive centre, as long as the rest of the country could be made to benefit from its growth. Although decentralisation would continue, it would have to be more discerning to avoid sapping the economic strength of Paris. The historic core would be preserved and enhanced, but much higher buildings than those allowed in the past would be permitted in the outer areas. Previous negative attempts to prevent peripheral sprawl would be replaced by planned expansion along corridors of growth.[81]

[78] For a detailed study of these recent administrative changes, see Annmarie Hauck Walsh, *Urban Government for the Paris Region* (1968); Préfecture de Paris, *De la Préfecture de la Seine à la Préfecture de Paris, 16 septembre 1966–20 février 1969* (1969).
[79] *Coopération technique*, nos. 46–8, c. 1966, pp. 22, 26.
[80] *Avant-projet de programme duodécennal pour la région de Paris* (1963).
[81] Paul Delouvrier, 'L'avenir de Paris: avenir spontané ou avenir concerté', in *Paris. présent et avenir d'une capitale* (1964), pp. 115–26.

In 1964 the *District* embodied these principles in its *Schéma directeur d'aménagement et d'urbanisme de la région de Paris*, which prepared for a possible doubling of the developed area by the year 2000.[82] It planned two main axes of growth running north-west towards the sea on either side of the Seine, but it retained the suburban nodes incorporated in earlier plans. Work now began on a *Schéma directeur* for the city itself, to embody these new conclusions. When the Paris interim development plan, which had been adopted by the City Council in 1962, was finally approved by a decree of 6 February 1967, its revision was immediately ordered and a series of new studies was undertaken.[83] The Paris *Schéma directeur* was published in January 1968. Like its regional equivalent it had no pretensions to being a development plan in itself, and was merely a collection of guidelines for the detail planners. In fact, its authors admitted that it conformed in many respects with previous plans.[84] But they claimed to have based their work on an analysis of current situations and trends to a much greater extent than their predecessors.[85] So their conservatism resulted partly from an appreciation of the aesthetic and historic value of much of the city, and partly from a realistic assessment of the amount of change that was feasible. The *Schéma* stated that the principal aims of town planning in Paris should be to disengage the centre and make better use of the periphery; to move the centre of gravity of tertiary activities more to the east of the city to compensate for the decline of industrial employment there; to obtain a more satisfactory balance of residence and employment, and to protect the city's architectural heritage.[86] Three or four 'poles of employment' (one of which—Maine-Montparnasse—was already being built) should be established just outside the historic centre near the railway termini and important *Métro* interchange stations, each providing between 20,000 and 40,000 jobs. This would allow the centre's excessive concentration of activities to be reduced, thus lessening congestion and allowing the restoration of buildings and amenities, and it would counter the unplanned conversion of dwellings into offices in the west. Traffic would be organised in a number of main thoroughfares planned for rapid movement, and through traffic would be discouraged from entering sidestreets. To this effect, existing improvement lines would be maintained in some streets but abandoned in those where heavy traffic flow was not desired.

[82] Peter Hall, *World Cities*, pp. 93–4.
[83] 'La Préfecture de la Seine 1967', special number of *B.M.O.*, March 1967, pp. 6–7.
[84] *Schéma directeur d'aménagement et d'urbanisme de la Ville de Paris* (1968), p. 118.
[85] *Schéma directeur (Paris)*, pp. 11–12.　　　[86] *Schéma directeur (Paris)*, pp. 82–3.

Throughout the *Schéma* a clear distinction was made between the treatment of the centre and that of the outskirts; indeed, the authors themselves stated, '. . . everything is dominated by the contrast between the centre and the periphery.'[87] For the first time an official planning scheme implying massive public expenditure[88] had consecrated the principle of preservation and even of active restoration of the historic core. But how far had this policy been established from first principles, and how far was it a rationalisation of an *état de fait* which made restoration or decay the only possible alternatives? To provide an answer we must look at the improvements that have actually been carried out in Paris since the war, and the share that the right bank centre has had in them.

As we have seen, the Government gave priority to public works in war-damaged areas after the Liberation.[89] Although the suburbs of Paris had been damaged by Allied air raids, the central areas were almost untouched, and other cities had been so much more heavily damaged than Paris that the capital had a very low priority. The City's finances were totally inadequate to finance all but the smallest improvement schemes. Revenue did not keep pace with the fall in the value of money, so that an increasing proportion of income had to be allotted to the maintenance of services while less was devoted to investment.[90] In 1938 wages and salaries had represented 13 per cent of the City's total expenditure on revenue account; by 1957 this proportion had risen to 32 per cent.[91] Moreover, the Government extended the control over the City's borrowing which it had established before the war, at first in the interests of national reconstruction, and later to slow down the growth of the city. From 1945 until the late 1950s the City was allowed to borrow no more than thirty to fifty million new francs a year, compared to a pre-war average of 1,000 million at current values.[92] Total capital expenditure was a mere 216·8 million new francs between 1946 and 1950, and 251·3 millions over the following five years, whereas between 1932 and 1936 it had totalled 2,629 million new francs.[93] In May 1952 the City Council called on the Prefect to

---

[87] *Schéma directeur (Paris)*, p. 34.   [88] *Schéma directeur (Paris)*, p. 115.
[89] For an account of national urban public works policy after the war, see Robert Auzelle, 'Town planning administration in France 1945–1955', *Town Planning Review*, vol. XXVIII, April 1957, pp. 7–36.
[90] Lafay, *Problémes de Paris*, p. 13.
[91] Brian Chapman, 'Paris', p. 471, in W. A. Robson (ed.), *Great Cities of the World* (2nd ed., 1957), pp. 451–86.
[92] 'Destin de Paris', p. 30, *Urbanisme*, no. 84, 1964; Alain Griotteray, *L'Etat contre Paris* (1962), p. 134.
[93] *Schéma directeur (Paris)*, p. 114.

establish a separate fund for town improvement schemes under the law of 15 June 1943, but in the following year a new Council was elected which throughout its five year term of office followed 'a reasonable policy of budgetary economies', and the fund never came into being.[94] On the other hand, the Government accepted the principle in 1946 that public works of general interest should receive a subsidy. But the subventions paid until the late 1950s were very small, and the Government's annual contribution of 400 million francs towards Paris street maintenance was discontinued in 1951.[95] Even in 1958, when investment was beginning to increase, subsidies amounted to only 16 per cent of the City's total capital outlay, including such headings as schools, housing and slum clearance.[96] But once the principle was established there was scope for further development.

The number of motorcars in Paris soon passed its pre-war level, and the City had to cope the best it could by advanced traffic control methods. From 1947, and particularly from 1949, many thoroughfares were converted to one-way operation.[97] Synchronised traffic lights were introduced to speed up flows. Parking restrictions were extended and in the mid-1950s Police Prefect Dubois took powers to tow away parked cars.[98] From the early 1950s some widenings were carried out at the expense of pavements and central reservations, and from 1954 a number of underpasses were built at the gates of Paris on the exterior boulevards.[99] But in the right bank centre, where no such improvements were possible without extensive compulsory purchases, nothing was done. While work went ahead on peripheral underpasses, one planned in 1950 for the Place du Châtelet[100] was quietly pigeon-holed, and still has not been built. Nothing was done to provide extra parking spaces in the centre.

After 1954 the City's investment budget began at last to rise slowly each year, and between 1956 and 1960 a total of some 680 million new francs (£48½ million) was invested. Then, from 1960, it began to climb rapidly, partly as a result of the expansion of the economy, and partly owing to the changed Government attitude towards Paris. The

[94] C.M. reports, 1953, no. 1, p. 18; 1958, no. 3, p. 3.
[95] *La direction générale des services techniques de Paris* (1958), p. 5 (supplement to the periodical *Travaux*, June 1958); Griotteray, *L'Etat contre Paris*, p. 135; Raiga and Félix, *Le régime administratif de la Ville de Paris* (1922), p. 632.
[96] (after Maurice Félix), *Le régime de Paris*, vol. IV, p. 8.
[97] See lists in Préfecture de Paris, *La circulation à Paris et dans le département de la Seine* (1953), annex 5.
[98] Philip J. Stead, *The Police of Paris*, p. 195.
[99] 'La Préfecture de la Seine 1967', special number of *B.M.O.*, March 1967, pp. 85–6.
[100] *La circulation à Paris* (1953), p. 28.

total capital outlay from 1961 to 1965 was 1,509·3 million new francs (£108 million), and the annual figure has continued to rise since then. A considerable impulse was provided by the Fourth National Plan (1962–5), and an even bigger one by the Fifth Plan (1966–70).[101] This increase was spread over the whole range of public works activities. Investment in water supplies, for instance, rose from an average of 24·8 million new francs a year in 1954–8 to a planned 587 millions a year for 1966–70. Capital expenditure on the Paris river port rose from nothing in 1954 to 189·6 million new francs in 1967. Work began on the east-west express *Métro* line. The growth of highway expenditure was also spectacular, rising from about five million new francs in 1954 to 100 millions in 1960 and over 300 millions in 1965.[102] Much of this investment was allocated to the circular motorway (*boulevard périphérique*) on the line of the city boundaries, fifteen kilometres of which were open in 1967. Completion was expected in 1970 or 1971. Another spectacular but less costly scheme was the Seine-side highway (*voie sur les berges*) running for several miles along the northern *quais*. This project was approved by the City Council in 1964 after similar but shorter sections had been built on the left bank, and it was opened in 1968. In both these schemes the City received a 40 per cent subsidy from the Government and 20 per cent from the *District*. The City also pressed ahead with the corollary of road improvements—the provision of parking spaces, which cost the taxpayer nothing. By 1967, 5,500 spaces had been provided in underground car parks, and 8,000 more were under construction.[103] Municipally guaranteed loans were made to private concerns to provide extra spaces. The right bank centre, however, was not allowed to share more than a small fraction of this increased investment. Apart from the Seine-side expressway it has seen no street improvements at all since 1945, despite its growing congestion. A large proportion of the underground parking spaces will eventually be provided in the centre, and work is now proceeding rapidly on several sites. But the only accommodation provided there so far has been the combined garage and car park built on the Place du Marché-Saint-Honoré in 1957.

It is clear from the schemes described so far that, despite the vast sums now being devoted to public works, the authorities do their

---

[101] *Schéma directeur (Paris)*, p. 114; 'Paris', *Coopération technique*, nos. 46–8, p. 20.

[102] Figures displayed at the exhibition 'Du Paris des projets au Paris des chantiers', Grand Palais, 22 March–20 April 1967.

[103] Figures displayed at Grand Palais exhibition, 1967. See also C.M. reports, 1965, no. 1, pp. 95–8; 1968, no. 1, pp. 12–13.

utmost to avoid the compulsory purchase of built property. It was estimated in 1962 that to build radial highways in Paris itself would cost at least sixty million new francs (£4·3 million) for every kilometre.[104] Despite the legislators' best efforts expropriation remains excessively costly. Although laws were passed in 1953, 1958 and 1967 to facilitate compulsory purchase, the compensation granted still often exceeds the estimated value of the property because of the extra indemnity paid for disturbance.[105] Sensibly, the authorities have been buying properties as and when they come on the market, and in 1962 a special agency was created to buy land in the Paris area on behalf of the Government and the local authorities. But its financial resources were insufficient,[106] and, in any case, property very rarely changes hands in the city centre where compensation costs are highest. The obligation to rehouse those displaced by public works remains a serious handicap in the continuing housing shortage. Recovery of betterment values is still limited despite new powers passed in 1961 and 1964.[107] And so by the mid-1950s planners and elected representatives had already lost all hope of ever undertaking big improvement schemes in the city centre. They looked back with nostalgia to the times of Haussmann and bemoaned the fact that they could never return.[108] At this time it was still the impossibility of changing the centre, as much as its undesirability, that dominated the official mind. Bernard Lafay, for instance, wrote of the first ten *arrondissements*:

> 'There exists a "crystallised" Paris, solidly implanted and often built to last, which it is difficult, and often undesirable, to touch.'[109]

Lafay recognised that public works had to be linked to the provision of dwellings rather than their suppression, which restricted them to the outer districts:

> 'Let us be realistic; it will be hard to obtain loan sanction to demolish a hundred buildings, even to open up an avenue. On the other hand, we shall get it if we want to erect one hundred

---

[104] Griotteray, *L'Etat contre Paris*, p. 73.
[105] See list of town planning legislation in Bastié, *Paris en l'an 2000*, p. 182. For an account of the difficulties which have surrounded the recoupment of betterment values in Britain, see Ralph Turvey, *The Economics of Real Property* (1957), pp. 102–48; Peter Hall (ed.), *Land Values* (1965), pp. ix–xix, 53–72.
[106] Bastié, *Paris en l'an 2000*, p. 118.   [107] Bastié, pp. 38, 117.
[108] See, for instance, Lafay, *Problèmes de Paris*, p. 51; Paul Haag, 'Un Préfet de la Seine— le baron Haussmann', *Revue politique et parlementaire*, July 1955, pp. 34–51. Lafay was President of the City Council, and Haag, Prefect of the Seine.
[109] Lafay, *Problèmes de Paris*, pp. 91–2.

buildings at a place where the avenue in question will then obviously be necessary.'[110]

Although Lafay was writing at a time of great financial stringency, the change of emphasis to the outer ring of *arrondissements* has not since been questioned even though much greater resources have become available in recent years. Instead of following the traditional policy of adapting the centre to the pressures placed on it, the City is now attempting to reduce those pressures in the hope of making improvements unnecessary. But so far it has been impossible to assess the results of this approach because the principal reduction of pressure, the departure of the Halles, did not take place until March 1969, and a final decision still has to be taken on the use of the site. To all intents and purposes, therefore, central Paris has been handed over to the preservationists. Even the Halles district, whose renewal is being discussed at the moment, has become much more of a restoration operation than was once anticipated.[111] Such, at any rate, has been the result of the long-delayed renewal operations in the unhealthy areas of the right bank centre.

3 THE UNHEALTHY AREAS

The City recognised the unhealthy areas as one of the most urgent of the problems facing it after the First World War. Louis Dausset was already suggesting in 1919 that they would have to be given a larger share of public works investment than in the past.[112] Tuberculosis mortality had increased in them during the war years, and conditions in them were likely to deteriorate still further as a result of the new rent control measures. But Parliament had now strengthened the inadequate powers that had held up clearance work before 1914. Siegfried's proposals were embodied in the law of 17 June 1915, which related compensation to the state of salubrity of the buildings. And the law of 6 November 1918 allowed the compulsory acquisition of whole areas without the requirement of establishing the insanitary state of every house.

In 1919 Councillor Rendu renewed his demand for the rapid demolition of the six unhealthy areas that had been designated before the war. But when the water and sewers committee reported in favour of this proposal other councillors demanded a totally new inquiry,

---

[110] Lafay, p. 11.   [111] See below, chapter 10.
[112] Louis Dausset, *Rapport général sur le projet de budget de la Ville de Paris pour 1920* (C.M. reports, 1919, no. 109), p. 28.

claiming that the number of unhealthy areas had certainly increased since the 1906 investigation. Their arguments persuaded the Council to refer the whole scheme back to the prefectoral administration, which undertook a new study.[113] In the meantime all clearance work was held in abeyance. The new survey took four years to complete. It showed that the problem had indeed become much worse than had been realised before the war, and strengthened the case for total demolition. It was now proved beyond all doubt that the traditional policy of creating parks and open spaces as reservoirs of pure air, and broad streets to allow the air to circulate throughout the city, was totally irrelevant to the struggle against tuberculosis. Detailed researches showed that houses on the banks of the Seine which received direct sunlight as well as fresh air had an extremely low incidence of the disease. But buildings which stood behind them, just twenty-five metres from the river yet screened from it by the first row of houses, had no benefit at all. The same phenomenon was apparent along the broad arteries built by Haussmann—only the houses directly fronting the street enjoyed a low incidence of tuberculosis. No completely effective chemical disinfectants had yet been developed, and it was now clear that there was no relation between tuberculosis and other infectious diseases. The report of the water and sewers committee concluded that completely new preventive techniques were needed, and that in future every house would need to have its own reservoir of air and light.[114]

The new inquiry designated a total of seventeen unhealthy areas, numbered in descending order according to their degree of tuberculosis mortality. They contained 4,290 buildings, occupied by 186,594 people.[115] None of the new areas was in the right bank centre and the increase resulted mainly from the addition of tubercular areas on the city outskirts. The boundaries of the old area number 1 (Saint-Merri) were modified, but it retained its position at the head of the list. In 1920 it had 12,653 inhabitants in 347 buildings, and its average annual tuberculosis death rate during the war had been 10·35 for every thousand inhabitants, the highest of all the unhealthy areas. The old area number 2 (Saint-Gervais) was extended and became number 16 in the new classification. It was still much smaller than area number 1, with 178 buildings and 8,698 inhabitants, and its average tuberculosis

[113] C.M. reports, 1923, no. 97, p. 54.
[114] C.M. reports, 1923, no. 97, pp. 43, 44, 66, 68, 83, 85.
[115] André Morizet, *Du vieux Paris*, p. 346.

11, 12 Paris in the 1850s. Rue de la Ferronnerie near the Halles (*above, left*), seen from the crossroads of the Rue Saint-Denis and the Rue de la Reynie. Rue Saint-Honoré (*above, right*), looking west from the Rue de la Ferronnerie. This street was the main east-west route across the centre of Paris before the Rue de Rivoli was built.

13 Paris in the 1850s. Rue Tirechape, from the Rue de Rivoli. This sinister alley is typical of many decrepit areas which stand just a few feet from Haussmann's new streets.

14 Paris in the 1850s. Rue Beurrière, seen from the Rue du Four, now in the VIe *arrondissement*. Note the contrast between the dark, cramped streets of the right bank centre, and the more open aspect of central districts on the left bank.

15 Paris in the 1850s. Rue du Mail, from the crossroads of the Rue Montmartre and the Rue du Cléry. The houses on the left stand on the line of the demolished rampart of Charles V.

16 Paris in the 1850s. Rue d'Argenteuil, on the flanks of the Butte des Moulins, near the Place du Théâtre-Français. This street was widened when the Avenue de l'Opéra was built in the 1870s.

(Marville collection)

(Marville collection)

17 Paris in the 1850s. Rue des Moineaux, seen from the Rue des Orties, at the summit of the Butte des Moulins. This whole area was demolished when the Avenue de l'Opéra was built.

18 (*above*) Work in progress near the Hôtel de Ville on the extension of the Rue de Rivoli, 1854. The roadway has been cleared, but has not yet been paved. Rapid progress is being made on new buildings fronting the street, which have been exempted from property taxation for twenty years. [*Illustrated London News*, 7 January 1854.] 19 (*below*) Rue Saint-Antoine looking west from the church of Saint-Paul and Saint-Louis in the late 1850s. The new Rue de Rivoli stretches away into the distance. It is at this point that the two streets merge almost imperceptibly into each other. The easternmost of the new Rue de Rivoli buildings are on the right, in contrast to the much older houses, on their narrow and irregular sites, which remain firmly entrenched on the left. [*Paris dans sa splendeur* (1861).]

20 (*above*) The Rue de Rivoli in 1871, looking east from the Rue Saint-Martin towards the Hôtel de Ville, after the capture of a Communard barricade by Government forces. **21** (*right*) Rue des Innocents, from the Rue Saint-Denis, near the Halles. The design of these buildings, built in the mid-seventeenth century, was fixed by an architectural ordinance.

22 (*left*) House with turret, Rue de la Tixéranderie, seen through the romantic eyes of Charles Méryon, from *Old Paris: twenty etchings by Charles Méryon*, plate 8. 23 (*below*) Avenue de l'Opéra under construction, February 1877. Removal of the Butte des Moulins, from *L'Illustration*, no. 1774, 24 February 1877, p. 124.

(*H. R. Walden*)

24, 25 Modern streets in contemporary Paris: (*above*) Place des Victoires and Rue Etienne-Marcel; (*below*) Avenue de l'Opéra from the Place du Théâtre-Français.

(*H. R. Walden*)

(*H. R. Walde*)

26, 27 Old streets in contemporary Paris: (*above*) Rue Montorgueil, looking south, towards the Halles, from Rue Réaumur; (*below*) Rue du Temple in the Marais, looking north. The arch on the left is the entrance to the Hôtel Saint-Aignan.

(*H. R. Walde*)

death rate had been only 5·56 during the war. The average for all seventeen areas was 7·09.[116]

Fortunately, the wartime mortality figures proved to be exceptionally high. As early as 1919 there was a sharp fall in the number of deaths from tuberculosis in all the unhealthy areas. So much of the panic atmosphere which seemed to be developing in the City Council in 1919 had been dispelled by the time it came to consider what practical steps to take in 1923. It was now estimated that complete demolition of all the areas would cost 1,000 million francs (£13·3 million). In the right bank centre alone, the clearance of areas numbers 1 and 16 would cost 167 and fifty-three million francs respectively. Yet only thirty million francs had been allocated to slum clearance from the new 1,800 franc loan, and the serious housing shortage made extensive demolitions out of the question. The City now carried out a new study to see whether the demolition of some houses and the reconditioning of the others could be as effective as total clearance and redevelopment. The prefectoral administration claimed that the results of the investigation showed that such methods, while not a panacea, would lead to a big fall in mortality. The Council had little choice but to agree, and in 1923 approved a scheme for the partial acquisition of area number 1 at a cost not exceeding twenty-one million francs (£280,000). Work also began on the preparation of similar schemes for the other areas.[117]

Modest though it was, the operation in area number 1 was considerably delayed. In December 1924 the City Council allocated nine million francs for the first instalment of acquisitions. These houses were sited in the sector bounded by the Rues Beaubourg, Simon-le-Franc, Saint-Martin and des Etuves-Saint-Martin which should have been demolished before 1914. The City now approached landlords in order to obtain as many properties as possible by negotiation, but it became clear that compensation costs would be much higher than had been expected, and the Council agreed to reduce the number of buildings to be acquired in the first instance to forty-four. On two occasions, in 1926 and 1927, the Council called on the administration to expropriate these properties, but after further financial difficulties and legal delays the City was given full powers to acquire by the civil tribunal of the Seine only in May 1930. Compensation was not fixed by the assessment panel until February and March 1931, although by this

---

[116] *Ann. Stat.*, 1920 (Îlots insalubres); C.M. reports, 1923, no. 97, p. 95.
[117] C.M. reports, 1923, no. 97, pp. 96–107.

9

time it had become possible to acquire a second instalment of forty-seven buildings to make up the full total of ninety-one in the 1923 scheme. There was now a further delay while tenants were rehoused, and the properties were not demolished until 1933–5.[118] And the delay might well have been longer if the City's resolve had not been strengthened by the desire to provide work for the unemployed. Slow progress could certainly not be blamed on public opposition to the demolition of ancient buildings. On the contrary, there was almost unanimous approval,[119] and the Old Paris Committee gave way with good grace in the interests of public health.

During the ten long years that it took to demolish less than one-third of the most lethal unhealthy area in Paris, discussions continued about the other sixteen. One of them, the small Clignancourt area, was hurriedly demolished in 1925 after an outbreak of plague, but nothing was done about the others. In 1926 the council of public hygiene and salubrity of the Seine *département* declared that only total clearance could provide a complete solution in the unhealthy areas,[120] and in 1928 several councillors called for the complete demolition of all of them within ten years. They proposed that the occupants should be rehoused in new workers' dwellings partly financed by the resale of cleared sites, even though this would have precluded the reaccommodation of those displaced in the same area.[121] On the other hand, Councillor R. Faillot argued that all except the most urgent demolitions should be postponed until the housing situation eased, or until the City was in a position to provide alternative accommodation under the Loucheur law.[122] He feared that if demolition proceeded regardless the only result would be to create new slum areas alongside the existing ones.[123] Reluctantly, the City Council admitted the good sense of this reasoning. In July 1930, when it approved a long-term plan for the construction of twenty thousand dwellings under the Loucheur law for those displaced by public works schemes, it agreed to slow down future demolitions. The Prefect of the Seine was even more pessimistic, believing that even when dwellings were built under the Loucheur law their rents would be too high for people from the unhealthy areas.[124]

[118] C.M. reports, 1931, no. 21, pp. 21–2; C.V.P., 28 January 1928, p. 4; *Ann. Stat.* 1932–4, p. 468.
[119] Louis Chevalier, in *La conjoncture économique dans le département de la Seine*, 1959, 3ème trimestre, p. 467.
[120] C.M. reports, 1932, no. 21, p. 23. [121] C.M. reports, 1928, no. 5.
[122] See below, chapter 9. [123] C.M. reports, 1928, no. 123.
[124] Fender, *Crise du bâtiment*, p. 290.

A further disappointment was the unexpectedly high cost of acquisition in area number 1, which seriously compromised even the modest clearance schemes envisaged. The City complained that the interpretation placed on the 1915 law by the independent valuers and the assessment panel was totally at variance with the legislators' intentions and even with the letter of the law. The Prefect took the case to the appeal court which ruled in his favour, but this gave no guarantee against future repetitions, and did not affect the compensation paid to tenants which had also been very inflated. The water and sewers committee even wanted the Prefect to postpone the acquisition of the second instalment of buildings in area number 1 until a new law had been passed to deprive the assessment panel of its right to decide on the state of insalubrity of a building, and to require all those concerned to follow precise rules of procedure. Without going quite this far, the Council decided to postpone all further slum clearance projects until the law was modified.[125] In 1931 a bill was introduced to modify the law of 1915, but it took four years for it to emerge as the decree-law of 8 August 1935. It gave the Prefect authority to undertake compulsory purchase without reference to the Government, and special powers to deal with unfit houses and unhealthy areas. The assessment panel was replaced by an arbitration tribunal which proved more reasonable in its adjudications, although its decisions did not always please the City. Another decree-law (30 October 1935) *required* the arbitration tribunals to subtract from an indemnity the total cost of the repairs that would be necessary to restore the property to a fit state, and the City's position was further strengthened by another decree-law of 24 May 1938.[126]

While waiting for these new enactments to come into force, councillors continued to suggest solutions for the unhealthy area problem. In 1934, for instance, Councillor C. Joly suggested that public gardens could be created in interior courtyards by the removal of sheds and other parasitic buildings, an idea that Albert Guérard had put forward in 1929.[127] But in the same year new hopes of a radical solution were aroused when the Prefect asked the Council to approve a scheme of works in several unhealthy areas at a cost of 300 million francs (£4 million) under the Marquet plan to reduce unemployment. The Council agreed to this expenditure, over two-thirds of which was to

[125] C.M. reports, 1932, no. 21; 1937, no 56; Lafay, *Problèmes de Paris*, p. 121n; Morizet, *Du vieux Paris*, p. 346.
[126] C.M. reports, 1937, no. 56; Lafay, *Problèmes de Paris*, p. 121.
[127] C.M. reports, 1934, no. 69; Guérard, *L'avenir de Paris*, p. 123.

be devoted to the right bank centre.[128] Shortly afterwards, however, the Government decided that the Marquet plan subsidies would be paid only in respect of the cost of new buildings, so that the full burden of site clearance would fall on the City. In November 1934 the Prefect put forward a modified scheme whose total expenditure would be reduced to 259 million francs, but it was severely criticised by the water and sewers committee and the Council referred it back in December. At the same time, the Council called on the Prefect to seek authority to borrow 300 million francs for slum clearance and improvement work.[129]

In December 1935 the City Council decided that it could safely go on to acquire the third instalment of area number 1, especially now that the new legislation had streamlined the procedure for representing unfit property. But the acquisition of further instalments now depended on the creation of new resources. Unfortunately, the Government was prepared to authorise a loan of no more than 150 million francs, and, even then, only on condition that cleared sites were laid out as public gardens. In June 1936 the Prefect proposed the allocation of this sum to the areas numbers 1 and 16 alone, but the scheme was referred back because the Council considered the creation of gardens to be uneconomic and ineffective. In July it called on the Prefect to renew his request for sanction to borrow 300 million francs and to seek a Government subsidy of 500 million francs for slum clearance. But the Prefect could obtain no satisfaction. By June 1937 the Council was reluctantly admitting that the City's growing annual deficits and the Government's refusal to authorise borrowing were destroying all chance of carrying out clearance operations. By this time the City had to abandon the 300 million francs subsidy offered under the Marquet plan, and the 10,000 dwellings built between 1930 and 1934 for displaced slum-dwellers had been used for general housing needs.[130] From then until war broke out again in 1939 all slum clearance was at a complete standstill.

Fortunately, there had been a considerable development of preventive measures against tuberculosis and other diseases since the Great War. In March 1915 the City Council adopted Rendu's pre-war suggestion that twelve tuberculosis dispensaries should be set up in Paris. Then, in July of the same year, the Prefect formed a committee

---

[128] C.M. reports, 1934, no. 133.
[129] C.M. reports, 1934, no. 133; 1937, no. 56, p. 32.
[130] C.M. reports, 1937, no. 56, pp. 1–6. The 10,000 dwellings were all that were built in the so-called '20,000 dwellings programme'.

to study the organisation of the struggle against tuberculosis in Paris and the Seine. The Government was also active, and set up in 1918 a bureau of social hygiene to direct preventive measures against all infectious diseases, and principally tuberculosis.[131] Further modifications were made to the sanitary code drawn up in 1904 under the law of 1902,[132] and the law itself was amended by the decree-law of 30 October 1935. The 1894 sewer law, which the City had been able to enforce only partially, was modified and complemented by the laws of 19 July 1923 and 13 August 1926. The second of these enabled the City to advance to landlords the cost of linking their properties to the sewers. And the law of 2 January 1928 extended the requirement of sewer links to properties in private streets and passages. This new legislation was very effective, and the proportion of buildings in Paris without a sewer link fell rapidly from 30 per cent in 1925 to 18 per cent in 1928.[133] Further control over private streets, of which a number still remained in the right bank centre, was afforded by the law of 15 May 1930, which gave the Prefect power to improve or take over any such street after an unfavourable report by the health inspector. And in 1937 the council of public hygiene drew up a model set of regulations for private streets.[134] But it must be borne in mind that the effect of much of this new legislation on the city centre was limited. Much of it was aimed principally at the private developers of suburban sites and estates rather than at Paris landlords. Any attempt by the authorities to coerce or encourage the owners of older buildings to improve them was doomed to failure because rent controls had sharply reduced the amount that landlords could spend on repairs. In 1939 only 10,000 workers were employed in Paris on repair work compared with 55,000 in 1914.[135] A law of 31 December 1937 allowed owners to raise rents to cover the cost of improvements, but it had little effect because they were required to obtain the prior consent of the majority of their tenants.[136] Equally abortive was a decree-law of 14 June 1938, which encouraged the formation of landlords' syndicates in street blocks where the public utility of sanitary improvement work had been declared. By the time France was invaded not one single request had been made for the application of this law.[137]

[131] (after Maurice Félix), *Le régime administratif et financier de la Ville de Paris* (1957–8), vol. I, p. 32.
[132] A.P.s., 19 March 1920, 7 May 1928, 7 May 1936.
[133] C.M. reports, 1928, no. 82, p. 3.
[134] Philippe Isaac, *Les problèmes de l'habitation urbaine en France* (1944), p. 58.
[135] Isaac, p. 187n.   [136] Isaac, p. 207.
[137] (after Félix), *Le régime de Paris*, vol. I, pp. 116–17.

The great epidemic diseases continued to fade away after the Great War. The authorities were convinced that the causes of all infectious diseases apart from tuberculosis were mainly superficial,[138] and they continued their efforts to improve water supplies, sewage disposal and street cleansing. With the development of prophylactic measures, especially vaccination, and the general improvement in hygiene and living conditions, the death rate contined to fall. In 1922 there were 139·6 deaths in Paris for every 10,000 inhabitants, compared with 157 in 1913, and by 1939 the death rate had fallen to 106.[139] The decline in mortality was equally marked in the right bank centre. Deaths from infectious diseases became increasingly rare. In 1939 only fifty-nine people died from typhoid in the whole of Paris, compared to 375 deaths in 1914. And although there were sixteen deaths from cholera in 1914, it disappeared completely as a lethal disease after about 1925.

Even more remarkable was the general fall in tuberculosis mortality. The disease killed 10,910 people in 1914, but no more than 4,087 in 1939. In the right bank centre the reduction was even sharper, the number of deaths falling from 1,130 in 1914 to 359 in 1939. However, there was very little improvement in the tuberculosis death rates of the unhealthy areas numbers 1 and 16 despite a substantial reduction in their population, and a big reduction in the average rate of all the unhealthy areas. It even seems likely that the toll in area number 1 would have been even higher in 1939 than in 1919 if the worst affected section had not been demolished in the early 1930s. But these gloomy prospects began to brighten in the early 1940s.

It is a paradox that the Occupation, which paralysed the evolution of Paris in almost every way, should have been a time of progress in the clearance of the unhealthy areas. This was because powers of requisitioning were introduced that would have been out of the question in peacetime. In July 1941 the whole of area number 16 was declared unfit, and the first requisition order was made in December. More orders followed at regular intervals until October 1943. They allowed the City to take possession after one month, and to use armed force if necessary to evict tenants. Yet in spite of this brutal but expeditious procedure the cost of requisitioning was higher than the City had expected. In the area number 16 the wartime evaluation committee

[138] See, for instance, a reference to rubbish dumps as one of the main causes of urban epidemics in Louis Girard, *Le nettoiement de Paris* (1923), p. 5.
[139] Figures taken from *Ann. Stat.*

ordered the City to pay up to twice as much as it had offered.[140] Experience here and in other parts of Paris showed that slum clearance still involved financial loss for the authorities, especially when the slums stood on potentially valuable sites.[141]

By October 1943 the City had requisitioned 221 buildings in the area number 16, but had demolished only 143 of them because of the shortage of accommodation at low rents and the continuing high cost of compensation for displaced tenants.[142] Demolitions ceased completely after 1943. And no properties at all were requisitioned in the area number 1 during the whole war.

After the Liberation the housing shortage immediately became even more serious than it had been in the last years of peace, and the City found it impossible to demolish most of the slum houses that it had requisitioned. On the contrary, it had to carry out expensive repairs in many of them to make them fit for more prolonged occupation. Outside the unhealthy areas the City was equally cautious. It was rare for an unfit house to be condemned or demolished, and the City preferred to compel landlords to make repairs.[143] Now that the retention of old buildings had become economically necessary, the City began to show greater interest in the preservation of their aesthetic qualities. The first sign of this change of heart was the decision to restore the buildings surrounding the former graveyard of the church of Saint-Gervais, in the area number 16, in 1945.[144]

Although the City did not lose its powers of requisition after the war it could make little use of them in the right bank centre. Only four more houses were acquired in the area number 16 between 1945 and 1947. The housing shortage, and the preparation of the Paris development plan, held up all further activity for some years. And, increasingly, the case against total demolition gained in credibility. Of course, the conventional preservationist arguments of writers like Georges Pillement had been heard, and ignored, before the war, but what now made them more acceptable was a sharp fall in tuberculosis mortality. This reduction was registered both in the city as a whole and, more spectacularly, in the unhealthy areas. By 1952 the annual number of deaths from the disease per thousand inhabitants in the

[140] Lafay, *Problèmes de Paris*, p. 123n.
[141] Isaac, *Problèmes de l'habitation urbaine*, p. 217. For similar British experience, see William Ashworth, *The Genesis of Modern British Town Planning* (1954), ch. IV, pp. 81–117.
[142] Lafay, *Problèmes de Paris*, p. 112.
[143] Isaac, *Problèmes de l'habitation urbaine*, p. 60.
[144] See Yvan Christ, etc., *Le Marais* (1964), p. 27.

unhealthy areas had fallen to 0·72, compared to an average of 6·75 in 1918–38. And this time the two unhealthy areas of the right bank centre reflected the general decline in mortality. In area number 1 the rate fell from 4·49 to 0·91, and in area number 16, from 4·32 to 0·66. This great improvement was the result of a further improvement in medical techniques, thorough disinfection, and the B.C.G. vaccination.[145] And the number of vaccinations continued to rise in the 1950s and 1960s.

As a result of this big fall in the number of deaths, tuberculosis mortality was by 1950 no longer a satisfactory index of the degradation of dwellings, and it became clear that housing conditions were as bad if not worse in some districts which had never been designated as unhealthy areas. In 1951 the Paris planning committee called for the complete revision of the delimitation of unhealthy areas, '. . . considering that tuberculosis mortality which was the basis of this delimitation has changed and can no longer be used as the basis of a new definition . . .'.[146] And the committee turned away from demolition as a solution in the old unhealthy areas:

> 'We believe that many old buildings in the Sainte-Avoie and Saint-Merri wards can be made healthy without demolition.'[147]

The first results of this new thinking, and the new researches that accompanied it, appeared in the draft development plan for the city in the early 1950s. It showed a large number of zones 'scheduled for special treatment', about eight of which were in the IIIe and IVe *arrondissements*, including the two old unhealthy areas. The public works committee expected that their number could be increased later, especially in the centre, but it made clear that wholesale demolition was no longer under consideration:

> 'From now on, the concept of the transformation of unhealthy areas has been extended into the idea of a planning zone more in accordance with the principle of a comprehensive renovation study.'[148]

This meant, as Lafay explained later, that the treatment of unhealthy areas would have to be incorporated in a broader scheme covering neighbouring wards.[149] The City Council accepted this case and in

---

[145] Lafay, *Problèmes de Paris*, p. 110.
[146] C.M. reports, 1952, no. 1, p. 10.
[147] C.M. reports, 1951, no. 2, p. 33.
[148] C.M. reports, 1953, no. 1, pp. 16–18.
[149] Lafay, *Problèmes de Paris*, p. 115.

March 1953 invited the Prefect to study the criteria that could be used to make a new delimitation of unhealthy areas, taking both hygienic and living conditions into account. In March 1954 it approved a set of new norms, and from 1953 the *Annuaire Statistique* ceased to publish separate mortality figures for the old unhealthy areas. Of course, all this did not mean that living conditions in the old unhealthy areas had improved; on the contrary, Bernard Lafay believed that they were far worse than in 1918.[150] But for the time being there was little hope of achieving any improvement, and Lafay accepted that only 'remodelling' would be possible. He considered that the emergency expropriation procedure was too brutal for regular use, and recognised that all compulsory purchases aroused great opposition.[151] Lafay hoped for much from the law of 6 August 1953, which was intended to allow the compulsory acquisition of slum properties at less cost than the value of the sites.[152] But the housing shortage and the Government's control of municipal borrowing greatly restricted the City's freedom of action. And in 1955 there were still no transit apartments available, and even no permanent accommodation for those displaced.[153] In addition, the redevelopment of central slum areas was affected by the special height restrictions enforced there, which prevented the rehousing of all those displaced on the same sites. Such restrictions also made redevelopment less attractive to private developers, whose participation could be obtained under the law of 1953. This was an important obstacle in the area number 16, where the City had already decided that redevelopment should conform to the aesthetic character of the district.[154]

Fortunately, the Government was about to give new encouragement to slum clearance. The year 1955 saw the birth of the modern concept of urban renewal in France. A decree of 20 May 1955 replaced the old principle of insalubrity by a broader definition which allowed much larger areas to be taken in. It attempted to obtain the participation of landlords in renewal, and, more important, offered subsidies to local authorities for renewal work. It was strengthened and amplified by further legislation in 1958. The City undertook a new programme of compulsory purchase orders in 1955, and properties were acquired in the XIIIe, XIXe and XXe *arrondissements*. The number of orders made rose rapidly from 1958.[155] But the City's attention had now

---

[150] Lafay, p. 110.   [151] Lafay, p. 123.   [152] Lafay, pp. 110–11, 115.
[153] C.M. reports, 1955, no. 5, p. 7.   [154] Lafay, *Problèmes de Paris*, p. 129.
[155] 'La Préfecture de la Seine 1967', special number of *B.M.O.*, March 1967, p. 10.

switched from the centre to the periphery, which was held to constitute the main problem. The City Council approved a new compulsory purchase instalment in the east of area number 16 in April 1957, but with the intention of spreading the operation over several years.[156] In fact, only six buildings were acquired there in 1957 and 1958. And in the old area number 1 all activity had long since ceased, in anticipation of the total reappraisal that would follow the departure of the Halles. Meanwhile, the City undertook a new study of the areas that were suitable for urban renewal so that they could be included in the development plan. It revealed that the zones of potential renewal covered about one-quarter of the city's area and housed about a million people.[157] But first of all the City had to deal with the hard core of the slum areas, which were still, in their essentials, the old unhealthy areas delimited after the Great War. By 1960 fifteen schemes had been begun, covering thirty-nine hectares. In the next five years eleven new schemes were started, covering 112 hectares, thirty-seven of which had been acquired by 1965. The total area cleared between 1955 and 1965 was fifty-seven hectares.[158] The law of 26 July 1962, by allowing the designation of long-term renewal zones, prevented speculation in condemned property which might force up values and compensation assessments. And a national slum clearance programme was embodied in the Third and Fourth Plans.[159] In January 1966 a new departure was made when the City Council approved the Prefect's proposals for the redevelopment of the 'Hauts-de-Belleville' and 'Italie' areas. In these schemes public and private initiatives are combined within an overall plan which will take twenty years to complete.[160] They mark a further shift in emphasis from the centre to the outskirts, where there are fewer restrictions on the scale of the redevelopment, and most of the dwellings can be provided in tower blocks. In the right bank centre the only urban renewal work still going on in a slum area in 1966 was in the old unhealthy area number 16, but this was admitted to be more of a restoration scheme than a normal renewal project.[161] In clearance operations in the decade preceding 1966 only 400 dwellings were demolished in the right bank centre (all in the area number 16),

---

[156] C.M. reports, 1958, no. 3, p. 24.
[157] For a plan of the areas to be renewed, see Bastié, *Paris en l'an 2000*, p. 197.
[158] *B.M.O.*, special number, March 1967, p. 11. See also *Atlas de Paris et de la région parisienne*, text, pp. 102–3.
[159] See 'La rénovation urbaine, I', p. 6, in *Seine et Paris*, no. 40, 4th quarter, 1966.
[160] See *Italie : secteur d'aménagement concerté Italie-Gobelins* (1967).
[161] *B.M.O.*, special number, March 1967, p. 15.

compared with 10,000 in the whole city.[162] So at a time when slum clearance was at last beginning to get under way in Paris, the oldest part of the city was being effectively excluded from it. And we shall see later, in chapter 10, how far this reprieve for the old houses of the centre reflected a positive desire for their preservation.

[162] *Atlas de Paris et de la région parisienne*, text, pp. 102–3.

9

The Approach of Obsolescence

Building was at an almost complete standstill during the war, and the economic boom of 1919–20 was not prolonged enough to allow the number of new buildings authorised to exceed 500 per year. In 1921 the total fell below 400, but activity expanded rapidly from 1922 to 1926, and over 1,100 buildings were authorised in this last year. Although building slumped severely in 1927, it recovered in the following year, and in 1929 over 1,250 permits for new constructions were issued. A more prolonged decline set in from 1930, with a serious deterioration in 1931 and 1932. Although the fall in the number of permits was halted and even reversed in 1933–4, it was renewed in 1935. In 1937, when only about 230 permits were issued, the Paris building industry was again almost as stagnant as it had been during the war. And it seems that the last two years before the Second World War saw only a very slight improvement.[1] After September 1939 building was again almost completely halted. In 1942 only fifty-three permits were issued for the whole of the city, and only thirty-nine in 1944. Even after the Liberation, conditions were not significantly more encouraging to building, and there was little sign of a recovery until 1948 (seventy-two permits). In 1949, 164 buildings were approved, but the number fell again in 1950, and only in 1951 did an extended period of expansion begin which lasted until 1956, when as many as 521 permits were issued. But the total again fell in 1957 and 1958. Even in 1956, the best post-war year so far, only about the same number of

---

[1] No building figures were published for 1938 and 1939 by *Ann. Stat.*, but the value of sites and properties, which had been declining, rose slightly in these years (G. Duon, 'Evolution de la valeur vénale des immeubles parisiens', *Journal de la Société de Statistique de Paris*, 1943, nos. 9–10, p. 180).

permits was issued in Paris as in 1932. After 1958 the decline continued despite the economic recovery which accompanied the change of Republic and the operation of the Common Market. In 1959, 1960 and 1961 the totals of permits issued for whole buildings were 330, 302 and 269. No further figures are available because the *Annuaire Statistique* ceased to publish Paris building permit statistics in 1962, a significant indication in itself of the extent to which new building had declined. This fall reflected mainly the shortage of suitable sites within the city, for building continued apace in the suburbs. Bernard Lafay wrote as early as 1954:

'. . . we have to recognise that free building lots are extremely rare, especially for the construction of *H.L.M.* or *Logéco* buildings which are the ones we most need.'[2]

Compared to the last two decades before the Great War, the years after 1918 were a time of considerable instability and generally low activity for the building industry. The number of buildings approved in the peak year of 1929 was exceeded in one year out of two between 1895 and 1914. The general paralysis of activity after 1945 was completely unprecedented in peacetime. Of course, the inability of private enterprise to construct dwellings for the working classes had become apparent long before 1914, and it was made even more intractable by the various rent control measures enacted during the war. Although rents of new buildings were not controlled, the diminished return on property investment resulted in the diversion of much capital to stocks and shares, which now, in contrast to the last years before the war, provided a better return than did buildings.[3] Many of the people of small independent means, who had been an important source of building investment before the war, had been ruined by 1918.[4] The only branches of construction which prospered were shops and offices, as a result of commercial and industrial expansion after the war, and small villas in the suburbs, which from the 1920s began to attract many of the working and lower-middle classes by the supposedly better living conditions which they offered.[5] Building was no longer an attractive long-term investment as it had been before 1914, and it could thrive

---

[2] Bernard Lafay, *Problèmes de Paris* (1954), p. 87. The buildings he is referring to are publicly built or subsidised types. The number of permits issued for these buildings fell from seventeen in 1956 to three in 1961.

[3] Emile-Xavier Fender, *La crise du bâtiment dans la région parisienne* (1936), pp. 71–2.

[4] Jean Bastié, *La croissance de la banlieue parisienne* (1964), p. 238.

[5] Fender, *Crise du bâtiment*, p. 79; see also Bastié, *Croissance de la banlieue*.

only when and where conditions were extremely favourable to speculation, or when share prices fell to a low level, as occurred in 1929. Many speculative development companies were founded, and the individual developer, who before 1914 had still been responsible for much new building, had almost disappeared by 1920.[6] The economic and financial instability of post-war France became a dominant influence on building. Contractors suffered from the rapid inflation of the 1920s, which often made their total building costs higher than the price agreed with the client, who usually could demand lengthy credit facilities from the contractor.[7] Building costs increased by over four times between 1914 and 1924, and by more than seven times by 1929, while rents rose only three times. *Crédit Foncier* loan interest rates, which had been 4·85 per cent in 1913, reached 7 per cent in 1918 and 8·25 per cent in 1921. In 1926, as the franc fell, the rate reached 10·60 per cent. After the franc was finally devalued in 1928, building began to expand in response to the overall growth of the economy, but the main spheres of activity were the building of luxury apartments and private mansions, and the modernisation of department stores and shops.[8] *Crédit Foncier* rates fell from 1927 onwards, and by 1930 had been reduced to 6·25 per cent.[9] Long-term interest rates remained generally low until 1931, but after that year the effects of the economic crisis spread to building. By 1935 the *Crédit Foncier* rate had again risen to 8·05 per cent. As early as January 1932 numerous abandoned building sites could be seen in Paris, and by 1933 the majority of building firms had almost completely stopped work. Developers suffered from deflation to the extent of a 40 or 50 per cent loss on capital invested in buildings constructed since 1926, and many contractors and development companies went bankrupt.[10] Then, from 1936, construction costs began to rise again after four years during which they had steadily declined.[11] After 1945, inflation and economic instability continued to restrict the building industry to a very low level of activity, and rent control had to be extended even further to protect the tenant from the astronomical rents that would have resulted from the operation of a free market in a situation of severe housing shortage. Only after about 1958 did the economic climate become more favourable to building enterprise, and even then

---

[6] Fender, *Crise du bâtiment*, p. 73.

[7] Fender, p. 161; for annual increases in retail prices, building costs, and rents, see Bastié, *Croissance de la banlieue*, p. 349.

[8] Fender, *Crise du bâtiment*, p. 164.   [9] Fender, p. 336.

[10] C.V.P., 30 January 1932, pp. 5–6; Fender, *Crise du bâtiment*, pp. 166–7, 210–12.

[11] In 1936 labour costs made up half the total cost of a building, excluding the price of the site (Fender, *Crise du bâtiment*, p. 39).

building did not enjoy the same prosperity as other sectors of the economy. The housing shortage has remained a serious problem. And although general economic factors such as bank loan charges, availability of credit, and inflation clearly had an influence on the building rate, they cannot alone explain the almost permanent malaise of building in Paris since 1914. Even if these external influences had been favourable, building would still have been less attractive to investment than it had been in the nineteenth century. Mainly responsible for this change were rent controls, public housing programmes, new obligations placed on landlords, higher taxation, land shortages, and stricter building regulations.

(a) Rent controls

From the very beginning of the Great War a general moratorium was declared on the rents of dwellings of mobilised personnel, and of all small dwellings. Under this moratorium, payment of rents was postponed until the end of the war.[12] Then, in August 1916, the rights of landlords to raise rents or give notice were restricted.[13] Although the rent law of 9 March 1918 aimed to bring about a progressive restoration of a free market, its rapporteurs realised that it would be difficult to reconcile the twin needs of cheap and salubrious accommodation:

> 'After the war, the housing question, and especially that of working-class housing, will arise in all its urgency.'[14]

The rapid rise in the lower rent ranges had been recognised as a problem before the war,[15] and it seemed advisable to keep rents at a low level until sufficient working-class dwellings had been built to allow the re-establishment of a free market. The legislature put off the moment when rents would be freed until 1922, when the law of 31 March 1922 established a transitional rent structure to prepare the way for the abolition of all controls.[16] But in December 1923 the first of a new series of laws limiting rent increases was passed. One of them extended control to commercial rents. Not until 1929 did it seem safe to envisage a progressive return to a free market, when the law of 29 June 1929 created a programme of staged increases for pre-war dwellings. The

[12] Fender, *Crise du bâtiment*, pp. 224–6.
[13] Law of 20 August 1916. It was extended by the law of 23 October 1919.
[14] Henry Chéron and Émile Bender, *La loi du 9 mars 1918 sur les loyers* (n.d.), pp. 7–8.
[15] See, for instance, C.M. reports, 1911, no. 76, p. 1.
[16] Pierre Maricourt, *Les charges de la propriété bâtie à Paris 1914–1925* (1925), p. 442.

first increase was planned for 1931, but it had to be postponed because of the economic crisis. A law of 31 December 1931, which allowed landlords who carried out improvements to raise their rents, remained almost a dead letter. In July 1935 the Government ordered a general *reduction* of 10 per cent in residential and commercial rents, and controls were retained until the declaration of war re-created the conditions which had originally made them necessary.

Although rent controls did not apply to post-war dwellings, they effectively limited the amount of new building undertaken. Investors had no guarantee that controls would not be extended at some stage to new buildings (as they actually were in 1941), and the low level of controlled rents had a depressive effect on those of new dwellings.[17] Tenants became accustomed to devoting a small proportion of their income to rent payments. Estimates have placed this proportion for working-class families at 15–20 per cent before 1914. By 1937 it had fallen to just over 6 per cent.[18] Although commercial rents rose more quickly than those of dwellings, they too failed to keep pace with rising costs.[19]

The declaration of the Second World War made the continuation of rent controls imperative. In February 1941 control was extended to modern buildings when a veto was placed on rent increases in dwellings built between 1914 and 1939. After the war the housing shortage was worse than ever, and inflationary trends began to accelerate. In 1948 rents were only 5·5 times higher than in 1914, although the cost of living had risen one hundred times. Their real value was only 4–5 per cent of what it had been in 1914, and they took up no more than 3–4 per cent of the income of a working class household.[20] It was to effect a progressive remedy of this situation that the law of 1 September 1948 established a new rent structure, and as a result of a series of six-monthly increases rents rose by an average of 12·8 times between 1948 and 1962, while the cost of living rose only 2·4 times.[21] But complete decontrol remained out of the question. Bernard Lafay, president of the City Council in 1954, estimated that there were still 120,000 homeless families in Paris.[22] In recent years the Government has continued the policy of progressive, stepped increases, which have been made

[17] Jean Bastié, 'Capital immobilier et marché immobilier parisiens', p. 241, *Annales de Géographie*, no. 373, May-June 1960, pp. 225–50.
[18] Institut de conjoncture, *Etude économique sur le problème du logement* (1944), p. 3; Philippe Isaac, *Le problème de l'habitation urbaine en France* (1944), p. 41.
[19] Bastié, 'Capital immobilier', p. 231.   [20] Bastié, p. 240.
[21] Bastié, *Croissance de la banlieue*, p. 367.   [22] Lafay, *Problèmes de Paris*, p. 240.

possible by the increasing prosperity of the economy. Modern dwellings have been exempt from control, but their rents are so high that they are beyond the reach of working-class and many middle-class families.[23]

(b) Public housing

This paralysing housing shortage, which has so far prevented the decontrol of rents which the Government and many economists see as the only complete solution to the relative inactivity of private enterprise in building,[24] would not have been so severe if the corollary of rent control—public provision of working-class housing—had been sufficiently recognised by the authorities. The Government had begun to take an interest in working-class housing as early as the 1880s. After the *Société Française des Habitations à bon marché* (working-class dwellings) was founded in 1889, the so-called Siegfried and Strauss laws of 1894 and 1906 were passed to facilitate the construction of such dwellings (*H.B.M.*).[25] In 1912 the Bonnevay law provided for the establishment of *Offices publics d'H.B.M.* by local authorities, and the City Council established that of Paris in 1913, with a loan of 200 million francs. After the war, State aid was increased by the law of 5 December 1922, and still further by the Loucheur law of 1928, which for the first time provided for the construction of dwellings (*habitations à loyer modéré—H.L.M.*) for the middle classes.[26] But the State subsidies offered were too small to encourage the erection of a sufficient number of these dwellings. Between the two wars no more than 85,000 public dwellings were built in the whole of the Seine, including Paris, and they housed only one-quarter of the total population increase in the conurbation.[27]

After the Liberation the Government fixed a modest national target of 150,000 dwellings a year, which was the most that had ever been achieved in any year between the wars.[28] Even this was too high a target at first, but in 1950 the Government instituted a scheme of bonus payments for new privately built dwellings, and other encouragements followed.[29] The building rate now rose more quickly. In the 1950s, after the original target figure had been reached, it was raised to 280,000 and later to 300,000, a total which was reached by about 1960. Under

[23] Gilbert Mathieu, *Peut-on loger les Français?* (1965), p. 27.
[24] See, for instance, Société de Statistique de Paris, *Paris 1960* (1961), p. 81, article by André Roussilhe, technical councillor in the Building Commissariat of the Paris Region.
[25] See Bastié, *Croissance de la banlieue*, pp. 190–92.
[26] Fender, *Crise du bâtiment*, p. 255.   [27] Bastié, *Croissance de la banlieue*, pp. 330–31.
[28] Mathieu, *Peut-on loger les Français?*, pp. 30–31.
[29] Bastié, *Croissance de la banlieue*, p. 367.

the Fourth Plan the objective was raised to 350,000 dwellings by 1965, but building starts already exceeded this figure by 1962, and completions did so by 1964. Now, under the Fifth Plan, the target has been raised to 480,000 dwellings by 1970.

Although the high building rate of recent years has done much to make up for the slow start in the 1940s and early 1950s, the Paris area has not always shared fully in this expansion. In the first years after the war it was national policy to concentrate on war-ravaged areas, and hardly any new dwellings were built in Paris. Between 1945 and 1963 only 6,000 were constructed in the city. This was only a temporary phase; between 1954 and 1964 nearly 100,000 were built.[30] But owing partly to the official policy of decentralisation, and partly to high land prices and administrative difficulties, the number of dwellings built in the *District* of Paris actually fell from 93,000 in 1959 to 71,000 in 1963.[31] The average value of building land in Paris increased by ten times between 1950 and 1960, while the cost of living only doubled. A number of pieces of legislation designed to recuperate betterment values remained a dead letter. More recently, the application of a plot ratio of 3–3·5 in Paris itself has brought about a relative decline in land values there, but there has been a corresponding increase in the suburbs.[32] Although the Third and Fourth Plans intended that about one-quarter of all new dwellings should be built in the Paris region, the proportion completed in most years was nearer one-fifth.[33] Moreover, direct Government aid to building has been restricted since the late 1950s. Between 1945 and 1955 a series of measures had increased this contribution, so that in 1957 two-thirds of the dwellings completed benefited from an important direct Government subsidy.[34] But after 1958 the Government acted to prevent the further growth of its direct contribution to housing, and to encourage more private investment by special guarantees, tax exemptions, and other indirect stimuli. Since 1965 this policy, which had come under heavy criticism, has been moderated, but the general effect of the Government's measures has

[30] *Schéma directeur d'aménagement et d'urbanisme de la Ville de Paris* (1968), p. 31. The Abbé Pierre's exposure of the scandal of Paris's homeless in 1953–4 was influential in persuading the authorities to play a more energetic part in the provision of housing. See Boris Simon, *Abbé Pierre and the Ragpickers* (1955). [31] *Schéma*, p. 34.
[32] *Schéma*, pp. 73–4; Bastié, 'Capital immobilier', p. 244; Bastié, *Paris en l'an 2000* (c. 1964), p. 39.
[33] Full building figures are published by the *Ministère de la Construction*. For details of completions in Paris and its area between 1945 and 1963 see Bastié, *Croissance de la banlieue*, pp. 351–3. In 1965, the terminal year of the Fourth Plan, starts were made on 100,000 dwellings in the Paris region out of a national total of 400,000 (*B.M.O.*, special number, March, 1967, p. 17). [34] *Schéma*, p. 55.

been to increase the number of dwellings built only by allowing a general increase in rents and property prices in both public and private sectors. So a chronic housing shortage remains for the working classes, especially in the Paris area. No complete decontrol of rents has been possible, and in the city centre, where high land prices have always prevented the construction of more than a handful of public working-class dwellings, the relatively lower rents of the existing older buildings have accelerated their decline into slumdom. And the construction of new dwellings there for the existing inhabitants by private enterprise has been almost impossible because of their inability to pay higher rents.[35]

Another of the Government's reactions to the housing shortage after the First World War was to control demolitions of dwellings and their conversion to other uses. In July 1924, when the immediate post-war housing crisis was at its height, a law was passed forbidding the conversion of a house to business use, or its demolition, unless the owner constructed a similar building in the same area for his displaced tenants. The law of 29 June 1929 confirmed and extended these regulations. It required the owner to pay compensation to the tenants for disturbance, and specified that each tenant should be provided with a similar dwelling to the one he had left, at the same rent, and in the same ward. As a result, voluntary demolitions ceased almost completely. These restrictions were maintained after 1945, and in the early 1950s all demolitions were made subject to prefectoral approval. In 1952 a prefectoral circular confirmed that a demolition permit for a dwelling-house would be granted only if the landlord undertook to rehouse the occupants and to rebuild as much dwelling space as had disappeared.[36] In the 1960s, as mentioned above, demolitions in densely built areas have been further slowed by the plot ratios applied to new constructions. The result of these measures has recently been summarised very bleakly by the City's planners:

> 'Spontaneous demolition takes place where densities are still rather low and the improved value of new buildings is considerable, whereas *no* demolition takes place where densities are very high and the building stock is at its oldest, *except where there is danger of collapse.*'[37]

[35] However, Bastié believes that the working classes have benefited indirectly from the great expansion of co-ownership housing schemes since about 1950 ('Capital immobilier', p. 247). [36] *B.M.O.*, 1952, pp. 441–2.
[37] *Schéma*, pp. 31–2. The italics are mine. Most of these enforced demolitions take place in the XIXe and XXe *arrondissements*. The right bank centre lost only 239 dwellings in this way between 1954 and 1964 (*Atlas de Paris et de la région parisienne*, text, p. 97).

At the rate of spontaneous demolition realised between 1954 and 1964, it would take eleven centuries to renew the buildings of the right bank centre.[38]

This brake on demolitions intensified the shortage of building sites. especially in the central areas where land values were already very inflated before 1914. In 1920 a law was passed to exempt gardens from the tax on the capital value of properties, which had been levied since 1900, where the owners were prepared to sign an undertaking to maintain them in their existing state for fifty years.[39] Although the tax had been rightly criticised as a levy on fresh air and open space, it had forced owners to make a large number of gardens and other spaces available for building. To terminate the tax completely could only aggravate the land shortage. There was a rapid escalation in land prices after 1919, which was halted only in 1931, by which time the average price of Paris sites had risen from 148 francs to 1,082 francs per square metre.[40] This factor helps to explain the high proportion of vertical extensions in the total of building operations authorised after 1918. Between 1895 and 1914 the proportion of vertical extensions never rose higher than one in six in any one year, but from 1922 it increased almost annually. It was of course higher in years when little new building was carried out, but even in 1926 and 1929, boom years for construction, nearly one operation in four was a vertical extension. In 1937 it was one in two. The land shortage helps to explain why less building was done in Paris during those years in the 1920s when conditions were very favourable to investment, than in similar years before 1914. And there was no change in the situation after 1945.[41] Indeed, it was aggravated, when building started to revive in the early 1950s, by town-planning and redevelopment schemes, which sterilised large areas within the city until definitive plans were approved.[42]. The value of 'free' sites rocketed; in just two years from 1952 it rose from 10,000 to 25,000 francs per square metre.[43] Between 1950 and 1960 average

---

[38] *Atlas*, text, p. 97, For details of demolitions in each *arrondissement* 1954–64, see p. 98.

[39] Law of 29 December 1920. See Maurice Félix and Eugène Raiga, *Le régime administratif et financier du Département de la Seine et de la Ville de Paris* (1922), p. 602.

[40] Edmond Michel, 'La valeur des terrains à batir à Paris', pp. 4–5, *Journal de la Société de Statistique de Paris*, 1941, no. 1, pp. 4–32. Retail prices increased by between two and three times during this period.

[41] For a comparison of the effect of land values on building costs in a number of European cities, which shows Paris as easily the least favoured, see *Atlas de Paris et de la région parisienne*, text, pp. 86, 94.

[42] Between 1945 and 1963 about six times as much building was done in the suburbs as in Paris itself (Bastié, *Croissance de la banlieue*, p. 18).

[43] Lafay, *Problèmes de Paris*, p. 87.

land values in Paris rose ten times, while the cost of living only doubled.[44] In 1964 the average sale prices of sites, including existing buildings to be demolished, varied between 607 new francs (£44) per square metre in the XXe *arrondissement* and 6,393 new francs (£463) in the VIIIe *arrondissement*.[45] As we have seen, a series of laws in the late 1950s and 1960s designed to ensure the return of part of this enhanced value to the community by some form of betterment levy have remained a dead letter,[46] though since 1962 the authorities have been able to prevent the inflation of land and property values in areas where they plan to intervene.[47]

(c) Building regulations

The recent imposition of plot ratios in Paris has been anything but a stimulus to construction. Georges Pilliet claimed in 1961 that they were holding up almost all planned building operations in the city.[48] They mark the most recent stage in a long development of building and town-planning regulations which, however necessary socially, have restricted the freedom of the developer to make the most of his site.

The first building regulations to apply to Paris were promulgated in a royal edict of December 1607. Their main aim was to stop building encroaching on the royal highway, to which all Paris streets belonged, and they instituted a procedure for the delivery of building permits, without which no construction could be undertaken.[49] Although this procedure was refined in 1706 and 1733, the first attempt to do more than control the site area occupied by a new building was not made until 1783. Several excessively tall apartment houses had been constructed in cramped positions in previous years,[50] and it was decided to restrict the height of buildings. A royal declaration of 10 April 1783[51] fixed the maximum height of new stone houses in Paris at twenty metres, and of timber-framed houses at sixteen metres. No house facing onto a street between eight and ten metres wide was to exceed

[44] Bastié, 'Capital immobilier', p. 244.
[45] Jean Cornu, *Evolution du parc-logements et démolitions d'immeubles dans le Département de la Seine: rapport analytique* (1966), p. 107. No estimate is available for the right bank centre and the IXe and Xe *arrondissements* because of the inactivity of the market.
[46] See Mathieu, *Peut-on loger les Français?*, pp. 73–4.
[47] Law of 26 July 1962 (see above, chapter 8).
[48] *L'avenir de Paris*, p. 145; see also *Urbanisme*, 1964, no. 84, p. 31.
[49] M. G. Jourdan, *Recueil de règlements concernant le service des alignements et de la police des constructions dans la Ville de Paris* (1900), p. 17.
[50] For instance, the nine-storey house in the Rue Radziwill, now occupied by offices of the Bank of France.
[51] Charles Magny, *La beauté de Paris* (1911), p. 20. These regulations were slightly modified by the *lettres patentes* of 25 August 1784.

sixteen metres in height, and in streets of less than eight metres the maximum height was fixed at twelve metres.

Many thought that even these maximum heights were excessive. The Committee of Artists wanted all buildings to be limited to eighteen metres,[52] and in 1842 a bill was drawn up to reduce the heights of new buildings, but had to be dropped in the face of opposition from property owners.[53] It was not until the building boom of the 1850s that the problem became so urgent that the imperial government decided to intervene. A decree of 27 July 1859[54] established the principle, which had been only implicit in earlier texts, that the height of houses facing onto public thoroughfares should be determined by the official width of those thoroughfares.[55] It also extended control to buildings facing onto interior courtyards, where no building could be higher than 17·55 metres, except in cases when the 'needs of art, science or industry' might justify a special dispensation. The same maximum height was fixed for buildings in streets of more than 9·75 metres in width, while for those in streets of between 7·80 and 9·75 metres, a height of 14·60 metres was the maximum. And in even narrower streets it was 11·70 metres. The decree also established a minimum ceiling height of 2·60 metres, and a procedure for establishing the maximum height and cross-section of mansard roofs, relating them to the width of the building. So in effect the 1859 decree confirmed the heights fixed in 1783 for narrower streets, and reduced them in wider ones. And by extending control to the interior of street blocks it represented an important restriction on the freedom of the builder.

The decree soon attracted criticism, not only because of its imprecision,[56] but because it was manifestly unfair to restrict heights in the new streets that Haussmann was building, many of which were thirty metres or more wide. So a further decree of 1 August 1864 allowed constructions of up to twenty metres in streets twenty metres or more in width, with the special permission of the City authorities, as long as the number of storeys above the ground floor, excluding the mansard roof, did not exceed five. These rules were embodied in a decree of 18 June 1872,[57] which had the subsidiary aim of ensuring adequate interior ventilation, especially in the taller houses. It required that a

[52] Gaston Bardet, *Naissance et méconnaissance de l'urbanisme* (1951), p. 369.
[53] Paul Léon, 'La beauté de Paris', *Revue de Paris*, 15 August 1910, p. 856.
[54] See Jourdan, *Recueil de règlements*, pp. 38–41n.
[55] The official width was the width between improvement lines.
[56] Magny, *Beauté de Paris*, p. 51.
[57] Jourdan, *Recueil de règlements*, pp. 38–41n.

building of twenty metres in height should incorporate a courtyard of at least forty square metres, and that in no building should the area of airshafts (*courettes*) be less than four square metres.

So in the 1870s maximum heights were still very similar to those fixed in 1783, despite the progress made in building techniques. On the other hand, many abuses still escaped regulation owing to the imprecision of the existing legislation. So in about 1880 the Prefect of the Seine set up a special committee, chaired by the director of public works, Jean Alphand, to draw up a new building code. It was approved by the City Council in 1881 and 1882,[58] and embodied in a decree of 23 July 1884.[59] It made the height of buildings strictly proportional to the width of the thoroughfares, private streets, or interior spaces onto which they faced. The maximum height remained at twenty metres, but the maximum permissible number of storeys above the ground floor was fixed at seven, including the mansard roof. An important innovation was that in cases where the builder was prepared to build his façade behind the official improvement line, the height would would be fixed in relation to the width of the street *plus* the setback. The procedure for fixing the height and section of mansard roofs was modified and tightened up, and the regulations relating to courts and airshafts were made more stringent, despite the protests of builders' organisations that they would result in higher rents without any improvement in salubrity.[60]

It soon became clear that this new legislation had fallen between two stools. It neither allowed the builder significantly greater freedom to build high when there was no danger to public health, nor ensured sufficient penetration of light and air to houses in cramped situations. From the early 1880s the development of iron-frame construction and efficient passenger lifts created a growing demand in building circles for freedom to build beyond the traditional Paris maximum of seven storeys.[61] A new study committee was set up by the Prefect in 1896, and in September 1897 the director of architecture, Joseph Bouvard, reported in favour of the revision of the building code. The guiding principle of the new regulations which emerged from these discussions was that public health regulations should be tightened up, particularly

---

[58] See reports of the architectural committee, 1881, no. 36, and the public works committee, 1882, no. 46.

[59] Jourdan, *Recueil de règlements*, p. 49.

[60] See C.M. reports, 1881, no. 36, annex.

[61] Magny, *Beauté de Paris*, pp. 61, 66–7. The world's first 'skyscraper' was built at Chicago in 1889.

with respect to courts and airshafts, but that builders should be compensated by more flexible height regulations, and greater freedom to build projections and bays above ground floor level.[62] The City Council approved the new code in December 1899 and the Prefect transmitted it to the Minister of the Interior in January 1900, declaring that it aimed to establish 'a more rational proportion between the height of buildings and the width of free spaces in front of them, in the interests of public health.'[63] It was embodied in the decree of 13 August 1902.[64] Although the maximum height of the façade in vertical line remained at twenty metres, a very close relationship was established between height and street width, with a hierarchy of twenty categories of width, from one to twenty metres, and the same number of height categories, from seven to twenty metres. The promised greater overall height was achieved by relaxing the restrictions on the height and section of mansard roofs, so that on large sites in very open situations, such as those facing a square or park, it became possible to include three or even more attic storeys. But the abuses of these regulations caused so great a public outcry that they had to be modified by a decree of 13 December 1907, which limited the height of roofs on aesthetic grounds, so that builders lost part of their quid pro quo. So Paul Léon could still write in 1910: ' . . . today's building heights are very much a survival from Old Paris.'[65]

The two decrees of 1902 and 1907 remained in force with no fundamental modifications until the late 1940s. Then, from 1948 onwards, a series of exceptions were enacted to favour the construction of taller buildings along very wide streets or facing open spaces. They were embodied in an order of 20 December 1958, which allowed buildings on streets of more than twenty-seven metres in width to go up to thirty-one metres, including the mansard roof. In the outer ring of *arrondissements* the limit was set even higher, at thirty-seven metres.[66] A number of special dispensations have been granted to allow heights in excess of these maxima, even in the central zone. But the right bank centre has been spared these extremely tall buildings on aesthetic grounds, with one exception, where the City has broken its own rules to allow a massively insensitive administrative block, the 'Cité Mor-

[62] See C.M. reports, 1899, no. 113. The new code was also intended to allow greater freedom to the architect for aesthetic ends (see below, chapter 10).
[63] Magny, *Beauté de Paris*, pp. 69–70.
[64] Magny, p. 75n; Léon, 'La beauté de Paris', pp. 855, 857; Albert Guérard, *L'avenir de Paris* (1929), pp. 67–8.
[65] Léon, 'La beauté de Paris', p. 857.   [66] Bastié, 'Capital immobilier,' p. 233.

land', to be built for the Prefecture of the Seine in the IVe *arrondissement*. However, even those taller buildings that have been erected so far in Paris are small by the standards of London and most other cities. Public conservatism and official inertia have prevented the combination of liberal height regulations and an adventurous plot-ratio policy which would have enabled Paris to follow other cities towards vertical development, as Le Corbusier had been urging for many years.[67] In the last few years attitudes have been slowly changing, and towers of several hundred feet have been built at the Défense, in the suburbs of western Paris, and even bigger ones are planned at Montparnasse and on the site of the *Santé* prison (XIVe). But such buildings are still considered to be out of the question in central Paris. The right bank centre, in particular, is unlikely to see them, partly because of their effect on the townscape, and partly because the area is no longer the city's prime business district. Although the reconstructed Halles site will almost certainly have some tall buildings, they will be very much smaller than those planned for the outskirts. In any case, what is done at the Halles will be totally exceptional in central Paris, because it will have been made possible only by massive public intervention. Throughout the rest of the area, where redevelopment has depended mainly on private initiative, the severe height restrictions have undoubtedly contributed to the absence of building activity. Until 1958 the maximum height allowed was hardly higher than at the end of the eighteenth century, and in the narrower streets it was considerably lower. Even after 1958 the right bank centre benefited very little from the relaxed regulations for houses built along very wide streets because its only thoroughfares to exceed twenty-seven metres were those built or planned by Haussmann, which were already lined with tall and relatively modern houses. Smaller vertical extensions of such buildings up to the maximum of thirty-one metres were of course allowed, and in some cases they have taken place.[68] But total reconstruction of such solid houses has been out of the question, and most central streets, of course, are so narrow that new buildings have not even been allowed to reach twenty metres in height. The City might have provided some encouragement by increasing the width between improvement lines of central streets beyond that fixed in the nineteenth century, yet this possibility has been strangely neglected despite the big increase in traffic. Between 1891 and 1951 the City increased the official width

---

[67] See, for instance, his *Destin de Paris*, (1941).
[68] One example is the *Bazar de l'Hôtel-de-Ville* department store in the Rue de Rivoli.

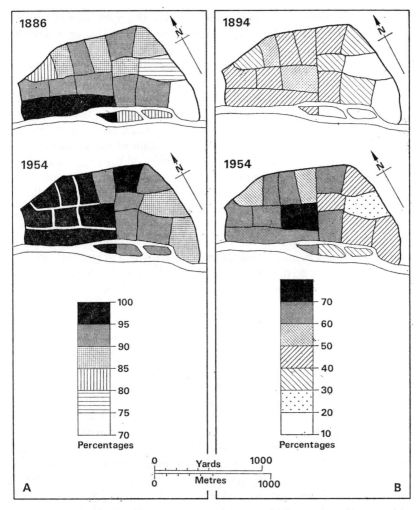

FIG. 4. *The growth of building congestion in the centre :* (*a*) Proportion of houses with more than four storeys above ground floor; (*b*) proportion of houses with more than six storeys above ground floor.

of only about forty streets or parts of streets in the right bank centre,[69] and most of these modifications were either very slight, or a formal prelude to widening schemes immediately carried out by the City. And there has been no change in the City's conservative attitude since 1951. Of course, there was nothing to stop owners setting their buildings back voluntarily to gain extra height, but this rarely happened in central districts because, owing to the high price of central sites, the developer stood to lose more than he could gain by building an extra storey or two. In the centre, of course, a high proportion of the houses dated from before 1783 in any case, and often infringed the regulations developed from that year onwards. In many cases, landlords knew that if they demolished a big, old building, the regulations would allow them to replace it only by a considerably smaller construction. The Extension of Paris Committee was aware of this danger before the Great War, and opposed any reduction of maximum heights in the narrower streets because it might encourage owners to retain their old houses.[70] It went on to state that height restrictions were 'doubtless the explanation of this surprising longevity of the buildings of Old Paris'.[71]

(d) Taxation

To all the above factors which reduced the intrinsic profitability of building was added an external discouragement—taxation. Towards the end of the nineteenth century public opinion demanded with increasing vehemence the abolition of the municipal customs dues (*octroi*), which for many years had been the City's most fruitful source of income. The socialist majority in the City Council attacked the unjust character of such indirect taxation. One councillor, for instance, argued in 1898 that the main burden of taxation should fall, not on the tenant, but on the landlord, who benefited from the untaxed betterment value of his property as the city prospered.[72] Even after the nationalists achieved a majority this demand was not abated. In December 1900 a law was passed to authorise the City to abolish part of the *octroi* by replacing the entry duties on beverages by new taxes.[73] These were taxes on buildings and undeveloped parcels of land, to be paid by the landlord, and a tax on dwellings to be paid by the tenant. In March

---

[69] This figure has been established by an analysis of the different editions of the *Nomenclature des voies publiques et privées*, 1891, 1898, 1911, 1928, 1951.

[70] Commission d'extension de Paris, *Considérations techniques préliminaires* (1913), p. 80.

[71] *Considérations techniques*, p. 82.

[72] C.M. reports, 1898, no, 2, p. 13. One of the traditional arguments in favour of the *octroi* had been that its product reflected changes in the prosperity of the city.

[73] Félix and Raiga, *Le régime de Paris*, p. 597.

1901 the City was allowed to levy a further tax, on the rentable value of commercial and industrial premises. The tax on undeveloped land was heavily criticised, and it was replaced in 1902 by a combined tax on the value of built and unbuilt properties, at a much lower rate.[74]

Before 1914 these new 'replacement taxes' were too small to compromise the net return on investment in properties. In 1909 they represented only 3·42 per cent of the gross revenue of a building. This was still less than the older taxes—property contribution, and doors and windows tax[75]—which together made up 5·98 per cent of gross revenue. So the total of direct taxes falling on the landlord still represented only 9·40 per cent of the total rentable value.[76] But after 1914 both the Government and the City increased their direct taxes on property. The Government impost was fixed in 1914 at 4 per cent of revenue, and it was later raised successively to 5, 10, 12, and 18 per cent. After the slump it was somewhat relaxed, but in 1934 it was still 12 per cent. Meanwhile, the City had increased the number of additional centimes from 73·5 in 1914 to 373 in 1934, which had the effect of doubling the property contribution.[77] Conveyancing dues had also been increased and were a serious source of annoyance. Service taxes —refuse removal, street cleansing, and sewers—made up 5·95 per cent of rentable value in the mid-1930s. The proportion taken by the 'replacement taxes' had risen from 3·42 per cent in 1909 to 6·5 per cent in 1936. After the landlord had paid this agglomeration of imposts, he found that he had lost 41·25 per cent of the total rentable value of his property. Property companies paid even more—50·95 per cent. By 1936 the net revenue of a new building had fallen to 5·20 per cent on the invested capital for an individual developer, and 4·60 per cent for a company. All new building would have ceased completely if new developments after 1921 had not been exempted from direct taxation for the first fifteen years.[78] But buildings erected before that year were

---

[74] Félix and Raiga, p. 601.

[75] These were two of the so-called 'quatre vieilles' taxes which were levied on landlords. For the origins and development of these and other taxes, see (after Maurice Félix), *Le régime administratif et financier de la Ville de Paris* (1959), vol. IV, pp. 145–201.

[76] Société de Statistique de Paris, *Notes sur Paris* (1909), pp. 46–7.

[77] See Maricourt, *Les charges de la propriété bâtie à Paris* 1914–1925 (1925); Fender, *Crise du bâtiment*, pp. 351–6, 368. Additional centimes could be added to the principal of each of the 'quatre vieilles' by local authorities, for their own use. An additional centime represented one-hundredth of the product of the Government tax.

[78] Law of 31 March 1921. It exempted from State and local authority property taxes (except service taxes), for fifteen years, all dwelling houses begun before August 1926 and finished before January 1930. The exemption was subsequently extended by stages until the Second World War (Félix and Raiga, *Le régime de Paris*, p. 602; Fender, *Crise du bâtiment*, p. 356).

required to support this crushing burden, with disastrous effects on the landlords' ability to carry out repairs and improvements, and invest in new constructions. The average net return on buildings fell from 5·6 per cent in 1914 to 1 per cent in 1939.[79] After the Second World War it disappeared completely for a time.[80] After 1950 there was some improvement in respect of new buildings, whose construction by private initiative was increasingly encouraged by the Government. The development of co-ownership also contributed greatly to reviving the property market, and it has since been extended in many cases to older buildings.[81] But dwelling houses are still far from being the attractive as well as secure investment that they were in the nineteenth century.

Throughout this period in which new building declined almost to nothing, the old houses of Paris continued to serve, especially in the central areas where they were clustered in large numbers. In most cases, no-one was prepared to demolish them, and few actually fell down of their own accord, or became so clear a danger to the public that they had to be condemned. For this, their solid construction was largely responsible. The Paris area had always been the source of excellent building materials, and, whatever might be said about the design of the older Paris houses, the quality of their construction was never in doubt. Indeed, it was a positive embarrassment when demolition was desirable for public health or social reasons. In 1914, for instance, Councillor B. Robaglia remarked that the houses in the unhealthy areas were 'very solidly built' and that they could 'still defy the test of time for many years despite their sordid appearance'.[82] Even when badly built houses began to collapse they were often supported by their neighbours.[83] And it has always been accepted that a well built Paris house will stand without difficulty for several hundred years.[84]

Another serious obstacle to reconstruction in the central areas was the extreme fragmentation of land ownership and the inconvenient shape of many sites. Building plots had often remained unaltered since the middle ages, and combined very narrow street frontages with very great depth. Many sites had a frontage of under ten metres, but were up to 100 metres long. Such a shape was not conducive to the construction

---

[79] Bastié, *Croissance de la banlieue*, p. 348.   [80] Bastié, 'Capital immobilier', p. 240.
[81] Bastié, 'Capital immobilier', p. 248.   [82] C.M. reports, 1914, no. 37, p. 3.
[83] See, for instance, the case of houses in the Rue Mathieu-Molé (C.M. reports, 1880, no. 22).
[84] See, for instance, Chambre de Commerce, *Statistique de l'industrie à Paris 1847-8*, p. 88; Fender, *Crise du bâtiment*, p. 66.

of a new building or buildings, especially as the most attractive sites, by the nineteenth century, were those with long frontages. Unlike London, most of the building land in Paris was and is freehold property, and, as we have seen, landlrods rarely controlled whole clusters or blocks of sites. So it was extremely difficult to form a number of narrow, inconvenient sites into one whose development would be more viable. Such fusions had been the effect and to some extent the object of Haussmann's street improvement schemes, but this means of compelling the rationalisation of sites became less and less productive after 1870, partly owing to the fall in the number of schemes carried out, and partly to legal restrictions on the amount of land that could be acquired outside the improvement lines. This problem has become increasingly serious over the years owing to growing restrictions on the proportion of the site that may be covered by buildings. Another limitation which, as we have seen, has particularly affected the city centre since 1945, has resulted from the prolonged preparation of town planning schemes, during which all rebuilding has been discouraged in the area likely to be affected.[85] And the building of commercial and industrial premises has been slowed down since 1955 by the Government's decentralisation policy. What is more, all these complications have had the result of extending the delay between the application for, and the granting of, the building permit. In the nineteenth century it had been granted within a few days; now it takes months or even years.

The time has now come to examine building in the right bank centre since 1914. Between 1915 and 1939 the level of building activity there was extremely unstable. General trends were similar to those in the city as a whole, but there were very great annual variations, and boom years were usually followed by periods of relative inactivity. The average number of permits issued each year was markedly lower than in 1895–1914. The lowest annual total in this latter period was registered in 1914, when only nineteen permits were granted, largely owing to the declaration of war. Yet this extremely low figure was subsequently exceeded only in 1923, 1925, 1929 and 1930. The proportion of permits issued in the right bank centre in relation to the whole city remained very low. In 1930, the best year during this period for building in the right bank centre, the permits issued there represented less than 3 per

---

[85] For a justification of this ban on new building, see Lafay, *Problèmes de Paris*, p. 87.

cent of the city total, even though the latter was lower than it had been in 1929. And in 1927, which was a bad year for both the whole city and the centre, the proportion was only 1·7 per cent. It is therefore not surprising that vertical extensions formed an even higher proportion of all building operations than before 1914, except during the years 1928 and 1930, when speculation was extreme. Between 1915 and 1926 the proportion of vertical extensions was 45 per cent in both the Ier and IIe *arrondissements*, and 41 per cent in the IIIe *arrondissement*, while in the IVe *arrondissement*, which was still less densely constructed than the others, it was only 26 per cent.[86] In the remaining years for which the *Annuaire Statistique* gives detailed figures—1927–31, 1934, 1937—the proportions in each *arrondissement* are 42, 37, 28 and 32 per cent. Another indication of the scarcity of suitable sites is the declining average height of buildings authorised, which is even lower than before 1914. Figures are available only for 1915–1926, but they show an average height of new buildings in the Ier *arrondissement* of 4·3 storeys, compared with 4·4 in 1895–1914, while in the IIe the reduction is from 5·5 to 4·4 storeys. In the IIIe *arrondissement* the average was still as high as 4·6 storeys, compared to 4·8 before the war, but in the IVe it was down from 5·1 to 4·3 storeys.

The east still predominated over the west in respect of the amount of building undertaken, although the IIIe *arrondissement* continued to lose its attractiveness to builders, a trend which had already been apparent before 1914. The IVe *arrondissement*, with over forty permits between 1915 and 1926, saw the most new building, and the Ier, with only twenty-six, the least. During the remaining years for which figures are available the IIe and IVe *arrondissements* predominated, with forty and thirty-nine permits respectively. Thirty-three permits were granted in the IIIe *arrondissement* and thirty in the Ier.[87]

The figures for these later years make a distinction for the first time between dwelling houses, and commercial and industrial buildings. As one would expect, they show rather more building for business in the west. In the IIe *arrondissement* twenty-three permits out of forty were for business buildings, and in the Ier, sixteen out of thirty. The proportion was almost as high in the IIIe *arrondissement*, with seventeen out of thirty-three, but the construction of dwellings predominated in

---

[86] The respective proportions of vertical extensions in each *arrondissement* in the 1895–1914 period were 39, 31, 32 and 31 per cent.

[87] These totals include a very small number of permits listed in the *Ann. Stat.* as 'extensions', separately from 'vertical extensions'. Because they imply an extension of the area of land covered by buildings, they have been counted here as total operations.

the IVe, with twenty-four out of the thirty-nine permits granted there being for residence. Part of the explanation for the low number of dwelling houses built in the right bank centre lies in the unattractiveness of the area for *H.B.M.* and *H.L.M.* enterprise. Not a single block of these types was built there between 1914 and 1939. Some were planned for the demolished section of unhealthy area number 1, but the cleared sites—in particular, the immense 'Plateau Beaubourg'—remained vacant. And elsewhere, high land prices and height restrictions discouraged public building organisms, which preferred the city outskirts. The relative decline of building in the east of the right bank centre, which was already apparent before 1914, reflects the general fall in the construction of houses, in particular for the working classes. The proportion of construction activity for business premises therefore increased both in west and east, but the west's predominance as a business district ensured it a higher number of such buildings. In these circumstances, scarcity of sites was a less crucial factor than before 1914, but the less densely constructed wards still saw more building. Between 1915 and 1926 the majority of permits granted in the IIIe *arrondissement* were in its two southern wards, and in the IVe almost as much building was done in Arsenal as in the other three wards together.

Any comparative study of building within the right bank centre becomes almost impossible after 1945. We have already noted that a slump of building in Paris is usually accompanied by an even bigger slump in the right bank centre. Between 1947 and 1950, only six permits were issued there for totally new buildings. A slight improvement followed, with ten permits issued in 1952, and as many as thirteen in 1956, a figure which represented only 1·4 per cent of the total building authorised in Paris. The subsequent depression was more serious in the centre than in the city as a whole, and by 1958 the number of permits issued had fallen to five, 1·1 per cent of the Paris total. The change of régime in that year produced no improvement, and only three permits were issued in 1959, and five in each of the following two years, after which the *Annuaire Statistique* abandoned the practice of publishing building figures for each *arrondissement*. There has been no change in this situation since 1962, and the undertaking of any building operation in the right bank centre still remains a source of wonderment to passers-by.[88] Between 1955 and 1964 23,752 square

[88] The almost complete stagnation of residential construction in the right bank centre is graphically illustrated by a map published in *Atlas de Paris et de la région parisienne*, maps, 31–5, showing the location of dwellings built in Paris from 1954 to 1965. Only sixteen developments are shown in the right bank centre, twelve of them in the IVe *arrondissement*.

10 36pp.

metres of floor space were built in the right bank centre, out of 4,375,248 square metres in the whole city (0·54 per cent).[89] Of the dwellings built in Paris between 1954 and 1964, only 0·66 per cent were in the right bank centre.[90] Even vertical extensions became rare. Hardly any were undertaken before 1956, after which they became slightly more numerous, but only in 1959 and 1960 did they represent more than one permit in four. They have remained few in number since 1961, despite the slight relaxation of height restrictions.

Although comparisons between the *arrondissements* have become almost meaningless, it is interesting to note the continuance of previous trends, with little building in the Ier *arrondissement*, less and less in the IIIe, while the IIe and IVe *arrondissements* emerge as the least stagnant districts, with roughly equal amounts of building. The totals of permits issued for complete buildings between 1947 and 1961[91] in each *arrondissement* are sixteen, twenty-two, nineteen and twenty-three respectively. In each the building curve follows in its general outlines that of the whole city, except in the IIIe *arrondissement*, where the situation is much more unstable. The decline of residential building in the west is even more pronounced than before the war. Of the permits issued for completely new buildings in the IIe *arrondissement* between 1947 and 1961, only three out of twenty-two were for residential or mixed residential-commercial developments. In the Ier *arrondissement* the proportion was only slightly higher—five out of sixteen. But in the IIIe *arrondissement* the figure was nine out of nineteen, and in the IVe, as one might expect, it was even higher, at fourteen out of twenty-three. The relatively high proportion of residential building here is due partly to the construction of several blocks of flats on cleared sites in the unhealthy area number 16.

The few buildings constructed varied very greatly in height, and to take averages would be meaningless, especially in view of several obvious printers' errors in the *Annuaire Statistique*. Most were very tall, of seven or eight storeys, but others, especially garages and certain commercial buildings, were of less than three storeys. A very clear contrast emerges between new buildings in the centre and the much higher constructions elsewhere. In 1961, for instance, the 112 blocks of apartment houses authorised in Paris totalled 1,125 storeys, an average of ten. Three blocks of publicly built dwellings totalled eighty-two storeys, an average of twenty-seven. These *averages* exceed the

[89] Cornu, *Evolution du parc-logements*, p. 53.
[90] *Schéma*, p. 31.
[91] Except for 1954—no figures published by *Ann. Stat.*

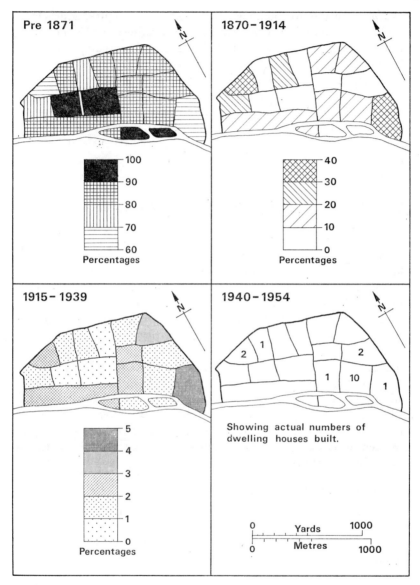

FIG. 5. *The centre's ageing buildings.* Proportion of houses constructed at different periods in each ward.

275

maximum heights for buildings in the right bank centre, and help to explain why building there remained so unattractive. In theory, of course, this restriction on height should have been compensated for by the resulting decline in land values. And, indeed, sites in the right bank centre have not enjoyed the same betterment value as those further west and in the suburbs, and in many cases their real value has not increased at all in the last hundred years.[92] But this has not encouraged building, because unconstructed sites are now almost completely non-existent, and declining land values have made it less economical to liberate and redevelop sites that are fully occupied by older buildings. Large-scale clearance by the public authorities, like that now planned near the Halles, will undoubtedly enhance the value of land in this area, but the clearance of individual sites does not produce the same effect.

So the centre still remains caught in the vicious circle of building stagnation—housing shortage—building stagnation, because the demolition of older buildings would only aggravate the shortage, yet without it building enterprise remains impossible. Between 1955 and 1964 a mere 6,546 square metres of floor space were demolished in the right bank centre, out of 377,016 square metres in the whole city (1·74 per cent). Only about 100 dwellings were involved.[93] An expansion of business might of course break the circle; but, as we have seen, the building figures reveal none of the massive construction of offices that has gone on since the last war in the City of London. Part of the explanation—direct restrictions on building—has now been examined. But what of the drift of business to the west that was already apparent in the nineteenth century? How far does the lack of office building in the centre reflect the movement elsewhere of the more dynamic and expanding enterprises?

2 BUSINESS, POPULATION, PROPERTY

The depopulation of the right bank centre accelerated after the First World War, accompanied by a slower decline in the city as a whole. Between the censuses of 1911 and 1936 it lost over a quarter of its population. The greatest reduction was again in the west, with 33 per

---

[92] See Bastié, 'Capital immobilier', p. 229. Land prices in the Halles area were recently estimated at 2–3,000 NF per square metre, compared with 10,000 NF in the Champs-Elysées area, whereas in 1860 land near the Halles had been the most expensive in Paris (Daniel Monteux, 'Les Halles et leur quartier', p. 278, in *Urban Core and Inner City* (1967), pp. 256–81).
[93] Cornu, *Evolution du parc-logements*, pp. 50, 53.

cent and 30 per cent losses in the Ier and IIe *arrondissements*. The 29 per cent fall in the IVe *arrondissement* was due partly to slum clearance in the unhealthy area number one, and the IIIe *arrondissement*, which was not affected by such demolitions, lost only 22 per cent. In 1936 the *arrondissements* had the following populations: Ier, 38,436; IIe, 41,280; IIIe, 66,233; IVe, 70,944. The reduction was particularly marked in Gaillon ward, where the population fell from 6,101 to 3,104, and in Place-Vendôme (11,845: 6,918). Palais-Royal's population also fell sharply, from 12,480 in 1911 to 7,055 in 1936. The explanation of this steady fall lies no doubt in the expansion of business activities up to 1929, and in the large number of dwellings that became vacant owing to the economic depression after that year. And even without commercial expansion, many richer tenants would have been attracted by the more modern and fashionable districts which had developed further to the west, and now in particular in the XVIe *arrondissement*.

Whereas in the west the richest and most commercial wards were losing their population quickest, in the east it was the poorest districts. In the IIIe *arrondissement* the biggest loss was in the Sainte-Avoie ward, and in the IVe, Saint-Merri, Saint-Gervais and Notre-Dame had a much greater rate of reduction than Arsenal. The depopulation of these poor districts was not accompanied by an increase of commerce and industry, and reflected a spontaneous movement to better accommodation, and a deceleration in the turnover of dwellings owing to rent controls, which resulted in an ageing population. On the other hand, the population in these areas was renewed to some extent by the arrival of successive waves of foreign immigrants, many of whom moved out to new areas after a short acclimatisation period.[94] But because most of the immigrants, both French and foreign, who came to Paris between the wars, were attracted by its need for industrial manpower,[95] the right bank centre, where industry was in decline, could have only limited attractions as a place of residence.

Compared to these big population changes, the number of commercial activities remains relatively stable. The Great War reduced the number of occupied commercial and industrial premises by about one-quarter in the IIe and IIIe *arrondissements*, and by rather lower proportions in the Ier and IVe *arrondissements*. But business returned after the war

[94] See Michel Coquery, 'Quartiers centraux et quartiers périphériques de Paris', p. 68, in *Urban Core and Inner City*, pp. 53–81; *Paris: présent et avenir d'une capitale* (1964), p. 40.
[95] Pierre George, 'Rapport introductif' at the *Table ronde de l'Association française de Science politique*, 29–30 April 1966 (circularised paper).

and, after a steady increase in the number of premises during several years, the total in each *arrondissement* in 1930 was slightly higher than before 1914. In this year the IIe *arrondissement* had 12,064 such premises (11,769 in 1910), and the Ier, 11,349 (10,220). In the IIIe *arrondissement* the total had risen from 10,244 to 11,019, and in the IVe from 6,932 to 7,682. This trend reflected a general increase throughout Paris, where the number of such premises had risen from 191,489 to 237,541. After about 1930, however, the depression brought about a reduction, and despite the economic recovery of the late 1930s the totals of occupied premises were lower in 1939 than at any time since the First World War. Worst affected were the IIe and IVe *arrondissements*, which had suffered losses of 20·9 and 28·4 per cent since 1930. In the Ier and IIIe *arrondissements* the totals fell by 18·4 and 17·9 per cent respectively. Yet the general reduction throughout the city was much smaller (14·3 per cent). The right bank centre had failed to share fully in the general expansion of commercial and industrial premises in the 1920s, yet now it was harder hit by the depression than Paris as a whole. As a result, by 1939 the right bank centre had only 33,344 commercial and industrial premises, compared to 39,165 in 1910—a loss of 14·9 per cent. During the same period the Paris total had increased by 6·4 per cent. And in the VIIIe and IXe *arrondissements* a much greater expansion took place. In the VIIIe the number of premises rose from 9,533 in 1910 to 12,595 in 1930, and by 1939 the total was even *higher*, at 13,569. This rapid growth reflected the growing importance of the Champs-Elysées as a business district. The IXe *arrondissement* was not quite so favoured, but its great predominance over each of the right bank central *arrondissements* was enhanced. The number of premises there rose from 16,849 in 1910 to 19,737 in 1930, but had fallen to 15,253 in 1939. To some extent, it too was beginning to suffer from the growing attraction of the VIIIe *arrondissement*.

The number of hotels and boarding houses in the centre also fell. In Paris as a whole, their number rose from 15,243 in 1919 to 20,600 in 1931, but after this year the total began to fall, so that in 1937 only 13,367 were left, a loss of 35·1 per cent.[96] In the IVe *arrondissement*, the traditional lodging-house district, the total rose from 525 in 1919 to 732 in 1925, but a subsequent decline had reduced it to a mere 393 by 1937. In the other three *arrondissements* the number of hotels and boarding houses rose quickly until 1925, followed by a period of stability or slow expansion until 1931. But from then on decline was rapid,

---

[96] *Ann. Stat.* does not publish figures for 1938–41.

so that by 1937 there were only 285 in the Ier *arrondissement,* compared
to 379 in 1919, a loss of 24·8 per cent. The reduction was slightly
smaller in the IIe and IIIe *arrondissements,* where the totals fell by
6·6 and 20·5 per cent respectively. The explanation for the fall in the
east lies in the steady depopulation of the area, and the slow decline
of its industries. In the west, it seems likely that hotels were affected
both by the depression, and by the growing favour accorded by tourists
to hotels in more fashionable districts.[97]

It is clear that the right bank centre continued to suffer after 1918
from the effects of the movement of the business centre to the west
and north-west. But this movement might well have been much more
rapid had it not been for the intervention of the legislature in the
interests of solving the housing shortage. As we have seen, a law of
20 July 1924 forbade the transformation of residential buildings into
commercial premises unless a similar residential building were erected
nearby, and was strengthened by further legislation in 1929.[98] Then
the law of 30 June 1926 extended rent controls to commercial leases.
This had the same effect as in the case of dwellings, and tenants hesitated to abandon their existing premises. The effect of this legislation
was to hinder the expansion of business in the densely built central
areas, and to encourage those enterprises that could not afford to pay
higher rents for modern premises to stay where they were. So although
the right bank centre was able to retain much of its former level of
activity, even during the 1930s, it tended to lose its more dynamic
enterprises to the new western business districts, and was left with
those that were incapable of moving, or did not need to move. Those
concerns which required to be highly accessible to their clientele, such
as luxury shops and agencies, were severely compromised if they did
not move north-west to the Opéra and beyond, or west to the Champs-
Elysées. The Avenue de l'Opéra itself lost even more of its cachet as
a luxury shopping street, and began to specialise in cheaper, mass-
produced articles. Contemporary observers were very struck by the
movement of fashion from the *grands boulevards* and the Avenue de
l'Opéra to the Etoile, while only the Rue de la Paix retained its former
elegance in the right bank centre.[99] Even the Place-Vendôme ward

[97] Several hotels were built along the extended section of the Boulevard Haussmann in
the 1920s (Harold Clunn, *The Face of Paris* [1933], p. 23).
[98] However, this legislation by no means halted such conversions. About 85,000 dwellings were converted into offices in Paris between 1920 and 1945 (Bastié, *Paris en l'an 2000*
[1964], p. 56).
[99] See George and Paul Adam, *A Book about Paris* (1937), p. 14; Jules Bertaut, *Paris
1870–1935* (1936), p. 280.

suffered from the competition of districts nearer the Etoile.[100] On the other hand, those activities which already had extensive buildings in the right bank centre, such as the larger banks and insurance companies, and department stores appealing to a less wealthy clientele, did not move. Nor did those which needed a central location, such as the businesses connected with the Halles, and the printing works associated with the big newspaper offices of the IIe *arrondissement*. In the east, expanding and capital-intensive firms were, as always, likely to move out, and there was now a growing temptation for highly labour-intensive enterprises to move to districts where the population was not so much in decline. But there still remained numerous undertakings, such as those involved in clothing manufacture, which needed to be near their retail outlets in the centre, and the slowly declining craft industries such as jewellery and fine metalwork whose firms were highly interdependent, and could survive only in an area of low rents.

Although the right bank centre retained much of its traditional level of activity, it suffered a certain relative decline, albeit a less rapid one than before 1914. In 1910 the product of the *patentes* tax there was 29·79 per cent of the Paris total. By 1930 it had fallen to 27·15, and by 1939 to 26·1 per cent. Meanwhile, the product of the IXe *arrondissement* remained stable at 19·53 per cent in 1939, compared to 19·83 per cent in 1910, and that of the VIIIe rose from 7·48 to 12·11 per cent. The relative decline was fairly evenly shared throughout the right bank centre. Between 1910 and 1939 the product of the *patentes*, grossly distorted by inflation, rose by 13·61 times in the IIIe *arrondissement* and 15·2 times in the IVe. In the Ier *arrondissement* it rose slightly faster, by 15.91 times, and in the IIe, by 14·96 times. In contrast, the total product in the VIIIe *arrondissement* rose by 28·05 times, and in the IXe by 17·06 times. Relative changes in property values were also less pronounced than before the war, because of the decline in building throughout Paris after 1914. In 1913 the right bank centre represented 15 per cent of the total value in capital of buildings and sites in Paris, and in 1938 it still stood as high as 13·5 per cent. On the other hand, total rentable values there fell from 17 per cent of the city total in 1913 to only 13 per cent in 1938, but this was probably due to the large amount of accommodation that became vacant there in the 1930s.

The declaration of the Second World War marked the beginning

---

[100] Michel, 'Valeur des terrains', pp. 13, 15.

of a period in which the ossification of the right bank centre became even more pronounced. With hardly any new building, and no public works apart from very limited slum clearance and redevelopment, there were few changes in the appearance of the area apart from the destruction of public conveniences and the cleaning of façades in recent years. Even the population stabilised for a time, after a fall everywhere during the war. In 1954 the Ier *arrondissement* had 38,926 inhabitants, compared with 38,436 in 1936. The population of the IIe *arrondissement* had actually increased from 41,780 to 43,857. That of the IIIe *arrondissement* had fallen slightly, from 66,233 to 65,312. Only in the IVe *arrondissement*, where a number of slum houses were demolished, was there an important reduction, from 70,944 to 66,621. The population still tended to fall in the poorest quarters of the east, just as it had before 1939, but there was no corresponding reduction in the western business wards. Indeed, the population of Gaillon *rose* from 3,014 to 3,589 between 1936 and 1954, and that of Place-Vendôme from 6,918 to 7,431. One may conclude that the transformation of dwellings into offices had almost completely ceased in the west. Although powers to limit conversions were re-enacted by a law of 1 September 1948, they were carried out in other parts of the city,[101] suggesting that it was in fact the *demand* for extra office space that was absent in wards like Gaillon. In the poor areas of the east the continued reduction in population was still due more to rising living standards, the disappearance of lodging houses, and an ageing population[102] than to anything else, though slum clearance certainly helped to reduce the population still further. The biggest fall occurred in Saint-Gervais, where most of this activity was concentrated, and the population there dropped from 29,588 to 24,689.

From the late 1950s the population began to fall again everywhere. At the time of the 1962 census all four *arrondissements* had lost between 3,000 and 4,000 inhabitants since 1954, with the exception of the IVe, where the population had been reduced by as many as 6,000. Even so, the population of the first three *arrondissements* was still only a few per cent lower than in 1936, and only the IVe *arrondissement*, where extensive clearance had been carried out, had lost more than ten per cent. This renewed fall appears to reflect a voluntary rejection of in-

---

[101] Bastie, 'Capital immobilier', p. 231.
[102] For this transformation of Old Paris into 'the Paris of the old', see *Paris: présent et avenir d'une capitale*, pp. 42–3. Also, the proportion of one-person households is higher in the centre than elsewhere, so that the number of births is lower (Coquery, 'Quartiers centraux', pp. 64–5).

ferior housing standards rather than an expansion of business in the right bank centre. Conversions of dwellings into offices were accelerated by the imposition of controls on new office building in 1958, but the right bank centre does not appear to have shared in this trend to any great extent.[103]

Commercial and industrial activities were, as we have seen, only just recovering from the depression when they were again decimated by the war and the Occupation. And after the Liberation a new period of economic difficulties prevented the rapid recovery of business in the centre. In 1947 the number of occupied business premises in the Ier and IIe *arrondissements* was slightly higher than in 1938, though lower than in the late 1920s, but in the east fewer premises were occupied than in 1938. The slow recovery of the late 1940s did not alter this general picture. By 1950 the IIe *arrondissement* had 10,516 premises subject to the *patentes* tax, compared to 9,540 in 1939, and the Ier had 9,607 compared to 9,260 in the earlier year. But these totals were still considerably lower than in 1930, when the Ier and IIe *arrondissements* had 11,349 and 12,064 occupied premises respectively. More serious, both the eastern *arrondissements* still had fewer occupied premises than in 1939, whereas in Paris as a whole the total had risen from 203,667 in 1939 to 221,652 in 1950.

During the 1950s there was at first a tendency for the number of business premises to increase everywhere in the centre except the IVe *arrondissement*, but this trend was reversed towards the end of the decade, no doubt owing to the provision of new office space elsewhere, and to the departure or dissolution of some industrial firms. In 1960 each of the four central *arrondissements* had fewer premises than in 1950, with a particularly marked decline in the Ier and IVe *arrondissements*. This trend reflected a reduction in the total of business premises in Paris which had begun in the mid-1950s, partly as a result of the Government's decentralisation policy, and partly owing to natural centrifugal tendencies affecting industry in particular.[104] The fall continued into the 1960s, and in 1964, the last year for which figures are available, the number of premises had sunk to a new low level both in the right bank centre and in the city as a whole.

The picture in the VIIIe and IXe *arrondissements* since the war has been very different from that in the old centre. The VIIIe, in particular,

---

[103] Georges Pilliet, *L'avenir de Paris* (1961), p. 26.

[104] According to INSEE figures, the number of establishments in Paris fell by 2 per cent between 1954 and 1958, but there was an increase in the Paris region (Pilliet, *L'avenir de Paris*, p. 60).

has been extremely dynamic. The number of its premises rose from 13,569 in 1939 to 15,557 in 1950. This was considerably higher than its 1930 total of 12,595. Since 1950 it has maintained this position, and in 1964 it had 15,694 premises. The IXe *arrondissement* has not exceeded pre-war figures, and it lost about 1,500 premises in the 1950s. But since 1960 the situation has stabilised, and in 1964 it still had 15,616 premises, compared to 15,253 in 1939. To some extent, it has continued to suffer from the attraction of its neighbour, the VIIIe *arrondissement*, and of the XVIe *arrondissement*, which has gained in importance as a business area since the war. But it still remains in a strong position compared with the right bank centre, where even the number of artisans has been falling, despite municipal encouragement of their activities. In 1958 their numbers varied from 840 in the Ier *arrondissement* to 2,420 in the IIIe, out of a Paris total of 44,620; but by 1964 their numbers in these two *arrondissements* had fallen to 620 and 2,205 respectively, while the Paris total fell to 36,550. There were similar falls in the other two *arrondissements*.[105] On the other hand, the number of hotels and lodging houses in the right bank centre did not fall so sharply as in the city as a whole, where the total fell from 13,367 in 1937 to 5,685 in 1964. As a result of a steady decline since before the war, the Ier *arrondissement* had 189 in 1964 compared to 285 in 1937. In the IIe the figure dropped from 328 to 182, and in the IIIe from 298 to 164. In the IVe *arrondissement*, the bastion of the lodging house, the reduction was from 393 to 176, which was clearly the result of the suppression of some of the poorest establishments. The smaller reduction in the west reflects the survival of many of its tourist hotels in an era of greatly facilitated travel.[106]

In terms of rentable value, the relative decline of the right bank centre's business activities has been more pronounced since 1945 than before the war. In 1939 the total product of the *patentes* tax in the right bank centre was 26·1 per cent of the Paris total. By 1950 it had fallen to 23·34, and by 1960 to 21·26. In 1964 it was 21·18 per cent. As we have seen, the decline between 1910 and 1939 was only from 29·79 to 26·1 per cent. Within the right bank centre the values of business premises in the east rose slightly faster than in the west, but without threatening the west's predominance. In 1958 the product of the *patentes* in the two western *arrondissements* was exactly three times

---

[105] *Ann. Stat.*
[106] For details of the distribution of tourist hotels, see *Atlas de Paris et de la région parisienne*, text, p. 835.

higher than that in the eastern pair. Average values also increased more rapidly in the east than in the west, no doubt as a result of the disappearance of some of the poorer establishments there.

In terms of total capital value of properties the right bank centre appears to have maintained its position relative to the city as a whole since the war, owing to the sharp decline in new building. In 1958 it still represented 14 per cent of the Paris total, compared to 13·5 per cent in 1938. And its share in total rentable values fell only from 13 per cent in 1938 to 12 per cent in 1958. Rent controls have probably been responsible for this crystallisation of values, but it is also possible that the stability is more apparent than real, owing to the fact that no complete reassessments have been made in recent years.

How can one explain the general stabilisation of the right bank centre's business importance in the last few decades? To a large extent, it reflects the decline in new building inside the city boundaries. The city has now become crystallised, and the frenetic business and population movements of the nineteenth century have faded away. The suburbs, of course, have continued to grow, but they seem to exercise less attraction on the centre of gravity of the business area than did the new western quarters of the VIIIe and XVIe *arrondissements* which were developed from the nineteenth century onwards. The pattern of communications has also helped to stabilise the centre. The area ringed by the terminal stations must inevitably contain a high proportion of places of work and service establishments, simply because so many people travel into Paris by train, despite (or perhaps because of) the very high motorcar ownership in the Paris area. The Gare Saint-Lazare alone was bringing in over a quarter of a million commuters a day by 1960.[107] The *Métro* network has also tended to tie the centre down. At the time it was planned the area between the Opéra and the Gare Saint-Lazare was the centre of the business district, and it was made the focus of several lines. A high concentration of stations was provided in the area. It is expected that the new east–west express *Métro* line will increase the attraction of this district, for the original plan was amended to take the line through it, with a station at Auber.[108] Clearly, the Champs-Elysées area has established itself as a strong rival, but Louis Chevalier, a great lover of the *grands boulevards*, argues that

[107] Peter Hall, *The World Cities* (1966), p. 73.
[108] Coquery, 'Quartiers centraux', p. 70. Work on this line began in 1962, and it will be finished in the early 1970s. The only other station in the right bank centre will be at Halles-Châtelet.

it has failed in its attempt to supplant them as the centre of Paris, and points to the almost total absence of theatres and newspaper offices there. Today, he says, most of the city's essential activities are still concentrated in a small area with the *grands boulevards* as its axis, just as they were in the nineteenth century.[109] Pierre Riquet believes that the transport network will reinforce the Opéra area as a district of trade and other activities depending on personal contact. So although it will continue to lose office workers, it will gain in commercial activity. But so, he believes, will many other districts, as the whole of Paris develops as a centre for a conurbation of 9,000,000 people.[110]

Another stabilising factor has been the tendency of the bigger enterprises, such as banks, insurance offices and department stores, to construct their own specialised premises, which they do not wish to leave, or are unable to sell to firms whose requirements would be less adequately satisfied by a second-hand building. So the larger concerns have tended to remain on their old sites, while smaller enterprises occupying rented accommodation have been able to move to other areas.

A further cause of crystallisation has been the Government's decentralisation policy, which has limited the creation of new office buildings, which are nearly always sited in the peripheral areas. Although the Government encouraged the decentralisation of industry from 1949, it did not impose actual restrictions on the expansion of industry in the Paris area until 1955. By a decree of 5 January 1955 all projects involving the creation of more than 500 square metres of factory floorspace, and extensions of factories of over 10 per cent of their existing area, within fifty kilometres of the centre of Paris, required a special permit from the Ministry of Construction, and the Government inaugurated a policy of administrative decentralisation under the direction of the Rivalland committee. In 1958 the controls of January 1955 were extended to offices, following official recognition of the rapid growth of jobs in the tertiary sector. Since 1960 even authorised schemes have had to pay a special tax of 50–200 new francs per square metre of floorspace. The controls were also extended to the re-utilisation of existing space, as, for instance, after a merger or a period of vacancy. The effect of these measures has been to slow down the provision of new office space, and enhance the value of older accommodation.[111]

[109] Louis Chevalier, *Les Parisiens* (1967), pp. 317–18.
[110] Riquet, 'Le quartier de l'Opéra', pp. 160–61.
[111] Hall, *The World Cities*, pp. 81–2; Bastié, *Paris en l'an 2000*, pp. 38, 85–6; *Atlas de Paris et de la région parisienne*, text, pp. 612–36.

So the right bank centre remains an important area of activity. In the Ier *arrondissement* the number of jobs of all types *rose* by 8·6 per cent between 1954 and 1962. The increase in the IIe was much smaller, but there was a similarly small rise in the VIIIe *arrondissement*, and there was actually a *reduction* of 2·8 per cent in the IXe.[112] The density of employment actually exceeds 100,000 to the square kilometre in the three western wards of the IIe *arrondissement* as well as in two wards of the VIIIe—a density as high as in the centre of New York.[113] Of the jobs in commercial establishments (excluding finance and insurance) in Paris, 8·7 per cent are in the Ier *arrondissement* and 7 per cent in the IIe. The proportion of those employed there in finance, banking and insurance is even higher—17·4 per cent of the Paris total in the IIe and 10·7 in the Ier *arrondissement*. But both are outstripped on all counts by their northern and western neighbours, which are, however, considerably greater in area. Of the jobs in commerce, 11 per cent are in the IXe *arrondissement* and 15 in the VIIIe. In finance, banking and insurance the IXe enjoys an extraordinary domination—39 per cent of all jobs in Paris—although the VIIIe, with 15·6 per cent, has a lower proportion than the IIe.[114] Of those employed in the IXe *arrondissement*, 30·57 per cent are in banking and insurance, compared to a Paris average of 7·28. In the IIe *arrondissement* the proportion is 22·95, and it is 14·31 in the Ier. The VIIIe has only 9·10 per cent in banking and insurance. The most specialised ward in the city is Gaillon, with 47·35 per cent of employees working in banking and insurance, but it is closely followed by Chaussée-d'Antin (IXe) with 40·77 per cent, and Faubourg-Montmartre (IXe) with 40·48. The next most specialised wards, varying from 31·47 to 13·99 per cent are, in descending order, Vivienne, Palais-Royal, Place-Vendôme, Saint-Georges (IXe), and Madeleine (VIIIe). Between 1962 and 1966 there was a discernible trend for banking to concentrate more in the VIIIe *arrondissement*, where banks rose from 26·5 to 29·3 per cent of the total number of establishments. At the same time, insurance concentrated more in the IXe *arrondissement*, for, although there was only a small increase in the number of establishments there, the total in the VIIIe *arrondissement* fell by forty-seven, and in the IIe by twenty-eight. The number of banks in the Ier *arrondissement* rose by nineteen to 185, and of insurance offices by twenty-five to 129, while the IIe had

[112] Coquery, 'Quartiers centraux', p. 62. The total employed in Paris as a whole rose by 6·6 per cent.
[113] *Schéma*, p. 42.
[114] *Atlas de Paris et de la région parisienne*, text, p. 118.

an increase of forty-eight banks to compensate for its loss of insurance establishments. Yet although the west of the right bank centre appears to be maintaining and even improving its position as a centre of financial activity, it still plays a minor role compared to the VIIIe and IXe *arrondissements* with their 1,193 banks and 1,223 insurance offices. And although the number of such establishments there may be stabilising, the new growth sector lies even further west, in the XVIe *arrondissement*, where between 1962 and 1966 the number of banks rose by fifty-three to 218 and of insurance offices by thirty-two to 181. So in terms of numbers of establishments the XVIe *arrondissement* has already overtaken the Ier, although the average size of establishment is still considerably smaller, especially in the case of banks. In fact, establishments are generally larger in the Ier and IIe *arrondissements* than elsewhere, with an average of about sixty employees per bank compared with only fifty in the IXe. This predominance is not so pronounced in insurance, but the Ier *arrondissement*, with an average of 32·4 employees, has the biggest units in Paris. It is followed by the IXe *arrondissement*, with 29·6.[115] On the other hand, the right bank centre is not predominant as a site for the head offices of industrial firms. Since the early 1950s there has been a discernible tendency for these firms to move their head offices even further west than banking and insurance concerns. They have moved, not only to the officially sponsored Défense project, but to other parts of the periphery as well, where they can group all their departments under one roof.[116] Pierre Riquet believes that this trend will continue, and that the centre will become more and more an area of banking and specialised commercial services, and also, possibly, a nursery for growing firms. The head offices of firms in new industries, such as oil and aeronautics, are mostly situated outside the right bank centre, which houses the offices of concerns in old or non-expanding industries, such as textiles, clothing, leather, furniture, foodstuffs, hardware, stationery and printing.[117] All these offices tend to belong to smaller firms, while those of larger firms are usually situated in the west of the business district, especially in the VIIIe *arrondissement*.[118] In fact, nearly one-third of the company head offices in the Paris region are situated in this area, while only

---

[115] Bernard Haumont, *Le tertiaire financier à Paris*: (1) *Les banques* (1968), pp. 6–16, tables.
[116] Riquet, 'Le quartier de l'Opéra', p. 154.
[117] Riquet, p. 146.
[118] A. Remberg and S. Goldberg, *Dépouillement du fichier INSEE des entreprises à établissements multiples: sièges sociaux, bureaux, usines* (1966), pp. 3–6.

11·6 per cent are in the four right bank central *arrondissements*.[119] So if the two western *arrondissements* of the right bank centre are not yet excluded from the predominant centre of activity,[120] they have become only a part of the central business core. The 'City' of Paris now lies, not inside the old fortifications, as in London, but astride them.[121] And the two eastern *arrondissements*, which are employing fewer and fewer people, while slowly losing both their biggest and their smallest establishments, are no longer counted as part of the central business district in such official publications as the *Atlas de Paris et de la région parisienne* and the *Schéma directeur d'aménagement et d'urbanisme de la Ville de Paris*. The number of jobs there fell by between 7 and 12 per cent during 1954–62, and the IVe was the only *arrondissement* not to show an increase in the ratio of active employed to active resident population.[122] Financial establishments there are few in number. In 1964 the IIIe and IVe *arrondissements* had respectively only twenty-four and twenty-three banking establishments, and they were small in size, employing an average of 12·2 in the IIIe and 14·0 in the IVe. And the insurance offices here were similarly small in number and size.[123] Although these activities showed a very slight tendency to expand in the IIIe *arrondissement* between 1962 and 1966, their numbers fell slightly in the IVe. Offices of industrial firms are more closely connected with actual production than in the west, and they employ fewer people. The average size of all establishments in the east is only five employees, compared to 7·8 and 10·0 in the Ier and IIe *arrondissements*, and 12·3 and 8·9 in the VIIIe and IXe.[124]

Of course, industrial activities provide a higher proportion of total jobs in the east of the right bank centre than in the west or in the VIIIe and IXe *arrondissements*. In the IIIe *arrondissement* over half the total

[119] For a table showing the distribution of offices in Paris for each group of industries, see Remberg and Goldberg, p. 43. The VIIIe *arrondissement* alone has a higher proportion of offices than the right bank centre in all groups except textiles-clothing, stationery-packaging, and printing and allied trades.

[120] The IIe *arrondissement* still has the highest employment density in Paris—1,000 jobs to the hectare (*Schéma*, p. 21).

[121] In 1899, 10 per cent of insurance offices were in the Ier *arrondissement* and 46 per cent in the IIe. The proportions have now fallen to 2 and 26 per cent. In the VIIIe *arrondissement* the proportion has risen from 5 to 16·8 per cent, and in the IXe, from 27 to 48 per cent (*Schéma*, p. 27).

[122] Coquery, 'Quartiers centraux', p. 62. The stability or decline of employment in the centre contrasts with increases of between 7 and 20 per cent in all of the ten peripheral *arrondissements*.

[123] Haumont, *Le tertiaire financier*, tables.

[124] *Schéma*, p. 119.

employed work in industry.[125] But the number of industrial jobs there is steadily declining. In part, this reflects a general decline in the city as a whole. Between 1954 and 1962 the number of industrial jobs in Paris fell by 54,000, and by a further 61,000 by 1966—an overall loss of 20 per cent in twelve years. Between 1950 and 1963, 678 firms were helped to move to non-metropolitan locations, and from 1962 to 1966, 222 requests were received for permission to move to the suburbs.[126] The departure of one firm will often lead to the extinction of various smaller firms carrying on specific processes on its behalf, or supplying it with materials or components. So, although firms large enough to be able to move to a new area are unlikely to be found in the centre, they can have a great influence over the destinies of smaller enterprises, many of which are located in the IIIe and IVe *arrondissements*. Some of the industries showing the biggest overall reductions in numbers employed are those traditionally located in the centre. Textiles and clothing manufacture lost 21,393 jobs in Paris—a quarter of their total in 1954—and all the branches of 'articles of Paris' manufacture lost between 15 and 30 per cent of their employees.[127] Most of this reduction has been the result of the disappearance of small, craft enterprises, a natural trend which has been accelerated by urban renewal operations.[128] In the branches showing a reduction, the fall in the number of establishments is steeper than in the number of jobs. It is no surprise, therefore, to find the most striking reduction in the number of industrial jobs in the IVe *arrondissement*, where there was a 25·4 per cent loss between 1962 and 1966. This was the biggest fall of any Paris *arrondissement*, but the IIe and IIIe, with 15·5 and 17·7 per cent reductions respectively, were among the five *arrondissements* showing the biggest losses. The Ier *arrondissement*, however, lost only 8 per cent.[129] By 1966 the IVe *arrondissement* had as few as 7,716 industrial jobs—a mere 1·28 per cent of the Paris total—compared to 24,975 in the IIIe. The worst affected sectors in the IVe were textiles, clothing, chemicals,

---

[125] *Schéma*, p. 41. The proportion is smaller in the IVe *arrondissement*, where one-third of the total employed are civil servants or local government officers.

[126] [Jacques Legru], *Le tertiaire induit dans les entreprises industrielles de la capitale* (1967), pp. 10, 86. However, the decentralisation policy has been estimated to account for only 15 per cent of the total reduction in industrial floorspace. In any case, it has been pursued with less urgency since 1963.

[127] *Schéma*, p. 25.   [128] Legru, *Le tertiaire induit*, p. 11.

[129] Legru, pp. 11–12. The usefulness of these figures is compromised by the inclusion of office workers, executives and technicians working at the head offices of industrial firms in the category of 'industrial workers'. In the VIIIe *arrondissement*, which had over 70,000 'industrial workers' in 1966, 71·9 per cent are estimated to be white collar employees (p. 48). But in the east of the right bank centre, where there are few head offices, the fall in the number of employees clearly reflects a fall in production.

furniture and metalwork. Decline in the same trades was largely responsible for the reduction of employment in the IIIe *arrondissement*, but there was also a fall in light engineering employment there which was not fully compensated for by an expansion of precision trades.[130] The fall in employment in the IIe *arrondissement* was caused almost entirely by a sharp contraction in the clothing trade, which in 1962 had accounted for nearly half the industrial jobs in the *arrondissement*. Textiles, another important branch here, also declined sharply. On the other hand, printing and allied trades, which provided 25·40 per cent of the industrial employment in the *arrondissement* in 1962, registered an increase of 5·46 in jobs by 1966, compared to an overall Paris increase in this sector of 2·5 per cent.[131] Textiles and clothing also contracted sharply in the Ier *arrondissement* but their effect on total industrial employment was less than in the IIe *arrondissement* because they represented a lower proportion of industrial jobs.

To sum up, a high proportion of the industries in the right bank centre belong to industrial sectors which are in general decline in Paris as a whole. The fall in the numbers employed there is not caused, by and large, by the movement of dynamic concerns to areas where expansion is easier, but by the disappearance of stagnant industries which are no longer viable in a modern economy. Those firms which move voluntarily out of the centre are often in highly labour-intensive industries, such as clothing manufacture, whose recruitment is affected by the decline in population in the centre. It would appear that the right bank centre, with its increasing stock of vacant industrial accommodation, is an ideal starting-point for firms beginning production on a small scale, but most of those that make the grade will lose no time in moving out of an area where traffic congestion, obsolescent premises, and restrictions on expansion are inimical to efficient production, except on a small scale. However, firms whose production is very closely linked to central retail or wholesale outlets will be more reluctant to leave the centre. So will those enterprises which value a central location because it makes them more easily accessible to skilled employees living

[130] For a detailed comparison of industrial concerns and numbers employed in the IIIe and IVe *arrondissements* in 1860 and 1956, see 'Le quartier du Marais', pp. 482–3, in *La conjoncture économique dans le Département*, 3rd *trimestre*, 1959, pp. 463–512. This reveals that the number of concerns has fallen from 22,351 to 9,721, and the number employed from 72,374 to 44,637. Only glass and ceramics, and chemical industries, employed more people there in 1956 than in 1860. The biggest falls in personnel occurred in musical instruments and furniture manufacture.

[131] But printing is expanding out of the *arrondissement*, and newspaper offices are tending to move west into the VIIIe *arrondissement* (*Atlas de Paris et de la région parisienne*, text, p. 570).

in different parts of the city. So although the decline in industrial employment in the right bank centre is likely to continue for some time, industry will not die away completely.

If right bank central business activities are likely to stabilise or decline even further, what is the future of the zone as a residential area? At present, the socio-economic structure of the right bank centre's population reflects the district's business activities, and is, therefore, in many ways a survival from an earlier Paris. It also reflects the dichotomy between east and west in the modern city. In 1954 all four *arrondissements* had more than the Paris average of industrialists, tradesmen and artisans, but less than the average of professionals and executives.[132] The two western *arrondissements* had an above-average proportion of office and shop workers, while their two eastern neighbours exceeded the average in foremen, and skilled, semi-skilled and unskilled workers. The Ier *arrondissement* had more industrialists, wholesale traders, professionals and executives, and fewer manual workers, than any of the other three, although the IVe *arrondissement* had a higher proportion of professionals and executives than the right bank centre as a whole. But compared to other parts of the city, the right bank centre had a homogeneous and balanced socio-economic structure. It had far fewer professionals and executives than fashionable western *arrondissements* like the XVIe, where over 18 per cent of the active population were professional people or senior executives. Even the Ier *arrondissement* could muster only 6·17 per cent in these categories. On the other hand, the eastern *arrondissements* of the right bank centre were not so predominantly working class as those further east. Even the IIIe *arrondissement* had only 15·57 per cent semi-skilled and unskilled workers, compared to nearly 19 per cent in the XXe and nearly 21 in the XIXe. And the city average of shop and office workers was exceeded in the Ier and IIe *arrondissements*, and almost attained in the other two.

Since 1954 the socio-economic structure of the right bank centre's population has been affected by the decline in industrial activities and the growth of the tertiary sector over the city as a whole. By 1962 the proportion of industrialists and wholesale traders had fallen both in Paris and in each *arrondissement* of the right bank centre.[133] But the

---

[132] Calculated from INSEE, *Données statistiques sur la population et les logements de la Ville de Paris* (1957).

[133] Calculated from INSEE, *Recensement général de la population de 1962: résultats du dépouillement exhaustif*, fascicules départementaux, tome VI.

fall was particularly marked in the industrial IIIe and IVe *arrondisse-ments*, and in the IVe the proportion in this category (1·94 per cent) had dropped lower than the Paris average of 2·05 per cent. The proportions of artisans, retail traders, foremen, and skilled workers also fell throughout the right bank centre and the city as a whole. At the same time, there was an increase in the proportions of executives, professionals, and office and shop workers not only in Paris but everywhere in the right bank centre. However, the numbers of professionals and executives in each of the first four *arrondissements* were still lower in 1962 than the Paris average. On the other hand, the proportions of office and shop workers were now higher than the city average except in the IIe *arrondissement*. This increase in the numbers of better-paid non-manual workers, although it was only slight and reflected a city-wide tendency, was encouraging. But there was also an ominous rise in the proportion of semi-skilled and unskilled workers throughout the right bank centre, which was much more pronounced than that in the city as a whole, where it had risen only from 13·06 to 13·60 per cent between 1954 and 1962. The increase was particularly marked in the two western *arrondissements*, but it was also above average in the east. In 1962 only the Ier *arrondissement* still had less than the Paris average in this category. These figures suggest that the advantages of a central residence have encouraged the middle classes to remain and even to increase their numbers in the right bank centre during the last few years, with the exception of those directly involved in industrial production and wholesale trading. But the even more pronounced increase in the proportion of the more depressed sections of the working class, despite the sharp fall in local employment opportunities for them, suggests that the degradation of large areas of the centre, both in east and west, is continuing. Many of these people are Portuguese or Algerian immigrants, who are generally less well paid than French workers, and who often live in overcrowded conditions. The average size of dwellings in all four *arrondissements* of the right bank centre is smaller than the Paris average of 2·43 rooms, and, despite the fall in overall population totals, slum pockets have expanded in the centre, and the overcrowding problem remains. In 1962 every right bank central *arrondissement* except the Ier exceeded the Paris average for the proportion of seriously overcrowded dwellings, and the reduction in overcrowding since 1954 was much less pronounced in the right bank centre than in the city as a whole, especially in the Ier and IIe *arrondissements*, where the biggest rise in the proportion of semi-skilled and unskilled workers took place. In the IIIe *arrondissement* as many as 14·7 per cent of all dwellings were seriously overcrowded (that is, having two or more habitable rooms less than the total of occupants), compared to a Paris average of 11·7 per cent. However, there has been a big improvement since 1954 in basic amenities, which has no doubt helped to consolidate the middle-class occupation of the centre. In 1962 between 80 and 90 per cent of dwellings in all four *arrondissements* had running water, whereas in 1954 only the Ier had more than 70 per cent. And this improvement was accompanied by an increase in the number of inside water-closets and baths or showers. Conditions also improved in the city as a whole, so that in 1962 the right bank centre was still, as in 1954, markedly inferior to the city as a whole. None of its *arrondissements* reached the Paris average of 90·9 per cent of dwellings with running water, of 34·8 with bath or shower, and of 58·0 with inside water-closet. In some parts of the right bank centre the inferiority of conditions was glaring; in the IIe *arrondissement* only 33·9 per cent of all dwellings had inside water-closets in 1962 (25·9 in Bonne-Nouvelle). And in the IIIe *arrondissement* only one dwelling in five had a bath or shower (16·0 per cent in Sainte-Avoie).

Of course, the under-equipment of central dwellings is partially off-set by the convenience of their location, and although the very rich are absent from the right bank centre, so (except for a few pockets) are the very poor. Most of the area, despite its steady decline since the nineteenth century, is still not a slum, and it retains a balanced community which very closely reflects the socio-economic composition of the whole of the population of Paris. In this respect it still resembles the central Paris of a century or more ago. But its generally poor living conditions, which have resulted from the steady fall in the number of new residential buildings erected,[134] will remain a discouragement to middle-class immigration on a scale large enough to revive the area. And the poor, working-class enclaves within the centre will continue to expand. The recent slight increase in the proportion of middle-class residents is at least an encouragement to the City's rehabilitation policy, but its application is very limited at the moment, and there is still a long way to go. It is certain that obsolescence has not yet reached its final stages in most of the right bank centre.

---

[134] In 1954, the proportion of houses built before 1871 exceeded 90 per cent in two wards of the right bank centre, and 80 per cent in nine more. Two more wards had over 70 per cent. None had less than 60.

So the outlook for the centre as a whole is a bleak prospect of stagnation and slow decline. In those few western-most wards which are still part of the central business district, further expansion of business activities is unlikely. Elsewhere they are threatened with further retrenchment. Industrial activities will continue to fade away. Accommodation standards will fall even further, and the population will become poorer, in relative terms. And so far, no measures have been put into effect or even suggested by the Government or the City that seem likely to halt this syndrome ⟨*see* plates 26, 27⟩.

10

Victory for Preservation

Before 1914 the survival of the historic centre of Paris was threatened principally by the City authorities—and its partial survival resulted from the practical impossibility of destroying it rather than any questioning of the desirability of doing so. From now on, the redevelopment of the centre becomes increasingly out of the question. Even the traditional enemy did not oblige by destroying it with bombs and shells in spite of having two opportunities to do so. And eventually, as the Parisians realised that they would have to live with it, they at last came to like it—'warts and all'. We have already covered the negative aspects of this development in other chapters, but now we must examine the impact of the conscious drive for preservation which gradually replaced modernisation as the planning aim in central Paris.

1 CONSCIOUS PRESERVATION 1915–39

Within a few weeks of the outbreak of war in 1914 the architectural heritage of Paris was in far greater danger than at any time since 1870–1. Although the battle of the Marne halted the German advance in late summer, the enemy remained within bombing distance of Paris for most of the war, and in its later stages they set out with Big Bertha and other guns to repeat the success of their 1870 bombardment. But once again, little damage was done to the city's historic core, though one shell penetrated the roof of the church of Saint-Gervais on Good Friday, 1918, killing dozens of worshippers and destroying several bays of the vault.[1] So while the citizens of such towns as Ypres and Arras were contemplating their almost totally demolished old quarters, Paris preservationists were able to pursue their efforts almost undisturbed. The main threat to their composure was not the enemy, but the City's

[1] Henri Sellier, A. Bruggeman, Marcel Poëte, *Paris pendant la guerre* (n.d.), p. 82.

optimism about the chances of carrying out the full pre-war improvement scheme once peace was restored. As early as April 1916 Prefect
Marcel Delanney called on the Old Paris Committee to support the
scheme which, he said, would certainly be carried out if Parliament
granted powers for the compulsory acquisition of whole areas. He
promised that the beauty of Paris would not suffer, as it had under
Haussmann, because the City had rejected rectilinear 'fetichism'.
Symmetrical perspective was necessary when a street was terminated
by a great monument, but in most cases it contributed to what the
Prefect called 'the frigidity of the main thoroughfare'.[2]

Delanney's new interest in the Old Paris Committee, which he had
attended only once in the previous five years, was a tribute to its
influence, which he wanted to divert away from criticism of the improvement scheme. To associate the Committee more closely with the
public works programme, he asked it to draw up a list of buildings
worth preserving, in cooperation with the City's architectural department and the Technical and Aesthetic Committee. The Prefect also
suggested that protected zones could be established around listed monuments to preserve their setting.[3]

The Old Paris Committee had decided before the war to draw up a
similar inventory of historic buildings, but the plan had fallen through
owing to bad coordination and lack of industry of individual members.
This time Louis Bonnier, head of the architectural department and a
member of the Committee, took responsibility for the work. He obtained the Prefect's agreement for an inventory of 'every building
having any historical or artistic interest, either as a whole or in one of
its parts', to be compiled by his staff and corrected by the Committee.[4]
There was a further word of warning from Delanney:

> ' . . . there can be no question of preserving every building about
> which we have some historical information . . . the Committee
> is dealing with an aspect of contemporary Paris, not of its history.'[5]

But these reservations did not alter the fact that the Committee was
being given an unprecedented chance to exert a positive influence on
the modernisation of Paris. The Prefect had agreed to Bonnier's proposed triple classification, in the first category of which would be
included buildings whose preservation would justify a change in the

[2] C.V.P., 8 April 1916, p. 3.   [3] C.V.P., 8 April, 1916, pp. 4, 6.
[4] C.V.P., 8 April 1916, p. 4; 13 May 1916, pp. 38–41.
[5] C.V.P., 10 June 1916, p. 61.

line of a new street.[6] The Committee stepped up the frequency of its meetings to two a month, and had finished the inventory of the first five *arrondissements* by May 1917. Although it subsequently slackened these efforts, it had almost finished work on Paris by 1924, when the suggestion was made to extend the inventory to the suburbs.[7]

After the war the outlook for preservation remained hopeful, partly owing to the City's continuing financial problems, but also because of its clear desire to conciliate the interests of past and present, and work more closely with historians and archaeologists. Marcel Poëte, who had proved indispensable to the Extension of Paris Committee before the war, was instrumental in transforming the City's library and historical department into an Institute of the History, Geography and Urban Economy of Paris in 1917. In 1919 urban studies courses were begun at the Institute, thus ensuring that students of urban problems and future town planners would have a measure of respect for the past, and an understanding of the historical factors affecting the development of cities.[8] When the Old Paris Committee formally presented the City with the first part of its inventory in December 1919, the preservation policy fathered by De Selves seemed to receive its consecration. The new Prefect, Auguste Autrand, was warmly applauded at the Hôtel de Ville by a distinguished audience, including Marshal Pétain, when he pledged himself to follow his predecessor's example, and added:

> 'The discussions of the Old Paris Committee have thrown too much light on *what used to be* for *what remains* not to be doubly dear to us.'[9]

Sceptics could of course argue that the City's new interest in old buildings reflected only its determination to demolish a large number of them. And fine words by the Prefect were certainly not enough to exempt his administration from criticism.[10] But during the 1920s, on the whole, municipal officials took greater care to ensure that public works did not disfigure well-known views, or destroy historic buildings.[11] The completed inventory and its staff were consulted very frequently by the City in town planning decisions, though it must be admitted that they rarely put up any opposition to changes. In the

[6] C.V.P., 10 June 1916, p. 55.
[7] C.V.P., 26 May 1917, pp. 209–10; 25 October 1924, pp. 119–21.
[8] *A.P.*s, 15 December 1917; 5 September, 1919.
[9] An account of this brilliant assembly is provided in C.V.P., 20 December 1919, p. 146.
[10] See, for instance, Léon Riotor's attack in C.M. reports, 1921, no. 49, pp. 1–3.
[11] See, for instance, C.V.P., 27 February 1926, p. 41.

late 1920s the inventory department dealt with about fifty enquiries a year. Its reaction was completely unfavourable in only nine cases during the years 1927–31, though in some instances approval was given with reservations.[12] In any case, the public works departments were not obliged to take any notice of its views. The basic cause of their greater deference to the past was their inability to carry out more than the smallest schemes, so they had plenty of time to play the game according to preservationist rules. Moreover, the official protectionist bodies set up before 1914 had lost so much of their impetus by the late 1920s that they could easily be browbeaten into submission when necessary. The work of the Old Paris Committee, in particular, lost much of its urgency as a result of the almost complete standstill of improvement schemes. As it had no control and hardly any influence over the so-called 'speculators' who were the main agents of change in the city centre,[13] it turned its attention more to historical studies and became less active as a campaigner for preservation. And its growing interest in the Seine *département* outside Paris tended to divert its attention from the historic core. Good relations with the City were maintained mainly because the Committee behaved itself. As Prefect Autrand had told its members in 1918:

> 'Your enthusiasm is subject to reason. You have no wish to remain bogged down in formulas which cannot be reconciled with the necessities of modern life.'[14]

And when the Committee was invited in 1938 to comment on the new Paris development plan it had to agree to mind its own business:

> 'It may point out how far a different line for a new street would result in fewer sacrifices of relics of the past, but without expressing any opinion on the general objectives of the planned street, which it cannot judge.'[15]

Although the Committee was occasionally taken into the City's confidence and asked to help in the detailed planning of a scheme affecting a historic site, it was more often presented with accomplished facts by the Council or the prefectoral administration. In 1938, for instance, it was invited to advise the City on a scheme to restore the Place des

---

[12] C.V.P., 25 February 1928, p. 50; 26 January 1929, p. 4; 22 February 1930, p. 22; 30 January 1932, p. 2.

[13] See, for instance, Jean Giraudoux's attack on the destructive results of 'individualism' in *De pleins pouvoirs à sans pouvoirs* (7th ed., 1950), p. 267.

[14] C.V.P., 11 May 1918, p. 90.   [15] C.V.P., 29 January 1938, section 8.

Victoires to something approaching its original appearance. But in 1939 it was told that it could do nothing to prevent the widening of the Rue Chanoinesse, in the Cité, because details had been passed to it 'for information only'.[16] It was equally powerless in its relations with the Government, and its protests against the deletion of buildings from the supplementary list of ancient monuments were ignored.

In spite of the growing interest in groups of old buildings, the Committee did little to encourage their protection. It even accepted so disastrous a scheme as the extension of the Rue Etienne-Marcel (Rue aux Ours) across the Marais. The chairman, Councillor Léon Riotor, said lamely that the scheme was to be regretted, 'but the Committee has never attempted to defend such large groups of buildings against improvements of such incontestable utility.'[17]

The other official organs of preservation were even more inactive. The Technical and Aesthetic Committee was made almost redundant by the lack of municipal improvement schemes. And the Sites Committee concentrated even more than before on rural areas.

The City maintained its opposition to the erection of excessively high buildings where they threatened a townscape or architectural composition. It even managed to compel the owners of the Astoria Hotel, at the Etoile, to demolish the upper storeys of their building, which had overshadowed the Arc de Triomphe since 1907.[18] In the right bank centre, the City continued to cooperate with the State in enforcing architectural ordinances in the Rue de Rivoli, and in 1916 one landlord was fined and ordered to demolish a vertical extension that he had built in infringement of them.[19] But it was more difficult to stop buildings of excessive height being erected in the great majority of streets, to which ordinances did not apply, even though after 1911 the City had power to refuse planning permission for buildings which would detract from the beauty of perspective views and townscapes. The establishment of protected zones appeared to provide the answer, especially as Prefect Delanney supported them in principle, even though he personally had no complaint about the 1902 building regulations.[20] In June 1916 the Old Paris Committee voted unanimously in favour of the creation of such zones, and a general restriction on the height of buildings. Although no zone was ever formally established, and Councillor Léon Riotor had to call (in 1921) for more vigilance by the City

---

[16] C.V.P., 26 February 1938, section 10; 28 January 1939, section 5.
[17] C.V.P., 29 October 1932, p. 125.   [18] C.V.P., 27 February 1926, pp. 34–43.
[19] C.V.P., 10 June 1916, p. 63.   [20] C.V.P., 8 April 1916, pp. 5–6.

in protecting Paris against the effect of new buildings,[21] the authorities appear to have exercised greater responsibility in the granting of building permits in the 1920s and 1930s. Criticism of their attitude became less frequent, and in the right bank centre the City intervened in two cases, in 1929 and 1934, where plans for large new buildings appeared to threaten traditional scenes. The Government, too, was more watchful. In 1928 the Minister of Education and Fine Arts re-established the special committee which coordinated the efforts of all the departments responsible for monumental perspectives in Paris, and which had not resumed its work at the end of the war.[22] The Government also agreed, in 1934, to modify article forty-three of the 1902 building regulations so that plans for Government buildings had to be examined by the Prefect of the Seine and the General Council of Civil Buildings.[23]

The Government continued to extend and modify its powers to protect individual monuments. In July 1914 a law was passed to set up a historic monuments fund in the form of an independent public corporation. It began operations in 1921 with an annual expenditure of 710,000 francs (£14,200), but it attracted considerable voluntary support and enjoyed a number of fixed revenues such as entrance fees. By 1932 its annual turnover had risen to 7,000,000 francs (£78,000).[24] The Government included preservation clauses in the town planning laws of 1919 and 1924, which provided powers to establish protected zones around monuments and safeguard groups of buildings. These new measures reflected a growing interest in buildings of secondary importance, and after the war the Ministry of Education and Fine Arts resumed the preparation of the supplementary list of historic buildings which had been authorised by the law of 31 December 1913. In 1921 the City of Paris was asked to help in this task. In fact, most of the necessary work had already been done in connection with the City's own inventory. The first buildings were placed on the Paris supplementary list in May 1927, and the 1913 law was modified and strengthened by that of 23 July 1927.[25] Property owners were required to give notice of their intention to demolish or alter scheduled properties, giving the Historic Monuments Commission the chance to place the

[21] C.M. reports, 1921, no. 49, pp. 1–3.   [22] C.V.P., 23 February 1929, p. 35.
[23] C.V.P., 30 June 1934, section 15.
[24] Paul Léon, *La vie des monuments français* (1951), p. 177.
[25] C.V.P., 26 November 1921, pp. 170–73; 31 May 1927, p. 66; Louis Réau, *Les monuments détruits de l'art français* (1959), vol. II, p. 277.

threatened buildings on the protected list. No compensation or maintenance grants were payable for scheduled buildings. Convenient
though this arrangement was for the State, the property owner was
often placed in an impossible position. He received no subsidies to
maintain his property, but if he attempted to modernise it the Government might decide to list it and he would lose all control. So the rentable value was effectively limited, and the temptation was to let the
building deteriorate, especially as rent controls had the effect of limiting
the amount that could be spent on maintenance in any case. Landlords
knew that the Historic Monuments Commission hesitated to spend
large sums on restoring buildings that were not of outstanding interest,
and would normally agree to demolition when a property reached a
dangerous state. From the late 1920s buildings were frequently removed
from the supplementary list and demolished, usually because their
owners wanted to rebuild, but occasionally because the City needed
their sites for improvement schemes. The Old Paris Committee was
horrified, but had to make strenuous efforts even to be informed of
such cases before it was too late. And in one instance a seventeenth-
century mansion was demolished because the Government and the
City could not agree on the financial and administrative arrangements
for listing it.[26] On the other hand, the supplementary list had the merit
of establishing the right of supervision of private properties, very few
of which had been listed owing to the high initial indemnity. By 1927,
only sixty-one of the 159 listed buildings in Paris belonged to private
landlords, and all but ten of these were already protected by ancient
architectural ordinances.[27] During the 1920s the Paris historical and
preservation societies campaigned for the abolition of this compensation, but in vain. The Government hesitated to list any building against
the wishes of its owner, because compensation would consequently be
higher, and the expense was worthwhile only for really exceptional
buildings. In 1925, for instance, a number of old houses on the Quai
du Louvre, needed for the extension of the *Samaritaine* department
store, had to be left to their fate because of 'the absence of any artistic
character'.[28] Only a handful of buildings were listed in Paris against
the owners' will in the 1920s. After 1930, such listings became even
rarer, though mainly because the building slump reduced the number
of demolitions, and buildings could be safely left on the supplementary
list. In fact, listing was used between the wars mainly as a means of

[26] C.V.P., 30 November 1929, p. 106; 22 February 1930, p. 24.
[27] C.V.P., 26 February 1927, pp. 45–7.   [28] C.V.P., 31 January 1925, p. 16.

strengthening existing architectural ordinances and restrictive coven-
ants. To limit compensation, protection was often restricted to
façades and roofs. Between 1928 and 1940 the exteriors of all the houses
of the Place-Vendôme were thus protected, while the interiors were
mostly ripped out and rebuilt for business use. The external appearance
of the Place des Vosges and the Palais-Royal was safeguarded in the
same way, though internal reconstruction did not ensue. Apart from
these, no more than three private buildings were listed in the whole
of the right bank centre between 1915 and 1939, and only one of them
was against its owner's wishes. Although a number of municipal and
State-owned properties were placed on the list, and the practice of
safeguarding the façades only became common, the very great majority
of old private houses still had no legal protection by 1939. And supplementary scheduling, by discouraging repairs, may well have accelerated deterioration in many cases.

Fortunately, the City continued to make up, to some extent, for the
Government's deficiencies. Even though financial stringency prevented
the City from acquiring buildings without very serious consideration,
it recognised the responsibility incurred by the Government's failure
to make any important acquisition in central Paris between the wars.
Even though André Hallays' assertion that the purchase of old mansions could be a paying proposition was contested within the Old Paris
Committee itself,[29] the City was able more often than not to make
good use of them. The Hotel d'Epernon, for example, was converted
into an annexe of the Lycée Victor Hugo with considerable success.[30]
The City's main acquisitions in the right bank centre were the Hôtel
Lauzun (1928), the Hôtel Lamoignon (1928) and the Hôtel d'Aumont
(1935). In the case of the Hôtel Lauzun half the cost of acquisition was
generously provided by the Government. And in 1935 the Government contributed half the cost of an eight million franc restoration
programme for old buildings owned by the City, under the Marquet
plan.[31]

Very little real progress was made in the protection of urban views
and groups of buildings, despite the powers contained in the town-
planning laws of 1919 and 1924, and in the law of 2 May 1930. This
act reorganised the preservation of areas of natural beauty and townscapes, and established the principle of protected zones around listed
monuments. But its application in Paris encountered the same obstacles

---

[29] C.V.P., 22 December 1923, p. 170.   [30] C.V.P., 16 March 1940, section 5.
[31] C.V.P., 26 January 1935, section 5.

that had thwarted previous attempts to place preservation orders on whole groups of buildings. As we have seen, by 1914 the Sites Committee had listed only two Paris views, and neither of them was in the right bank centre, or included any buildings. Even though the Committee's terms of reference included townscapes, it had called in vain for the listing of the western end of the Cité and the surroundings of the Pont-Neuf. It experienced the same frustrations after the war when the Government refused to allow this part of the island to be listed because it held the freehold of most of it, and maintained that the State's property could not be made subject to any restriction.[32] The City was equally uncooperative. In 1932, for instance, the Prefect of the Seine refused to apply to the Minister of Fine Arts for the listing as a townscape of the *grands boulevards*, because they were a centre of activity in constant evolution, without original architecture. He defined a townscape as 'above all, a harmonious composition, a beautiful decor in whose creation nature and time have played as big a part as the hand of man.' It should also display some uniformity.[33] So it is hardly surprising that no townscape of any kind was listed in Paris between the wars.

More significant in the long term than unenforceable legislation was the growing interest of informed opinion in the aesthetic aspects of town planning. Writers on town planning and Paris attempted to define the true nature of beauty and its importance for the citizen. Jean Raymond, for instance, wrote in 1934 that beauty was an essential factor of happiness in a town, and 'paid' in the long run. The aesthetics of a city gave it its soul, and often influenced its evolution.[34] In 1929 Albert Guérard urged that building regulations should control external appearance as well as height and ventilation, to prevent an un-Parisian proliferation of different styles of architecture.[35] In the absence of big public works schemes the building bye-laws of 1902, even when modified, remained a target for criticism. Linear aesthetics and geometrical street planning were even further discredited by the official admission, voiced by Prefects Autrand and Juillard in 1919 and 1922, that Haussmann had destroyed too much.[36] Even one of Haussmann's admirers,

[32] C.V.P., 31 January 1925, pp. 16–17.
[33] C.V.P., 28 May 1932, pp. 71–3.
[34] Jean Raymond, *Précis d'urbanisme moderne* (1934), pp. 44, 56.
[35] Albert Guérard, *L'avenir de Paris* (1929), p. 73.
[36] C.V.P., 27 January 1923, pp. 37–9.

Marcel Poëte, had to admit that in the Cité the great Prefect had 'destroyed as much as he created'.[37]

As before 1914, the esteem in which old buildings were held was a function of their rarity. In 1935, for instance, it was suggested that the Old Paris Committee should draw up a list of timber-framed buildings like the medieval house in the Rue Volta (IIIe).[38] The Committee itself became less purist in its attitude to old houses which had no particular architectural interest, although it still considered their preservation to be virtually out of the question. It also showed an interest in relatively recent buildings such as the Art Nouveau creations of the turn of the century. In 1928 it called for the listing of the nondescript façade of the *Variétés* theatre because of the memories it evoked of the *grands boulevards* in the good old days. And the Gaillon fountain in the Rue de la Michodière was actually placed on the supplementary list in 1926 because of its historical and traditional interest, even though it had little architectural value.[39] This liberalisation of preservation criteria was also reflected in the growing interest in groups of old buildings. Such groups could be placed on the supplementary list of historic monuments, and a number of writers emphasised that they were an essential element in the beauty of Paris. For instance, Albert Guérard, who was by no means an extreme preservationist, urged their protection.[40] And in 1937 Georges Lenôtre, who *was* an extreme preservationist, wrote of:

'. . . the indescribable attraction of these old houses which have no architectural particularity to draw the onlooker, but which we love because they have witnessed the past; they retain the trace of lives which ended long ago, and our ancestors loved them.'[41]

The interest in the preservation of Montmartre before 1914, which stemmed from the growing number of artists, intellectuals and bourgeois who lived there, was paralleled after the war in the Île Saint-Louis. Although most of the original middle-class residents had left the island in the nineteenth century, such people were now attracted to it once more by its convenient and healthy situation, and absence of industry. This return, after about 1920, reinforced the post-1902

---

[37] Marcel Poëte, *Une vie de cité* (1931), Album, p. 476. Other strong critics of Haussmann's rectilinear planning were L. Dubech and P. d'Espezel, in their *Histoire de Paris* (1926), p. 424, Albert Guérard, in *L'avenir de Paris*, p. 14, and Louis Bonnier, in C.V.P., 29 January 1938, section 8.

[38] C.V.P., 25 May 1935, section 2. [39] C.V.P., 28 May 1932, p. 71.

[40] *L'avenir de Paris*, p. 29. [41] Georges Lenôtre, *Paris qui disparaît* (1937), p. 12.

campaign against high buildings in the island which would have ruined the view from the *quais*. Some of the newcomers, of course, wanted to extend their properties as well as modernise them, but excesses were resisted by the City, supported by the great majority of influential residents who wished to see the authentic appearance of the island preserved. They were happy to stand idly by while the poor Marais quarter deteriorated, but they had not bought apartments in the Île Saint-Louis just to see it ruined by modern 'skyscrapers'. In 1923 the City laid down very precise guidelines for the construction of new houses in the widened Rue des Deux-Ponts,[42] and refused permission in 1925 for the addition of extra storeys to a house on the Quai d'Orléans, even before the Old Paris Committee had passed a resolution to that effect.[43] In the early 1930s a proposal by Councillor G. Lemarchand[44] generated hopes that the whole island would be listed as a monument, and the Director of the Paris Plan approved the general lines of a protection scheme prepared by the Old Paris Committee.[45] But practical difficulties caused the project to be dropped, so that in 1934 nothing could be done to prevent the demolition of the Hôtel Hesselin on the Quai de Béthune.[46]

The appreciation of groups of old houses did not yet extend to the unhealthy areas. The Old Paris Committee was given prior warning of demolitions there, and the chance to earmark for preservation any portable details of condemned buildings. It expressed regret at the loss of historic central districts, but agreed that total destruction was necessary to eliminate tuberculosis. And when, in 1934, the Committee visited fifty condemned buildings in unhealthy area number 1 it found hardly anything worthy of preservation.[47]

The official view that the demands of preservation and modernisation were not contradictory was rarely questioned between the wars, although, as has already been pointed out, it probably would have been if more improvement work had been carried out. Nearly every Prefect of the Seine assured the Old Paris Committee, as Paul Bouju did in 1925, that he wanted to 'bring the grandeur of the past closer to the equally glorious needs of powerful and magnificent evolution'.[48] And this view was supported with rather less grandiloquence by several writers on town planning and allied subjects. Albert Guérard thought

---

[42] C.M. reports, 1929, no. 77, p. 4.   [43] C.V.P., 28 November 1928, pp. 98–9.
[44] C.M. reports, 1929, no. 77.
[45] C.V.P., 31 January 1931, pp. 18–19; 28 November 1931, pp. 143–8.
[46] C.V.P., 2 June 1934, section 5.   [47] C.V.P., 24 November 1934, section 9.
[48] C.V.P., 28 November 1925, p. 94.

that every town planner should have tradition in his blood, but criticised André Hallays' gospel of total preservation, which he thought could perpetuate the past only in a faded and discoloured form.[49] Jean Raymond called for demolition to improve traffic flows, but without destroying a city's character.[50] Guérard suggested that the whole of Paris should be listed as a historic and monumental site, not to prevent all change, but to ensure that every scheme was submitted to a special supervisory planning committee. In his opinion, preservation and progress could be married if the city's area continued to expand as it always had done in the past.[51]

The inter-war period saw a new development in the form of nationally based societies which acted positively to ensure the protection of various historic monuments by their own efforts, instead of appealing to the Government or local authorities. Limited though their influence was in Paris, they set an example which was to be followed in the capital after 1945. In the 1920s were created the 'Sauvegarde de l'Art français' society, which was interested in various aspects of national art, and the 'Demeure historique', which concentrated more exclusively on historic buildings. Both were organised and supported by nobles and other leisured individuals.[52] In the 1930s the Society for the Protection of the French Countryside and the 'Société pour l'Esthétique générale de la France' were set up.[53] A new periodical, *Pierres de France*, was founded by an architect, Achille Carlier, to attack vandalism, and *Le Temps* also joined the struggle with a noisy press campaign in favour of preservation conducted by Léandre Vaillat.

Of more direct interest to Paris was the society of the Friends of Old Paris Houses, founded in 1922, and the Society of Historical and Geographical Studies of the Paris Region, which appeared in 1929. This latter society was intended mainly to interest primary school-teachers in the Paris area, so that they would eventually teach their pupils to respect the past.[54]

2 CONSCIOUS PRESERVATION 1940–69

The Second World War was potentially an even greater threat to the historic heart of Paris than the First. In 1940 the city could well

---

[49] *L'avenir de Paris*, pp. 14–15.
[50] Jean Raymond, *Précis d'urbanisme*, p. 43.
[51] *L'avenir de Paris*, pp. 72, 330.
[52] For a more detailed description of these societies, see Réau, *Monuments détruits*, vol. II, pp. 279–80; Georges Pillement, *Saccage de la France* (1943), p. 207.
[53] See Pillement, p. 207, and Réau, *Monuments détruits*, vol. II, p. 282.
[54] Réau, vol. II, p. 280; C.V.P., 29 April 1927, p. 58; 21 December 1929, p. 122.

have suffered the same fate as Rotterdam or Coventry, but its artistic importance helped to save it, not because the Germans would have refrained from damaging it, but because the French decided not to defend it. Subsequent air raids by the Allies damaged installations in the suburbs, but bombs fell in the centre only by accident and very little damage was done there. In the last stages of the Occupation, the city's most important buildings might have been blown up if General von Choltitz, the commander of the garrison, had not chosen to disobey Hitler's orders. So historic Paris emerged unharmed from a war which destroyed so many architectural glories elsewhere.

All effective preservation measures were paralysed during the war, but demolitions also ceased, except in the unhealthy areas. The Old Paris Committee continued to meet, and the City created a post of inspector-general to coordinate its functions with those of the Sites Committee.[55] But their activities had a purely academic interest. The renewal of the threat to the city's old buildings was further postponed for some years after 1945 by the post-war paralysis of public works and the construction industry. Although a number of buildings were pulled down in unhealthy area number 16, demolition was much less comprehensive than in area number 1 before the war, and the City's decision to restore a block of old buildings next to the church of Saint-Gervais in 1945 indicated a change of heart and a willingness to retain the old structures where possible, when they had some historic interest. But this operation was the only one of its kind to be carried out in the 1940s, because of the halt in slum clearance acquisitions after 1943. The City began to show a renewed interest in preservation towards 1950, in connection with the preparation of the development plan, which included a number of 'remodelling' schemes in the east of the right bank centre. By now the old unhealthy area policy of total clearance had been abandoned, and the new schemes involved only partial demolition. So some measure of preservation, both of individual buildings and of townscapes, could easily be incorporated in them. At the same time, public interest in the Marais was being aroused by the work of writers such as Georges Pillement and Jean Giraudoux, whose attacks on bureaucratic muddle and individual philistinism seemed particularly apposite under the Fourth Republic. Acknowledging this new climate of opinion, the City prepared a special town planning scheme to preserve the appearance of area number 16, and its different

[55] *A.P.*, 29 November 1941.

departments at last began to coordinate their conservation efforts.[56] The draft development plan presented to the City Council in December 1951 contained several large-scale schemes of modernisation, including a number of new traffic arteries, but in general it was extremely favourable to the preservation of historic areas. At last, the City seemed to recognise the importance of groups of buildings; the Halles, for instance, should be rebuilt on the same site but 'with all care being taken not to shatter an area that is so loaded with history'.[57] The Opéra district would be preserved as a whole, and all improvement lines would be redrawn to this effect. The Place des Victoires would be rebuilt in its original form, and the old houses in streets such as the Rue du Caire and the Rue d'Aboukir would be preserved.[58] Improvement lines would also be redrawn in the Rue Saint-Honoré. As for the Marais, it would be re-established by degrees as a middle-class residential area by restoring its old buildings and freeing its courtyards and gardens of outbuildings. But the traditional local trading and artisanal activities would be retained. In the Cité, new erections in the Place Dauphine would be forbidden, and owners of existing buildings there would be required to reduce their height to the original three storeys within fifty years.[59] Of course, such a measure would almost certainly have been unenforceable. Equally Utopian was the suggestion that the cost of restoring old buildings (defined as having been built before 1815) should be met by an extra charge on the rates.[60]

Reaction to the plan was mixed. The idea of preserving the Opéra area was too far ahead of its time to arouse much enthusiasm, but the plans for the Marais were welcomed by councillors and public alike. The report as a whole was given only qualified approval by the Council, and it was regarded in any case as only an advance plan. Its conservation proposals would certainly have involved the City in very great expense, and would have created various legal and political problems. Yet, although it was succeeded later by totally new plans, it represents a first step towards the definitive preservation of the Marais and similar areas.

For the time being, Montmartre was still much further along the path to overall conservation than the Marais. As early as 1942 Claude Charpentier, architect and Montmartre resident, had produced a town planning scheme for the area which aimed to recreate its mid-nineteenth century appearance. This plan was passed on to the City

---

[56] 'Le quartier du Marais', *La conjoncture économique dans le Département*, 1959, 3ème trimestre, p. 469; Paul Léon, *Vie des monuments*, p. 356.
[57] C.M. reports, 1951, no. 2, p. 17.   [58] C.M. reports, 1951, no. 2, p. 24.
[59] C.M. reports, 1951, no. 2, pp. 26–8.   [60] C.M. reports, 1951, no. 2, p. 27.

authorities by the Old Paris Committee. After representations in the early post-war years by the Committee and the Ministry of Fine Arts, the Sites Committee obtained the City's agreement to the listing of the whole of Montmartre as a picturesque townscape in 1949. In 1951 the Prefect asked Claude Charpentier and Jacques Ogé to prepare an official planning scheme, which was approved by the Sites Committee in 1952. In 1956 the City Council accepted the plan and voted the necessary financial resources. This success encouraged the hopes of all those who wished to see similar schemes elsewhere in the city, and in 1956 the Old Paris Committee called for the preparation of a conservation plan for the Palais-Royal area.[61] But nothing more was to be achieved until the 1960s.

The protection of individual buildings was made much easier by the small number of voluntary demolitions and the City's greater readiness to cooperate with the preservationists. In 1956, for instance, the City agreed to send the Old Paris Committee photographs of all buildings for which demolition permits had been requested.[62] Most mansions were no longer in danger of total demolition, but the City endeavoured to prevent their deterioration and degradation. Wherever possible it tried to convert those used for industry or commerce into residential accommodation,[63] although the law of commercial property made this both difficult and costly. Complete restoration was still, in the late 1950s, too onerous for the City's limited resources. In 1959, although work was continuing at the Hôtel d'Aumont, it had been halted at the Hôtel de Lamoignon owing to lack of finance. As a rule, the Government refused to sanction such outlay.[64] But there was a considerable increase in expenditure on restoration in the 1960s as the financial situation improved.

Lack of resources also stopped the City acquiring more than a handful of ancient buildings after the war. It had enough difficulty in maintaining those that it already owned. However, in the right bank centre it purchased the Hôtel Bertier de Sauvigny, Rue Béranger, as

---

[61] C.V.P., 1 February 1956, *B.M.O.*, 13 April 1956, pp. 747–8; 6 June 1957, *B.M.O.*, 15 January 1958, pp. 110–11.

[62] C.V.P., 1 February 1956.

[63] C.V.P., 16 January 1958, *B.M.O.*, 16 December 1958, pp. 2438–9. Purists like Yvan Christ were no longer satisfied with the conversion of mansions into municipal offices (Y. Christ etc., *Le Marais* [1964], p. 18).

[64] 'Le quartier du Marais', *La conjoncture économique dans le Département*, 1959, 4ème trimestre, p. 662.

an annexe of the *mairie* of the IIIe *arrondissement*,[65] and after the war it bought the Hôtel de Beauvais and the Hôtel Salé. It had these former mansions listed and restored in 1964.[66]

The City's continued inability to carry out improvements in the city centre limited the number of occasions on which the Old Paris Committee could attempt to influence its actions, just as it had before 1939. On the other hand, cooperation between the City and the Committee became more sincere and productive now that the former was directly concerned in the conservation of historic areas. But the Committee remained powerless in the face of a firm decision by the City or the Government. It was, for instance, unable to influence the Finance Ministry's decision to expand its city centre offices at the expense of a group of old houses.[67] It continued to cooperate in the preparation of the city development plan by drawing up a scheme of architectural and aesthetic ordinances, but even here its role was very restricted:

'It really has to consider the city's past, and not its future.'[68]

In 1954 the Committee had to make a 'voluntary' restriction on the freedom and range of its discussions after the administration criticised it for dealing with various important questions without giving prior warning. It then agreed to send a written question to the relevant department before discussing any matter which did not lie within its own terms of reference.[69] In 1959 Albert Laprade complained that the Committee was powerless, and called for its complete reorganisation.[70] It has continued to meet regularly in the 1960s, but has not been able to increase its direct influence over the City.

The City's extensive commitment to conservation since 1945 has limited the significance of the Government's role, but this has continued to develop. The Vichy Government's enthusiasm for town planning resulted in the provision of some protection at last for the surroundings of historic monuments. The law of 25 February 1943 created special controls for all constructions visible from a listed or

---

[65] C.V.P., 27 November 1941, section 6.
[66] Léon, *Vie des monuments*, p. 271; Christ, *Le Marais*, pp. 227, 250.
[67] C.V.P., 29 May 1941, section 7; 7 January 1955, pp. 7–12.
[68] C.V.P., 29 May 1941, section 10.
[69] C.V.P., 18 March 1954, pp. 37–9.
[70] C.V.P., 2 February 1959, *B.M.O.*, 21 March 1959, pp. 651–3.

scheduled building within a radius of 500 metres. All modifications to buildings within this distance needed the approval of the Minister of Fine Arts. The law also provided powers of compulsory purchase to rearrange the surroundings of a monument. On the other hand, the listing of private buildings remained very difficult after the war, and no legislation has so far made it appreciably easier. But the addition of buildings to the supplementary list proceeded apace. By 1955, 231 buildings or parts of buildings in the right bank centre were on the supplementary list. It was still difficult to apply the legislation on townscapes, but the western extremity of the Cité, excluding the river bank and the *quais*, was finally listed in 1958.

The rarity of additions to the primary list of protected monuments after the war was due largely to the fact that the Historic Monuments Commission had insufficient resources to maintain those that had already been listed.[71] Actual acquisitions were even more infrequent, although the Hôtel de Fontenay was purchased in 1946 by the *Archives Nationales*, and the Department of Fine Arts bought and restored the Hôtel de Sully, Rue Saint-Antoine, in the 1950s.

We have already seen how public opinion was coming to favour comprehensive preservation before 1939. But it was after the war that the movement reached its apotheosis. During the years of reappraisal after the debacle of 1940, Jean Giraudoux and Georges Pillement published works which had a considerable influence on public opinion. Giraudoux attacked the banality of modern architecture and urged that the masterpieces of the past should be preserved. He wanted to see Paris expand on the outskirts, allowing the conservation of the centre.[72] In about 1940 he founded the Urban and Rural League, which aimed to provide better environmental amenities. Pillement's attacks were much more violent. He pilloried both middle-class materialism and administrative incompetence: '. . . the civil service is a monster which destroys everything around it.'[73] He painted a melodramatic picture of a massive conspiracy against old buildings of beauty and historic interest. And although his near-hysterical writings often weakened the case for preservation rather than strengthening it, they effectively made the public aware of the issues at stake.

The liberalisation of the criteria of preservation continued after 1940.

[71] C.V.P., 24 February 1955, pp. 64–5.
[72] Jean Giraudoux, *De pleins pouvoirs à sans pouvoirs* (7th ed., 1950), pp. 62, 69.
[73] Georges Pillement, *Destruction de Paris* (1941), p. 113.

Both Pillement and Giraudoux favoured the conservation of whole groups of buildings, and their demands were echoed by many others. In 1946 Claude Charpentier could even call for the listing of part of the XVIIe *arrondissement*, dating from the Second Empire, not because it was considered of any architectural interest, but because future generations might be glad to have it passed down to them intact.[74] This was an extreme view. But even without an official preservation order there was little chance that such areas would be modified in the foreseeable future. Town planners and city councillors agreed that little change was possible in the centre and west of Paris, and began to question whether change was actually desirable, even for areas which did not have the same architectural distinction as the Marais. Such was the view of Bernard Lafay, president of the City Council, who wrote in 1954 that in the centre '. . . one finds the "old stones" adored by all Parisians . . . it has that indefinable atmosphere which is the charm of Paris'.[75] On the other hand, most opinions rejected the idea that the centre should be turned into a museum, and the presence of artisans, in particular, was encouraged.

In earlier times an increase in public works investment on the scale realised in the late 1950s would have aroused the fears of preservationists. But, as we have seen, very little of these resources was devoted to the city centre, and public feeling in favour of conservation was now strong enough for a keen fight to be put up against those few changes that were approved. Only the approaching departure of the Halles threatened to disturb the old buildings of the centre, as we shall see later.

(a) The Marais

By now, the Marais was no longer protected only by the inability of the City and private builders to redevelop it, but by a positive recognition of its architectural and historic value. In 1956 the City Council made the whole area a protected zone in the development plan,[76] and a ten-year conservation scheme was presented to the Council in December 1961. It involved the preservation of over 100 mansions, nearly one-fifth of which already belonged to the City or the State, and the exclusion of wheeled traffic from many of the narrower streets.[77] The

[74] *Urbanisme*, no. 84, 1964, p. 32.
[75] Bernard Lafay, *Problèmes de Paris* (1954), p. 199.
[76] *B.M.O.*, special number, March 1967, p. 8.
[77] Jean Bastié, *Paris en l'an 2000* (1964), p. 156.

Council approved this overall plan, which covered an area of 129 hectares, as well as a detailed rehabilitation scheme for four street blocks adjoining the Place de Thorigny (IIIe).[78] This decision, incidentally, marked the final abandonment of the extension of the Rue aux Ours, which had been planned by Haussmann and actively pursued until 1939. Its completion would have caused the demolition of many of the houses whose restoration the Council had now approved.

So the future of the Marais was already assured when new legislation on the preservation of France's architectural heritage, the 'Malraux law', was enacted in August 1962. But the law strengthened the City's powers to prevent undesirable changes by creating 'protected sectors', for which perpetual preservation plans were to be prepared, and in which no demolition or construction work could be undertaken without prior authorisation. Grants would be made to landlords who were prepared to renovate their properties. This law was applied to the Marais by a ministerial order in July 1965.[79] In the same year, the City started work on the restoration of the Place de Thorigny sector, covering three and a half hectares. The scheme was planned to take five years, with just over half the cost borne by the landlords, and the rest shared between the Government and the City. Restoration work was carried out by a specially created public corporation, which also directed the operations of those landlords who chose to renovate their own properties under the law of 1962.[80] By-products of the work were to be the creation of a large area of gardens by the removal of outbuildings, and an underground car park for 500 cars. It was planned to re-let the ten mansions to be restored to wealthy tenants prepared to pay highly for a prestige dwelling.[81] Much of this scheme has now (1970) been completed, and its results are especially spectacular in the Rue du Parc-Royal where a whole row of mansions has been restored. All of them would have been condemned to demolition by the abandoned street improvement scheme.

The City's efforts were accompanied by a quickening of public interest in the Marais which began to take a very positive form in the early 1960s. Discussion of André Malraux's proposals focused attention on the area of Paris which was likely to be the first to benefit from

[78] C.M. reports, 1965, no. 1, p. 33.
[79] C.M. reports, 1965, no. 1, p. 33; *B.M.O.*, special number, March 1967, p. 9.
[80] Paul Chatelain, 'Quartiers historiques et centre ville: l'exemple du quartier du Marais', p. 352, in *Urban Core and Inner City* (1967), pp. 340–55; *B.M.O.*, special number, March 1967, p. 9.
[81] Albert Laprade, 'Vieux quartiers et techniques modernes', p. 60, *Coopération technique*, nos. 46–8, pp. 57–60.

their enactment, but the preservationists realised that more publicity was needed for the Marais, which still remained unknown to many Parisians. Their solution was to launch, in 1962, the Festival of the Marais. Concerts and plays were held in the courtyards of some of the larger mansions and in the churches of the district, and it was hoped to devote any profits to the restoration of individual buildings. In the event, the success of the Festival exceeded the organisers' hopes. The numbers attending rose from 10,000 in 1962 to 72,000 in 1965.[82] The Festival Association was soon able to begin restoring two old houses in the Rue François-Miron (IVe) with the help of volunteer labour and a generous municipal subsidy.[83]

Most of the interest in the preservation of the Marais came from people living elsewhere in the city. Of the 5–10,000 people signing petitions organised by the Association, only 8 per cent lived in the first four *arrondissements,* and one in four of this minority resided in the Île Saint-Louis.[84] Of course, the manifestation of greater interest by the inhabitants of the area would have justified greater confidence in the chances of preventing its degradation, but it was unreasonable to expect it from the present inhabitants, most of whom were of very limited means. And the interest taken by middle-class people from other districts was encouraging to those who hoped to base the regeneration of the Marais on an influx of wealthy residents. Indeed, the southern part of the Marais, between the Rue Saint-Antoine and the Seine, was already benefiting from an extension of the spontaneous renovation work which had already taken strong root in the Île Saint-Louis. The City's decision not to proceed with the total clearance of unhealthy area number 16, and to rebuild on cleared sites in a harmonious style, opened up great possibilities for private enterprise to co-operate with the authorities. Indeed, hardly any of the dwellings constructed there since the war have been subsidised (*H.L.M.*), and most appear to be let at high rents to well-off tenants. The City has even had to delineate a *ZAD* (long-term redevelopment zone) of fifteen hectares to prevent speculation in the area.[85] But in general this new flow of investment into the Marais is most encouraging to the City, in view of the limitations on the resources it can devote to the area when so much remains to be done elsewhere in the city. It has been possible to plan the extension of positive restoration works beyond the

[82] Chatelain, 'Quartiers historiques', p. 352.
[83] *B.M.O.*, special number, March 1967, p. 70.
[84] Chatelain, 'Quartiers historiques', p. 353.
[85] Chatelain p. 353.

Place de Thorigny sector, and in early 1968 work began on studies for the restoration of houses in the Place des Vosges.[86] The first results of this new enterprise can already be seen.

(b) The Halles area

Although the preservationist victory has been almost total to the east of the Boulevard de Sébastopol, battle is still joined to the west, where the odds might appear at first sight to be stacked in favour of redevelopment. The west of the right bank centre is too much a part of the central business district to be left entirely in the hands of the preservationists. However, few spontaneous changes would have been made to its buildings had it not been for the decision to remove the Halles.

The Halles had gradually extended their influence over the rectangle bounded by the Rue Etienne-Marcel, the Boulevard de Sébastopol, the Rue de Rivoli and the Rue du Louvre. Nearly all the commercial activities here were connected with the markets and the inconvenience, noise and dirt of the district had driven out all but a very poor population, many of whom worked at the Halles. The few middle-class residents who remained were mostly market traders. So it was clear that the departure of the Halles would deprive the area of its activities and some of its population, after which it could only degenerate into a total slum. At the same time, property values would slump so dramatically that the authorities would have a heaven-sent opportunity to acquire and redevelop the whole area. There were many worse areas in the city—indeed, the Halles ward had had more attention from Haussmann than almost anywhere else. But to regenerate this area might halt the decline of the whole of the right bank centre by providing a nucleus of first-class residential and business accommodation, open space, and cultural equipment. It might even help to halt the drift of business to the west of the city centre and encourage landlords outside the improvement area to modernise and reconstruct their properties.

The City Council gave its approval in 1961 for studies of the renovation of the Halles area to begin. A coordinating committee representing all interested departments was set up in the following year, and in 1963 the City set up a corporation to carry out detailed preparatory studies.[87] As usual, individual architects and planners published their

[86] Conseil de Paris, reports, 1968, no. 1, p. 16.
[87] C.M. reports, 1965, no. 1, p. 32.

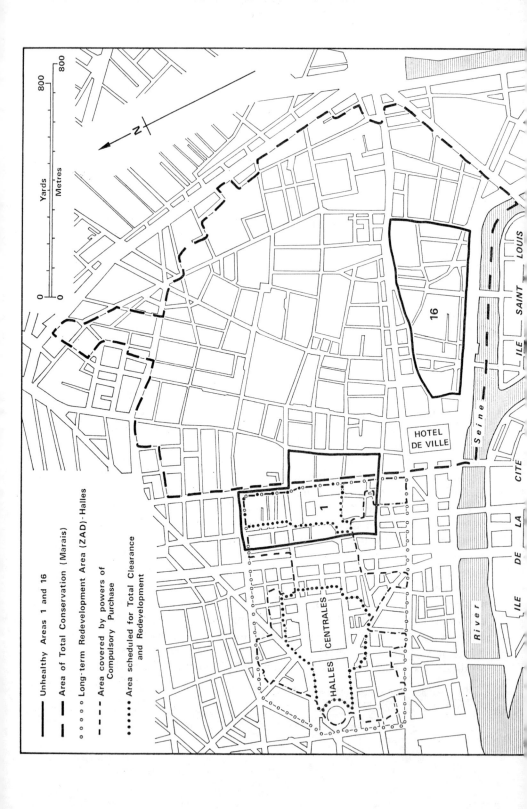

	Unhealthy Areas 1 and 16
	Area of Total Conservation (Marais)
o o o o o	Long-term Redevelopment Area (ZAD)-Halles
--- ---	Area covered by powers of Compulsory Purchase
••••••	Area scheduled for Total Clearance and Redevelopment

800

800

Yards

Metres

N

HOTEL
DE VILLE

16

1

HALLES

CENTRALES

Seine

River

ILE SAINT LOUIS

ILE DE LA CITE

own schemes. Some were very ambitious. The Lopez and Rotival schemes, for instance, involved the renovation of 250 hectares, from the Seine to the Gare de l'Est.[88] But the City was thinking along much more modest lines. A decision was not immediately urgent because the Halles were not due to move for some years, and the City Council was not called upon to pass further policy resolutions until 1966. Then, on 23 December, it invited the Prefect to seek powers of acquisition within an area of 35·4 hectares, and to designate as a long-term redevelopment zone (*ZAD*) a slightly larger zone of forty-three hectares, including the area to be acquired. This zone covered nearly all the area bounded by the Rue de Rivoli, Rue Beaubourg, Rue Etienne-Marcel and Rue du Louvre. It was also agreed to establish the corporation studying the renovation of the area on a firmer basis. By July 1967 the Prefect had obtained the required powers, and the Council then decided that negotiations with landlords should be conducted by the new corporation.[89] Some urgency was necessary by now because it was still hoped that the Halles might be vacated by the end of 1967 or early 1968. The City Council approved the establishment of a further public corporation to carry out the work of renewal and restoration, and agreed that some fifteen hectares should be acquired within five years.[90] But it also insisted that 10,000 people should be accommodated in the redevelopment area, in dwellings or hotels, after completion of the work, compared to 18,000 at present. The Prefect agreed that this was a reasonable stipulation.[91] The City now asked six architects to take part in a competition for the best redevelopment scheme for the first fifteen hectares. Even if no clear winner emerged, it would be possible to combine the best points of various schemes, and also to designate one architect-planner to direct the whole operation. The architects were required to conform to a ceiling of twenty-seven metres, which was the general maximum for the historic city centre, but buildings might rise in exceptional cases to thirty metres. Among the buildings which they were instructed to include were a new office block for the Ministry of Finance, which wished to vacate its quarters in the Louvre but remain in the city centre, and an embryonic 'international commercial

---

[88] Daniel Monteux, 'Les Halles et leur quartier', p. 280, in *Urban Core and Inner City*, pp. 256–81.
[89] *Mémoires du Préfet de Paris au Conseil de Paris*, 1968, no. 2, p. 2.
[90] *B.M.O.*, 24 July 1967, pp. 377–414; 10 August 1967, pp. 1450–51.
[91] *Mémoires du Préfet de Paris*, 1968, no. 2, pp. 3–4.

FIG. 6. *Special zones in the right bank centre.*

centre', which meant more offices. The retention of churches and a number of other important monuments was stipulated, as was the preservation and restoration of four groups of old buildings. Four other groups were pointed out as being suitable for restoration, but it was left to the participants to decide whether to retain them.

One of the competitors was Claude Charpentier, the prominent preservationist architect, whose renovation techniques were already being applied with great success elsewhere in the city. He produced a characteristic plan involving almost no demolition and the construction of new buildings in a neutral style. The other architects were more iconoclastic.[92] In February 1968 the Prefect reported to the Council on his reactions to the schemes. Although he dismissed Charpentier's project as too conservative, he did not swing completely to the other extreme. He told the City Council:

> 'The historic centre must play a mixed role as an area of residence, business, and great national and international institutions. The treatment of the centre is a matter of renewal just as much as of restoration. We have to set off our architectural heritage by forward-looking architecture, but while retaining the spirit and the pattern of the urban tissue in order not to destroy continuity by a conflict of different scales.'[93]

Although the Prefect considered that none of the schemes was really satisfactory, he suggested that two architects who had produced coherent and ambitious plans, Du Marien and Faugeron, should be asked to modify them to include more open space and to conform with the organisation of the whole of central Paris outlined in the *Schéma directeur*. After some grumbling about lack of consultation, the Council agreed. The architects quickly made the required modifications, and the redevelopment project for the fifteen-hectare sector was finally approved by the City Council in July 1969.[94]

In the meantime, some progress was made in obtaining control of the area under discussion. Before compulsory purchase procedure was set in train, all landlords were offered the chance to participate in the improvement scheme. Some showed interest, and various associations

---

[92] For details of the schemes, see *Mémoires du Préfet de Paris*, 1968, no. 2, pp. 14–26; *Architecture d'aujourd'hui*, no. 138, June–July 1968, pp. 52–72, 74–9.

[93] *Mémoires du Préfet de Paris*, 1968, no. 2, p. 28.

[94] *Le Monde*, 13–14 July 1969. However, the Prefect had to promise to produce an area plan to show how the Halles project would fit in with the rest of the right bank centre. This was potentially a cause of further delay.

of property owners were set up. Then, early in 1968, acquisition of a first instalment was undertaken. The sector to be acquired housed 7,600 people—over one-third of the population of the redevelopment area. Work is expected to take until 1978, and will result in the provision of 1,200 new dwellings. The first buildings to be demolished will be in three streets on the site of the Halles-Châtelet station of the express *Métro* line, which is due to be constructed by the cut-and-cover method just to the south of the Halles.[95] But demolition is not planned to begin until late 1970, at which time work will also start on the demolition of the few remaining houses on the 'Plateau Beaubourg'—the only part of the old unhealthy area number 1 to have been cleared during the 1930s. This site will be used for a new public library and a group of workers' dwellings.[96]

Meanwhile, the City Council and the prefectoral administration were discussing what was to be done with the remaining twenty hectares for which compulsory purchase powers had been obtained. The cost of comprehensive redevelopment here was certain to be much higher than in the fifteen-hectare zone centred on the Halles, because very few sites and properties were already owned by the City. Moreover, the preservationists argued strongly against total clearance. So on 24 October 1968 the City Council agreed that the twenty hectares should be designated a zone of rehabilitation and restoration. Although final details still have to be worked out, it is clear that a minimum of demolition will be involved.

It would seem, therefore, that the complete demolition of the Halles district is a long way off, even if the scheme that is finally adopted requires it. Many of the residents are already mounting a campaign against the transformation of their ward, which they know will banish most of them to the suburbs. It is too early to judge how the district will look in ten or twenty years' time, but the City's recent record would suggest that the more ambitious schemes will slowly be forgotten, and that the element of restoration in the plans will grow in importance. And even if the whole area is rebuilt, it seems unlikely that it will bring about the spontaneous reconstruction of neighbouring districts. Moreover, the difficulties and delays encountered in the Halles ward may well discourage the City from undertaking similar schemes elsewhere in the centre.

To conclude, the situation in 1970 is that the Government and the

[95] *Mémoires du Préfet de Paris*, 1968, no. 2, pp. 3–4.
[96] *France-Soir*, 17 March 1969.

City have approved the conservation and restoration of most of the eastern half of the right bank centre. In the west, their only plans are for the long-term redevelopment of one ward out of eight. The other wards are likely, as we have seen, to remain as they are for several decades to come, if not longer. As time passes, the preservationist case will grow in influence, so that protection may be extended beyond the Marais. Preservation and restoration may well even emerge as the quickest, cheapest and most effective form of redevelopment in the city centre. It is on these grounds that one may conclude that in central Paris the cause of preservation has triumphed.

11

Conclusion

For over 100 years, we have followed the development of four *arrondisse-ments* in the heart of Paris. During this time they have changed very little. Their boundaries, their wards and their names have remained exactly the same. Nor have their industries and business activities changed very greatly. Even their streets and houses are little different from a century ago. Their appearance is an astonishing survival from the past that is unique among the centres of the cities of northern Europe. Yet by remaining almost unchanged in a city that has been transformed, they have lost the pre-eminent position that used to be theirs. They were once a centre both of residence and of business for the whole city. Now they have lost much of their population, but have not gained in business to an equivalent degree. In 1850 they were not so much central Paris as Paris itself; between them and the city gates lay districts that still retained a certain rustic air. But in 1970 their claim to centrality is based more on geography and geometry than on their function.

The whole period studied here has been one of rapid urbanisation throughout France, in which Paris has had a bigger share than most cities. The area of the Paris conurbation has increased many times. In such a time of expansion—affecting the area of the city, the number of its inhabitants, the amount of work done, and the total of money made—the right bank centre, by remaining almost the same, has declined in relation to Paris as a whole. But such a decline was not inevitable. The area might have been redeveloped with tall and massive buildings, and thus have achieved so great an increase in accommodation that it could have maintained its position relative to the rest of the conurbation, at least in business if not in population. This, after all, was what occurred in Manhattan, and, to a lesser extent, in the City of London, during the same period. But everything was against such a transformation. Paris had always been a city of tall houses, and the building regulations developed from the 1780s were designed mainly to check excessive heights, for reasons of public health. During most of the nineteenth century these bye-laws were not restrictive in comparison with those of other European cities, and before the development of efficient passenger lifts and the spread of steel-frame construction in the 1880s it would have been difficult to build much higher than they allowed. But from then on the regulations fell increasingly out of step with technical possibility and economic reality. After the defeat of a half-hearted attempt to liberalise them in 1902, in the first serious battle between the forces of progress and of conservation, they were not substantially modified until after 1945. And by this time the preservationist influence on the authorities was so strong that height restrictions were hardly relaxed at all in the city centre, even though this was the area where encouragement to building was most urgently needed.

The impossibility of greatly increasing the amount of accommodation in the right bank centre meant that business had to set up outside it as Paris developed as the commercial and industrial, as well as the administrative, capital. The right bank centre dominated Paris until the early nineteenth century, until which time urbanisation had been slow and the French economy, in comparison with England's, retarded. But when France began to catch up this lost ground, a process which was greatly accelerated from the 1850s, the right bank centre could no longer maintain its position. Many concerns began operations in the more spacious areas to the west and north-west, where street congestion was less, and close to the terminus of the city's main suburban railway network. Prominent among these enterprises were the sophisticated financial institutions that grew up in the nineteenth century, the offices of big industrial firms, and luxury shops. In comparison to London, Paris had not been an important financial and commercial centre before the nineteenth century, and its central areas had never had the same pronounced business functions as the City. So when a Parisian West End grew up, and, like London's, became an important business area, it overshadowed the right bank centre and diminished it. Many of the firms that had grown up in the right bank centre went out of business, or moved to the west.

Until the nineteenth century the industries of Paris had produced almost exclusively for the local market. So most firms had been able to handle the distribution of their own goods, and production was closely linked with wholesale and even retail trade. Even where distribution was in the hands of specialist merchants, these tended to operate from the industrial areas, for without the help of sophisticated banking services they needed close contact with the manufacturers. All production and trading processes were organised on a small scale. The Parisian industries were predominantly finishing trades, with a strong bias towards luxury products—a natural result of the lack of local raw materials and the numerous nobility and bourgeoisie who lived in or near the city. So they were highly labour-intensive trades, and were usually fragmented into small, interdependent units, with many functions performed by outworkers. And this meant that industry was closely linked with residence as well as trading. Without cheap public transport, employees had to live near their work, or the traditional gathering-places where they could obtain it. This confusion of industry, commerce and residence was made possible by the great density and height of buildings. A single house could contain ground-floor shops, a first-floor apartment for the landlord or a rich trader, several floors of lesser apartments, some of them occupied by working craftsmen, and servants' quarters in the roof. And the courtyard or garden would often be filled with workshops. Within such an urban structure, segregation of classes was vertical rather than horizontal, although certain areas were more favoured by the rich than others. Even though this structure of activities and residence had already been breaking down before the nineteenth century, the trend was greatly accelerated after 1800. The disruption produced by the Revolution and the propagation of egalitarian and socialist ideas frightened the middle classes and made them want to live separately from the workers. Their departure from the old central areas was accelerated by fear of disease, which medical opinion began to associate in the nineteenth century with bad housing, overcrowding, dirt and polluted air. They could still return daily to work in the centre by using the omnibus services that were developed from the 1820s. But as they moved to new residential areas in the west, the shops and services which depended on their patronage moved with them. The commerce that remained in the centre was either that which could not afford to move to the rich areas of the west, or the trading activities that were intimately linked with industrial production. And even these began to leave or disappear. Increasing mechanisation forced certain production processes to move to the outskirts in the north and east, and municipal taxation of raw materials encouraged others to leave the city altogether. Many of the workers moved with them to new, poor residential areas which had few middle-class residents. Only the traditional, craft industries remained in the centre, but most of them were in relative, or even actual, decline.

By the middle of the nineteenth century the right bank centre was already beginning to reflect the cleavage between east and west that existed within the city as a whole, but without reproducing the extremes of poverty and riches that were visible elsewhere. The first two *arrondissements* were an area of prosperous business and well-to-do residence. Their two eastern neighbours had less commerce but more industry, and a poorer population. A few wards did not fit in with this pattern completely; the two eastern wards of the IIe *arrondissement* had much in common with the IIIe, and the residential east of the IVe *arrondissement* was very much like parts of the Ier. And there were still slum districts in the west, and middle-class areas, such as the Marais, in the east. But as time went on, these anomalies became less noticeable, and the segregation of classes and activities was increasingly transferred from a vertical to a horizontal plane. So as the city's population and economy expanded, the right bank centre was bound to lose its original focal function, and become simply a fringe district of the western business centre and of the eastern industrial complex.

The desertion of the right bank centre was accelerated by the decline in the amount of new building there in the second half of the nineteenth century. To some extent this reduction resulted from a fall in demand owing to the early departure of some of the more prosperous residents and concerns. But initially its main causes were lack of sites, great congestion of buildings, and restrictive building regulations. It meant that residential and business accommodation in the centre diverged increasingly from modern standards as time went on. A vicious circle was created; inadequate conditions accelerated the desertion of the centre, which in turn confirmed the trend towards obsolescence, for only the presence of prosperous residents and businesses could have made it worthwhile for landlords and developers to pull down the older houses and redevelop their sites. But the advantages to certain types of firm of a location on the fringes of the central business district, and the continued demand for central residential accommodation, kept rents higher than in districts further to the east and north. Of course, as the central business district moved even further west, and the structural condition of the buildings deteriorated, parts of the right bank centre were bound to degenerate into a slum. Values would then fall low enough to allow redevelopment, but private enterprise would be afraid to undertake it piecemeal because of the depressive influence of surrounding old houses on the rents of new properties. Only in the final stages of degeneration would values fall low enough for the municipal authorities to be able to envisage total clearance and redevelopment with working-class housing, which could not possibly make a profit.

But in central Paris the municipality chose to intervene partially long before this final stage was reached. At first, during the Second Empire, its aim was to arrest the decline of the centre, by linking it to the outskirts, improving communications within it, and encouraging private building. This policy was based on a scheme of street improvements. In the mid-nineteenth century the streets of the right bank centre corresponded even less to modern needs than did the houses. They had been adequate in the days when people did not need to move beyond their own ward or even their own street, because work, shops, and entertainments could all be found there, but their congestion had become part of the cause of the departure of population and business. So the City decided to provide a network of wide streets in the right bank centre, which appears to have slowed economic decline there. Now, large units, such as department stores, serving the population of very wide areas, were established in the right bank centre as well as outside it, and did not fail to prosper. The convergence of a number of new streets on the right bank centre helped to reinforce its business activities against slow erosion. But in other ways the Haussmannic street improvement policy was a failure. It did not bring about the spontaneous redevelopment of the centre, but rather discouraged it by depriving the older streets of much of their commerce, and displacing thousands of tenants who further accentuated overcrowding in the old houses nearby. And the policy was self-defeating, for it caused property values to increase everywhere, and especially in the vicinity of streetworks, hindering their further extension. Moreover, in the long run Haussmann's policies encouraged the westward movement of the business centre. Many of his new streets were built on the western outskirts of the city, in the VIIIe, XVIe and XVIIe *arrondissements*, whose middle-class residential development was thereby accelerated. This enhanced the value of a west-central location for luxury commerce and financial houses. The growth of new, fashionable areas of residence was accompanied by the departure of the rich in increasing numbers from districts nearer the centre, which allowed the conversion of their dwellings to business use. But only the extreme west of the right bank centre was

325

able to share in the creation of a west-central business district. The rest, despite the construction of new traffic arteries, was still difficult to reach from the western outskirts, and even more so now that it was necessary to cross the new business centre to reach it. The reconstruction of the Halles on their original site multiplied congestion in the centre as the city grew, and although it stimulated activities in the immediate vicinity, it hindered expansion in the wards lying to the north and east.

The right bank centre would have been slightly better off if Haussmann had been able to complete his plan, as he would have done if he and the Second Empire had been allowed a further ten years. In particular, he left unfinished a number of schemes in the east of the centre, an area to which he had never accorded priority. He had been right to draw up a complete plan of improvements for the whole city, but after his departure the plan was something of a hindrance. Compulsory purchase powers had been obtained for many streets, and the City thought it best to make use of them for fear that, if they were annulled, they might not be renewed later. The existence of these powers established a somewhat artificial order of priority for public works. The very comprehensiveness of Haussmann's plan seems to have caused officials and councillors to stop thinking about its relevance to the city's problems—they sought only to carry it out. Parliament, which exercised an increasing control over the City after 1871, was also impressed by Haussmann's plan, and could usually be relied upon to support the execution of improvements contained in it. This was because it could be convinced that Haussmann's schemes, concentrated as they were on the centre and centre-west of the city, were of national interest. It was less enthusiastic about projects planned in the interests of public health in the proletarian east. The conversion of most other European cities to Haussmann's concepts and methods seemed to confirm that the City was right to continue in the same path. Until the 1890s the disadvantages of Haussmann's approach were not fully apparent—traffic congestion was not too serious, public health standards seemed to be improving, and the cost of public works was not yet prohibitive. The only force to combat this inertia was the section of the City Council which represented the outer districts. These councillors urged that their areas, which Haussmann had largely ignored, should be given priority over the centre. To some extent they obtained satisfaction, for they could often command a majority in the Council. But the odds were stacked against them. Although the Council had the ultimate sanction over municipal expenditure, it suffered from its lack of control over the administration. Time after time it had to bow to the technical expertise of the officials, many of whom had been trained by Haussmann and were devoted to his ideals. And it often came into conflict with a Prefect appointed by a Government which usually did not share the radical or socialist views of its majority. Yet, paradoxically, although the Government wanted to see Haussmann's plan carried out in preference to new schemes, it declined to provide any financial help. The provinces have always been jealous of Paris, and have objected strongly to the devotion of public resources to its further improvement. Under an authoritarian, personal régime, the provinces cannot make their voice heard, and the Government is prepared to devote resources to the capital which gives it its home and much of its glory. But democratic constitutions have always allowed provincial representatives to dominate the legislature and prevent the diversion of funds to Paris. During the period studied here, national subsidies have been granted for public works in Paris only under the Second Empire and the Fifth Republic, which were ruled by similar personalities eager to exalt Paris. During the Third and Fourth Republic no subsidies were granted, except in the totally exceptional circumstances of the 1930s.

So owing to planning inertia the right bank centre continued after 1870 to enjoy a very generous share of the Parisian total of public works. Their emphasis switched slightly from the west to the east as the outstanding large-scale schemes were completed in the west. And it was much cheaper to work in the east. But by the early 1890s much momentum had been lost. Legal and financial difficulties limited the acquisition of properties, and piecemeal widening was increasingly preferred to the construction of completely new streets—even though Haussmann had shown that this was a false economy. In any case, the primary imperial network was nearly complete. Haussmann had planned his main thoroughfares as a mere skeleton on which would be constructed a grid system of smaller streets, but the City was now tempted to rest on its laurels. It hoped that spontaneous rebuilding and the application of improvement lines would take care of the rest. Moreover, the opportunity to build the *Métropolitain*, which was at last offered to the City in the 1890s, was a powerful distraction. For a time it even seemed, like street improvements in the 1850s, to be a new panacea. It would provide work for the unemployed, stimulate the city's economy, render irrelevant the long dispute with the General Omnibus Company, reduce surface congestion, *and* pay for itself. The only disadvantage was that it would not contribute to slum clearance, but it could be hoped that the slum problem would fade away now that the epidemic diseases had been checked, or that the divorce of clearance from street works would allow resources to be devoted more effectively to the comprehensive improvement of obsolete areas. But within a few years of the opening of the first line in 1900, disillusionment was complete. The *Métro* was proving a useful, indeed essential, means of transport, but it was no panacea. It did not diminish street congestion but accentuated it, by encouraging movement. The multiplication of motorcars created traffic problems that had not been foreseen in the 1890s. And the slum problem now appeared not on the way to being solved, but more intractable than ever, since it had recently been proved that tuberculosis thrived in poor and overcrowded living conditions.

To contemporaries, it seemed that not much time had been lost, and that it could be made up quickly by an energetic return to street improvements. And such a change of course was possible because it had the approval of most city councillors, of the officials, and of the Government, all of whom now recognised that there was only one solution to the growing traffic problem. But within five years of the inauguration of the new programme, war interrupted the work and overthrew the foundations on which the Haussmannic improvement policy had been based. Admittedly, so far as the execution of Haussmann's primary network was concerned, the right bank centre had not been ill served. By 1914 it was almost complete. However, the largest gaps were in the east, which was more in need than the west of the limited economic benefit that could result from improvements. And the right bank centre as a whole had not benefited economically from the concentration of improvement resources within its boundaries. The building rate remained high, although with a tendency to decline, until 1914, but this was mainly the result of the clearance of sites in connection with streetworks. New building had almost completely ceased away from the new streets owing to the absence of virgin sites and congestion of existing constructions. So modern accommodation was not being provided fast enough to encourage business to expand, or even to remain in the centre. And as the obsolescence of central residential accommodation became more pronounced, and congestion increased, the richer residents also left in increasingly larger numbers. This departure was a further discouragement to luxury commerce in the centre, although it revived in the extreme west just before the war. Not only had the street improvement policy failed to ensure the spontaneous renewal of the centre, but it had positively retarded it by accelerating the development of densely populated slum areas inhabited largely by poor tenants displaced from the areas affected by the works.

As time went on, the redevelopment of the centre by private initiative became harder to envisage, for the departure of expanding businesses and rich residents deprived the area of the only clients who might have commissioned such enterprise. So municipal intervention was even more necessary after the First World War than before. But it was precisely at this time that massive obstacles grew up in the path of such an initiative. The unprecedented inflation of the 1920s and the unprecedented depression of the 1930s replaced the more stable pre-war economic conditions which had encouraged an ambitious policy of long-term borrowing. The Government intervened increasingly in the national interest to control the City's capital expenditure. With the building of dwellings to let almost at a standstill, there was a big expansion of the construction of small houses for sale in the suburbs, creating new urban problems which diverted attention away from the old city. The City began to concentrate its effort more on the adequate planning of new areas and less on the renewal of the old. But, above all, the lack of resources produced a kind of torpor that seems to have been shared by officials and councillors alike. No individuals emerged from the general mediocrity to provide a lead.

The city of Paris itself (though not, of course, its suburbs) had stopped growing, and its population was already starting slowly to decline. In relative terms, of course, the right bank centre benefited from the deceleration of change in the whole city. Its proportion of the economic activity of Paris declined more slowly than before 1914, and the building stagnation which had long affected the centre became apparent elsewhere. In the absence of new means of transport the existing network of streets, railways and the *Métropolitain*, which converged on the old centre, decelerated the westward movement of the business district. But such a state of affairs could not serve the long-term interests of the right bank centre, for in the absence of new building and improved communications, it was becoming increasingly ill-fitted to serve as a business area. If ever conditions of expansion were restored, it would be deserted with relief by many of the enterprises that had been compelled to remain in it.

The restoration of normal conditions was delayed by the Second World War, which, like its predecessor, held up the city's natural evolution. It was followed by a period very much like the 1920s, in which inflation, economic instability, and Government policies inimical to the expansion and modernisation of Paris reduced capital expenditure almost to nothing. Building was halted during the war, and did not subsequently recover within the city boundaries, although the suburbs were more favoured. So the right bank centre remained almost unchanged, both in relative and in real terms, except that its population continued to decline very much faster than that of the whole city. But during the 1950s the City started to prepare for the day when restrictions on investment would at last be relaxed, as they would eventually have to be when the results of years of neglect of the capital's problems became intolerable. The centre of Paris was by no means ignored in these plans. But after years of inaction the objects of the planners were now very different from what they had been before 1914, and no longer involved an ambitious remodelling of the city centre.

During the decades in which the historic centre of Paris had been so markedly transformed, public indignation grew from almost nothing under the Second Empire to a mighty movement of opinion by 1914. The concentration of historic buildings had always limited the scope of replanning in central Paris, although Haussmann had cleverly incorporated the biggest of them in his improvements. But now more and more buildings came to be considered worthy of preservation by scholars and enlightened laymen. The City had been forced to take account of public opinion after the *Métro* interlude by seeking to make modernisation and preservation mutually compatible. The terms of the compromise were certainly less satisfactory for the preservationists than for the supporters of change, but they had accepted it because in a city that had been in a constant state of transformation for nearly half a century, total conservation was hard to imagine. After 1914 the situation was very different. The city stopped changing, and conservation was transformed from a pipe dream to the natural state of affairs. The preservationist movement lost some of its momentum now that there was little to protest about, but its philosophy became more acceptable to those who governed the city as they renounced their hopes of being able to pursue ambitious modernisation policies in the foreseeable future. The natural conservatism of the Parisian was encouraged by the ossification of the historic centre, and even the inhabitants of the poorer districts became attached to their traditional appearance.

The planning policies developed from the 1950s took this new situation into account. Partly out of respect for the historic areas, and partly because of the high cost and limited return of carrying out improvements in the centre, the City developed a policy for the historic core which increasingly acquired a character of out-and-out conservation. The centre of gravity of slum clearance operations was switched from the right bank centre, where it had been until 1945, to the proletarian eastern outskirts. Tertiary sector employment was encouraged outside the centre. The plans made for the centre represented a retreat from the problems that its modernisation would have involved. The decentralisation of the Halles, represented by the City as a positive contribution to the replanning of the centre of Paris, was really an attempt to make replanning less urgent. The redevelopment scheme connected with it has already been transformed largely into a conservation project. In the east of the right bank centre, where the architectural heritage is richer, this process has gone further. The main slum clearance operation there has been slowed down and converted into a restoration and reconstitution programme designed to attract private investors and encourage cooperation with existing landlords. Elsewhere, in the Marais, programmes of total conservation are under way, and the whole area has been made a protected zone. It is very probable that within twenty years the whole of the right bank centre, which in the meantime will hardly have changed at all, will be protected. The present ossification of the area will have been legalised and exalted, as a result of over a century of failure to cheapen compulsory purchase, to recuperate betterment values, and to restrict residential densities in order to reduce the dimensions of the rehousing problem. The success of the conservation policy will depend mainly on its attracting middle-class residents to an area which is at present largely deprived of them. This movement is now becoming possible to envisage as more and more families acquire a second home. An apartment with a central position, even in a closely-built area, will become increasingly attractive to those who can afford to maintain a country villa for their periods of leisure. The traditional development of the centre will thus be reversed, as business gives way to residence.

But such a destiny for the centre is still a long way off. In the years to come, rather less resources may be available for investment in Paris than there have been in the 1960s. If the development of new office areas slows down, activities will still remain in the right bank centre, although a marked expansion will not take place there. The population will decline further and grow poorer, and the present areas of foreign immigrant occupation will expand. This will prolong the present ossification of the centre and accentuate the deterioration of its fabric. If positive conservation does not proceed rapidly, a stage may well be reached when certain areas of the centre can no longer be preserved —though this would require several decades of total neglect. But whatever changes of population and employment take place there, it is very unlikely that the appearance of the right bank centre will be modified appreciably in the next half century. Whether or not this can be regarded as a satisfactory state of affairs depends on whether one can reconcile the survival of one of the oldest and most fascinating city centres in Europe with the tribulations of many of those who have to live and work there.

Appendix 1: Sources

I HISTORICAL SOURCES

(a) Secondary

Secondary sources are not very helpful for the history of Paris since 1850. The city has always been a magnet for the antiquarian, but has frightened or discouraged the social and economic historian. For a valuable general survey of the current state of urban historiography in France, including numerous references to Paris in the period covered in this book, see François Bédarida, 'The growth of urban history in France: some methodological trends' in H. J. Dyos (ed.), *The Study of Urban History* (1968), pp. 47–60. The general histories of the city, of which the best are Marcel Poëte, *Une vie de cité: Paris de sa naissance à nos jours*, 3 vols. and album (1931), Louis Dubech and Pierre d' Espezel, *Histoire de Paris* (1926), and Pierre Lavedan, *Histoire de Paris* (1960), are not very informative after the mid-nineteenth century. Fortunately, they have been supplemented in the last few years by two symposia published by Hachette in the series 'Colloques: cahiers de civilisation', *Paris: croissance d'une capitale* and *Paris: fonctions d'une capitale*, which are frequently but erratically helpful. Town planning has received more attention, because of the unique importance of the improvement work carried out during the Second Empire, but Haussmann's predecessors and successors have been almost completely neglected. Even Pierre Lavedan's monumental *Histoire de l'urbanisme* fades away after 1870. The only book of importance to cover the sequel to Haussmann's work is André Morizet, *Du vieux Paris au Paris moderne* (1932). It should be read in conjunction with two important works on Haussmann and Napoleon III (although it is invidious to choose from so many): David H. Pinkney, *Napoleon III and the Rebuilding of Paris* (1958), and Louis Girard, *La politique des travaux publics du Second Empire* (1952). Pinkney's book is the best general survey of the imperial improvements in French or English, and Girard has provided an indispensable analysis of their economic and financial aspects. For the effect of street improvements on population and property values, both before and after 1870, it is essential to consult the pioneer work of Maurice Halbwachs, in his *Les expropriations et le prix des terrains à Paris 1860–1900* (1909), and *La population et les tracés des voies à Paris depuis un siècle* (1928). For years these volumes remained unemulated, but recently Adeline Daumard has adopted Halbwachs' methods of disciplined statistical analysis in her *Maisons de Paris et propriétaires parisiens au XIXe siècle* (1964) and *La bourgeoisie parisienne de 1815 à 1848* (1963). Even more recently, a number of important contributions on the evolution of the centre of Paris have appeared in *Urban Core and Inner City*, the proceedings of an international study week at Amsterdam in 1966, published by E. J. Brill of Leiden in 1967. For the demography of Paris in the nineteenth century, Louis Chevalier's *La formation de la population parisienne au XIXe siècle* (1949) and *Classes laborieuses et classes dangereuses à Paris pendant la première moitié du XIXe siècle* (1958) are indispensable. The history of the administration of Paris until recent years is covered exhaustively by the new and greatly augmented edition of a work by Maurice Félix and Eugène Raiga first published in 1922, *Le régime administratif et financier de la Ville de Paris et du Département de la Seine*, 4 vols. (1957–8). A comprehensive study of vandalism and preservation movements, in which Paris figures prominently, is provided by Louis Réau in his *Les monuments détruits de l'art français*, 2 vols. (1959), and by Paul Léon in *La vie des monuments français* (1951). For the history of individual Paris buildings one may consult the work of an army of scholars, but among the most useful are the books of Georges Pillement and Jacques Hillairet's *Connaissance du Vieux Paris*, 3 vols. (1951–4). The development of public transport is covered in Pierre Merlin's *Les transports parisiens : étude de géographie économique et sociale* (1966), but its historical sections are often superficial, and one can still draw much useful information from René Clozier, *La Gare du Nord* (1940), which is much wider in its treatment than its title suggests.

It is the absence of general historical works that has forced Jean Bastié to provide what constitutes in a very large measure a history of modern Paris in *La croissance de la banlieue parisienne* (1964). This is likely to remain a key tool of any student of the city for many years to come. Bastié also provides the most complete up-to-date bibliography of the history of Paris, which forms a useful complement to Marius

Appendix

Barroux's *Le Département de la Seine et la Ville de Paris: notions générales et bibliographiques pour en étudier l'histoire* (1910).

(b) Primary

Much of this study has been devoted to the actions of the local government authorities, which have been the predominant influence on the evolution of the right bank centre since Haussmann's time. It is more difficult to study municipal policies before 1871 than after, because many records were lost in the Hôtel de Ville fire of that year, and because minutes of the proceedings of the City Council were not published during the Second Empire. Some details of the Prefect's reports to the Council were published in the press, and notably in the *Moniteur*, and other information on its activities is to be found in the collection of *Documents administratifs* (B.A. 21,522) published by the Prefecture of the Seine during Haussmann's term of office. The Library of the City Council at the Hôtel de Ville has preserved the summonses (*arrêtés de convocation*) for the years 1862–70 (no. 1579), each of which contains an agenda. The minutes of the General Council of the Seine, on the other hand, were published throughout this period, and they contain useful annual reports from the Prefect on the progress of public works in Paris.

For details of new streets, one should consult the *Atlas des grands travaux* (1889), whose preparation was directed by Jean Alphand, and the different editions of the City's *Nomenclature des voies publiques et privées*, which have appeared regularly since 1845, and contain full details of the length, width, numbering and date of construction of streets, and all changes therein. And further useful information of a more general nature appears in the two editions (1844 and 1855) of the Lazare brothers' *Dictionnaire administratif et historique des rues et monuments de Paris*. Documents relative to the construction of streets are preserved at the *Archives de la Seine* in the series VO 11. Where no original records are available, the Lazare collection of newspaper cuttings and miscellaneous information, classified under streets, is very informative. This also is kept at the *Archives de la Seine*, at D1Z. Another of the activities of the Lazare brothers during these years was to publish a semi-official periodical, the *Gazette municipale* (1843–50), merged in 1851 with the *Revue municipale* (1848–61). It contained full details of street schemes as well as other information on the work of the City. Details of compulsory purchases and compensation can be found in another periodical, the *Gazette des Tribunaux*.

After 1871 it becomes much easier to study City policies. A verbatim transcript of debates is provided in the minutes (*procès-verbaux*) of the City Council (1871–1939, continued by reports in the *Bulletin municipal officiel de la Ville de Paris*), and the texts of resolutions are published in its *Délibérations* (1880–). The more important committee reports and propositions by individual councillors are published in the series *Rapports et documents* (1871–), and prefectoral memoranda have recently been published in a further collection, *Mémoires du Préfet de la Seine au Conseil municipal* (1925–). Orders made by the administration, including compulsory purchase orders, are recorded in the *Recueil des actes administratifs de la Préfecture du Département de la Seine*, and may also be checked in the daily *Bulletin municipal officiel*. Information on the careers and views of individual councillors is to be found in a number of handbooks, the most notable of which were those edited by Ernest Gay under the title *Nos édiles*, which were succeeded from 1913 by Paul Robert's *Le Conseil municipal de Paris*. Also useful are the reports of the *Commission des logements insalubres* and of the *Commissions d'hygiène du Département de la Seine*, both of which were published from the early 1850s, and the two reports of the special *Commission d'extension de Paris* which appeared in 1913. The reports of the Prefect of Police's *Conseil de salubrité* were published from 1829 until 1894, when they were replaced by those of the *Conseil d'hygiène publique et de la salubrité*. There also exists a separate series of reports of the *Commission du Métropolitain*.

The VO 11 series of the *Archives de la Seine* remains very useful for the study of street schemes until 1920, but later documents are not yet available for consultation. No equivalent of the *Atlas des grands travaux* was published after 1889, but it has been possible to map changes in the street pattern carried out after that date by comparing different editions of the *Atlas municipal des vingt arrondissements de Paris*, which were published every few years from the Second Empire. Information on legislation and other regulations concerning streets can be obtained from A. Deville and Hochereau, *Recueil des lettres patentes, ordonnances royales, décrets et arrêtés préfectoraux concernant les voies publiques* (1886, and supplement of 1889), and the three editions (–1900) of Gustave Jourdan's *Recueil de règlements concernant le service des alignements et des logements insalubres de la Ville de Paris*.

There are numerous sources of statistical information. Between 1821 and 1860 six volumes were published of *Recherches statistiques sur la*

Ville de Paris et le Département de la Seine. They contain mainly demographic material, but also a great variety of additional information.
They can be supplemented by the *Statistique de la France*, which is
particularly informative on mortality. From 1865 there began to appear
the monthly *Bulletin de statistique municipale*, which was supplemented
by annual summaries until the *Annuaire statistique de la Ville de Paris*
was created in 1880. The *Annuaire* has continued to appear ever since,
and since 1956 has been accompanied by a statistical publication with a
more flexible formula, *La conjoncture économique dans le Département
de la Seine*, which appears three times a year. Much of the information
contained in the published census returns is reprinted in the *Annuaire
statistique*, but the City published separate volumes for Paris figures
abstracted from the censuses of 1881, 1886, 1891 and 1896. And since
the last war the *INSEE* has published three editions of *Données
statistiques sur la population et les logements de la Ville de Paris*, containing material abstracted from the censuses of 1946, 1954 and 1962.
Demographic information is available in graphic form in *Atlas de
statistique graphique de la Ville de Paris* (1889) and *Cartogrammes et
diagrammes relatifs à la population parisienne et à la fréquence des prin-
cipales maladies à Paris pendant la période 1865–1887* (1899). The above
sources, used in conjunction with certain others (see sections II and
III), can be used to establish series of statistics of demolitions, new
building, and changes in rents, property values and use of accommodation. Information on industrial and commercial activities is much
harder to obtain, except for the mid-nineteenth century, when it is
possible to consult the results of two surveys by the Paris Chamber of
Commerce, the *Statistique de l'industrie à Paris* in 1847–8 (1851) and
in 1860 (1864), and for the last few years, the most useful source for
which is the text and maps of the *Atlas de Paris et de la région parisienne*
(1967). The *Atlas* also contains a great variety of other information,
and is the most comprehensive publication of its type published so far
in Paris. For general information on the city the Baedeker and Joanne
guides are particularly useful and authoritative.

The main source used here for the history of conscious preservation
has been the *Procès-verbaux de la Commission du Vieux Paris*. They
were published in full between 1898 and 1932, and shortened versions
have appeared since 1955 in the *Bulletin municipal officiel*. The secretary of
the *Commission*, Michel Fleury, very kindly communicated the typescript
minutes of the intervening years. The activities of the preservation

societies have been studied through the *Bulletin de la Société des Amis des Monuments parisiens*, 1885–1900, and the monthly *Les Amis de Paris*, 1911–23. Details of architectural ordinances can be obtained from M. L. Taxil's *Recueil d'actes administratifs et de conventions relatifs aux servitudes spéciales d'architecture* (1905). Listed and scheduled buildings are to be found in *Liste des immeubles protégés . . . dans de Département de la Seine*, published in 1955 by the *Ministère de l'Education nationale*, and *Immeubles protégés au titre de la législation sur les sites* (1960), published by the *Ministère des Affaires culturelles*.

II CONSTRUCTION AND DEMOLITION FIGURES: A NOTE ON SOURCES

Any attempt to establish a continuous series of building, demolition and compulsory purchase statistics is plagued by various omissions and changes in definitions. The object of this note is to explain what sources have been used to compile the series used here, together with their imperfections and limitations. Wherever possible, I have used published sources, for reasons which will become apparent.

The principal source of information during the Second Empire is Haussmann's annual reports to the General Council of the Seine, published in the minutes of that body from 1853 to 1869. They give the annual totals of demolitions and constructions in Paris until 1860, and the totals of buildings demolished after compulsory acquisition, but do not distinguish between complete and partial operations. From 1860, separate totals are given for each *arrondissement*, with the exception of the figures for compulsory purchases by the City, which become very erratic. Fortunately, complete tables of expropriations for each *arrondissement* for the years 1860–1900 are to be found in Maurice Halbwachs, *La population et les tracés des voies à Paris depuis un siècle* (1928), pp. 189–90.

After 1870 the statistics are much more complete, but their interpretation is complicated by changing definitions and categories. Annual totals for the whole city of constructions and demolitions from 1869 to 1894, making no distinction between complete and partial operations, are provided in C.M. reports, 1895, no. 170, annex 1. Separate figures for total and partial demolitions and constructions in the years 1872–1909, and for total and partial constructions *only* in 1913, are published in two budget reports by Louis Dausset; 1910, no. 91, annex, and 1913, no. 120, facing p. 42. This source also provides the total rentable value of accommodation demolished and erected. The same figures, but without the rentable values, are provided for the shorter range of years

1872–1900 in the *Livre foncier de Paris*, first part, 1900, graph no. 14. However, this series of statistics does not coincide completely with the figures in report no. 170 of 1895. Between 1873 and 1889 the Dausset figures are consistently one year behind those of report no. 170, and also the totals published for 1870–75, 1877–9 by the *Annuaire de l'économie politique*, and for 1880–88 by the *Annuaire statistique de la Ville de Paris*. But from 1891 to 1894 the Dausset and the report no. 170 figures for complete and partial constructions coincide. It would seem, therefore, that a trivial error had crept into the Dausset figures, and I have used the report no. 170 totals for those years when the two sources disagree. The Dausset figures also appear subject to the same error in respect of complete constructions. From 1878 to 1888 they can be checked against figures published by the *Annuaire de l'économie politique* and the *Annuaire statistique*, which reveal the discrepancy of one year; but they are the only available source for the years 1872–7 and 1889–1909. It is reasonable to assume that from 1891 the discrepancy has been corrected, just as the total of complete and partial constructions has been. Similarly, it seems fair to assume that the figures for 1872–7 and 1889–91 apply in fact to 1871–6 and 1888–90. But this leaves two loose ends to be cleared up. Firstly, I have preferred the corrected Dausset figure for 1877 to the *Annuaire de l'économie politique* figure for that year, which is slightly higher, because all the totals for the other years in the *Annuaire* coincide with the corrected Dausset figures. Secondly, I have fixed an arbitrary figure of 1,500 total constructions for 1890, a year for which no information is available once the Dausset figures have been corrected.

Even more complications arise in establishing series for each *arrondissement* after 1870. For the years 1872–9, I have used the totals of constructions and demolitions published in the *Annuaire de l'économie politique*. But this source does not always distinguish partial from total operations, and gives no figures at all for 1876. For the years 1877–88 this series is continued by the City's *Annuaire statistique*. But from 1889 it is discontinued, although the *Annuaire statistique* continues to publish building permit statistics, which it had begun to do in 1882. Although this means that no demolition figures are available after 1888, the building permit material is much more complete than the series it replaced, which was prepared by the rating department. Not only does it provide information for each ward, but it distinguishes complete buildings from vertical extensions of existing buildings (*surélévations*), and indicates the height in storeys of the structures authorised.

But a comparison of the two series over the years 1882–8, the only ones for which both are available, shows that the sum of permits for new buildings and vertical extensions is very much lower than the figure for total and partial building operations prepared for tax purposes. Whereas, in Paris as a whole, only one building permit in five is for a vertical extension, one building operation in two is 'partial' according to the tax figures. In the right bank centre the discrepancy is even greater. Between 1882 and 1888 the tax authorities registered 244 complete constructions and 422 partial operations there, while 228 permits for whole buildings and seventy-five for vertical extensions were issued by the City. This difference arose because the municipal rating department (*Service des contributions directes*), like similar departments everywhere, was very quick off the mark in noting very small changes which might affect the rateable value of a property, even when they could not be defined as structural alterations and so did not require a building permit. So far I have not been able to trace the original building permit records, but the *Contributions directes* returns for the years 1846, and 1852–, are preserved in the *Archives de la Seine* at D7P2. They confirm that many alterations and additions were included for which no permit would have been required, but they cannot be used to establish annual totals even for single *arrondissements* or wards without a prohibitive amount of drudgery. New constructions did not become taxable until three years after they were built, and so most of them are mentioned at least twice in the returns, first in the year of their completion, and again three years later when they are finally assessed. However, there is no rule about this, and some buildings appear only once, while others are mentioned three or four times. To establish accurate totals would mean keeping a check on each house, and even then there would be no guarantee of complete accuracy, as the officials responsible for the different wards varied greatly in their efficiency. On the whole, it would seem that the permit statistics give the more accurate measure of actual structural changes, which are what one usually understands by building, but one must also be aware that the issue of a permit is not always followed by its use.

Halbwachs does not provide statistics of expropriations for each year after 1900, although he does give them for groups of four or five years in his *Les expropriations et le prix des terrains à Paris* (1909), p. 251. So I have established annual totals for 1901–14 from the lists of vesting orders (*arrêtés de cessibilité*) published in the *Recueil des actes administratifs du Préfet de la Seine*. But I have not prolonged this series beyond

1914, owing to the almost total absence of compulsory acquisitions in the centre after that year.

The *Annuaire statistique* continues to publish building permit figures during and after the Great War, and even provides details of the use for which the accommodation is intended, but it no longer breaks them down into wards from 1927 onwards. Moreover, during the 1930s so little building was being done that this source does not even break the Paris totals down into *arrondissements* in the years 1932, 1933, 1935, 1936, 1938 and 1939. Further disruption was caused by the war, and no building figures at all were published for 1940 and 1941. Separate *arrondissement* figures were not given again until after the war, and ward totals were never resumed. And since 1962 the *Annuaire statistique* has once again ceased to break down the Paris total into *arrondissements*, probably on account of the small amount of new building that is taking place within the boundaries.

III SOURCES FOR CHANGES IN USE OF ACCOMMODATION, RENTS AND PROPERTY VALUES

The main source of information on the value and use of Paris buildings is provided by the returns of the municipal rating department (*Service des contributions directes*). Although the *octroi* was the main provider of revenue in the last century, and various other indirect taxes have been since, a significant proportion of the City's income has always come from the so-called 'quatre vieilles'—taxes on property originally levied by the State, part of whose product went to the City. These taxes originally were:[1]

(1) a tax on the revenue of buildings and lands, payable by the landlord;
(2) a 'personnelle-mobilière' tax composed of two separate elements:
   (a) a poll tax originally equal to three days' work,
   (b) a tax based on the rent of the taxpayer's dwelling;
(3) a tax on doors and windows, payable by the landlord;
(4) a tax on business premises, payable by the occupier.

The returns of the door and window tax are not of use for present purposes, but the other three can help to provide a clear picture of changes in the number and value of buildings and premises, especially

[1] See (after Maurice Félix), *Le régime administratif et financier de la Ville de Paris* (1959), vol. IV, p. 146.

as they are levied throughout the period studied here. After about 1900 they are supplemented, but not replaced, by a number of new taxes, most of which were created to replace *octroi* taxation.[2] A tax on the value in capital of buildings and lands was set up in 1902 to replace a tax on lands alone, created in 1900, which had been heavily criticised. Also instituted in 1900 was a tax on the rentable value of dwellings payable by the tenant. Other new taxes were simply additional to the existing 'quatre vieilles', and were levied on the same assessments.

Until the First World War the returns of all these taxes provide a very rich source of information. The historian's task is made even easier by three detailed abstracts produced by the City which provide a register of changes from 1860 to 1910. These are *Les propriétés bâties de la Ville de Paris en 1889 et en 1890* (1890), which contains retrospective tables, *Le livre foncier de Paris*, 2 vols. (1900, 1902), and *Le livre foncier de 1911* (1911). At this time reassessments were carried out very frequently. The tax on the revenue of buildings and lands was reassessed in 1865, 1879, 1891, 1901 and 1911, and on each of these occasions the assessed value of existing properties was raised by between 5 and 15 per cent.[3] Moreover, the annual figures are continually adjusted to take account of buildings erected or demolished. And between 1898 and 1901 a completely new cadastral survey was carried out. It was the great accuracy of these assessments which encouraged the City to abstract and publish them in regular volumes before 1914, together with a variety of other statistics relating to the buildings of Paris. Details of the number, nature and condition of properties and units of accommodation can also be found in the published census returns, although they do not always correspond with figures abstracted from the tax assessments.

After the First World War the City no longer published separate taxation abstracts, but the returns continued to appear each year in the *Annuaire statistique*. Unfortunately, separate figures are not given for each ward, and these returns are in a number of other ways less informative than those published in the old *Livres fonciers*. Since 1918 the assessments have tended to become more formal, rather like rating assessments in this country, but although they no longer fully reflect changes in actual values, they are still useful for comparative purposes. And they do at least make it possible to establish continuous series of

[2] See *Le régime de Paris*, vol. IV, pp. 177–201.
[3] Louis Dausset, *Rapport général . . . sur . . . le projet de budget de la Ville de Paris pour 1911*, p. 37 (C.M. reports, 1910, no. 91), and *Rapport général* for 1913, facing p. 92 (C.M. reports, 1912, no. 95).

the number and taxable value of properties and of business premises in each *arrondissement*. It is more difficult to follow changes in the value of residential accommodation because the lowest-rented dwellings are exempt from tax. But the biggest problem which arises in interpreting these figures is common both to the years before and after 1914. This is the difficulty of distinguishing the industrial from the other forms of business premises.

The *patentes* tax has always been levied on persons carrying on a commerce, industry or a non-salaried profession, and is based on the rentable value of the premises occupied. When it was first instituted, there was very little distinction in many cases between a commercial and an industrial activity, and the two have never been separated in the returns. The pre-1914 *Livres fonciers* break down the overall totals into three classes, but as the biggest of these groups offices and work-shops together, the problem remains as intractable as before. And after 1914 there is no means of breaking down the totals at all. It is true that separate statistics can be obtained for 'factories' (*usines*) before 1914; this class includes not only manufactories, forges and mills, but also abattoirs, wholesale and retail markets, baths and laundries.[4] This gives a somewhat distorted picture in the right bank centre where there were always relatively few manufactories, forges and mills, but a high concentration of markets, baths and laundries resulting from the great density of population there. Unfortunately, alternative sources of information are incapable of providing a complete answer. Two exhaustive surveys of Paris industry were carried out by the Chamber of Commerce in the late 1840s and the late 1850s, but no similar work was done until the *Institut national de la Statistique et des Etudes économiques* (*INSEE*) began to keep a full register of the city's industrial activities in the mid-1950s. The Chamber of Commerce survey of 1847-8 is difficult to use because figures are given for the pre-1860 *arrondissements* and wards, which in no way correspond with the present administrative divisions. And the *INSEE* statistics of industrial establishments and employees do not distinguish between white-collar and manual workers, in that the offices of an industrial concern, even when separate from the works, are counted as industrial establishments, and their employees as industrial workers. It would be possible to eke these sources out by using the *Bottin* directories to locate industrial firms, but their lists are incomplete and do not include many of the smaller firms which have always been a key element in the industrial structure

[4] *Les propriétés bâties de la Ville de Paris en 1889 et en 1890*, p. 1.

of the city centre. The only solution is to go back to the original taxation assessments for each building, which are available for the nineteenth century and have been used for selected areas by Mademoiselle Daumard in her *Maisons de Paris et propriétaires parisiens au XIXe siècle*. But to build up a picture for the whole of the right bank centre from them would be a long and tedious task, and I have not attempted it here.

Sources used to supplement the statistical series described in this appendix are detailed, where relevant, in the footnotes.

Appendix 2 :
Graphs and Diagrams

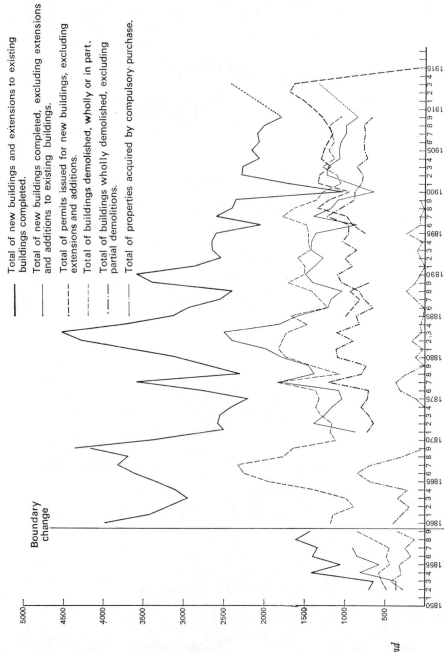

Total of new buildings and extensions to existing buildings completed.

Total of new buildings completed, excluding extensions and additions to existing buildings.

Total of permits issued for new buildings, excluding extensions and additions.

Total of buildings demolished, **wholly** or in part.

Total of buildings wholly demolished, excluding partial demolitions.

Total of properties acquired by compulsory purchase.

FIG. 7. *Building and demolition in Paris, 1852–1915.*

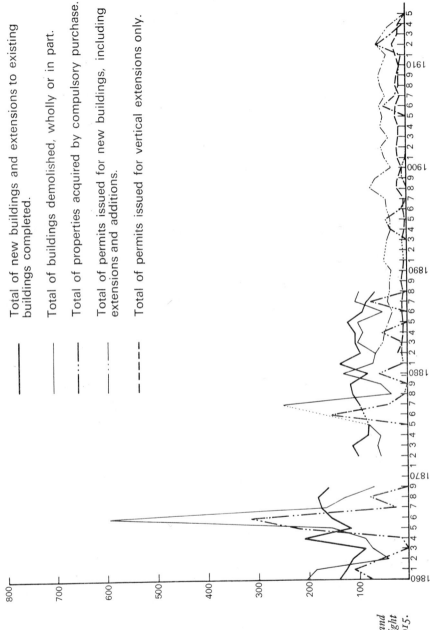

Total of new buildings and extensions to existing buildings completed.

Total of buildings demolished, wholly or in part.

Total of properties acquired by compulsory purchase.

Total of permits issued for new buildings, including extensions and additions.

Total of permits issued for vertical extensions only.

FIG. 8. *Building and demolition in the right bank centre, 1860–1915.*

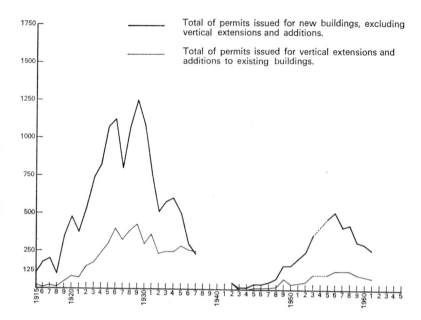

FIG. 9. *Building in Paris, 1915–61.*

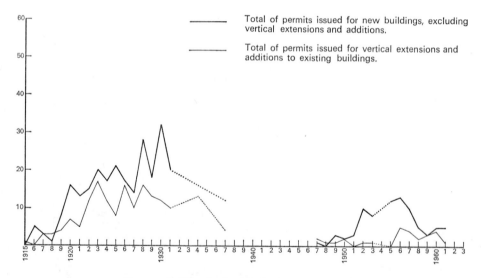

FIG. 10. *Building in the right bank centre, 1915–61.*

348

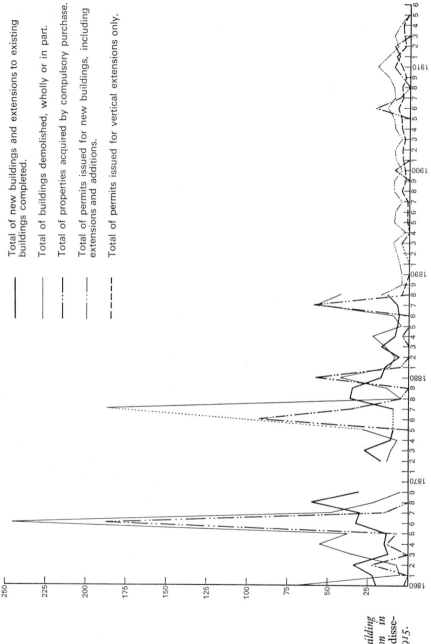

Total of new buildings and extensions to existing buildings completed.

Total of buildings demolished, wholly or in part.

Total of properties acquired by compulsory purchase.

Total of permits issued for new buildings, including extensions and additions.

Total of permits issued for vertical extensions only.

FIG. 11. *Building and demolition in the Ier arrondissement, 1860–1915.*

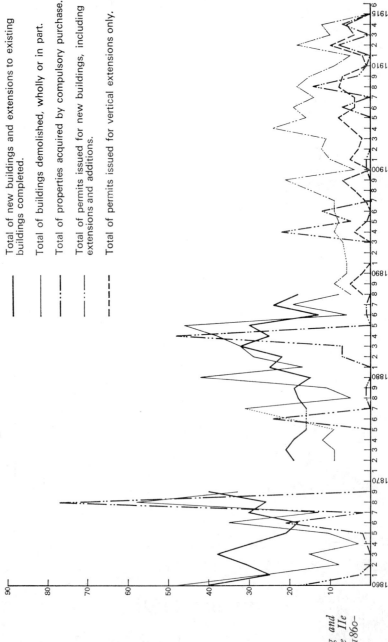

Total of new buildings and extensions to existing buildings completed.

Total of buildings demolished, wholly or in part.

Total of properties acquired by compulsory purchase.

Total of permits issued for new buildings, including extensions and additions.

Total of permits issued for vertical extensions only.

FIG. 12. *Building and demolition in the IIe arrondissement, 1860–1915.*

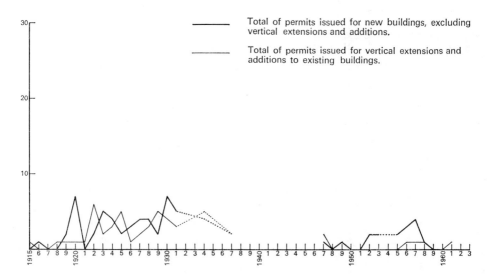

FIG. 13. *Building in the Ier* arrondissement, *1915–61.*

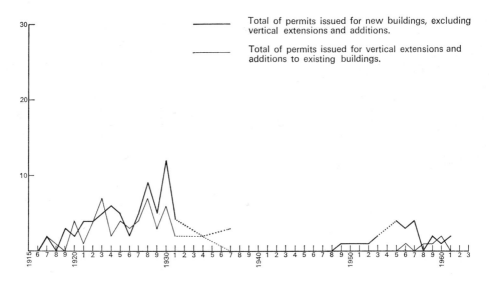

FIG. 14. *Building in the IIe* arrondissement, *1915–61.*

351

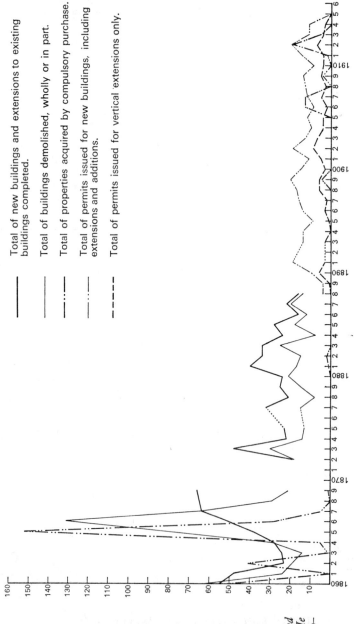

Total of new buildings and extensions to existing buildings completed.

Total of buildings demolished, wholly or in part.

Total of properties acquired by compulsory purchase.

Total of permits issued for new buildings, including extensions and additions.

Total of permits issued for vertical extensions only.

FIG. 15. *Building and demolition in the IIIe arrondissement, 1860–1915*

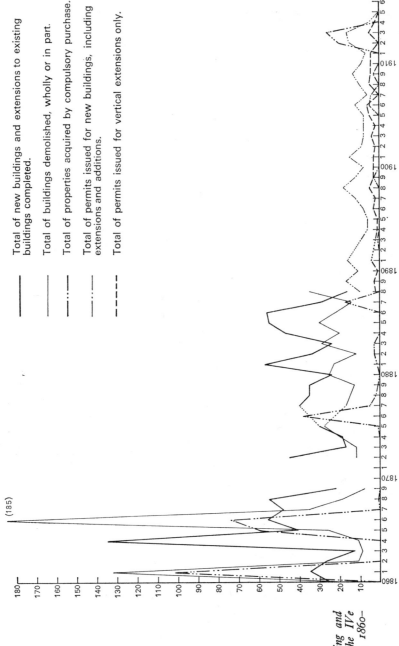

(185)

Total of new buildings and extensions to existing buildings completed.

Total of buildings demolished, wholly or in part.

Total of properties acquired by compulsory purchase.

Total of permits issued for new buildings, including extensions and additions.

Total of permits issued for vertical extensions only.

FIG. 16. *Building and demolition in the IVe arrondissement, 1860–1915.*

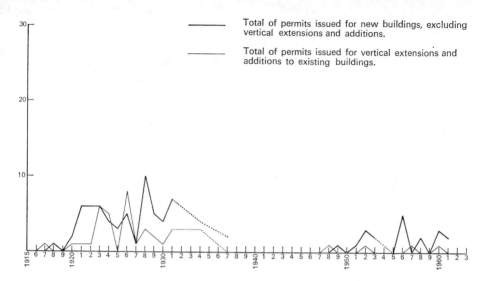

FIG. 17. *Building in the IIIe* arrondissement, *1915–61.*

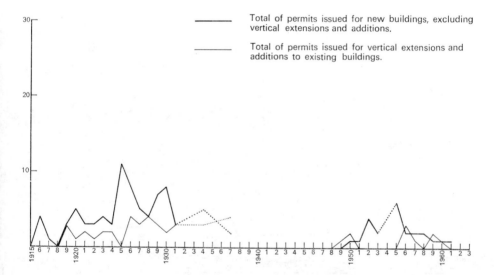

FIG. 18. *Building in the IVe* arrondissement, *1915–61.*

354

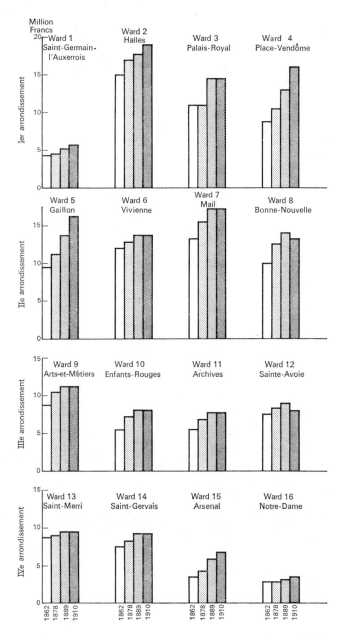

FIG. 19. *The total value of houses and factories in each ward of the right bank centre in 1862, 1878, 1889 and 1910.*

355

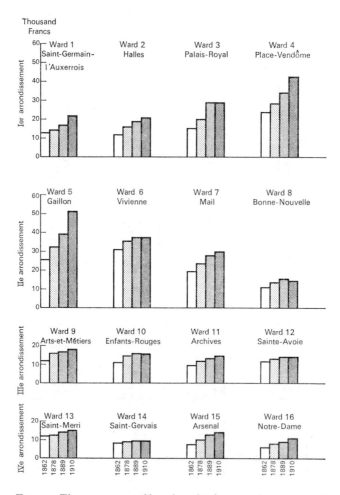

FIG. 20. *The average rentable value of a house or factory in each ward of the right bank centre in 1862, 1878, 1889 and 1910.*

Index

Coquillière, rue, 89
Cornu, Jean, 262*n*
Councillors, *see* City councillors
Cour de cassation, 41
Cour des comptes, 63, 186
Courcelle-Seneuil, Jean, 200
Cousin, Jules, 204
Coventry, bombing of, 307
Crédit Foncier, 43–6, 55–6, 58, 68, 71–2, 76, 87, 118–19, 255
Credit institutions, 117–19
see also Crédit Foncier; Sous-comtoir des entrepreneurs
Crédit Lyonnais, 119, 162, 172
Croisée de Paris, *see* Paris cross
Croissant, rue du, 149, 152
Croix-des-Petits-Champs, rue, 217
Cunin-Gridaine, minister, 16
Curinier, C. E., 70*n*

Daniel, civil servant, 17
Dante, rue, 93
Daumard, Adeline, 115*n*, 116*n*, 138–9
Dauphine, place, 308
Dausset, Councillor Louis, 86, 90–1, 94–5, 174, 213, 221, 239
De Amicis, Edmondo, 165*n*
De Beauvoir, Roger, 184*n*, 187
De Gaulle, Charles, 233
De Guilhermy, M. F., 182*n*, 185, 187, 190
De la Gournerie, Eugène, 182*n*
De Lasteyrie, Ferdinand, 35, 35*n*, 185
De Pontich, Henri, 31*n*
De Selves, Justin, Prefect of the Seine, 88, 196, 207–8, 220–1, 297
Debré, Michel, prime minister, 232
Decentralisation of employment, 228, 231–2
criticism of, 232
legislation, 285
modifications of the policy, 232–6
see also Industry; Offices; Halles centrales
Défense, La, development at, 266, 287
Delanney, Marcel, Prefect of the Seine, 296, 299
Delarue, Jacques, 109*n*
Délibérations du Conseil municipal de Paris, 336
Delisle, Léopold, 204
Delon, Charles, 188, 188*n*
Delouvrier, Paul, Delegate to the District of Paris, 233, 233*n*
Demeure historique, society, 306
Demolitions
control of, 260
reluctance of owners to demolish, 138–9, 140–1
see also Arrondissements; Arcis; Cité

Department stores, 154, 162
see also Bazar de l'Hôtel de Ville; Belle Jardinière; Bon Marché; Magasins du Louvre; Magasins Réunis; Samaritaine
Des Cilleuls, Alfred, 12*n*, 15*n*, 94*n*
D'Espezel, P., 304*n*
Deux-Ecus, rue des, 89
Deux-Ponts, rue des, widening, 93, 216, 218, 305
Deville, Councillor, 70, 90
Deville, A., 336
Dictionnaire administratif et historique des rues et monuments de Paris, 335
Disease
asthma, 104
bronchitis, 104
cancer, 104
catarrh, 104
children's diseases, 104–5
cholera, 61, 103–4, 106
epidemic of 1832, 14, 97
epidemic of 1848, 20, 29, 98–100
effect on public health policies, 97–8
convulsions, 104
diptheria, 105
enteritis, 104
fevers, 103
heart diseases, 104
infectious diseases, 104–5, 107, 246
phthisis, 104
plague, 242
propagation of disease, 29, 107
pulmonary diseases, 103–4
respiratory diseases, 104–5
smallpox, 105
treatment of disease, 106
tuberculosis, 104–5, 107–8, 111, 222, 239–41, 246–8
measures taken against, 109–14, 240, 244–5, 248
propagation of, 104–5, 108–9, 112, 240
typhoid fever, 104, 107
vaccination, 246, 248
District de la région de Paris
establishment, 233–5
subsidies for public works, 237
Districts of Paris, *see Arrondissements;* Wards
Dix-Décembre, rue du, 39, 156, 158
Dreyfus, Councillor Camille, 65
Dreyfus affair, 220
Du Marien, architect, 318
Du Sommerard, Alexandre, antiquary, 183
Dubech, L., 304*n*
Dubois, Prefect of Police, 236
Duon, G., 123*n*
Dussoubs, rue, 92, 135
Duveau, Georges, 34*n*

Index

Michodière, rue de la, 304
Middle classes, areas of residence, *see* Chaussée-d'Antin; Socio-economic structure
Monasteries, 3, 12
Mondétour, rue, 58, 73, 75
Monge, rue, 186
Moniteur universel, 22, 155, 335
Montagne Sainte-Geneviève, society, 206
Montalembert, 179, 182
Mont-de-Piété, 125, 188, 204
Monteux, Daniel, 317n
Montmartre, faubourg, 286
Montmartre, rue, 63, 67, 126n
improvement, 18–19, 95, 97, 126, 224
Montmartre, village, 126n
preservation, 198, 304, 308–9
Montmartre, ward
building, 126–7
industry, 149
Montorgueil, rue, 63
Montparnasse, 266
Montrésor, Hôtel de, 204
Morizet, André, 31n, 86n
Morris, William, 188
Mortality
causes, 104
infant mortality, 103
local variations, 76
rates, 76, 103–4, 107, 111, 246
recording of, 101, 103, 107
Moulin de la Galette, 208
Museums, development of, 183–4, 204

Naples, embassy of, 169
Napoleon Bonaparte, 13
Napoleon III, 11, 187
aesthetic qualities, 180, 187
control over Paris, 6
fall of, 42
public building, 102, 117
public works policy, 20–5, 27, 30, 32, 36, 49, 51, 103, 116, 179, 180
National Academy of Medicine, 99, 99n, 110
National Assembly, 16, 27, 45, 49, 62–3, 196, 202, 207, 226, 232
National Plans
third, 250, 259
fourth, 237, 250, 259
fifth, 237, 259
National Workshops, 19
New York, *see* Manhattan
Newspaper offices, 290n
see also Arrondissement II
Nomenclature des voies publiques et privées, 335
Normand, Charles, preservationist, 190, 195, 200, 205–6, 211
North Tramways Company, 82

Notre-Dame, ward
building, 134, 136
business premises, 164
lodging houses, 175
population, 277
property values, 158, 161, 173
slum clearance, 113
socio-economic structure, 163

Occupation, 246, 282, 307
Octroi, *see* Taxation, municipal
Odéon, 167
Offices, administrative, *see Arrondissement* VII; Cité Morland
Ogé, Jacques, architect, 309
Old houses, survival of, *see* Archives, rue des; Beaubourg, rue des
Old Montmartre Society, 206
Old Paris Committee, 195, 197, 199, 202–4, 207–8, 209–10, 242, 296–9, 301–2, 304–5, 307, 309–10
Omnibuses
characteristics, 81–2
origins, 79
see also General Omnibus Company
Open space, effect on public health, 30
Opéra, 49–50, 53, 145, 152, 164–5, 169–70, 176, 185, 191, 218, 231, 279, 284–5, 308
Opéra, avenue de l'
business premises, 164
commerce in, 155
construction, 39, 47, 49, 52, 54–5, 57, 75, 76, 132, 140, 191
decline, 170–1, 279
demolitions, 162
property values, 160, 168
traffic, 165
Opinion nationale, L', 185
Opportun, Councillor, 93
Orléans, quai d', 305
Orsay, quai d', 63
Ours, rue aux, 56, 63, 67, 67n, 69, 92, 299, 313
Overcrowding, 27, 115–16
cause of disease, 101–2, 105, 107, 110
result of public works, 42, 136–8, 178

Paix, rue de la, 151n, 156, 171, 279
Palais, boulevard du, 38
Palais de Justice, 15, 36–7
Palais-Royal
preservation, 302, 309
prostitution in, 152n
street improvements near, 64, 92, 218
Palais-Royal, ward
building, 126–7, 132, 135, 141
business premises, 164–5
employment, 286
entertainments in, 145, 152